On Stone by W L Walton.   Hullmandel & Walton Lithographers

CATARACT OF THE WHITE WATER.
London: Richard Bentley, 1846.

A CANOE VOYAGE
UP THE
MINNAY SOTOR

WITH AN ACCOUNT OF
THE LEAD AND COPPER DEPOSITS IN WISCONSIN;
OF THE GOLD REGION IN THE CHEROKEE COUNTRY;
AND SKETCHES OF POPULAR MANNERS

By George W. Featherstonhaugh

With an Introduction by William E. Lass

Volume 1
REPRINT EDITION
MINNESOTA HISTORICAL SOCIETY ST. PAUL
1970

2004 reprint of 1970 edition

New Material Copyright © 1970 by the Minnesota
Historical Society, St. Paul

THIS WORK WAS FIRST PUBLISHED BY RICHARD BENTLEY
OF LONDON, ENGLAND, IN 1847.

Library of Congress Catalog Card Number: 71-111618
Standard Book Number: 87351-057-7

CONTENTS - FIRST VOLUME

INTRODUCTIONS

Introduction to the Reprint Edition by William E. Lass . . xv
Author's Introduction lxv

CHAPTER I.

PAGE

The Author proposes to make a Tour of Exploration to the Côteau de Prairie, at the Sources of the Minnay Sotor, or St. Peter's River, a N. W. Tributary of the Mississippi 1

CHAPTER II.

Embarks upon the Canal at Georgetown, near Washington.—Beautiful Scenery of the Potomac.—Action of the River upon the Rocks near the Great Falls.—A sociable Quaker.—Fossil Plants in Silurian Sandstone.—Calcareous Breccia formed by the eastern Ridge of the Alleghanies coming up through the Limestone.—Harper's Ferry.—Characteristic story of a German Settler 5

CHAPTER III.

William's Port.—Clear Spring.—Bath Springs.—Arrive at Cumberland.—Fucoidal Fossils in place.—Frostburgh.—Great Bituminous Coal-field.—Remarkable Section of Coal Seams on the Potomac . 14

CHAPTER IV.

Interesting Escarpment on the Banks of the Potomac.—A singular Public Dinner.—The Gorge of Will's Mountain.—Bedford Springs.—Valuable Mineral Waters.—Cross the Backbone Mountain.—The Contorted Strata become horizontal to the west of the Alleghanies.—Arrive at Pittsburg 23

CONTENTS.

CHAPTER V.

Visit Braddock's Field.—Events which led to the Expedition of that General 36

CHAPTER VI.

His ill-judged March to the Ohio.—Reaches the Mononghahela . 47

CHAPTER VII.

The Influence which that Defeat had in producing the Revolt of the British Colonies in 1776 56

CHAPTER VIII.

Visit to the German Society of Economy.—Its Origin . . 62

CHAPTER IX.

Count St. Leon, a singular Adventurer.—Sows Dissension in the Society, with the Intention of plundering it 70

CHAPTER X.

Prosperous State of the Society.—Interview with its Head, George Rapp 79

CHAPTER XI.

Reach Ravenna, the Summit Level of the Country.—Cross the Lake Ridges, and reach Cleveland on Lake Erie.—Reach Detroit . . 90

CHAPTER XII.

Agreeable American Society.—Manners of the French Canadians residing at Detroit 101

CONTENTS.   ix

CHAPTER XIII.

PAGE

Domestic Connexion of the French with the Aborigines.—Their early Explorations of the West.—Pondiac, a celebrated Ottaway Chief.—Massacre of the English Garrisons.—Death of Major Dalyell .   . 105

CHAPTER XIV.

Embark for Lake Huron.—Intelligence in Pigs.—Great Lacustrine Deposit.—Christian Indians.—Embark on Lake Huron   .   .   . 122

CHAPTER XV.

Captain and Mrs. Dingle and Co.—Reach Michilimackinac.—Fine Salmon Trout.—Voracity of Fish   134

CHAPTER XVI.

Embark for Lake Michigan.—Violent Storm.—Reach Navarino.—Flux and Reflux of the Waters of Green Bay.—Fort Howard.—Purchase a Bark Canoe and engage a Company of *Voyageurs* .   . 148

CHAPTER XVII.

Ascend Fox River.—Voracity of the *Voyageurs*.—Drunken Winnebagoes.—Explanation of the Arrangements for a Canoe Voyage.—Lake Winnebago   160

CHAPTER XVIII.

Droll Disaster of an Indian Chief.—Butte des Morts.—Remedy against Mosquitoes.—Immense Fields of Wild Rice   172

CHAPTER XIX.

Reach Fort Winnebago.—Meet with the first Tetrao.—Slight Elevation of the Land separating the Eastern and Western Rivers.—Embark on the Wisconsin.—Horizontal Sandstones.—A Shot Tower excavated in the Rock.—Beauty of the Valley of the Wisconsin.—Reach the Mississippi   188

CONTENTS.

CHAPTER XX.

PAGE

Reflections on the Policy to be observed for the Development of British North American Commerce, and for the Protection of our Colonies 204

CHAPTER XXI.

Kindly received by the Officers of the American Garrison of Prairie du Chien.—An Assiniboin Irishman.—Talent of the Indians for imitating the Cries of Night Birds. 213

CHAPTER XXII.

An intelligent Indian and his Family.—Reach Wabeshaw's Band.—Scaffolds for Dead Bodies.—Carver's supposed Fortifications . . 228

CHAPTER XXIII.

Reach Lake Pepin.—Hear the Cataract of St. Anthony.—Reach Fort Snelling.—Engage Milor as a Guide, and get into very bad Lodgings 247

CHAPTER XXIV.

An Evangelical Pretender to Sanctity.—The Falls of St. Anthony . 263

CHAPTER XXV.

On the ancient State of the Mississippi and other American Rivers, and the manner in which their present Channels have been modified . 270

CHAPTER XXVI.

Embark on the Minnay Sotor.—Reflections on the Ruin impending over the Indians.—The proper Name of the Sioux, "Nahcotah."—The Geomys, or Mus bursarius 278

CONTENTS.

CHAPTER XXVII.

Pass Chagnkeeoota.—Trees taking the Autumnal Tint.—Traverse des Sioux.— Immense Abundance of Boulders.—Reach the Makatoh. —Le Sueur's Copper-Mine, a Fable 292

CHAPTER XXVIII.

Ascend the Makatoh again.—The *Voyageurs* unwilling to proceed.—Milor's good conduct.—Minday Mangwah, or "Swan Lakes."—Pahkah Skah, a beautiful Half-breed, abandoned by her Father.—Cameron's Grave.—Milor's Escape from Starvation.—Granite in Place . . 305

CHAPTER XXIX.

How to cook a Racoon.—Make a *Cache* of our heavy Articles.—A Granite Country.—Prowlers about our Camp.—The *Grand Portage* . 321

CHAPTER XXX.

Camp nearly burnt.—Reach Lac qui Parle.—Turbulent Conduct of the Savages.—Danger of being plundered.—The Author's Speech to the Chief 335

CHAPTER XXXI.

The Chiefs present their Pipes in token of Friendship.—Huggins, a Yankee Missionary.—Three Ojibways scalped.— A Scalp-Dance.—Pleasing Music of the Squaws 346

CHAPTER XXXII.

The Author permitted to see the Braves attire themselves for the "Dance of the Braves" in honour of his Arrival.—Dance of the Squaws. —Matrimonial Negotiations 358

CHAPTER XXXIII.

Leave Lac qui Parle —Exposed to the Danger of being frozen to Death.—Excellent Conduct of Milor.—Reach a few Trees, and make a Fire. 372

CHAPTER XXXIV.

Reach the Summit Level dividing the Waters which flow into the Gulf of Mexico from those flowing into Hudson's Bay.—Migration of Musk-rats.—Two Buffaloes killed by One Draft of an Arrow.—Leave Lake Travers.—Buffalo Skeletons.—Reach the Sources of the Minnay Sotor on the Côteau du Prairie.—Milor advises our Return . 382

CHAPTER XXXV.

Reach Big Stone Lake on our Return.—Symptoms of Winter.—Immense Masses of Granite, from whence the Lake takes its name.—Prairies on Fire.—Supposed Origin of the Word "Missouri."—Reach the Wahboptah.—Egregious Pride of the male Indians . 396

CHAPTER XXXVI.

Reach Lac qui Parle.— An Indian Marriage.— Dependence of the Indians upon the Traders.— Re-embark on the Minnay Sotor.—Immense Quantities of Wild Fowl.—Reach Mr. Moore's and find Pahkah Skah there 405

ILLUSTRATIONS

Volume 1

Cataract of the White Water, North Carolina	Frontispiece
George W. Featherstonhaugh	xix
Title Page of the 1847 Edition	xlvii
Dan's Mountain Coal Beds, Maryland	21
Along the Potomac River near Cumberland, Maryland	25
Will's Mountain near Cumberland, Maryland	29
Braddock's Field, Pennsylvania	60
Fort Michilimackinac, Michigan	148
Le Grand Gres Pillar, Minnesota	290

Maps

The Minnay Sotor or St. Peter's River between 288 and 289

INTRODUCTION
TO THE REPRINT EDITION

DURING the era of Jacksonian Democracy, the United States was visited by many Europeans led by their natural wanderlust to view the largest republic of the western hemisphere. English travelers came in the greatest numbers, and some of their published impressions have come to be regarded as classics in the historical literature of the time. Captain Basil Hall, on leave from the Royal Navy, wrote an account entitled *Travels in North America* (1829) which became the model for many later visitors. In 1837 Harriet Martineau, an English reformist and philosopher, published *Society in America,* and the following year Frances Trollope, a well-known novelist, contributed *Domestic Manners of the Americans.* Frederick Marryat, a novelist famed for his tales of the sea, toured the country and wrote *A Diary in America* in 1839. Three years later Charles Dickens revealed his impressions in *American Notes.* Because many of these people were literary figures well known to the public, their accounts were received with great enthusiasm.

Dozens of travel books by lesser known Englishmen were also published. Some of these minor figures left memorable impressions of the United States and in many instances reported on aspects that had been neglected by the famous writers. George William Featherstonhaugh was one such individual.[1] His *Canoe Voyage up the Minnay Sotor*, published in 1847, has never been accorded the notice it deserves. Well written and entertaining, it describes his extensive travels in Wisconsin, Minnesota, and various southern states in 1835 and 1837.

Featherstonhaugh, an Englishman by birth, rearing, and temperament, and a geologist by profession, was well qualified to comment on the American scene.[2] By the time of his travels in the 1830s, he had lived in the United States for nearly thirty years and had participated actively in the country's business, social, and political life. A professional scientist, he was also a linguist with an attentive ear for the speech of the white and red men he encountered. In performing his duties as a geologist for the United States he visited remote sections of the frontier that few other trained observers had yet had an opportunity to see.

While Featherstonhaugh's account has unique qualities, it also resembles the writings of some of his more

[1] Most Americans pronounce this name phonetically "Feather-stonhaugh." Some members of the English branch of the family, however, pronounce it "Fanshaw," and residents of southern England who have a public school education would say "Feaostanho." John H. Bliss, who traveled with the author in 1835, recorded the English pronunciation as "Frestonhaw." George W. White, Research Professor of Geology, University of Illinois, Urbana, to the author, December 23, 1969; Daniel Jones, *Everyman's English Pronouncing Dictionary*, 175 (London, 1963); John H. Bliss, "Reminiscences of Fort Snelling," in *Minnesota Historical Collections*, 6:350 (St. Paul, 1894).

[2] Biographical information in this introduction was obtained mainly from J. D. Featherstonhaugh, "Memoir of Mr. G. W. Featherstonhaugh," in *American Geologist*, 3:217–223 (April, 1889); W. H. G. Armytage, "G. W. Featherstonhaugh, F.R.S. 1780–1866, Anglo-American Scientist," in *Notes and Records of the Royal Society of London*, 2:228–235 (March, 1955); George P. Merrill, *The First One Hundred Years of American Geology*, 136–138, 161–165 (Reprint, New York, 1964); George W. White, "Editor's Introduction," in the *Monthly American Journal of Geology and Natural Science*, 1:xi–xiv (Reprint, New York, 1969).

celebrated contemporaries. Despite his long residence in the United States, Featherstonhaugh followed the examples of Trollope, Marryat, Dickens, and others who judged the country by English standards. He was repelled by what he derisively referred to as the "Republican America" of the Jacksonian era with its mass democracy and cultural backwardness. Though his criticisms often accurately reflected the nature of life on the frontier during what has been called "The Age of the Common Man," they also revealed Featherstonhaugh's own prejudices and Tory sentiments.

Featherstonhaugh's travels were so extensive that he could have justifiably selected a broader title — one which would have more accurately described the scope of his journeys. In fact, it would appear that he had chosen just such a title, for in the contract he signed with London publisher Richard Bentley three months before the book appeared the title was given as "A Canoe Voyage in North America." The agreement stipulated, however, that the title was to be modified, perhaps because the publisher did not feel the suggested one was romantic enough. In any event, the title finally selected, *A Canoe Voyage up the Minnay Sotor*, emphasized the farthest point reached by Featherstonhaugh — the headwaters of the Minnesota (St. Peter's) River — and employed the mysterious sounding Sioux Indian name "Minnay Sotor." A lengthy subtitle was then added which included references to Wisconsin and the "Cherokee Country" of Georgia, but which still did not fully delineate the breadth of Featherstonhaugh's rambles.[3]

[3] "Memorandum of Agreement between George William Featherstonhaugh and Richard Bentley," September 28, 1846, in Bentley Papers, vol. 46614, folio 336, in Department of Manuscripts, British Museum, London. The Minnesota Historical Society has a typed copy.

In reality, the book here reprinted chronicles two separate expeditions — a geological investigation in 1835 of the area from Lake Michigan west to the Coteau des Prairies at the headwaters of the Minnesota River, and a tour in 1837 of the mineral lands of Wisconsin, Missouri, Georgia, and the western Carolinas. On July 8, 1835, Featherstonhaugh left Washington, D.C., for his outfitting point at Green Bay, Wisconsin, on the shores of Lake Michigan. For the first hundred miles or so he traveled by canalboat from Georgetown to Williamsport, Maryland, then by stage through the mountains via Cumberland, Maryland, and Bedford, Pennsylvania, to Pittsburgh. Despite the lateness of the season and his desire to be out of the wilderness before winter, he dallied for a time in the Pittsburgh area, visiting the sites of General Edward Braddock's defeat in the French and Indian War and J. George Rapp's utopian community, Economy. He then moved rapidly by stage across Ohio to Cleveland, where he booked passage for Detroit on a lake steamer. There he again interrupted his journey to look over the town, cross into neighboring Canada, and visit historic spots which called to mind Detroit's role in the history of the Great Lakes frontier. He then sailed to Mackinac, where he met Henry Rowe Schoolcraft, the discoverer of the source of the Mississippi, whom he puzzlingly identified only as "the Indian agent." Schoolcraft accompanied the Englishman to Green Bay, an outfitting point which they reached on August 18, 1835, about six weeks after the geologist set out from Georgetown.

At Green Bay, Featherstonhaugh and his fellow geologist, William Williams Mather, purchased a large birch

GEORGE W. FEATHERSTONHAUGH
Photograph in the Minnesota Historical Society's collections

bark canoe and, with the assistance of Daniel Whitney, the founder of the village, hired five voyageurs to paddle it through the lakes and streams to the west. Proceeding by way of the Fox River and the celebrated portage to the Wisconsin River and thus to the Mississippi, Featherstonhaugh followed the historic route of Jacques Marquette and Louis Jolliet, passing through the Winnebago Indian lands. He stopped briefly at Fort Winnebago, at Helena near present-day Spring Green, Wisconsin, where he saw a famous lead-processing shot tower, and then journeyed to the Mississippi at Prairie du Chien, Wisconsin. There he tarried from August 31 to September 2, calling on Colonel Zachary Taylor, the commandant of Fort Crawford, before proceeding upstream to Fort Snelling in present-day Minnesota, where he arrived on September 12.

At that time Fort Snelling, the northwesternmost military post in the United States, represented the edge of the wilderness; few of its officers had traveled much beyond that point. After obtaining information, supplies, and a local half-breed guide named Milor,[4] Featherstonhaugh continued his canoe voyage up the Minnesota River to its source in Big Stone Lake on the present South Dakota-Minnesota border. The river journey and the return trip to Fort Snelling took approximately a month. During this time Featherstonhaugh examined the site of French explorer Pierre Le Sueur's supposed copper mine, met numerous Sioux Indians and fur traders, visited the

[4] Very little is known of Milor. It is possible that he may have been the William Meyer who served as one of the witnesses to the signatures on a Sioux treaty signed by Zebulon M. Pike in 1805. See Donald Jackson, ed., *The Journals of Zebulon Montgomery Pike*, 1:246 (Norman, Okla., 1966); Edward D. Neill, *History of Minnesota*, 276 (Philadelphia, 1873).

Lac qui Parle mission to the Sioux, and ultimately went as far west as the summit of the Coteau des Prairies, the ridge that separates the watersheds of the Missouri and Minnesota rivers.

Traversing the Minnay Sotor, as he sometimes called it, took the geologist beyond the fringes of frontier settlement into the most primitive sections of country he had seen. Only Stephen H. Long's expedition of 1823 had preceded Featherstonhaugh in formally exploring the area. Although the Minnesota River Valley was raw and undeveloped, it was no longer an unsullied wilderness. White fur traders had lived among the Sioux for years and the army had left its mark. The missionaries at Lac qui Parle had preceded Featherstonhaugh by only a matter of weeks. Thus the observant Englishman witnessed and recognized the transitional trader-military-missionary frontier while it was in the process of forcing the Sioux out of their traditional tribal ways toward an unpromising future in the white man's world.

After returning to Fort Snelling on October 12, 1835, Featherstonhaugh went by canoe down the Mississippi to Galena, Illinois, where he dismissed his voyageurs with no particular regrets and, much to his delight, met Charles Augustus Murray, a fellow countryman who had just completed a western trip.[5] The two men then boarded a steamboat bound for St. Louis, where Featherstonhaugh spent a week and a half visiting with such notables as

[5] Murray later described his journeys in a two-volume work entitled *Travels in North America during the Years 1834, 1835, & 1836. Including a Summer Residence with the Pawnee Tribe of Indians, in the Remote Prairies of the Missouri, and a Visit to Cuba and the Azore Islands* (London, 1839). Issued by Bentley, who was also Featherstonhaugh's publisher, the book was evidently quite popular since a third edition with a new introduction was printed in 1854.

artist George Catlin, explorers Stephen W. Kearny and Joseph N. Nicollet, fur trader William H. Ashley, and Sir William Drummond Stewart, a Scottish sportsman. The geologist ended the account of his 1835 trip on November 16, the day he left by steamboat for Louisville and Pittsburgh, en route to Washington, D.C.

In 1837 Featherstonhaugh started again from Washington but this time did not describe the trip until he reached Galena on May 19. With his compatriot Richard Cowling Taylor, he spent about three weeks traveling by horseback through the lead mining region of northwestern Illinois and southwestern Wisconsin. He visited Belmont, the original capital of Wisconsin Territory, Mineral Point, where he met territorial governor Henry Dodge, and the Four Lakes region, where the new territorial capital was taking shape at Madison. Though Featherstonhaugh's purpose in Wisconsin was to survey the lead formation and compare it with those of Missouri and Iowa, he seems to have been more interested in observing frontier speculative activity and the colorful personalities he chanced to encounter.

Despite his instructions to survey the Cherokee lands of Georgia during the season, Featherstonhaugh went from Galena to Prairie du Chien, where he discussed with Zachary Taylor and trader Joseph Rolette Sr. the possibility of realizing his ambition to travel to the Missouri River. Receiving nothing but discouragement from both men, Featherstonhaugh resumed his surveying task, going by steamboat to St. Louis. After spending five days there, he left on June 24 to employ the next three weeks investigating the Missouri iron deposits in the vicinity of Pilot Knob, west of Ste. Genevieve, and visiting at the home of United States Senator Lewis F. Linn. The latter was particularly interested in the commercial development of his state's lead and iron deposits and was one of the key congressional supporters of geological surveys like that in which Featherstonhaugh was engaged. Featherstonhaugh had certain misgivings about Linn, particularly because of the senator's involvement in a pistol duel between two youths (2:160). In spite of his reservations, the Englishman's respect for position was so great that he neither named the senator nor used his initials in the book, even though Linn was dead by the time it was published.[6]

On July 9 Featherstonhaugh departed Ste. Genevieve for the Cherokee country. He traveled via steamboat to Paducah, Kentucky, then up the Tennessee River to Tuscumbia near the foot of Muscle Shoals in northern Alabama. Because these rapids were unnavigable, he then went by rail some forty miles to Decatur, Alabama, before resuming river travel. He left Decatur on July 22, but three days later low water below Chattanooga, Tennessee, forced Featherstonhaugh to complete his trip into the Cherokee country of northwestern Georgia by canoe, horseback, and stage.

The geologist spent most of August and September, 1837, in Tennessee, Georgia, and the western Carolinas, primarily for the purpose of surveying the gold diggings. As usual, however, he availed himself of every oppor-

[6] The geologist provided enough clues, however, so that the senator's identity must have been very apparent to those conversant with Missouri politics — his residence at Ste. Genevieve, his interest in mineral lands, and his participation in the duel as both second and surgeon. On Linn, see *Dictionary of American Biography*, 11:282 (New York, 1933); Dr. Robert E. Schlueter, "Lewis Fields Linn (1795-1843), Physician and Statesman," in St. Louis Medical Society, *Weekly Bulletin* (January 25, 1935).

tunity to meet and observe people and to note significant events. Featherstonhaugh's work in the Cherokee country gave him an opportunity to view a civilized Indian tribe and to observe one of the last acts in the great Cherokee removal drama. At the time Featherstonhaugh visited the Cherokee in 1837 they had received their removal orders. The Van Buren administration had made clear its determination to enforce the controversial New Echota treaty, which had been signed in 1835 by an extremely small tribal minority. John Ross and other tribal leaders journeyed to Washington to protest the implementation of the treaty, and when Ross returned to the tribe, the government—fearing a possible rebellion—declared martial law in the area and sent John Mason, Jr., as a special agent to explain the government's position. Featherstonhaugh, realizing the significance of the conference held in October at Red Clay—in what is now southern Tennessee—made it a point to attend, and here he met Ross and other Cherokee leaders such as the Reverend Jesse Bushyhead. Although he had no official capacity at the conference, Featherstonhaugh occasionally leaves the impression that he was part of the group of commissioners which included Mason, Colonel William Lindsay, and General Nathaniel Smith.[7]

After the council the Englishman was the guest of Langdon Cheves, former speaker of the United States House of Representatives, and of John C. Calhoun, staying for a time at the latter's mansion near Pendleton, South Carolina. The geologist then quickly concluded his 1837 trip, moving by stage across North Carolina

[7] See Grace S. Woodward, *The Cherokees* (Norman, Okla., 1963).

from Asheville to Raleigh to Gaston and by rail to Washington, arriving there on October 9.

The scope of these journeys and the liveliness of Featherstonhaugh's observations on the diverse regions he saw in 1835 and 1837 make *Canoe Voyage* a book well worth reprinting. Within a short period of time, Featherstonhaugh toured widely separated sections of the frontier, many of them well off the main travel routes. His comments range from an appreciation of the beauty and productivity of the land to descriptions of life among the various Indian tribes and caustic remarks about frontier morals and manners. His book captures the essence of American frontier materialism and expansionism, and it contributes to an understanding of the inexorable westward push of Anglo-American culture. Its geographic range makes the work an important source for many states that were part of the frontier in the 1830s. The volume is liberally laced with humor and anecdotes, most of them based on Featherstonhaugh's own firsthand experiences, and it contains many comments on the well-known people whose company the snobbish Englishman so highly valued.

Indeed, Featherstonhaugh's vivid word portraits of people constitute one of the most valuable features of the book. He took pains to find out who the leading men in a particular area were, and he assiduously wrote ahead to make his arrival known, no doubt pointing out his government mission. He seemed to derive special pleasure from these contacts with what he regarded as the "better classes" of America, and such men of position as Calhoun, Cheves, Zachary Taylor, Henry Dodge,

INTRODUCTION TO REPRINT   xxvii

Henry H. Sibley, and Major John Bliss were either praised or treated deferentially.

Featherstonhaugh was middle-aged when he made the geological reconnaissances on which this book is based. His long, varied career and his scientific training singularly qualified him for the task. Born in London on April 9, 1780, Featherstonhaugh received an academy education and was graduated from Oxford University. His study of the classics, his command of Latin, German, and French, and his musical accomplishments reflect the man's broad interests and abilities. It is possible, too, that he began the formal study of geology in these early years, for he spent four years on the continent, primarily in France and Italy, before traveling to the United States in 1807.

Provided with proper letters of introduction, Featherstonhaugh — the epitome of the European gentleman — was soon known and accepted in rather exclusive social circles of the eastern United States. Standing over six feet, the handsome, urbane, aristocratically minded youth willingly displayed his linguistic talents and musical skill. Instead of returning to England as he had originally planned, Featherstonhaugh married in 1808 and stayed on in the United States.

His wife Sara was the daughter of James Duane, who had been a wealthy New York landowner, jurist, politician, and onetime mayor of New York City. She had inherited a thousand acres of land at Duanesburg near Schenectady, New York, and there the couple took up residence. Featherstonhaugh became well known as a gentleman farmer in the lower Mohawk Valley, an advocate of scientific agriculture who imported and raised purebred cattle and sheep.

The prominence of his wife's family provided him with valuable social contacts, and he soon became associated with Stephen Van Rensselaer, scion of the famed patroon family. The two men shared an interest in improving farming methods. When the New York Board of Agriculture was formally organized in 1820, Featherstonhaugh was elected corresponding secretary and Van Rensselaer president. Among other things, these two recommended the study of geology as a means of bettering agriculture.

A few years later they were again associated in a plan to build a railroad between Schenectady and Albany. At the time Featherstonhaugh was keeping abreast of European geological developments through correspondence with English associates and periodic visits to England. On one such trip the inquisitive scientist became aware of English efforts to build railroads. He concluded that a steam railway would solve the problems of Schenectady and Albany merchants hurt by the new Erie Canal which diverted considerable commerce to the rival city of Troy. Featherstonhaugh believed that a sixteen-mile railroad between the two cities would re-establish Albany as the entrepôt for western trade by providing a shortcut to the Erie Canal and make Schenectady a significant depot on the canal. In late 1825 Featherstonhaugh publicly advertised that he would ask the next New York legislature to charter the Mohawk and Hudson Rail Road Company. With the backing of Van Rensselaer and a number of Albany merchants, he spent several trying months lobbying in the state legislature, and in April, 1826, the railroad was incorporated.[8]

In September, 1826, Featherstonhaugh and his wife went to England, where they remained until March, 1828, while he studied British railroad developments. This was a difficult time for the couple because their two daughters had died of diphtheria in 1825, but the long sojourn abroad permitted Featherstonhaugh to renew his friendships with leading English geologists such as Roderick Impey Murchison and Adam Sedgwick. In 1827 he was elected a Fellow of the Geological Society of London.

After returning to New York, Featherstonhaugh entered a period of misfortune. His wife died in June, 1828, and a year later his beautiful home at Duanesburg was destroyed by fire. Difficulties with his associates led to his abrupt resignation from the railroad directorship on August 1, 1829, and to his removal to Philadelphia. Although Featherstonhaugh resigned two years before the railroad was operative, it was he who began the short line that ultimately grew into the New York Central system. In 1926 when the New York Central observed its centennial, appropriate tributes were paid to Featherstonhaugh as the railroad's founder.

In Philadelphia Featherstonhaugh became associated with an intellectual circle and renewed his deep interest in the classics. His translation of Cicero's *Republic* was

[8] For further information on Featherstonhaugh's railroad venture discussed here and below, see David M. Ellis, *Landlords and Farmers in the Hudson-Mohawk Region 1790-1850*, 175 (Ithaca, 1946); Alvin F. Harlow, *The Road of the Century: The Story of the New York Central*, 2-10 (New York, 1947); Codman Hislop, *The Mohawk*, 265-270 (New York, 1948); and Frank W. Stevens, *The Beginnings of the New York Central Railroad*, 1-19 (New York, 1926).

published in 1829, and a drama, *The Death of Ugolino: A Tragedy*, appeared the next year. The play described the end of Ugolino della Gherardesca, a Pisan politician whose death by starvation in a dungeon in 1289 was immortalized in Dante's *Inferno*.

As the decade of the 1830s dawned, Featherstonhaugh's life took yet another turn. In 1831 he married Charlotte Carter, daughter of Bernard Carter of Virginia. At about the same time, as a result of a series of well-received lectures on geology, he established the *Monthly American Journal of Geology and Natural Science*. This short-lived publication furnished a reputable outlet for his geological essays and also carried reports by such men as explorer Stephen H. Long and artist John James Audubon. Largely because of the journal Featherstonhaugh became widely known as one of the foremost advocates of geology, at that time a revolutionary new science.[9]

Several major developments that were to give geology its characteristics as a modern professional science occurred in Featherstonhaugh's lifetime when geologists generally abandoned the Neptunian theory of the earth's formation in favor of uniformitarianism and the systematic study of historical geology through paleontology and stratigraphy. During Featherstonhaugh's youth, geological theory was dominated by Abraham Gottlob Werner, a German who held that the earth's crust had been formed by chemical deposits from a primeval universal

---

[9] On the emergence of geology as a science and on Featherstonhaugh's role in disseminating geological information discussed here and in the next four paragraphs, see Merrill, *American Geology*, 136; White, "Introduction," in *Monthly American Journal* reprint, 1:xi–xiv; Martha Bray, "Joseph Nicolas Nicollet, Geologist," in American Philosophical Society, *Proceedings*, 114:37–59 (February 16, 1970).

ocean. Werner's simplistic Neptunian theory, which coincided so neatly with the belief in the biblical flood, was challenged successfully by James Hutton, an Englishman whose ideas were set forth in his *Theory of the Earth* (1795). Hutton was an advocate of uniformitarianism, holding that the phenomena which had shaped the earth were still operating in varying degrees; hence, such geological processes as water action, wind, and volcanic upheavals were observable. Hutton's concept of geological evolution as distinct from Werner's static world had several significant effects: it contributed to a dramatic upsurge of interest in field work, and it changed the entire notion of the earth's age since the existence of slow-working natural processes made necessary the hypothesis of a world millions of years old.

A ferment of activity got under way. Following Hutton's lead, other geologists turned to field studies and soon sophisticated their discipline by dating and describing strata according to fossil remains. The pioneer of fossiliferous stratigraphy was William Smith, "the Father of English Geology," who identified the proper stratigraphical sequence of the secondary formations in England and published a geological map of that country in 1815. Smith's work stimulated the efforts of Murchison and Sedgwick who identified and described the Silurian and Cambrian formations. Featherstonhaugh knew these two men well and was apparently aware of some of their conclusions before they were generally known, for he was able to study the Silurian system in the United States before Murchison's monograph on the subject was published in 1839.

While England moved to the forefront in geological

thinking, noteworthy developments also occurred in the United States, where scientists were acquainted with the work of Hutton and Smith. When the American Geological Society was organized in 1819, some politicians were becoming increasingly interested in the new science. Amos Eaton, perhaps the leading American geologist of the 1820s, was commissioned by Stephen Van Rensselaer to make a geological and agricultural survey of the Erie Canal route. Through his friendship with Van Rensselaer, Featherstonhaugh must have known Eaton. Certainly he was familiar with Eaton's work, which he refers to in the volume here reprinted (1:128).

Perhaps Featherstonhaugh's greatest service to geology was the dissemination of the new developments in England to an American audience through the *Monthly American Journal*. He was, however, somewhat ahead of his time. There was no particular demand for a scientific publication intended for a lay audience, and Featherstonhaugh's project failed with the June, 1832, issue. His attempts to revive the journal by seeking federal funds to underwrite it likewise failed, but in the course of his dealings with government officials he successfully called attention both to geology and to himself as a geologist.

Some federal officials and congressmen were interested in the science primarily because it promised to unlock the potentially vast mineral treasures of a virtually unexplored nation. Featherstonhaugh's strongest supporter was his close personal friend, Lieutenant Colonel John J. Abert, Chief of the Bureau of Topographical Engineers. Abert, whose principal duty was the supervision of road and river surveys, also wanted to secure funds to make geological surveys of the known lead deposits in the Mississippi River Valley and to acquire additional knowledge of the nation's copper resources. He was rewarded when Congress, in a rivers and harbors act of June 28, 1834, appropriated $5,000 for such studies. Evidently, however, there was some question about the legality of funding geological surveys as part of a rivers and harbors act, for this method of financing them did not continue. In subsequent years Congress funded them by making appropriations under an earlier act of April 30, 1824, which empowered the president to authorize surveys. Thus, through a unique provision in the 1834 rivers and harbors act and a rather liberal congressional interpretation of the 1824 survey act, Abert gained the financial support necessary for federally sponsored geological expeditions, as distinct from exploration in general.[10]

Featherstonhaugh had apparently been negotiating with Abert before passage of the 1834 act, for within a matter of days after its approval Abert notified the Englishman: "I am directed by the Honorable Secretary of War to inform you, that you have been selected, as principal Geologist, to aid in carrying into effect the directions of the law in relation to Geological and mineralogical researches." Abert subsequently referred to Featherstonhaugh as United States Geologist, and Featherstonhaugh himself used the title. It was, however, only an informal designation, for the War Department did not officially have such a position. Abert felt, however, that since Featherstonhaugh was the first geologist to be

[10] On the 1824 and 1834 acts, see United States, *Statutes at Large*, 4:22, 702, 777.

hired by the department, he could properly be referred to as the United States Geologist.[11]

While working in this capacity within the Bureau of Topographical Engineers, Featherstonhaugh in the years from 1834 to 1837 made the three extensive survey trips upon which his later literary works were based. His first geological reconnaissance of the Ozark area carried him to Missouri, Arkansas, and Texas. Two publications resulted from this expedition. The first was his official report which was printed as a congressional document in 1835; the second was a successful two-volume literary version entitled *Excursion Through the Slave States*, which was published in 1844.[12] Featherstonhaugh makes numerous references to this earlier trip throughout *Canoe Voyage*.

Abert was well pleased with the Ozark report. He described Featherstonhaugh as a man of "known intelligence, great zeal and untiring perseverance," and on July 7, 1835, he gave the geologist the additional instructions which eventually resulted in the publication of the book here reprinted. As his principal assignment in 1835 Featherstonhaugh was to obtain "some knowledge" of the mineral structure of the Coteau des Prairies. He was also to make a mineralogical investigation in the "vicinity" of the Wisconsin River and to observe the gen-

[11] Abert to Featherstonhaugh, July [8?], 1834, October 24, 1837, in United States Topographical Bureau Papers, 1829–70, Letters Sent, in National Archives, Washington, D.C., NARG 77, microfilm copy in Minnesota Historical Society.

[12] Featherstonhaugh, *Report of Geological and Mineralogical Survey of the Elevated Country between the Missouri and Red Rivers*, in 23 Congress, 2 session, *House Executive Documents*, no. 151 (serial 274). The report was also separately printed by Gales & Seaton of Washington, D.C., in 1835. On *Excursion Through the Slave States*, see p. xlv, below.

eral geology of the country along his route from Washington to Green Bay. Lastly, he was advised to collect specimens of "metals and mineral substances." [13]

While Abert did not mention it in his instructions to Featherstonhaugh, the two men had obviously also talked about determining the nature and site of Le Sueur's famed copper mines. In the opening pages of this book Featherstonhaugh appears to describe that task as one of his major goals, and Abert, who had some rather vague notions of history and geography, later wrote to Secretary of War Lewis Cass that "Early history has mentioned the 'Coteau de Prairie' as a locality rich in its deposit of copper in its various forms. Records which are presumed to be deserving of confidence state that many tons of this mineral had been taken at an early period of our history to France, and there smelted to advantage." Not doubting the existence of copper in the coteau region, Abert noted that the quantities and specific locations had yet to be determined.[14]

The results of the survey became publicly known in 1836 when Featherstonhaugh's official report appeared. Those who anticipated a succinct document must have been amazed, for the author did not reach the subject of his investigations until page 95. Showing his preoccupation with general stratigraphy and the philosophy of geology, Featherstonhaugh prefaced the description of his 1835 activities with what he described as "a somewhat elementary exposition of the principles of the sci-

[13] Abert to Featherstonhaugh, July 7, 1835, Letters Sent, NARG 77; Abert, "Report from the Topographical Bureau," November 2, 1835, in *American State Papers: Military Affairs*, 5:713 (Washington, 1860).

[14] Abert, "Report," in *American State Papers*, 5:713.

ence," justifying it on the grounds that there was a need to call "public attention" to geology.[15]

Once into the actual events of the expedition, Featherstonhaugh wrote chiefly of his day-to-day activities, devoting scant space to geological observations. The report, which was lucidly written in concise lay language, offers little more geological data than appears in this book. There is virtually no technical terminology. Although the geologist did not copy them word for word, many passages are quite similar to those printed here. Most of the same individuals are also described, but in more restrained language and with none of the social commentary and character assessments that make these volumes so lively.

The scientific significance of Featherstonhaugh's 1835 reconnaissance is questionable. He extended existing knowledge of North American formations, related strata to comparable European formations, and collected rock and fossil specimens in some quantity. Perhaps his greatest accomplishments were negative. He examined and identified Le Sueur's "copper" as a worthless iron silicate. Rather rashly, he concluded that since he had identified it, so obviously had Le Sueur. Instead of reasoning that the Frenchman was uninformed in such matters, he depicted him as a knave who probably invented "fables to give him influence at the court of France." Featherstonhaugh's failure to find copper or other mineral deposits either along the Minnesota River or on the Coteau des

---

[15] Featherstonhaugh, *Report of a Geological Reconnaissance Made in 1835, from the Seat of Government, by the Way of Green Bay and the Wisconsin Territory, to the Coteau de Prairie*, in 24 Congress, 1 session, *Senate Executive Documents*, no. 333, p. 5 (serial 282). The report was also separately printed by Gales & Seaton of Washington D.C., in 1836.

Prairies dispelled any notion of obvious mineral wealth in these regions. However, in both accomplishments, his conclusions had been anticipated by William H. Keating, a member of Stephen Long's 1823 expedition. In his detailed and informative report published in 1824, Keating had also presented considerable data on the natural history and Indian life of the area. Though Featherstonhaugh's report contained a map, even this contribution was soon completely overshadowed by that of Joseph Nicollet. The French-born Nicollet, as a result of explorations in 1836 and 1838, made a monumental contribution to cartography in 1843 with the publication of an accurate and complete map of the Minnesota region.[16]

Perhaps Featherstonhaugh should be judged, however, primarily by what his superiors expected of him. Writing to the secretary of war while Featherstonhaugh was on the expedition, Abert noted that since the Englishman would have to contend with an unknown wilderness and an early winter, his report would probably be quite general. Abert seemed satisfied with the expectation that Featherstonhaugh would merely provide a basis for further and more specific studies.[17]

The release of Featherstonhaugh's official report brought to light a strange situation that has fascinated historians to this day — the feud between Featherstonhaugh and William W. Mather, his professional com-

[16] *Report*, 1836, p. 145. See also Keating, *Narrative of an Expedition to the Source of St. Peter's River . . . under the command of Stephen H. Long*, 2 vols. (Philadelphia, 1824). Nicollet's map appeared in his *Report Intended to Illustrate a Map of the Hydrographical Basin of the Upper Mississippi River*, in 26 Congress, 2 session, *Senate Executive Documents*, no. 237 (serial 380). The map has been reprinted by the Minnesota Historical Society.
[17] Abert, "Report," in *American State Papers*, 5:713.

panion on the 1835 expedition. Featherstonhaugh failed to mention his fellow geologist's name or even to acknowledge the fact that he had been accompanied by another scientist. One would believe from Featherstonhaugh's account that he alone set out with the voyageurs from Green Bay.

When he was put on detached service to accompany Featherstonhaugh, Mather — a thirty-one-year-old United States army lieutenant and a descendant of the famous New England Mathers — had already earned a respectable reputation as a geologist. He had contributed numerous articles on various scientific topics to professional journals and had written a text entitled *Elements of Geology for the Use of Schools* (1833). He had also taught chemistry, mineralogy, and geology at West Point for six years, and in 1833 while on leave from the army taught geology at Wesleyan University, Middletown, Connecticut. The following year he conducted a geological survey of a Connecticut county.[18]

On July 3, 1835, Abert, having secured Mather's release from his regular unit, instructed the young scientist to "repair to Green Bay, Michigan Territory, to aid in the Geological and Mineralogical investigations to be made between that place and the Coteau des Prairies, in relation to which you will receive and conform to the instructions of G. W. Featherstonhaugh, Esq." Mather was expected to assist in all aspects of the expedition, but he was specifically directed to make a detailed map of the Minnesota River area.[19]

[18] For detailed information on Mather's life, see C. H. Hitchcock, "Sketch of W. W. Mather," in *American Geologist*, 19:1–15 (January, 1897); John H. Newvahner, "William Williams Mather," in *Ohio Archaeological and Historical Quarterly*, 40:190–199 (April, 1931).

[19] Abert to Mather, July 3, 1835, Letters Sent, NARG 77.

It was soon obvious that Featherstonhaugh and Mather were incompatible. Writing from Detroit, Featherstonhaugh complained to Abert that Mather had been trying to tell him how to organize the expedition and he further commented: "Desirous of doing justice to Mr. Mather, who is in the most exact sense of the word a *steady* man, a strict Presbyterian, a member of the temperance society, and who, young as he is, would absolutely faint away at the sight of any woman's legs excepting Mrs. Mathers, and who, I really say it from a sense of justice to him, is a kind, respectful companion to myself. I must to you whom I have no concealments with, *say*, that he is a man unpracticed with the world, and of course dull." In the same letter, Featherstonhaugh called Mather "incurious," "unteachable," and "pedantic" and said that he was "like a fifty lb. shot hanging over my back." Then, with the expedition less than a month old, Featherstonhaugh asked that Mather be excluded from assisting in the compilation of the final report because "it is morally impossible he can ever suggest an idea for my report."[20]

Relations between the two did not improve after they left Detroit, for Featherstonhaugh later wrote that "we sit in the boat for hours without speaking." Finally, on their return down the Mississippi, Mather was told by Featherstonhaugh that his services would not be needed in compiling the report of the expedition. The men quarreled bitterly over this decision, and on this note the journey ended. Mather was understandably angered. He was ambitious and naturally sought the recognition that

[20] Featherstonhaugh to Abert, August 2, 1835, in Mrs. Dana O. Jensen, ed., "Letters from the First United States Geologist: W. G. Featherstonhaugh to Colonel J. J. Abert," in *Bulletin of the Missouri Historical Society*, 8:275 (April, 1952).

his participation in the expedition should have brought. Furthermore, this curt dismissal obviously inferred an unsatisfactory performance which would adversely affect his future military career.[21]

After spending some time at the federal arsenal at St. Louis, Mather was transferred to the infantry at Fort Gibson in what is now Oklahoma. He believed he had been unjustly treated. He relayed various grievances about Featherstonhaugh to Abert only to be met with the rebuff, "you are essentially wrong in every position you have taken." Mather reluctantly sent Abert his map of the Minnesota River and his journal of the expedition. Thinking that Featherstonhaugh would benefit from the information in the journal, Mather asked Abert not to allow Featherstonhaugh to see it. Abert complied. On learning of this request, Featherstonhaugh responded that since Mather was unco-operative he would not mention him in the official report, and Abert apparently did not question this decision.[22]

After resigning from the army in August, 1836, Mather had a freer hand in airing his complaints. Among other things he publicly charged that Featherstonhaugh had assumed the title of United States Geologist when in fact such a position had not been authorized by Congress; that he, as well as Featherstonhaugh, should have participated in writing the final report; and that Featherstonhaugh had appropriated his map of the Minnesota River. Abert, as usual, defended Featherstonhaugh and reiterated that Mather had been hired only as an assistant and

[21] Featherstonhaugh to Abert, September 1, 1835, in Jensen, ed., *Bulletin of the Missouri Historical Society*, 8:281.
[22] Abert to Mather, December 2, 1835, February 25, 1836, Letters Sent, NARG 77.

INTRODUCTION TO REPRINT xli

that the so-called map was really nothing more than a sketch that had been extensively revised by compilers. Furthermore, Abert commented that Mather should have realized that the map was public property, so Featherstonhaugh could not possibly have "appropriated" it.[23]

It would be difficult, if not impossible, to fix the blame in the Featherstonhaugh-Mather dispute. Featherstonhaugh was haughty and difficult to get along with, but Mather himself was somewhat egocentric and, at least in this matter, lacked objectivity. In addition to the personality clash between the two men, it is likely that they held opposing views concerning geological work. Featherstonhaugh was interested in the broad picture. He was more concerned with stratigraphic sequences than with the collection of specific data. His criticism that Mather was too much of a "schoolmaster" may very well have meant that Mather placed a greater premium on the details of field work.[24] In any event, Featherstonhaugh remembered their differences. Mather was given the same treatment in *Canoe Voyage* that he had received in the official report. He was not mentioned anywhere in the book.

Featherstonhaugh spent most of 1836 in Washington, D.C., working on the report of his 1835 activities, but on October 25 Abert instructed him to make a mineral survey of the recently ceded Cherokee Indian lands in North Carolina and "other Southern states." The approach of winter precluded an extensive tour, so Feath-

[23] Abert to Featherstonhaugh, October 24, 1837, Letters Sent, NARG 77; [William Williams Mather], "Protest of Lt. Mather," in *American Journal of Science and Arts*, 33:205 (January, 1838).

[24] Featherstonhaugh to Abert, August 2, 1835, in Jensen, ed., *Bulletin of the Missouri Historical Society*, 8:276.

erstonhaugh was advised to do some preliminary investigating with the idea of completing the survey at a later date. After working briefly in western North Carolina, he returned to Washington to prepare for his third major expedition in four years.[25]

The 1837 survey had two broad objectives: to study the Wisconsin and Missouri mineral lands in order to obtain more data on the similarities and differences of the various formations in the Mississippi Valley, and to continue the survey of the Cherokee lands. The tour was also an outgrowth of Featherstonhaugh's 1835 and 1836 explorations and was part of his continuing assignment of investigating mineral deposits in the public lands and territories. The geologist made a series of reports by letter in 1837, but the government never published a comprehensive summary of his third, and last, survey; thus the second volume of this book constitutes the sole published record of this activity.

Although his geological excursions were the high lights of Featherstonhaugh's career, it by no means diminished after he left the service of the United States. In the spring of 1839, expressing a desire to see his aged, blind mother and to renew associations with the scientific friends who had elected him a Fellow of the Royal Society in 1835, he returned to his native land after having lived abroad for a total of thirty-six years. Featherstonhaugh moved his second family to England, leaving behind two mature sons of his first marriage. One son, James Duane Featherstonhaugh, continued living at Duanesburg, New York, and later wrote an informative memoir about his father, whom he liked and respected.

[25] For material here and in the next paragraph, see Abert to Featherstonhaugh, October 25, 1836, April 29, 1837, Letters Sent, NARG 77.

INTRODUCTION TO REPRINT   xliii

The other son, George William, Jr., who had worked on surveys for the Topographical Bureau, moved to Calumet County, Wisconsin, in 1839 to manage extensive land holdings that his father had acquired there. Playing the role of a country squire, he soon entered politics and served in the last Wisconsin territorial legislature and as a member of the second constitutional convention in 1847–48.[26]

Featherstonhaugh had been in England only two months when he was sent back to North America as a boundary commissioner for the British government. He and Lieutenant Colonel Richard Z. Mudge of the Royal Engineers were assigned by the Palmerston government to survey and map the St. Croix River separating Maine and New Brunswick. The boundary had been in question since the Paris Treaty of 1783, but the conflicting claims of Americans and Canadians had culminated in the so-called Aroostook War of 1839, which made urgent a settlement of the controversy. Featherstonhaugh and Mudge were generally praised for their work by British officials, but they were roundly condemned by Americans. The Massachusetts legislature characterized the survey as being "calculated to produce, in every part of the United States, . . . a state of the public mind highly unfavorable" to the creation of a "conciliatory temper." Featherstonhaugh was especially denounced, probably because of his American background and government service. Daniel Webster, who finally negotiated a boundary settlement in the Webster-Ashburton Treaty

[26] See note 2, above. On George William, Jr., see H[orace] A. Tenney and David Atwood, *Memorial Record of the Fathers of Wisconsin*, 213 (Madison, 1880); "George William Featherstonhaugh, Jr.," a biographical sketch prepared by WPA workers, in the manuscripts collection of the State Historical Society of Wisconsin, Madison.

of 1842, later wrote that he was surprised the British government had chosen Featherstonhaugh as a commissioner. "It did not know him as well as you and I know him," Webster said. "He is shallow and conceited, with quite a lurch toward mischief." [27]

At the time the geologist seems to have reacted calmly to the criticism, and he defended his work in public appearances. It is likely, however, that he was rankled by the American reaction and that some of his venomous comments about the United States in this volume can be traced to the American reception of his boundary survey. To provide historical background for the boundary dispute and to defend the Webster-Ashburton Treaty, Featherstonhaugh wrote two booklets in the early 1840s. The first, entitled *Historical Sketch of the Negotiations at Paris in 1782*, was published in London in 1842 and may well have been intended to bolster the British position during the treaty negotiations with the United States. A somewhat shorter treatise of 119 pages, entitled *Observations upon the Treaty of Washington* (Webster-Ashburton Treaty), was released in 1843. In this work Featherstonhaugh reviewed the history of the boundary controversy from the end of the Revolutionary War, making the point that because of the long-standing contentions and confusions over the St. Croix River boundary the treaty was very reasonable and that neither country could have expected more from a settlement.

At the conclusion of his boundary duties Featherston-

[27] "Resolves of the Legislature of Massachusetts, Concerning the North Eastern Boundary," June 21, 1841, in 27 Congress, 1 session, *House Executive Documents*, no. 18 (serial 392); 27 Congress, 3 session, *House Executive Documents*, no. 2, p. 17–23 (serial 418); George T. Curtis, *Life of Daniel Webster*, 2:170 (New York, 1870).

INTRODUCTION TO REPRINT　　　　xlv

haugh turned his attention to writing the first of his major travel books, *Excursion Through the Slave States*, which was based on his 1834 reconnaissance of the Ozark region. This work of approximately 750 pages was published by John Murray of London in 1844. In the same year a shorter volume bearing the same title was also published in the United States by Harper & Brothers. Featherstonhaugh set the critical tenor for his treatment of the United States in his introduction. He explained that he had thought of publishing such a book while living there but had refrained for fear of offending the sensibilities of "a powerful interest." Instead, he had waited until he was home where "he could express with perfect freedom any opinions that were on the side of humanity, of rational liberty, and the moral government of mankind." [28]

During the year in which *Excursion* was published, Featherstonhaugh, as a reward for his boundary services, was appointed British consul for the Department of the Seine at Havre, France, a position he held until his death on September 28, 1866. Apparently the consular duties were not too demanding, for he soon found time to write the volume here reprinted. It bears a publication date of 1847, twelve years after the first of the expeditions on which it was based. This lapse of time, said Featherstonhaugh in his introduction, indicated that he was not "anxious to appear" in print. He was, he said, "less influenced by personal motives than by those of a higher character" (1:lxv), for he wished his experience to be useful to his countrymen. They should be made aware of the great power and aggressive tendencies of the

[28] *Excursion*, xii.

United States, a country prone to reckless diplomacy because of imperfections of its governmental system. Featherstonhaugh did admit that he was also influenced by the favorable reception of *Excursion* in his native country. In spite of his avowed reasons for the belated publication of *Canoe Voyage,* it is quite unlikely — in view of his geological work and his later duties — that he would have had time to write the account much earlier than 1845 or 1846.

The book bore the imprint of Richard Bentley, one of England's most reputable publishers, who was famed for the quality of his work. Bentley's outstanding reputation was built in part upon his association with Charles Dickens, who for a time edited the company's literary magazine, *Bentley's Miscellany.* Richard and his older brother Samuel had earlier operated as a partnership, but in 1832 the latter — with his nephew John and others — established the printing firm of S. & J. Bentley, Wilson and Fley. In subsequent years Richard as publisher and Samuel as printer co-operated on many publications, including Featherstonhaugh's *Canoe Voyage.* Samuel Bentley was widely known for his meticulous craftsmanship, and he was one of the "three different printers" recorded as having produced the work.[29]

The firm issued the book in a deluxe two-volume edition which contained two folding maps and twelve lithographs and woodcuts. A compact $5\frac{1}{2}$ by $8\frac{1}{2}$ inches in size, the work sold for £1. 8s. 0d. While the exact number of copies published is uncertain, an approximation

[29] On the Bentleys, see *Dictionary of National Biography,* 4:316 (London, 1885); Richard Bentley and Son, *A List of the Principal Publications Issued from New Burlington Street During the Year 1846* (May, 1896), in the Bentley Papers, Rare Book Room, University of Illinois Library, Urbana. The Minnesota Historical Society has a Xerox copy of the latter.

A CANOE VOYAGE

UP

THE MINNAY SOTOR;

WITH
AN ACCOUNT OF THE LEAD AND COPPER DEPOSITS IN WISCONSIN ;
OF THE GOLD REGION IN THE CHEROKEE COUNTRY ;
AND SKETCHES OF POPULAR MANNERS ;
&c. &c. &c.

BY G. W. FEATHERSTONHAUGH, F.R.S., F.G.S.
AUTHOR OF "EXCURSION THROUGH THE SLAVE STATES."

IN TWO VOLUMES.
VOL. I.

LONDON:
RICHARD BENTLEY, NEW BURLINGTON STREET,
Publisher in Ordinary to Her Majesty.
1847.

TITLE PAGE OF THE 1847 EDITION

INTRODUCTION TO REPRINT xlix

can be based on Bentley's account with the engraving firm of Hullmandel & Walton. In 1846 the lithographers billed Bentley for 400 copies of the two maps and the two lithographs used as frontispieces, and three years later Bentley was billed for an additional 260 copies. It is unlikely that any copies of *Canoe Voyage* were made up after 1849 since sales were evidently quite slow. In 1854 Featherstonhaugh's royalty, which was one-half of the profits after production and promotion costs had been deducted, was only £3. 1s. 6d.[30]

Although the title page of *Canoe Voyage* carries the date 1847, the book was actually published late in 1846. It appears on Bentley's *List of Principal Publications Issued . . . During the Year 1846*, with December 26 as the publication date, but with the notation, "Dated '1847' on the title-pages." Apparently the book was completed slightly earlier than Bentley and the printers anticipated, or perhaps the publisher, for promotional purposes, deliberately used 1847 so the book would still be recognized as new after the turn of the year.

The lithographs of the "Cataract of the White Water" in southwestern North Carolina and "The Pilot Knob" in Missouri which appear as frontispieces were prepared from Featherstonhaugh's sketches by the firm of Hullmandel & Walton. Charles Joseph Hullmandel, the head of the firm, was a famous pioneer lithographer. The son of a German immigrant to England, Hullmandel took up lithography within twenty years of its invention in Germany in 1796. He was not only an accomplished artist,

[30] For information here and in the following paragraph, see *English Catalogue of Books*, 1:253; *List of Principal Publications in 1846* and "Statement of Hullmandel & Walton," in Bentley Papers, University of Illinois Library; vol. 46676A, folio 31, Bentley Papers, British Museum.

but also the developer of new methods of preparing lithographic stones and the author of a technical work entitled *The Art of Drawing on Stone* (1833). Featherstonhaugh, who must have been a rather talented artist in his own right, makes numerous references throughout the book to various sketches which he made while on the scene. It is obvious that the frontispieces as well as all the smaller sketches came from his pen.[31]

Although at least one edition of Featherstonhaugh's first book was printed in the United States, *Canoe Voyage* was not — nor has it ever previously been reprinted either in this country or in England.[32] The present edition has been reproduced photographically from a copy in the Minnesota Historical Society's library. No changes have been made in the text, which appears here exactly as it was originally published. The lithographs and maps have been carefully reproduced to match as closely as possible the size and color tones of the original. The first edition did not contain an index. That supplied at the end of volume 2 was prepared especially for this reprint by the Minnesota Historical Society's editorial staff.

By the time Featherstonhaugh wrote this second travel book, he had no desire to assert that he had been an employee of the United States government, preferring rather to leave the impression that he had made the grand tour at his own expense. Though the critical tone of the work concerning things American was undoubtedly partially contrived to appeal to an audience that had welcomed comparable fare from other English travelers, it

---

[31] On Hullmandel, see *Dictionary of National Biography*, 28:199 (London, 1891).

[32] It may be of interest that in 1960 University Microfilms of Ann Arbor, Michigan, microfilmed *Canoe Voyage* as part of its American Culture Series.

reflected in large part the author's own convictions and personality. While in the field, his arrogance and fastidiousness were as evident as he later made them in the book. Though much of what Featherstonhaugh had to say about the United States was not flattering, he acknowledged the natural beauty which abounded and recognized the country as a potentially powerful nation. He also praised the "real gentry" of America, referring with a kind of awe to such statesmen as John C. Calhoun and Langdon Cheves.

Featherstonhaugh's greatest scorn was lavished on the political changes wrought by Jacksonian Democracy, for he was openly contemptuous of "Republican America." The common class, Featherstonhaugh argued, had deprived the intelligent well-bred minority of its rightful rule. The faceless, nameless mass which he called the "Sovereign People" suffered frequently from the venom of his pen. He observed cynically that "if the devil kept pigeonholes with *improved* forms of government in them, as the Abbé Siéyes is said to have done, he could not have imagined anything more fatal to religion, morality, integrity and sober manners, or more sure to accomplish the ruin of a nation, than frequent elections, universal suffrage, and perfect equality." (2:347)

The excessive democracy in the United States, reasoned Featherstonhaugh, posed a direct threat to Great Britain, for "in a republic founded upon universal suffrage, demagogues will always be found contending for power and emolument, seeking to become the leaders of the masses by flattering their cupidity and their prejudices." (1:209) The demagogue, in turn, he contended, would be inclined to satisfy the aggressive tendencies of

Americans, who with reference to Canada "must always remain doubtful and dangerous neighbours." (1:210)

In Featherstonhaugh's view, the United States was not only shackled by the tyranny of the "Sovereign People," it was also afflicted by the "all-absorbing passion for money" which had created a class of "go-ahead" men who lived "only to carry out their own base and selfish manœuvres." (2:97, 99) Featherstonhaugh told his readers that these "smart men" received the "most unbounded admiration" from the public (2:99).

While maintaining a careful distinction between the "Sovereign People" and the cultured minority, Featherstonhaugh related that crudeness and vulgarity were national hallmarks, noting that some members of the "lower classes" were "scarce above the level of savages, either in manner or appearance." (2:173) Those with the least education bore the brunt of his ridicule. Once, whiling away time on board a steamer, Featherstonhaugh played an accordion. A Tennessee woman admired his instrument, but in so doing revealed not only her language deficiencies, but her musical ignorance as well. Cuttingly Featherstonhaugh quoted her as saying: "Well, if that ain't the leetelest piazzur-forty (piano-forte) I ever seed: don't it beat all, now don't it, Miss Kittle?" (2:175) In the same vein, he remarked that in the South "the English language is in a strange way." (2:188)

Featherstonhaugh's scientific training did not temper his many prejudices, which included an intolerance of tobacco, drunkenness, obscenity, bawdiness, and dirt. Firmly convinced that cleanliness was next to godliness, he had adventure after adventure in his persistent quest for comfortable lodgings. He recalled a situation where a landlord had proffered: "'Squire, I reckon you'll get up quite lively in the morning.' And so I did, for on awaking, such a spectacle presented itself of bugs running all over me and over every thing else, that I jumped up as lively as a parched pea." (1:23) In Pittsburgh he stayed at a tavern with "an exterior so filthy that I was ashamed to enter," and he commented that the entire city was befouled by what he called "fuliginous matter" from the forges (1:33). Combining his prejudices on another occasion, Featherstonhaugh observed that "Democracy and dirt have a great regard for each other; and where the first has the upper hand, the second never fails to assert its authority." (1:95)

Of the many things he abhorred, however, tobacco smoke seems to have led the list. He wrote that "nothing would frighten me more than to apprehend an eternity of tobacco-smoke." (2:23) It made him physically nauseous, and he was repulsed by tobacco chewing and spitting. Though Featherstonhaugh regarded these habits as highly undesirable, he managed to deliver his antismoking diatribes with good humor; he speaks of a God of Nicotinia and recounts the height of unpleasant experiences—waking in his room in St. Louis in the dark of night faced by smoking Indians who had been billeted with him after he had gone to sleep! (2:61).

While he could be humorous about tobacco, Featherstonhaugh was grimly serious about the evils of liquor. He associated many of the shortcomings of the "Sovereign People" with their penchant for intemperate drinking and reported a pathetic young housewife as having said that laboring men were too lazy to raise potatoes, but "'if it's plenty of whisky they can get, they are satisfied.'" (1:15) Perhaps Featherstonhaugh's most detested experience occurred aboard a river steamer where he was forced to live with a rowdy lot under crowded conditions; the boat, he said, became a "Babel of noise and vulgarity; drinking, smoking, swearing, and gambling prevailed from morn to night." (2:45)

One gets the impression, however, that Featherstonhaugh's objections to such practices were not basically religious in nature. His comments on religion seem to have been dictated by his aristocratic background rather than by strong moral convictions. He described the Episcopal church as "a strong bond of union amongst the educated and well-bred" (2:269), and he reacted favorably to a Roman Catholic service which he attended in Detroit. On the other hand, the revival efforts of Major Gustavus Loomis at Fort Snelling offended him, and he was critical and even scornful of some missionaries he met. Indeed, he is rather consistently mistaken about the various church affiliations of those he encountered, labeling the Presbyterian missionaries at Lac qui Parle as Methodists, and those near Camp Wool, Tennessee, as Moravians when they were Presbyterians.

He was especially caustic about Alexander G. Huggins at Lac qui Parle, whom he described as "an odd, long-legged, sharp-faced, asparagus-looking animal," a "quaint, drawling, vulgar Jonathan," who, in speaking used "interjections and grunts" instead of yes and no. Featherstonhaugh claimed a conversation with Huggins in which "I asked him why he had not taken a young Indian girl to wife? 'Stranger,' said he, 'I allow them har young painted Jizzabuls aint just up to missionarying.'" (1:348, 349) Dr. Thomas S. Williamson, Huggins' compatriot at Lac qui Parle, fared only slightly better. The doctor gave the impression of being an extremely earnest young man, and Featherstonhaugh seemed to derive a certain satisfaction from poking fun at clergymen who took themselves seriously. As a result, the geologist spurned Williamson's invitation to attend Presbyterian services in favor of a Sioux scalp dance.

Though the missionaries and many others received the rough side of Featherstonhaugh's tongue, at least one man — Milor, his half-breed guide on the Minnesota River — was singled out for consistent and lavish praise. The guide, in Featherstonhaugh's opinion, had uncommonly good judgment. Aside from his invaluable experience with the Sioux, Milor was apparently properly courteous and respectful, traits which weighed heavily with his demanding master. The voyageur crew Featherstonhaugh had recruited at Green Bay was not so lucky. Obviously enjoying his role as *bourgeois*, Featherstonhaugh tongue-lashed them frequently, both on the trip and in the book.

Several rather prominent Minnesota men also incurred Featherstonhaugh's wrath. For some unknown reason, he conceived an intense dislike for Joseph Renville, the *bois brulé* trader at Lac qui Parle, and his animosity seems to have resulted in several errors of fact. He implied that Renville had hampered the missionaries, whereas the trader had actively helped Williamson establish the mission just weeks before Featherstonhaugh's arrival. It seems virtually impossible for the geologist not to have known this; yet he makes it appear that Renville and his pagan braves stood in the way of Christianity. Nor did he approve of Joseph R. Brown, the trader he met near Big Stone Lake. He accepted an erroneous story that Brown, who was considered a ladies' man among the Indian girls, had been married several times before he went West, apparently not realizing that Brown was only fourteen when he arrived in Minnesota.

Loomis, the psalm-singing officer at Fort Snelling who was responsible for assigning Featherstonhaugh to uncomfortable quarters in a storeroom, was described as "a long-legged, self-sanctified, unearthly looking mortal." (1:265) He was, however, accorded a certain anonymity because Featherstonhaugh, following a literary practice common in his day, used only the initial of Loomis' surname. Considerable efforts have been made by the Minnesota Historical Society's editorial staff to identify as many of these people as possible, and the results are evident in the index printed at the end of volume 2.

Because he too often trusted his ear and did not question local orthography, Featherstonhaugh made numerous odd errors. For example, he recorded Hercules Dousman of Prairie du Chien as "Mr. Douceman," Hazen Mooers as "Mr. Moore," and Jean B. Faribault as "Terribaux." He evidently did not learn Louis Provençalle's name or else he chose to avoid it in favor of the more colorful "Le Blanc," a sobriquet used by the Indians for the illiterate Traverse des Sioux trader. In addition, Featherstonhaugh (or perhaps his typesetters) had some difficulty in correctly dating Jonathan Carver's search for the western sea in 1766–67, and the author is incorrect in thinking that the cavern he visited near Fort Snelling was Carver's Cave. In reality Featherstonhaugh saw and described nearby Fountain Cave in present-day St. Paul, Minnesota.

While its author was often critical and sometimes wrong about the people and places he visited, the book offers a great deal of valuable and useful information. Featherstonhaugh knew the men of whom he wrote; he did not invent characters or situations. He kept a meticulous journal, with great effort and uncommon discipline, so his chronology is very accurate. His descriptions of terrain and physical objects were discerning and, in some instances, remarkable; an example is his depiction of the shot tower hill at Helena on the Wisconsin River (2:110). Although his examination of the Wisconsin lead mines with Richard C. Taylor in the spring of 1837 was rather cursory and his conclusions somewhat superficial, he did secure information on the methods used to obtain and smelt lead, and he saw something of the extent of the lead formations.[33]

Featherstonhaugh made notes on the major geological formations of every region he visited in the hope that Congress would authorize the compilation of a geological map of the United States.[34] He made a real effort to relate strata to the recently determined Cambrian and Silurian systems of Sedgwick and Murchison, and he consistently observed the drainage patterns of the Wisconsin-Minnesota region, logically concluding that the area had held far greater amounts of water in a prior

[33] For some Wisconsin reactions to Featherstonhaugh's observations, see Harold L. Geisse, "Featherstonhaugh and His Critics," and "Featherstonhaugh in Tychoberah," in *Wisconsin Magazine of History*, 45:164–185 (Spring, 1962). The journals kept by Featherstonhaugh during his geological expeditions are now in the possession of Mr. James D. Featherstonhaugh of Albany, New York.

[34] See Featherstonhaugh, *Report*, 1836, p. 13.

geologic age. In the same vein, while contemplating the general water diminution of North America, he referred to the old river valleys, where the landscape caused him to think in Huttonian terms of millions of years (1:276). This time concept in itself would not have been possible too many years before Featherstonhaugh's time, since geological chronology had been ensnared in the Neptunian theory and its natural association with the Noachian flood. Featherstonhaugh, working before the compounding of glacial theories, recognized that the land surface had been altered by a "denuding force," which he infers was probably water action (1:204). Once — and there is a question as to whether he was serious or merely twitting his learned peers — he reverted to Wernerian thought and seemingly found some satisfaction in a scripture-related interpretation of geological phenomena (2:336).

A complex man of intense feelings, Featherstonhaugh saw a great variety of life and successfully captured with his mind and his pen a blend of the bizarre, the humorous, and the miserable. Determined to tell a good story, he related numerous anecdotes, sometimes at his own expense. He caught the grand tragedy of the Indians, and he succeeded also in recreating the essence of frontier informality, crudeness, materialism, and speculative mania.

A substantial amount of space in this volume is devoted to generally sympathetic observations on various Indian tribes — especially the Sioux, the Winnebago, and the Cherokee — and particularly to native-white relations. Though Featherstonhaugh clearly recognized the plight of the red man, he thought of their decline as the

INTRODUCTION TO REPRINT   lix

natural order of things. Rather than placing the blame entirely on the whites, he also criticized the Indians for their short-sightedness in relying upon the traders. Featherstonhaugh had obviously devoted considerable thought to the exploited natives; in several passages (notably 1:188) he aptly described the cruel dilemma of their transition. His conclusions about the red men of Wisconsin and Minnesota have the advantage of being based almost entirely on his own observations. A realist rather than a romantic, he emphasized the squalor of Indian society. When he visited the Sioux, he saw numerous villages and bands, but he evidenced no awareness of the various tribal divisions. He was especially interested in Indian languages, and he made conscientious efforts to record and translate Indian words, especially for the names of geographic features.

As might be expected, a book written by a fastidious Englishman who used tooth and nail brushes even in the wilderness, who insisted on the daily regimen of making his "toilette," and who was overly concerned about comfort and courtesy was not well received by many American readers. They criticized both the man and the work. Henry H. Sibley, the cultured Minnesota trader who was to become the state's first governor, had no reason to be offended by Featherstonhaugh's comments about him. He nevertheless reacted sharply to the Englishman whose "appearance and manners," he said, "were ill calculated to ensure him a favorable reception among plain republicans. He was both aristocratic and conceited." Sibley noted that Featherstonhaugh's book was "characterized by abuse of American society and of particular individuals," and he took sides in the Mather-

Featherstonhaugh feud by stating firmly: "All the information embodied in it of any value to Minnesota, was the result of the labor of Lieut. Mather." Lawrence Taliaferro, the Virginia gentleman who served as Indian agent at Fort Snelling, wrote that Featherstonhaugh's report "was made up mostly from construction and not from actual observation or geological research. He was obviously not flattered with his reception at Fort Snelling, or in the Indian country. He attempted to pass current for that which he possessed not — superior talent and modesty in his profession." On the other hand, the agent regarded Mather as "solid, clear-headed, scientific, with a modest, unassuming gentlemanly bearing."[35]

The opinions of these two men were recorded after they had ample opportunity to reflect on Featherstonhaugh and his book, but the missionary Thomas Williamson reacted to the geologist soon after meeting him. Within weeks after the Englishman's stop at Lac qui Parle, Williamson wrote his superior that both Featherstonhaugh and Mather "appeared to be men of good education and genteel manners [and] were sociable and pleasant but from some remarks of Mr F I thought at the time he was not a man of much principle." The missionary also noted that Featherstonhaugh had purportedly "circulated" at Fort Snelling "reports highly injurious to Mr. Renvilles character." Concerned about criticism of his missionary effort, Williamson observed that "I have not heard that he [Featherstonhaugh] had said anything injurious to us but it is highly probable he may do so as he may

[35] Sibley, "Reminiscences; Historical and Personal," in *Minnesota Historical Collections*, 1:393 (St. Paul, 1872); "Auto-Biography of Maj. Lawrence Taliaferro," in *Minnesota Historical Collections*, 6:245.

INTRODUCTION TO REPRINT　　　　　lxi

probably have observed the [sic] we felt more regard for Lieu. Mather than himself which was really the case though we did not design to show it." Williamson was no doubt primarily concerned that Featherstonhaugh somehow might cause Renville, the mission's protector, to be removed from the Indian country. Edward D. Neill, Minnesota's pioneer historian, noted that Featherstonhaugh was the only individual who ever criticized Renville and characterized the geologist as a "dyspeptic and growling Englishman" whose book portrayed a "filthy imagination," and was "only remarkable for its vulgarity." [36]

Most of the frontiersmen who met Featherstonhaugh knew him but briefly. An exception was John H. Bliss, son of the Fort Snelling commandant, who as a twelve-year-old boy traveled with Featherstonhaugh from Fort Snelling to Pittsburgh by way of St. Louis. Bliss lived with the scientist for some weeks. He later remembered him as a "large, fine-looking and determined man, with many excellent qualities, but with an unfortunate disposition to bully and domineer over those who were under him." By nature, Bliss wrote, Featherstonhaugh was "admirably calculated to get along with the Canadian voyageurs, whom he treated like brutes, as they deserved, and they consequently feared and respected him." Bliss readily recalled the Englishman's "weaknesses and peculiarities," but he felt "bound to say, that from beginning to end he did the fair thing by me." [37]

[36] Williamson to Rev. David Greene, October 15, 1835, in American Board of Commissioners for Foreign Missions Papers, typed copy in the Minnesota Historical Society, original in Congregational House, Boston; Neill, "A Sketch of Joseph Renville," in *Minnesota Historical Collections*, 1:162; and Neill, *History of Minnesota*, 416.

[37] Bliss, in *Minnesota Historical Collections*, 6:353.

Featherstonhaugh was sixty-seven when *Canoe Voyage up the Minnay Sotor*, his last literary effort, was published. He then carried on the quiet duties of his consular post only to become involved in the most notable incident of his extraordinary career. The French revolution of 1848 forced the abdication of King Louis Philippe, and the monarch and his family, fearing for their lives, fled to Havre where Featherstonhaugh aided in their successful escape abroad. The imaginative Featherstonhaugh escorted the disguised king to a waiting ship, posing Louis Philippe as his visiting English uncle. Featherstonhaugh's role in the escape became well known, and he was later rewarded by the royal family. Geologist Roderick Murchison was delighted by his friend's adventure, for Featherstonhaugh—ever the scientist—had given Louis Philippe not his uncle's name but that of William Smith—the father of English geology!

It is easy to see why Featherstonhaugh's American contemporaries were often offended by his personal vanities, his barbed pen, and his antirepublican sentiments. In fairness, however, it should be pointed out that his criticisms of American democracy and of the crudity and materialism of frontier society were shared by many Englishmen of his generation—as was his extreme respect for men of breeding and position. Thus the animosity he aroused in many frontiersmen would probably have been directed at most Englishmen of his upbringing and bearing in similar situations. In an age of Anglophobia, it was unlikely that the frontier inhabitants of a nationalistic "Young America" would see much virtue in any Englishman. The Sibleys, Taliaferros, and Williamsons of the 1830s and 1840s were, after all, conditioned by the anti-British heritage of the Revolutionary War and the War of 1812.

Even his severest contemporary critics, however, would have had to admit that Featherstonhaugh was intelligent, capable, observant, and adventurous. He entered a new profession relatively late in life and followed it enthusiastically into little-known regions where few had gone before. Though his scientific observations now seem obvious and dated, it must be remembered that in his day he was one of the foremost men in his field. His activities in promoting the "new geology" won him appointment as the first geologist employed by the federal government.

In spite of the fact that Featherstonhaugh's *Canoe Voyage up the Minnay Sotor* was rather severely condemned by some of its contemporaries, the volume has stood the test of time. It remains a valuable source of historical information for a considerable geographic area of the midwestern and southern United States. It is also an entertaining and well-written book which reflects many of the social attitudes and employs many of the literary techniques typical of the bygone days of the mid-nineteenth century.

WILLIAM E. LASS

Mankato, Minnesota
January 15, 1970

AUTHOR'S INTRODUCTION

THE criticism of the Public is sometimes deprecated by travelled Authors, upon the plea that their original notes were not made with a view to publication. Without claiming any indulgence upon this ground, the writer of the following pages can truly state, that they are almost literally transcribed from the Journals he kept during the period of his observations; and he hopes that he may claim some confidence upon this point, since it is obvious, that, if he had been particularly anxious to appear as an Author, he would scarcely have permitted so many years to elapse before presenting his narratives to the public; for ten years had already passed away when his "Excursions through the Slave States" were published, and this "Canoe Voyage" was commmenced the same year that those Excursions terminated.

In determining to publish his Travels, the Author has been less influenced by personal motives than by those of a higher character. The greater part of his life having been passed in distant foreign lands, and his deep attachment to his native country having increased with absence, he always cherished the natural English feeling, that he was bound—according to the degree of his ability—to make his experience useful to his country. It was only, therefore, when an appropriate moment seemed to be arrived for the accomplishment of that duty, that he ventured upon the experiment of drawing the attention of his countrymen to the serious considerations suggested by his knowledge of America, which, independent of them, he should most probably never have attempted.

During the ten years which have elapsed since the Author visited the countries he has described, the reading public has had its attention occupied by various tourists in the United States in works principally descriptive of the manners, customs, and progress in the useful arts of the American population settled upon their Atlantic frontier; those features of civilization, which, with the exception of some strong shades of difference arising from climate and form of Government, forcibly remind the English traveller of those commercial communities in his own country, which owe their high prosperity to the enterprise and persevering character of its distinguished merchants and manufacturers.

The pleasing pictures furnished by these writers of the stirring activity of the people of the Atlantic coast, of the intelligence and hospitality of the better classes, of the excellent administration of justice in the superior courts, and of the generally successful manner in which the better classes of Americans have applied the religion and laws which they derived from their British ancestry to the high purposes of civilization, are most satisfactory, and seem largely to flatter the opinion which is so well established in Republican America, that it is the happiest country in Christendom.

Divided as the Americans are by their struggles for political power, yet, the occasions are frequent which evince their attachment to their country: for in no part of the civilized world, is there found a people indulging in such unqualified exultation, when writing or speaking of themselves, or which is more unanimous, when the object is territorial aggrandisement.

We rarely, however, find them inquiring whether that growing power, which is the source of their national pride, is likely to contribute to the happiness of mankind: that, indeed, seems to be a question which more nearly concerns those who contemplate their future strength as pregnant with some danger to it. Enough has already transpired to create the justest apprehension of this character. We have seen conterminous states in North America in turns the object of that rapacious policy, which is sure to be generated by an inordinate cupidity. Scarcely had it been appeased by the conciliatory conduct of our own country, which Providence appears to have constituted at this time the especial guardian of the peace of Christian countries, than, refreshed as it were by its prey, the government of the United States, with no plea more intelligible than that which determines the strong man when he assaults his weaker neighbour, dismembers and invades a sister Republic—first making annexation the cause of war, and then making war the immediate motive for further annexation. Thus has a country, which came into existence with a promise of moral greatness, already stained its history by acts that revive the indignant remembrance of the worst of European political transactions!

How often have not the orators of the model Republic, in their 4th of July orations, denounced the spoliation of Poland as the most execrable public act that ever was perpetrated? and how often have they not predicted, that, although Poland has been suppressed, no physical power can extinguish the deep hatred of the Poles, or avert the fearful consequences that one day will overtake their oppressors? Hereafter, perhaps, it will be seen that the unprincipled invasion of Mexico will produce no permanent consequences, save the planting of an inextinguishable hatred in the future generations of its people.

For some time past the attention of the world has been turned to the tendencies of the Republican Government of the United States: no one, indeed, who has observed them, and who associates those tendencies with the possible misapplication of the immense resources which another generation or two will place at its command, can shut his eyes upon the future. The English traveller, above all, who has advanced to the distant confines of that Government, who has trod over many thousand miles of its unrivalled fertility,—who has traversed its Coal-fields, occupying an area larger than Great Britain,—who has seen its inexhaustable supply of Iron and Copper ores, its productive Lead district extending at least eight hundred miles, its Gold regions nearly equally long,—and who foresees what a prodigious population will hereafter be assembled amidst these elements of power, cannot but be deeply impressed with the fact that every popular election in Republican America exposes all these immense resources to fall under the controul of men little disposed to honour the principles that alone bind nations to the maintenance of the peace of mankind; men who, within another generation, may attempt upon the British North American provinces as lawless an invasion as that which they have set on foot against their presumed feeble sister Republic of Mexico! In the following pages the reader will see how vast the future resources of the United States will be; and, if he has attended to the progress of events, will be prepared for the warnings which the Author has given in the 20th Chapter of the first Volume.

It was reflections of this kind that first led the Author to revise his old notes, with a view to their publication. In the introduction to the "Excursions through the Slave States," Universal Suffrage and the Government of an uncontrolled Democracy were spoken of with freedom. Since the publication of that work, events have taken place on the American continent which have confirmed the Author in his opinions, and determined him to offer to the public a second Narrative, where an extensive tour through a different part of the American continent will be described. To this he confesses he was also partly induced by the somewhat unexpected approbation with which his first work was received in his native country. In the United States that work on its appearance, was represented as an illiberal attack upon the nation, and the Author spoken of in acrimonious terms. This he somewhat expected, and submitted to, in the confidence that time would produce a juster feeling towards him in liberal minds there. In this he has not been disappointed, having received the most satisfactory assurances that he is acquitted in the judgment of the good and wise of any intention but that of holding up just principles to the veneration of all men. He trusts, therefore, that the present work also will be considered in America as a not unfaithful representation of what is described, and that no passage in it will be construed as justly offensive to honourable minds, or bring into doubt the Author's lively admiration for a country he knows so familiarly, where he has left so many valued friends, and whose future glory and prosperity he prays may be founded upon those great principles which alone secure the happiness of a people and the respect of mankind.

Dec., 1846.

A CANOE VOYAGE
UP THE
MINNAY SOTOR

A CANOE VOYAGE

TO THE

SOURCES OF THE MINNAY SOTOR.

CHAPTER I.

THE AUTHOR PROPOSES TO MAKE A TOUR OF EXPLORATION TO THE CÔTEAU DE PRAIRIE, AT THE SOURCES OF THE MINNAY SOTOR, OR ST. PETER'S RIVER, A N.W. TRIBUTARY OF THE MISSISSIPPI.

At the close of the winter which succeeded to the excursion I made in 1834 through the Slave States to the then frontiers of Mexico, which has been already laid before the public, I turned my attention to those countries watered by the principal tributaries of the Mississippi river, which descend from the elevated land to which the old French *voyageurs* had given the name of *Côteau de Prairie*, and from which are thrown down the waters of Red River, of *Lake Winnipeg*, several important tributaries of the *Missouri* river, and the *Minnay Sotor*, or St. Peter's River, first visited by Carver in 1778. With the exception of the huried *reconnaissance* of the country adjacent to this last river by that intelligent American officer, Colonel Long, no account existed of the nature of the country and its capabilities for settlement but in the meagre pages of Hennepin and Carver.

SUPPOSED COPPER-MINES.

Charlevoix, it is true, in his "Histoire de la Nouvelle France," had asserted that Le Sueur, in 1698, had entered the *Makatōh*, a tributary of the St. Peter's, and had discovered near its mouth a copper-mine, at the foot of a mountain ten leagues long, which appeared to be composed of a green cupreous earth; and further added, that Le Sueur, having received a commission from the French Court to open these mines, had entered the Makatōh on the 19th of September, 1700, with a party of workmen that had accompanied him from France, had erected Fort *L'Huillier*, named after one of the farmers-general who was his patron, and having taken 30,000 pounds' weight of the ore, descended to the mouth of the Mississippi with it, and selecting 4000 pounds of the best kind, had proceeded with it to France.

If this extraordinary statement were founded in truth, the locality well deserved to be investigated. Unfortunately Colonel Long's party, who were acquainted with Charlevoix's statement, had not found it convenient, when passing through the country, to enter the Makatōh and convince themselves of the probability of such an extraordinary deposit of cupreous ore existing; so that Charlevoix, whom I had found in my previous excursion accurate in many things, had hitherto not been contradicted.

Although the impostures of La Hontan, and the exaggerations of other French adventurers who in the early periods of the domination of the French crown in Canada had penetrated to the Mississippi, had too frequently led me to place little confidence in their descriptions of the unknown countries they asserted themselves to have visited, yet Hennepin and La Sale were good authorities; and as it was possible that Charlevoix's statement was founded in fact, I was desirous of personally settling this very interesting mineralogical question. The whole geology, too, of this part of America was unknown; and a tour of observation for the purpose of examining it could be made to comprehend an investigation of the lead region of Wisconsin, which I had found reason to believe, during my examination of the mines in Missouri in 1834, was an extension of one great galeniferous deposit at least of from six to seven hundred miles in length. In the pursuit of these objects I could not fail to acquire a great deal of information; and, by selecting a route to those remote countries through the most unfrequented and undescribed settled districts of the central parts of the United States, it was probable I should be able to acquire the knowledge of many things interesting both to America and Europe, and see a good deal of the manners and customs of the inhabitants.

It was my desire to commence this journey of from fifteen hundred to two thousand miles from Washington to the sources of the St. Peter, by ascending the Potomac river to the great bituminous coal-field commencing at Cumberland. I had before been much struck with the sections of rock this river had made at Harper's Ferry, and was desirous of inspecting those which had been created by its passage through the Alleghany Mountains and the enormous coal-field extending along the whole course of their western flank. Fortunately for my purpose, some gentlemen of my acquaintance, who superintended the construction of the Chesapeake and Ohio Canal, a very extensive work, then in progress along the margin of the Potomac, for the purpose of transporting the coal from Cumberland, were on the point of proceeding on the canal as far as it was finished, to inspect their works, and most kindly offered to conduct me on my way as far as they were themselves bound. These were not only intelligent, but amiable men, such as the better classes are formed of in the United States : so, independent of the great convenience which thus presented itself, I should, by accepting their offer, have the advantage of enjoying for several days the society of cheerful and well-informed companions. One of them was a near relative of the celebrated George Washington, and not only bore his name, but a strong family resemblance to him, which, apart from his intrinsic good qualities, always interested me deeply; so charmed are we to trace in living expression some of the lineaments of departed greatness. Another of the party was a distinguished topographical officer, in the service of the United States. A third was a very remarkable Quaker gentleman from Virginia, shrewd, well-informed, full of wit and repartee, and quite capable of unbending into a fair share of discreet joviality. The rest of the party was composed of men of great worth, and who, with those I have named, had been selected by the stockholders of the canal and by the Government of the United States to manage the construction of this important undertaking.

CHAPTER II.

EMBARKS UPON THE CANAL AT GEORGETOWN, NEAR WASHINGTON.—BEAUTIFUL SCENERY OF THE POTOMAC.—ACTION OF THE RIVER UPON THE ROCKS NEAR THE GREAT FALLS.—A SOCIABLE QUAKER.—FOSSIL PLANTS IN SILURIAN SANDSTONE. — CALCAREOUS BRECCIA FORMED BY THE EASTERN RIDGE OF THE ALLEGHANIES COMING UP THROUGH THE LIMESTONE.—HARPER'S FERRY.—CHARACTERISTIC STORY OF A GERMAN SETTLER.

July 8, 1835.—This morning we all embarked upon the canal at George Town, near Washington, in a commodious iron boat, eighty-five feet long. The weather was clear and sunny, and we glided agreeably on in the midst of the most charming scenery, with that fine river, the Potomac, flowing within the distance of a few yards on our left. The gneiss and hornblende rocks which prevailed at George Town continued to the *Great Falls of the Potomac.* The strata were generally inclined at an angle of about 50°. About eleven miles from George Town we reached the termination of the first plane, containing seventeen well-constructed locks : here the west side of the canal was walled up next to the river by masonry 100 feet high ; and I soon began to understand how such massive constructions must necessarily have occasioned, upon so long a line, the expenditure of the many millions of dollars which had been talked of. The contrast between nature and art was very striking here ; for by the side of these ponderous displays of human enterprise, the river wound about in a beautiful manner, to escape by a narrow and picturesque gorge. Further on, the stream was running amidst thousands of very small islands, consisting of gneiss covered with wild grass exceedingly verdant.

Ere we reached the Great Falls the rocks lay bared for a great distance, as ruggedly as if they were upon their edges, somewhat resembling the effect that would be produced by the instantaneous congelation of a sea highly cuspated. As my friends very kindly permitted me to leave the boat whenever I desired to examine any locality, I descended to these rocks, and found reason to believe that they had been brought to that state by the action of the water: remains of pot-holes were numerous, some of which had been two and three feet in diameter. Here, undoubtedly, had been a ledge across the river, which at this place is 168 feet above the level of tide water, giving about 14 feet slope per mile for the distance from George Town. Like most other streams, the Potomac has worked its channels through the rocks by retrocession, and in long periods of time has worn down this ledge by first forming pot-holes, and then attenuating and breaking them up. In this particular place the very rugged appearance has been materially caused by the inclination of the strata, formed of a coarse micaceous slate.

Having gratified myself with the inspection of many curious geological phenomena along the channel of the river, I re-ascended the bank, and after a sharp walk overtook our party. We now, all seated in the comfortable cabin of our nice floating hotel, proceeded to discuss a cold collation, consisting of a great many good things; some very choice old Madeira not being wanting to crown our repast. We all got very merry, and began singing songs as we glided along the pleasant canal. I found my companions an amiable jocose set of men, without prejudices, quite disposed to make the excursion a pleasant one, and full of kind attentions to myself. But we none of us could hold the candle to our worthy friend the Quaker, whose dry facetious manner was inimitable : he was the life of the company, full of repartee and anecdote. Now and then our mirth was suspended for a short time by these gentlemen leaving the boat to inspect the works, and when, upon their return, I inquired how far it was to the next lock, our dry friend would say, "Thee may'st put it down in thy book, that it will take us just two bottles of Madeira to get there." One of our party was a General S., who had commanded a body of fifteen hundred American militia, when in 1813 the gallant General Ross captured the city of Washington. Amongst the amusing anecdotes he told us, was that of a party of his men, who slipped off to play at "all-fours:" some of our light troops coming upon them unawares, fired a volley and killed the corporal, with " high, low, Jack, and the game " in his hand! It was a day of uninterrupted enjoyment and happiness to me.

Towards evening we arrived at Seneca Falls, where a wide dam was thrown across the river for a feeder, raising a fine expanse of water for several miles, and giving it all the character of a broad glassy lake. The hills recede here, and the country assumed an aspect different from that given by the imposing primary rocks amidst which we had hitherto been moving. The country had the appearance of a basin, and I thought it not improbable that it might be an extension of the bituminous coal-field which passes through Virginia to the south; for on reaching Seneca Creek, I found it divided the micaceous slate from a red slaty sandstone, that had evidently been disturbed from a horizontal position. Near this place we slept at a country tavern, far inferior, however, in cleanliness and resources, to our own floating hotel.

July 9.—The next day we stopped at a romantic place called *The Rock*, belonging to a gentleman of the name of Lee, who has a pretty cottage at the top of a narrow path, fancifully cut in the hill-side. I was curious to visit this place, having before examined at Washington some stone intended for the public works that came from the quarries Mr. Lee had opened here. The rock was a silurian sandstone, containing seams of anthracite coal, with many traces of carbonate of copper. Calamites and other fossil plants were not unfrequent, and I brought away a few good specimens.

On leaving this place we passed for a dozen miles through a rich agricultural country, some fine farms having been established upon the fertile alluvial bottoms. For the first nineteen miles we had a tolerably level country, having had to pass only three locks. The *Bignonia radicans* was everywhere abundant and showy. Five miles before arriving at *Monocasy* Creek, a calcareous breccia occurs dipping to the east, in broad beds; these are sometimes separated by seams of red shaley argillaceous sandstone, which on the other side of the Monocasy we found in places without any breccia, dipping equally to the east. This breccia, which has furnished the beautiful columns of the Senate-Chamber at Washington, again occurs near to the *Point of Rocks*, dipping to the west, and completing the anticlinal axis.

At the Point of Rocks the river passes through the *Cotoctin* Mountains, formed here of an unctuous and

ORIGIN OF THE BRECCIA.

shining chloritic talcose slate. The canal is constructed in this rock all the way to Harper's Ferry, where we arrived about sunset. The whole of this day was replete with geological interest to me: the broad Potomac had laid open the structure of the country in a much more complete manner than investigations made on land could have done. This breccia, too, was a very interesting feature in the geology of the country. From the irregular calcareous seams in it, it was evident that after its first consolidation it had undergone another movement, which, in giving it an anticlinal form, had produced fissures, that, being subsequently filled up by calcareous solutions, formed the irregular seams so frequent in it. A similar breccia, but composed of rocks not calcareous, is found at various points in Virginia and the southern States south-west from this. Near Buckland, in Virginia, there is a fine instance of it. It may, therefore, be inferred that the most eastern of all these Alleghany ridges, which I have upon other occasions called the Atlantic slope or chain, has been upraised through the silurian limestone of this part of the country, and through the slates farther to the south, and has carried their fragments to its eastern side, where they have been deposited in beds, and consolidated into rocks; and that the anticlinal structure of these beds has been occasioned by a subsequent movement.

July 10.—Having passed the night at Harper's Ferry, I arose early to have an opportunity of again looking at the lofty escarpments of the Shenandoah, which here joins the Potomac, and the rocks of what is called the *Blue Ridge*, opposite to Harper's Ferry, which present a mural escarpment of about 900 feet. After breakfast we returned to our boat, and pursued our way until we had passed through all the chloritic slates of the ridge, when we again came upon the silurian limestone, about a quarter of a mile from an important feeder of the canal, which confirmed me in the opinion I had formed of the origin of the breccia we had left behind. Further on, we passed on the Virginia side of the Potomac immense deposits of bog-iron ore, which it is probable had a contemporaneous origin with the red argillaceous matter in which the beds of breccia were occasionally inclosed.

The country and river here were both very beautiful, and the district we passed through was singularly fertile, teeming with heavy crops, whilst the scene was much embellished by the fine limestone escarpments on the right bank of the river. On our arrival at Shepherdstown, there being yet some daylight left, I walked to the escarpment, which contained large proportions of hydraulic lime, of a good quality, that had been made serviceable in the construction of the canal. Shepherdstown is an old Virginia village, built upon the fertile limestone valley that traverses the country, and which is filled with rich farms. The Potomac is deep here, and wound in a pleasing serpentine course. It was too evident, however, that every advantage was not taken of the great fertility of the soil, and that slovenly farming kept down its productiveness.

July 11.—Pursuing our route, we came at no great distance to a place where the canal had been cut through a stout bluff of limestone 85 feet high, that had projected into the river. Several caves were in the rock, into one of which I entered, but found nothing but stalactites. Everywhere nature was beautiful, the weather was delicious; and although the sun was rather inconveniently hot, a belt of graceful trees, entwined from top to bottom with vines and creepers, which extended along the edge of the tow-path next to the Potomac, gave us a grateful shade, with occasional lovely peeps at the river. We endeavoured to do honour to all these attractions, by sacrificing sundry bottles of excellent wine, and being as merry and facetious as good wine and good company could make us. Every man was strong in his way, but for a good crack our excellent friend the Quaker was without a rival. If any one made us roar by a story, our demure-looking companion was sure to follow with a supplementary joke of a higher caliber.

This fertile land, on the Maryland side of the river, which bore such heavy crops of wheat and maize, was valued, I found, at fifty dollars an acre, and belonged principally to the descendants of Germans who had strayed from Pennsylvania,—a thrifty, but, generally speaking, a coarse, ignorant race of men. We passed the house of an opulent settler of this kind, of whom they related the following story, which, although rather vulgar, is quite characteristic of the ways and manners of these people.

He was notorious for his stinginess, and had never been known, when any one entered his house whilst he was at table, to practise those rites of hospitality so common amongst country-people. He was in the habit, however, of getting over the omission by an impudent sort of turn, that was inimitable. If a traveller entered the house about noon, which is the usual hour for dinner with American farmers, who are generally a very hospitable race of people, he would say, in his Anglo-Germanic dialect, "How t'ye do? Heb you make your dinner?" and if he received an affirmative answer, would say, "Well den, you peats us." If he got a negative answer, his regular response was, " Well den, we peats you." With this established character, an impudent Yankee tin pedlar once tried an experiment upon his patience.

This fellow had a prodigious canine appetite, and was, for this reason, the dread of the whole circuit in which he was accustomed to sell his tins. He had therefore thought it prudent to annex to his perambulations a new district in Maryland; and hearing of this German farmer, and being in his neighbourhood, he one day presented himself just at the dinner-hour. " How t'ye do ? Heb you make your dinner ? " said the farmer. " I guess I have," answered the pedlar. "Well den, you peats us," he replied. " You see," said the Yankee, " I'm one of them critturs that likes his dinner as soon as he can git it; howsumdever I'll jist take a look at your taturs till the woman has done, and then, perhaps, we can trade a little." Upon this he sat down, and helping himself to one half of the pork that was on the table, he shot it down so rapidly, that all eyes became fixed upon him, little suspecting that the corned beef on the table was doomed to follow it instanter. Having achieved the beef, he perceived near to him two fine young cabbages, the first that had been gathered that summer : these, which were the German's own dear dish, he had the inexpressible horror to see disappear in a twinkling down the implacable throat of the omnivorous tin pedlar. Rising from his seat, full of wrath, the farmer now shoved a huge dish of unskinned seedy potatos to the fellow, that were there for the family, and screamed out, " Will you swallow de botatos too, you duyvel's kind, mit de dish und de skins ? I should like to see dat." " No," said the Yankee, " I guess I telled you I'd only jist look at your taturs; it ain't so long to supper-time but I can hold on. So I'm ready for a trade whenever you please." " If you makes your subber as you makes your dinner, and if you trades in de same way," roared the German, " I dink I shall hab de worst of de pargin; so I'll not trade mit you at all." This story, which was related to us with good effect, produced much merriment.

The evidences were very frequent, along the line we were proceeding upon, of the greater degree of violence which had operated upon the crust of the earth on the eastern flank of the Alleghanies, at the time when the chain was upraised. Towards their western flank I had, upon various occasions, observed fine anticlinal segments of arches, denoting a regular and more tranquil movement; but here the beds of limestone frequently dipped both ways in very short distances, and sometimes portions of an arch had taken an almost vertical position by subsidence.

At William's Port, one hundred miles from Georgetown by the canal, beds of laminated slate came into the limestone, which, a little further to the west, began to change its character, and become partially fossiliferous. The Conococheague Creek, a fine rural stream, empties itself into the Potomac at William's Port; and here we had to leave the canal, to my great regret, it being finished no further.

CHAPTER III.

WILLIAM'S PORT.—CLEAR SPRING.—BATH SPRINGS.—ARRIVE AT CUMBERLAND. —FUCOIDAL FOSSILS IN PLACE.—FROSTBURGH.—GREAT BITUMINOUS COALFIELD.—REMARKABLE SECTION OF COAL SEAMS ON THE POTOMAC.

July 12.—We slept at William's Port, and whilst the gentlemen in the morning were giving directions about their works, I walked out and loitered amongst the rocks, where I was overtaken by a violent thunder-storm, and got thoroughly soaked with rain. Seeing some small rough cabins, or shanties, on the side of a hill, erected for the accommodation of the Irishmen who worked on the canal, and some of whom had been thus engaged for three years, I entered one of them to dry my clothes. I found an Irishman and his wife within, who received me civilly, but were evidently ashamed of the miserable manner in which they lived. A beautiful young child was lying in a rude cradle, and the rain, which soaked through every part of the roof, was falling down upon his face; but the little fellow did not seem to mind it much, it probably not being the first time he had felt it there. Having made my wishes known, the woman made the fire up; but the smoke almost choked and blinded me, and the hearth was so uneven, that I could scarce sit upon a little bench which I drew to it. On the man's going out, observing that she seemed fond of her child, I got up a sort of friendly conversation with her, and having said, "What! have you got no potatos to eat? Why, you certainly could grow them on this good soil!" she replied, "Heaven's blessing on the potato I've clapped my eyes on, sir! The truth is, the men are too lazy to raise them: if it's plenty of whisky they can get, they are satisfied." "You have very fine children, I perceive," said I; "what do you feed them with?"—"Faith, sir," she replied, "it's just the children that are raised aisier than the potatos." Then seeing the rain fall on her pretty child, she exclaimed, "God bless my father and mother! Sorrow the day I left them to come a canalling in this country! If I had been in their house, not a drop of this rain would fall on me or the babe." She said America was a fine country, if the men would only take care of what they earned; that the wives of the other men were all dissatisfied, because their husbands were neither sober nor prudent; and that but one thought occupied their minds, which was to save money enough to get back to Ireland with.

Numerous curious appearances of the strata presented themselves within a short distance, all proving what a crushing movement the rocks have once undergone here.

I was sorry we were to leave the canal here and our agreeable boat. Although America is a country where the geologist finds fewer opportunities for investigation in quarries, and sections made by human art, as they occur in Europe, yet, in ascending an immense stream like the Potomac, which has worn its way through the strata, and laid them bare for inspection, the grandest field is presented to him; and the difficulties which anomalous cases present to the observer, when walking over the face of the country, are on these great fluvial excavations generally accompanied with their solution.

July 13.—Having exchanged our boat for a stage-coach, we proceeded this morning to a place called *Clear Spring*, where we breakfasted at a very dirty tavern. There was a fine limpid spring here, very much loaded with calcareous matter; and, being hot weather, we all drank too freely of it. Some it purged violently; upon my stomach it sat heavily and created nausea. Preferring to walk, in two or three miles from this place I began the ascent of the *North Mountain*, formed of what used to be called grauwacke, and which are now known as silurian sandstones. These beds continued to *Hancock*, a village on the Potomac. We were here about 400 feet above the level of tide water. Finding I was not far from *Bath Springs*, in Berkeley county, Virginia, I forded the Potomac, which was rather shallow here, and in about five miles reached this pleasant-looking rural place, which is in a narrow valley, confined by two small ridges, and where I found a tolerably clean and commodious hotel. The springs, which are numerous, rise through the slate which had accompanied us so long; and finding a pretty good-looking bath, I entered it, but it was excessively cold, and I was glad to get out again, which I did at the end of five minutes, dressing with a charming glow upon me. This is considered a fashionable watering-place, but the season for company appeared not to have arrived yet. Upon asking if I could have some refreshment, I was shewn to a public room, which I had no sooner entered, than the most execrable music I ever heard was struck up: however, I got a cup of tea, and took up my line of march again for the Potomac, which having crossed, I rejoined my friends at the village.

July 14.—This day we proceeded along the national road, crossing the ridges of the Alleghanies, of which one,

AN ATTRACTIVE VALLEY.

called *Town Ridge,* was a rather imposing one. The rocks here changed to red shale and sandstone. It was a wild country, less thickly wooded, and containing a great many beautiful dells and valleys. In the afternoon we drove down a rapid slope, and entered a beautiful vale called Flintstone Spring Valley; and finding a comfortable inn, with a spacious garden well stocked with abundance of ripe raspberries and currants, we determined to remain all night at a place so remarkable for its amenity and air of comfort. I found the calcareous beds highly fossiliferous here.

July 15.—We left this pretty place after breakfast, and a few miles from it ascended an elevated ridge, from whence we looked down upon a very attractive valley, resembling some of those I had frequented when wandering in the Tyrol. It was embosomed amidst lofty hills, whose slopes were covered with bright verdant foliage, whilst a gentle brawling brook wound its way through the fertile bottom. A cottage peeped out here and there with its tiny agriculture about it; and the smoke just then curling gracefully from some of their chimneys, awakened an interest for the individuals who had selected a situation so sequestered, and to which no road could be seen either for ingress or egress. Coming unawares upon such lovely visions, Nature seems to touch with her most delicate hand the finest chords of our humanity, and to bring us under the influence of inexpressible feelings, where admiration of what she has rendered exquisitely beautiful contends for expression with gentle emotions of kindness and sympathy towards our fellow-creatures.

Upon such occasions experience has taught me that it is wise to surrender oneself altogether to that charm which the mind, investing everything around with touching attributes, enchants us with. For if we mutiny against the dominion of imagination, and would too curiously inquire into the connexions betwixt our feelings and the realities they are associated with, the imagination, like an offended beauty, breaks with us upon the first slight. It is prudent, therefore, to lend to such scenes the advantage of distance, and not to enter such cottages, lest our material senses, taking cognizance of the filth of their insides, should destroy the illusion created by external appearances. It is unfortunate that too many of our disappointments should spring from our own race, for Nature, always glorious and true, becomes the more attractive the more she is investigated.

As we approached Cumberland the calcareous beds became very slaty and fossile, and alternated with shale and sandstone, the beds being often contorted and disturbed. Having alighted at a tolerable hotel, I sallied out to look at the place. Cumberland is an old village, and was a post of some celebrity in the time of the Indian wars, in the middle of the eighteenth century. It lies close to the Potomac, in a depressed basin, surrounded by lofty hills, and the situation is quite beautiful. To the west rises a lofty ridge, about 900 feet in height, called Will's Mountain, with an immense gap, through which flows a stream called Will's Creek. East of this mountain is a smaller ridge, with a valley on its west and east side. The waters that have in ancient times come down the Potomac, and the various valleys and gorges, have washed away more than a mile and a half in breadth of this ridge, the continuation of which is seen on the other side of the river. Being composed of shale and limestone, the first friable mineral would easily give way, as

STRATA CONCENTRICALLY BENT.

it has done at Niagara, and the limestone losing its support would fall down. In this way the basin of Cumberland has been scooped out. On the west side of a bridge built across the creek is a *plateau*, consisting of the detritus of this operation. The north part of the ridge is highly fossiliferous.

July 16.—Having now reached the point where the canal was to terminate, I prepared this morning for an excursion to examine the extensive coal-field which lay a short distance from this place, for the transportation of the products of which the canal was projected, and my companions were obliging enough to accompany me. Proceeding through the great gorge, watered by Will's Creek, to Frostburgh, about ten miles from Cumberland, I was much struck by its imposing character. On each side the escarpments were about 900 feet in height, about 100 feet of red shale visible, superimposed by 800 feet of grey sandstone. There was a great deal of flexure in the rocks, the strata being concentrically bent, and the summit of the mountain exhibiting the apex of the arch imperfectly, showing that the summit of the ridge had been lowered. Towards the further end of the gorge I found fine specimens of fucoidal fossils. Ascending the mountain, we reached Frostburgh, which is elevated almost 1900 feet* above tide water. Towards the summit frequent beds of limestone, alternating with shale and micaceous sandstone, announced the approach to a coal-field.

The seams of bituminous coal are numerous here : one of them, including a narrow subordinate seam of compact

---
* Cumberland is 573 feet above tide water.
Frostburgh is 1275 feet above Cumberland.

1848.

bituminous shale in its centre, is about 10 feet thick. The bands of argillaceous iron-stone are also numerous. A few miners were at work in an irregular manner, having run adits upon the principal seam. I made an interesting collection of coal plants,* and we then pursued our way to Western Port, an obscure village on the Potomac, about eighteen miles from Frostburgh. The road lay down the pretty valley of George's Creek, hemmed in by lofty hills close on each side, containing many seams of coal. Western Port contained about twenty old log-huts and framed buildings, without a pane of glass in any one of the windows. Still there was an appearance of rurality about it, and it would have produced some effect seen at a distance. But our party was too numerous to find accommodation here; and hearing that a Mr. De Vickman, the son of a Frenchman, had a house and mill about two miles off, at the mouth of Savage River, a few of us proceeded thither, with the intention of throwing ourselves upon his hospitality.

As soon as it was ascertained that we could be received here, I went about a mile further up the *North Branch*, as it was called here, where the Potomac had cut a gap through what they called *Dan's Mountain* at least a mile wide. That part of the mountain which was on the opposite or right bank of the river appeared to be about 750 feet high, and presented an escarpment of the most extraordinary kind. To examine this I had to ford the river, the bed of which, although only about 120 feet in breadth, was filled with rolled rocks, which made it a very difficult undertaking. The face of this escarpment contained no less than six seams of coal, sepa-

* Calamites, lepidodendron, stigmaria, and various species of ferns, many of which appear to agree specifically with European coal plants.

rated by beds of sandstone and limestone, the lowest seam being not more than 10 feet from the water's edge, near to which was a fine horizontal band of argillaceous iron-stone.

The following section presents the order in which these seams of coal occur, without reference to the thickness of the other mineral beds.

I was told that one of the seams had something more than a foot of compact bituminous shale in the centre, and that one of the lowest seams contained sulphuret of iron. The deficiency in America of the geological beds lying in other countries above the coal measures, will be found exceedingly advantageous when the mines at some future day require to be vigorously worked. The coal from the seams in this escarpment, which has its correspondent exposition on the left bank of the river, can be quarried by adits run into the hills, and shot down from situations of this kind by inclined planes into barges placed below. An Englishman, accustomed to place great value upon such remarkable deposits of coal, is somewhat astonished at seeing the representative of so much wealth lying dormant.

On recrossing the river I went to see a curious mystical

German quack, named Brandt, who I was told was the proprietor of 2500 acres of coal land, including this escarpment. He wore an immense beard, and wanted nothing but a black cat on his shoulder to have passed for Katterfelto. He said that he would sell me all his coal lands for ten dollars an acre, and seemed very anxious to part with them, which was natural enough, for he derived no profit from them, and was not a very likely person to keep anything out of pure regard for posterity. There is such an enormous quantity of coal in the country, and the competition to get it to market will be so great when the canal is finished, that it is quite evident no one will make any money by it but the canal company, who will receive the tolls; so that, in fact, these seams of coal will for a long time be in the hands of speculators, who, purchasing the land at agricultural prices of a few dollars per acre, will exert themselves to sell them again, at mining prices of a higher rate per acre, to persons who desire to keep them for another generation.

On returning, a little fatigued, to Savage River, I found there was no room for me at De Vickman's, and that I must go back to Western Port.

CHAPTER IV.

INTERESTING ESCARPMENTS ON THE BANKS OF THE POTOMAC.—A SINGULAR PUBLIC DINNER.—THE GORGE OF WILL'S MOUNTAIN.—BEDFORD SPRINGS.—VALUABLE MINERAL WATERS.—CROSS THE BACKBONE MOUNTAIN.—THE CONTORTED STRATA BECOME HORIZONTAL TO THE WEST OF THE ALLEGHANIES.—ARRIVE AT PITTSBURG.

July 17.—The place where I slept was humble enough, being a very low sort of country tavern, kept by a most unsophisticated piece of rustic ignorance called Hammel. What with getting wet, fatigue, and want of proper refreshment, I had a headache at night, and the last thing he said to me, on lying down upon a very extraordinary sort of bed, was, " Squire, I reckon you'll get up quite lively in the morning." And so I did, for on awaking, such a spectacle presented itself of bugs running all over me and over every thing else, that I jumped up as lively as a parched pea, and rushed out to the well. Having made my ablutions, I walked out on the adjacent mountains, and was sketching an outline of the noble hills around, when a sottish-looking man on horseback approached, dismounted, and began to look over my sketch in a very impudent sort of way; upon which I closed my portfolio, and taking out my pocket-compass, began to take the bearing of some hills. "I see," he now growled, in a coarse tone, " you are one of those that draw by the rule of thumb."—" I shall be very much obliged to you," replied I, "if you will tell me what that means, for I do not know." Upon which he began to curse and swear, and hope that "West Point, that —— Institution, would be pulled up by the roots, and not one stone left upon another." I mentioned this on my return to the tavern, and our host told me he was the country surveyor, but that he had taken umbrage at the appearance of the United States engineers, who laid out the line of the canal, and who were all trained at the National Institution of West Point. He had never been employed to assist them—a piece of neglect that had made a hole in his temper, and let in an undue portion of envy and malice. He had, therefore, taken to console himself with strong morning drams, under the influence of which I saw he was when he accosted me—thinking, no doubt, that I was one of his detested rivals in the surveying art.

Having made a very humble sort of breakfast, our party re-assembled, with the intention of returning to Cumberland, keeping, as far as we could, the left bank of the Potomac. The scenes around us were picturesque and wild; the streams came rushing down from the mountains; and at every turn a new object full of amenity and beauty presented itself. We had to travel about twenty-eight miles to get to Cumberland, and kept a pleasant path close to the edge of the river, which sometimes flowed between narrow gorges, at other times through ample and fertile bottoms teeming with heavy crops of wheat and maize. Sometimes the hills came down with a sharp slope to the river, leaving no room for a path, and then we were obliged to ford the Potomac into the state of Virginia, to be in an hour or two driven back into the state of Maryland from the same cause.

Upon one occasion, where the gorge was very narrow,

the mountain side was sharpened to an angle of about 50°, and as there was no path, we had to ascend the hill by a narrow bridle-path, which in more than one place did not admit of a horse being turned if two persons mounted were to meet. This was the case at a particular point, 500 feet above the level of the river, with a precipitous slope down the whole way to the bottom. Occasionally we had glorious views of the river and country. On descending this hill, which appeared to be the eastern limit of the coal-field we had just left, we came upon compact limestone exceedingly contorted, with occasional beds of shale. Having reached the bottom of the hill, I observed an escarpment opposite to us on the right bank of the Potomac, that exhibited

a remarkable flexure of the beds, preserving to a great extent the regular arch of a rainbow. In the background was a view of distant and lofty mountains, well wooded. The western end of this arch was covered with trees, but the beds had the appearance of bending regularly down to the river. I was so pleased with the view, that I took a sketch of it.

At another point on the left bank was a mass of contorted beds, most strangely twisted about, with a base of about 150 yards, in an escarpment which went vertically down into the water, and around which I forded to obtain a good opportunity of examining it. I have never seen in any part of America contorted beds more worthy of examination by those who think that the study of them may reveal the nature of the movements by which they have been produced. Passing through Cresaptown, a lone, decayed village, containing half-a-dozen tenements, we reached Cumberland again about 4 P. M.

Here another sort of scene. awaited us. We learnt that, in honour of the president and directors of the canal, a grand dinner was to be given to them the day of our return; and anxious for repose as we were, it was necessary to dress, as the leading men of the place were expected to be present. An amusing part of the affair was, that not a single soul of our party knew whether the dinner was to be given by the inhabitants or the directors. The first was not probable, as no invitation had been received from them, and the second was as unlikely, as no invitation had been given. We sent, however, to the tavern where the dinner was said to be prepared, and were told that certainly a grand banquet was to be given to these gentlemen at 5 P. M. This was satisfactory enough to us after a journey of about thirty miles, fording rivers, performing various other travellers' feats, and fasting from 6 A. M.

On reaching the tavern we found a crowd about the door, and entering the house found no one there to receive us. By-and-by several persons dropped in,—men and boys of all descriptions; and about six o'clock the landlord himself made his appearance, and said he had "made up his mind" to put Mr. Such-a-one, who had formerly been in Congress, in the chair as president of the day, and to make some other person whom he named, and who was a lawyer and a member of the Temperance Society, vice-president. We all followed him after this declaration to a room with a long narrow table, to which we with a motley crowd enough sat down. A single glance at the dinner and company induced me to take my seat close to the door, that I might make my retreat without being observed. The meat, the puddings and pies, with every thing that had been prepared, were placed on the table together. I tried one or two of the messes, and tasted some atrocious stuff the landlord called sherry, but which I had no doubt was some preparation of whisky made at the doctor's shop; but there was nothing fit to eat or drink, and hungry as I was, I was deliberating with myself whether I could with propriety leave such a coarse affair and go to our lodgings for a comfortable cup of tea, when two or three noisy fellows, exactly opposite to me, began to smoke some execrable tobacco. This terminated my share of the grand dinner, and taking my travelling-cap out of my pocket, I walked quietly out of the door. On reaching our lodgings, I learnt that the dinner was nothing but a speculation of the landlord's, and that every guest was expected to pay for his dinner.

My companions, who did not find it convenient to act as independently as I had done, very good-naturedly remained at the dinner, and acquired golden opinions from the company. They gave me, on their return, an amusing account of the entertainment; and just as I was going to bed, the vice-president, who was the principal man in getting up the temperance society at this village, came to our quarters most outrageously drunk, and told us of a toast he had given after the directors had left the table, which met great applause. "I gave them," said he, "The Chesapeake and Ohio Canal, and the president and directors, and may the impediments in their progress be prosperous and eternal." In this mutilated sentiment I immediately recognized the sherry I had tasted. Of the fallibility of these leaders of temperance societies, our landlord, Hammel, had given us another amusing instance when we were at Western Port. The member of the Maryland legislature for that district was a pious Methodist, and very strict member of the Temperance Society; but at the last election, finding that the patriotism of the voters could not be brought to his side without libations of whisky, he directed the landlord to give whisky to those who insisted upon having it, but to charge it to him in his books under the head of "oats;" and Hammel actually exhibited his books to us, where there was a long column of charges against the candidate for oats, all of which he said were for whisky. These specimens of the "conscientious principles and temperance" of those demagogues, who flourish by encouraging vulgar country-people in running after some novelty or other in religion, morals, or politics, are to be found in every district where I have been.

July 18.—Having breakfasted, I had the painful task before me of parting with the kind friends who had accompanied me from Washington, and who had placed me under so many obligations. Having received their hearty good wishes for a prosperous return from my tour, they drove away, and I proceeded to that remarkable gorge in Will's Mountain of which I have before spoken, to examine it more in detail. It is about 3000 paces in length, and in some parts is 500 in width, Will's Creek running through it, with the summit of the mountain rising about 850 feet above the level of the water. At the eastern end the beds rise into a regular curvature, the lowest being a red shale, and the uppermost a gray quartzose sandstone. On the south side of the creek the curvature is most remarkable, presenting a magnificent segment of an arch, the base of which would measure about 10,000 feet. On the north side there is a regular mural escarpment from the summit, of about 300 feet, with an immense talus of fallen masses extending beneath it and forming a slope to the bottom.

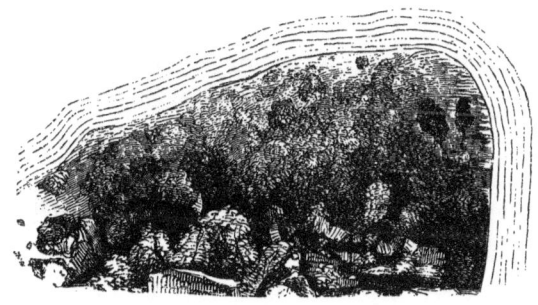

On reaching the point at the western end, where I had before observed the specimens of fucoidal fossils, I observed that the flexure of the beds had collapsed, and that for a thickness of about 200 feet they were hanging vertically upon the flattened side of the arch. It was at the foot of this vertical part of the segment that I had, on a previous occasion, found the fucoides, and I now determined to see if I could find the bed from which they had been detached. Having climbed the hill, I looked diligently about, and at length had the satisfaction of finding them in place on the outside bed. This was very interesting, since here was a proof that an ancient flat bed of the sea, bearing fucoidal plants, had been bent with the subjacent strata into the form of an arch, and that, from some inequality in the movement, or perhaps from subsidence, the sides had collapsed towards the centre, in such a manner, that, if it had been hidden from view, the beds would appear to be in a vertical position.

July 19.—I left Cumberland this morning for Bedford Springs, the road lying principally on the red shale that underlies Will's Mountain. The knolls of fossiliferous silurian limestone were numerous in the valleys, all closely hemmed in by the Alleghany ridges, with here and there the never-failing German farmer. I reached Bedford Springs towards evening, and was shewn into a building containing rows of pigeon-holes, about spacious enough for a cobbler to draw a wax thread in. The furniture, consisting of one chair, and a table just two feet square, with the bed and bed-clothes, might be worth ten or a dozen dollars; but, as it was a clean place, and I could be alone in it to read and write, I was quite satisfied. Having taken a moderate repast and looked at the place, I retired early.

July 20.—This day I devoted to the examination of the vicinity. The hotel was built in a neat and narrow little valley, containing various lofty knolls. That to the east has a small stream, called Shover's Creek, running at its base; and the mineral springs come down from the base of the ridge in that direction. The principal spring, which is called Anderson's, has a temperature of about 58° Fahrenheit: it contains a little carbonic acid, with small proportions of neutral salts; sulphate of magnesia, however, is its principal solid ingredient. Of all the mineral waters I have ever tasted in America or Europe, this is the most agreeable and efficacious, and the celebrity it has attained is well deserved. The other springs have different properties; one is highly calcareous, another contains sulphuretted hydrogen. In relation to the value of the mineral waters, I think this the most remarkable place of the kind in the United States; and the confidence I found reason to place in the water of Anderson's Spring, according with the experience of many persons I found there, induced me afterwards to recommend the use of it upon many occasions to invalids suffering from indigestion and liver complaints.

July 21.—I lost no time in making various excursions in the neighbourhood. It is worthy of remark, that, although there is a general parallelism in these Alleghany ridges, yet the deflexions from their north-east course are numerous, and in some instances ridges are found running transversely to the general direction,—circumstances which will exercise the ingenuity of future geologists. Many of the calcareous beds about Bedford had strong seams of chert running in them, with cherty masses resembling alcyonia. Curvatures were common in the strata, and I was able to make a very fair collection of fossils in this valley. A short distance from the springs the vale widens out into a well cultivated country, where the small village of Bedford is built.

July 22.—Having obtained a carriage, I left this place, on my way to Pittsburgh, crossing Will's Mountain, the general rocks being limestone, red shale, and sandstone. At fifteen miles from Bedford we commenced the ascent of what is called the Backbone Mountain, which is twelve miles from base to base. This is a remarkable feature in this mountainous country: first, because the waters from the western side run to the Ohio; and, secondly, because it is the eastern edge of the great coal-field of the western country. At the base the red shale is seen, which in other parts is directly connected with the old red sandstone; and higher up are important beds of grit and conglomerate, with pebbles of a medium size. The summit of the mountain presents a table land, eight miles in breadth: here, a little to the right, I examined a seam of bituminous coal, 7 feet thick, with 2 feet of compact bituminous shale in the centre. It was perfectly horizontal, as well as the beds further west, from which it was evident that the complicated movement which had contorted and otherwise disturbed the more eastern ridges of the Alleghanies, had ceased to act here, and in the country further to the west, where all the beds are horizontal. As we advanced, coal constantly cropped out by the side of the road.

July 23.—I slept at a small place called Staystown, from whence the country to Pittsburg was an irregular surface of knolls and vales, that had apparently been modified when the surface was beneath the ocean. Everywhere coal was to be seen. It was harvest-time, and the population was busily engaged in the fields. The wheat crops were heavy, as well as the meadows; and so many fields were standing quite ready for the harvest scythe, that it was evident labour was not very abundant. The people were a stout healthy-looking race, and the villages numerous, but the houses were generally poor and shabby-looking. Greensburg is an old and rather extensive place, but did not appear to be very inviting as a residence. At half-past 5 P. M., having passed the United States Arsenal, with its admirable wall and neat-looking interior, I drove into the dusty, dirty, coal-hole-looking place called *Pittsburg*.

When we reached the tavern to which I was directed, the exterior was so filthy that I was ashamed to enter; but every one having told me it was the best inn in the place, no choice was left. The great number of forges and manufactories established here, and the imperfect manner in which the combustion of the coal is effected, cause the atmosphere to be constantly loaded with flakes of soot, which not only get into your throat and nostrils, but defile your clothes and linen in the most provoking manner. It was hot, and I threw up the window of my bed-room; but in five minutes the fuliginous matter began to float in and alight upon the bed-linen. I wanted some linen washed immediately, but was told it could not be done in a hurry, as it had to be dried and got up in the house, the state of the atmosphere not admitting of its being done out of doors. Having made up my mind to bear up with all sorts of inconveniences before I commenced my tour, I determined to resign myself to these, and walked out to look at the place.

Pittsburg is built upon a wedge of alluvial land, lying betwixt the *Mononghahela* and *Alleghany* rivers, just before they mingle with each other and take the name of *Ohio*. The streets are exceedingly narrow, badly paved, and in every way disagreeable; the population hurrying about in a restless manner from morn to night. Market Street, which is called the principal street, is about as narrow and dirty as the worst in any other town. But the industry and activity of the inhabitants is great, and coal being to be obtained almost for the price of quarrying it, it is delivered to the inhabitants for domestic uses for four cents, or twopence, a bushel. Pittsburg will, in time, be the great manufacturing place of America. Here will be sent the iron smelted from the furnaces that will soon be erected all over this region of coal and iron; and cannon foundries, rolling-mills, nail-manufactories, and heavy machinery of various kinds, will soon make it the Birmingham of America.

July 24.—I devoted this day to a more minute examination of the neighbourhood. The triangular wedge of alluvial matter upon which the town stands is the site of the celebrated Fort Duquesne, erected by the French in 1755, and intended as one of their principal posts upon the extensive military line from which they proposed to operate upon the British Atlantic colonies. Being erected at the very point of the triangle, it was protected from Indian warfare on both sides by the water. At the other end of the alluvial deposit, the triangle shoulders itself up against the high land which constitutes the banks, 400 feet in height, of the Monongahela and Alleghany rivers. In old times, when the rivers of America were at a much higher level, the confluence of those two streams was probably at the base of the high land called now Grant's Hill, when the whole flat part of the triangle must have been under water in a broad bay. This locality affords an additional proof, to be added to those which all the rivers and lakes present, of the great diminution of the waters of this continent.

An excellent bridge is thrown across the Monongahela, and two across the Alleghany. I crossed over one of them to a new settlement called Alleghany, where the streets are wider and the houses better than at Pittsburg; many of whose inhabitants, feeling themselves cramped and choked with the smoke of their own manufactories, are seeking elbow-room and purer air at this place. At present the population of Pittsburg is of a motley kind: the Irish seem to be the most numerous; the number of Germans also is very great; then come the indefatigable New Englanders, with their restless enterprise and ingenuity. How all these are ever to assimilate and make one people, is to be proved by time; but ere long a great population will have assembled here; for never was there a locality better calculated to maintain one, supported as it will be by a fertile country, manufactories of every kind that require steam power, and enjoying unrivalled facilities of water and railway communication to New Orleans, Philadelphia, and New York.

The environs would be beautiful but for the smoke, which defiles every thing. The irregularities of the surface are of the most graceful kind; charming wooded knolls and hills, with lovely vales, are all around, and beautiful rivers flowing between lofty banks.

CHAPTER V.

VISIT BRADDOCK'S FIELD.—EVENTS WHICH LED TO THE EXPEDITION OF THAT GENERAL.

BEFORE I left Pittsburg I devoted one day to a visit to Braddock's Field, about nine miles distant, in the valley of the Mononghahela river, and universally known in the neighbouring country by that name. After going about six miles on the turnpike-road, I turned down on the right to the valley, which is generally about two miles broad, including the beautiful slopes on the north or right bank, that terminate in frequent intervals of rich bottom land close to the river, most of which were covered with fine crops, the whole presenting one of the sweetest scenes I ever saw. The summit of the bank is perhaps 350 feet above the level of the river, and distant from it about 2000 yards, sloping for the greatest part of the way gently down, interrupted by a somewhat flat sort of terrace, about two-thirds of the distance from the river, along which there is now a road; and from it the ground goes by an easy descent to the water. At the period when General Braddock attempted to reach Fort Duquesne, the whole distance from the summit to the stream was densely wooded.

The causes which led to the unparalleled disaster that befel the enterprise conducted by General Braddock, and the remarkable results which it probably led to, have been so little noticed, that a brief account of the circumstances which led to this unfortunate campaign, and some details of the defeat itself, will be interesting to the English reader.

The surrender of Louisbourg, in the island of Cape Breton, to the British arms under General Pepperell, in 1745, by giving England the command of the Gulf of St. Lawrence, was a blow which laid the axe to the root of the French power in Canada; and, if it had been followed up by the retention of that island, would probably have so crippled the French in that quarter, that they never would have been troublesome again to the British colonies. But at the Peace of Aix la Chapelle, in 1748, the island was restored; and very soon after evidences were not wanting of the determination of the crown of France, not only to secure their possessions in Canada, but to drive out the English from their Atlantic colonies. To effect this, great pains were taken to conciliate the Indian tribes, who occupied the western country behind the English settlements; and in 1751 the English Ohio Company were driven from the banks of that river.

The arrival, in August 1752, of the Marquis du Quesne in Canada, as Governor-General, gave a new impulse to the exertions of that gallant people. Du Quesne was a very enterprising person, and was bent upon establishing a line of forts and communications from Niagara to the Missisippi, thereby encircling all the English colonies, with the intention of destroying, by incursions of hostile Indians, their western trade and back settlements. This unpromising state of things created much alarm in Virginia; and in October, 1753, the Governor of that province wrote to the French commandant on the Ohio, to remonstrate against his proceedings, sending the letter by Colonel Washington, at that time a youth of only twenty-one years of age; but whose prudent and resolute character, even at that period, had acquired him the confidence of all who knew him. The mission of this distinguished young Virginian was undertaken at a period, not only of great public anxiety, but at a season of the year when the winter was momentarily expected to set in, and when, in addition to the dangers he was exposed to from the hostile Indians, he would have to contend against the severity of the weather, the deep snows, and the half-frozen rivers, before he could possibly accomplish his return. And never was a mission executed with greater resolution and excellent judgment than he displayed upon this occasion,—giving a foretaste to his countrymen of those great qualities which he afterwards displayed in a career made for ever renowned by his illustrious name. Leaving Williamsburg, the seat of government of Virginia, on the 1st of November, 1753, he, after various adventures upon the land and the rivers, on the 11th of December reached one of the French forts on French Creek, a tributary of the Alleghany river, about fifteen miles distant from Presque Isle, on Lake Erie. This was on the line by which the French intended to penetrate—from Niagara to Presque Isle, and thence by Fort Le Bœuf, down French River, to the Alleghany and the Forks of the Ohio.

The French commander, Monsieur Legardeur de St. Pierre, was a Knight of St. Louis, and is described by Colonel Washington as an "elderly gentleman," having "much the air of a soldier." Upon receiving the letter of the Governor of Virginia, he sent for the commanding officer of the fort at Presque Isle; and a council being held, a written answer was returned, declaring in polite terms that they should not retire, but should carry out the instructions of the Marquis du Quesne.

Colonel Washington had now to return as quick as possible; and some idea may be formed of the hardships he had to encounter, and the determined spirit with which he surmounted them, by the following extract from his Journal :*—

"*December* 23.—When I got things ready to set off, I sent for the Half King, to know whether he intended to go with us or by water. He told me that *White Thunder* had hurt himself very much, and was sick and unable to walk; therefore he was obliged to carry him down in a canoe. As I found he intended to stay here a day or two, and knew that Monsieur Loncaire would employ every scheme to set him against the English, as he had before done, I told him I hoped he would guard against his flattery, and let no fine speeches influence him in their favour. He desired I might not be concerned, for he knew the French too well for anything to engage him in their behalf; and that though he could not go down with us, he yet would endeavour to meet at the Forks with Joseph Campbell, to deliver a speech for me to carry to his Honor the Governor. He told me he would order the young hunter to attend us, and get provision, &c., if wanted.

" Our horses were now so weak and feeble, and the

---

* This extract will show that at the age of twenty-one, Washington felt himself equal to a task that required the greatest degree of fortitude and prudence.

baggage so heavy, that we doubted much their performing it : therefore myself and others (except the drivers, who were obliged to ride) gave up our horses for packs, to assist along with the baggage. I put myself in an Indian walking-dress, and continued with them three days, till I found there was no probability of their getting home in any reasonable time. The horses grew less able to travel every day ; the cold increased very fast, and the roads were becoming much worse by a deep snow, continually freezing. Therefore, as I was uneasy to get back, to make report of my proceedings to his Honor the Governor, I determined to prosecute my journey the nearest way through the woods on foot.

"Accordingly I left Mr. Van Braam in charge of our baggage, with money and directions to provide necessaries from place to place for themselves and horses, and to make the most convenient despatch in travelling.

"I took my necessary papers, pulled off my clothes, and tied myself up in a match coat. Then with gun in hand, and pack at my back, in which were my papers and provisions, I set out with Mr. Gist, fitted in the same manner, on Wednesday the 26th. The day following, just after we had passed a place called the *Murdering* Town, (where we intended to quit the path, and steer across the country for *Shannapins* Town,) we fell in with a party of French Indians, who had been in wait for us. One of them fired at Mr. Gist or me, not fifteen steps off, but fortunately missed. We took this fellow into custody, and kept him until about nine o'clock at night; then let him go, *and walked all the remaining part of the night without making any stop,* that we might get the start so far as to be out of the reach of their pursuit the next day, since we were well assured they would follow our track as soon as it was light. The next day we continued travelling till quite dark, and got to the river about two miles above *Shannapins*. We expected to have found the river frozen, but it was not, only about fifty yards from each shore. The ice, I suppose, had broken up above, for it was driving in vast quantities.

"There was no way for getting over but on a raft, which we set about with but one poor hatchet, and finished just after sunsetting. This was a whole day's work. We next got it launched and went on board of it, then set off; but before we were half way over we were jammed in the ice, in such a manner that we expected every moment our raft to sink, and ourselves to perish. I put out my setting-pole to try to stop the raft, that the ice might pass by, when the rapidity of the stream threw it with so much violence against the pole, *that it jerked me out into ten feet water*, but I fortunately saved myself by catching hold of one of the raft logs. Notwithstanding all our efforts we could not get the raft to either shore, but were obliged, as we were near an island, to quit our raft and make to it.

"The cold was so extremely severe, that Mr. Gist had all his fingers and some of his toes frozen; and the water was shut up so hard, that we found no difficulty in getting off the island, on the ice, in the morning. We met here with twenty warriors, who were going to the southward to war; but coming to a place at the head of the Great Kunnaway, where they found seven people killed and scalped, (all but one woman with very light hair,) they turned about and ran back, for fear the inhabitants should rise, and take them as the authors of the murder. They report that the bodies were lying about the house, and some of them much torn and eaten by hogs. By the marks which were left, they say they were French Indians of the Ottaway nation who did it.

"As we intended to take horses here, and it required some time to find them, I went up about three miles to the mouth of Yaughyaughgane, to visit Queen *Alliquippa*, who had expressed great concern that we passed her in going to the fort. I made her a present of a match coat and a bottle of rum, which latter was thought much the best present of the two."

At this period, the colonists of Virginia, being more exposed to the hostile proceedings of the French than those in the other provinces were, felt exceedingly interested in their movements: in most of the other colonies there was a general ignorance of, and indifference respecting the frontiers; and even Pennsylvania, which was deeply concerned in these hostile measures, when called upon by the crown to succour Virginia, sought to excuse itself from so expensive a duty, by professing to doubt whether the Ohio was within the British limits. The province of Virginia, however, lost no time in raising three hundred men, and placing them under the command of Colonel Washington, who, with these, and two independent companies from New York, marched on the 1st of May, 1754, for the frontiers, sending an officer and a small party in advance, with instructions to build a fort at the confluence of the Mononghahela and Alleghany rivers, where the town of Pittsburg now stands, and the importance of which, as a military post, had not escaped his attention on his previous visit. This service had scarce been performed, when M. Contrecœur, having marched with a strong force and eighteen pieces of cannon from Presque Isle, on Lake Erie, to the head of the Alleghany river, descended that stream, and appearing before the fort, it was surrendered on the 17th of April. Colonel Washington, however, continued to advance, and on the 28th of May had a successful skirmish with a body of the enemy, who lost their commander, and about thirty in killed, wounded, and prisoners. During his further progress, he learnt that M. de Villier, with a body consisting of nine hundred French and Canadians, and two hundred Indians, was advancing to meet him; so falling back to the Great Meadow, and hastily constructing a work to which he gave the name of Fort Necessity, he there waited his arrival; and after an obstinate conflict of three hours, against more than twice his number, was compelled to enter into a capitulation with the honours of war.

This reverse, which was owing to the parsimony of the other colonies, caused a general defection of the Indian tribes, and gave the French possession of the whole line of the Ohio.

The alarm now became general throughout the British dependencies; the evil consequences of a line of French forts, and the hostility of the Indian tribes from Niagara to New Orleans, became obvious to all; and, with the concurrence of the crown, measures to establish a more efficient union amongst the colonies, to conciliate the Indians, and to make a general attack upon the French possessions, were earnestly agreed upon. A force was ordered to Nova Scotia. Crown Point, a strong French fort at the southern termination of Lake Champlin, was directed to be invested by Colonel, afterwards Sir William Johnson. Sherley's and Pepperell's regiments were to proceed to Lake Ontario and reduce Niagara ; and General Braddock, an officer of a very energetic character, was appointed to drive the French from the Ohio ; and in the first instance from the fort which M. Contrecœur had taken possession of at the Forks of the Ohio, and which he had strengthened and named Duquesne, in honour of the Governor-General of Canada.

Many persons of great experience, upon consideration of the immense difficulties which General Braddock would have to encounter in traversing the Alleghany Mountains, and afterwards in advancing through a rugged wilderness without roads, continually exposed to ambush from wily Indians in the numerous defiles that were upon his line of march, were at that time of opinion that it would have been a wiser plan for him to have advanced upon the French line of communication through the state of New York, since by that road he would have found greater facilities for his movements, and perfect security from attack ; indeed it would seem now to be certain, that if he had advanced in that direction, he would have effectually broken up the communication of the French betwixt Canada and their posts on the Ohio, and that the garrisons of these last must have surrendered on being summoned, or have abandoned their posts and descended the Ohio and Missisipi to New Orleans.

But at the consultation which the General held, in April 1755, on his arrival in Virginia, with some of the governors of the colonies, at Alexandria, in that province, it appeared that his orders were to advance immediately to Fort Duquesne. To these instructions he determined to adhere; and being an experienced soldier, and a person of undaunted resolution, he resolved to proceed without delay, and to encounter every obstacle, in the confidence that they must all yield to his perseverance. The possibility of his being defeated, and of being compelled to retreat through a barbarous country, harassed by the ferocious savages in the French interest,—a disadvantage he would not have been exposed to, if he had failed in his attack upon advancing by the line of Lake Ontario,—most probably never occurred to him. Had his instructions pointed out to him the object he was to accomplish, without tying him down to the route by which he was to advance to it, this most disastrous campaign would, most probably, not only have been a very successful and glorious one, but would have been unattended with consequences, which, as will be hereafter adverted to, have been amongst the gravest which have hitherto affected mankind.

On his arrival in Virginia, from Ireland, this unfortunate but gallant officer brought with him the reputation of a resolute and experienced soldier. Being a strict disciplinarian and observer of military etiquette, he was not a little disgusted to find that the assistance he had been taught to expect from the province of Virginia was likely to be uncertain, depending upon legislative concurrence, and the conciliation of persons very much at variance in their opinion of the manner in which the service ought to be performed. The colonists were brave men, and anxious to repel the French, but were accustomed to conduct their military undertakings by provincial expedients, which were not likely to find favour with a commander accustomed to the measured proceedings of a regular army. All the contracts, too, for provisions and transportation of the *matériel*, were to be made with interested persons, not very scrupulous in keeping their engagements ; and long before the General commenced his expedition, he had conceived as contemptible an opinion of the knowledge amongst the colonists of the art of war, as they had of his fitness to carry on Indian warfare in the woods, without resorting to the precautions they had always found necessary to ensure success. Colonel Washington offered his services as a volunteer, and a corps of Virginia riflemen marched with the army.

CHAPTER VI.

HIS ILL-JUDGED MARCH TO THE OHIO.—REACHES THE MONONGHAHELA.

HAVING reached Fort Cumberland, distant about one hundred and twenty miles from Fort Duquesne, the General, on the 10th of June, put his troops, consisting of two thousand two hundred men, and a few pieces of artillery, in motion; and hearing soon afterwards that the French garrison expected a reinforcement of five hundred men, he separated his army into two divisions, leaving Colonel Dunbar to follow with the provisions, stores, and heavy baggage, and commenced a series of tedious marches at the head of twelve hundred men and his artillery. It was remarked of General Braddock, that he neither attempted to conciliate the Indians, in order to prevent their joining the French, nor the provincial troops. These last were clad in buckskin jackets, and were armed with tomahawks as well as rifles, most of them being accustomed to Indian warfare; being ordered to move in the rear, a post peculiarly unsuited to their qualifications, they considered it as a mark of the General's contempt for them. It is sufficiently obvious, that, if he had carried along with him the smallest body of Indian warriors, they would have seasonably detected every ambush; and that even if he had permitted the provincial riflemen to be in the advance, these, who had been accustomed to the Indian practice of each man skirmishing with his rifle from behind a tree, would have given abundance of occupation to an Indian enemy, until a convenient disposition could have been made of the regular troops. But Braddock took counsel only from his courage, and burning with ardour to drive the French from their garrison with the British bayonet, he continued to advance through the wilderness, without any other information than that which he derived from three or four guides who accompanied him; opening and levelling roads with superfluous *accuracy*, as if in fastidious disregard of the *simple* expedients of the provincials; wearing out his troops, already discontented with their provisions and their hard duty, and irritated by the jeers of the provincial soldiers, who openly predicted that the regulars would be tomahawked and scalped.

On the 9th of July, a memorable day, and pregnant with events both immediate and remote, this gallant officer, with his fated troops, reached the left bank of the Mononghahela, only nine miles from Fort Duquesne, at a shallow ford now called the Ripple, and detached Lieutenant-Colonel Gage across the river with three hundred men—afterwards reinforced with two hundred—with orders to open a road to a trading-path, called Grant's Road, which led to the French fort. The opposite bank, close to the water, consisted of a piece of flat alluvial land, excessively choked with shrubs, saplings, and briars, that masked the ground : from thence a slope rose, very thickly wooded, which continued to where the ground formed the terrace before mentioned, which ran parallel with the river, and distant about twelve hundred paces from it. From that edge of this terrace, which is furthest from the river, the land rose rather more abruptly to the crest of the valley, the whole surface being densely

AMBUSH OF INDIANS.

covered with trees and underwood. About midway betwixt the river and the crest of the valley were three ravines, numbered in the plan 2, 3, 4, (*vide* the plan.) In No. 2 is a fine spring of clear cool water : No. 3, distant only 200 paces from it, lies betwixt the terrace and the river ; and No. 4, 150 paces still further, partly intersects the terrace. Lieutenant-Colonel Gage having opened a road some distance, the general, with the artillery, and the waggons containing the baggage and provisions, crossed the river with the main body, and reached the right bank about 1 P.M.

The troops, being hot with getting through the thick bottom, rushed to the spring, forming as soon as they had drunk, for the purpose of following the vanguard under Lieutenant-Colonel Gage. Here it was that the fatal error of not employing the Virginia riflemen to scour the woods in advance became obvious. Whilst the troops at the spring were preparing to move, and not suspecting that an invisible enemy, contemptible in numbers, but combining the resources of Europeans with the cunning and ferocity of savages, were laid within gun-shot in silent ambush in the ravine No. 3, Lieutenant-Colonel Gage was slowly advancing : he had been permitted to pass the head of this ravine without interruption, and had advanced 150 yards further to ravine No. 4, where an ambush was posted equally strong of French and Indians ; but it being necessary to cross this last, the men had only just begun to enter it, when the ambuscade suddenly fired, and immediately setting up one of those hideous yells, till then unheard by those unfortunate British soldiers, took to the trees to load again. The troops, seeing their comrades in the front drop around them, and astounded by the yells of an enemy no longer visible, fired a volley into the trees, and fell back in great confusion, pursued, shot down, and tomahawked by their fiend-like enemies. The main body, part of which had formed, whilst others were seated on the ground waiting for their comrades, who were drinking at the spring, hearing this firing and the yells, hastened on as quick as they could be formed to the assistance of the advance, and hurrying unconsciously past the ravine No. 3, received a deadly fire from the ambuscade there, which yelled and disappeared in the same manner. The confusion soon became overwhelming; the retreating advance, mixed up with Indians bearing uplifted tomahawks, rushed upon the main body, and embarrassed them still further; whilst the enemy in No. 3, perceiving the confusion, delivered another fire, and springing into the column, instantly began the work of tomahawking and scalping. The troops, unaccustomed to this kind of warfare, soon lost all confidence in themselves; being shot down almost as fast as they formed, they believed the woods to be filled with savages; and, overcome with terror, fired their muskets at random amongst the trees, where no enemy had appeared. At length, the panic becoming universal, they broke and fled, abandoning their artillery; nor could they be stopped until they reached the guard which had charge of the waggons. Here a stand was made to cover the baggage, whilst every exertion was employed by the General and his officers to rally and tranquillize the men; but, thoroughly unmanned, they were as insensible to persuasion as they were to commands.

The person from whom I had many particulars of this disaster informed me, that Colonel Washington now respectfully asked permission of the General to cover the troops with the riflemen, and engage the Indians in their own way, until the men could be formed again: irritated, however, by the general insubordination, he answered, "High times, indeed, when a young buckskin wants to teach an old general!" and urging on his horse, regardless of danger, seemed absorbed in the idea of bringing his men to their duty by his own personal exertions. He was everywhere; and whilst alternately upbraiding and entreating the soldiers to be calm, had five horses shot under him. Touched with his gallantry, his officers seconded him in the most devoted manner; many of them, hoping to inspire the men by their example, advanced in a body to recover the artillery, but they sacrificed themselves in vain. An old Canadian, whose father was engaged in the affair on the side of the French, told me at Detroit that he had heard him say, " Cela faisoit pitié le voir!" After three hours of this horrid massacre—for it deserves no other name—General Braddock received a mortal wound in the lungs, and, being taken to a white oak tree,* was placed at its foot. At this time the loss of officers had been very great. Colonel Sir Peter Halkett and many gallant gentlemen were already slain, together with Mr. Shirley, an amiable youth, who was secretary to the General, and who received a ball in the head. Amongst the wounded were Lieutenant-Colonel Gage, Lieutenant-Colonel Burton, Sir John St. Clair, with Captains Orme† and Morris, the General's two aids,—all of them severely hurt.

* *Vide* plan, No. 5. The stump of this tree was standing when I was there. Some one had cut the tree down to get a hive of honey the bees had made in it.

† The following official letter of Captain Orme, addressed to Governor Morris, confirms in many of the particulars the narrative I have drawn up:—

"Fort Cumberland, July 18, 1755.

" DEAR SIR,—I am so extremely ill in bed with the wound I have received

Colonel Washington, who had greatly distinguished himself, and who had had, as he afterwards wrote to his mother, two horses shot under him, and his clothes riddled with balls, was almost the only officer who had not been wounded; and General Braddock, finding himself incapable of further exertions, now sent for him, and consulted him as to what was best to be done. He advised an immediate retreat across the river, and the conduct of it being given to him, measures were instantly taken to effect it; but the French and Indians, perceiving

in my thigh, that I am under the necessity of employing my friend, Captain Dobson, to write for me.

"I conclude you have had some account of the action near the banks of the Mononghahela, about seven miles from the French fort. As the reports spread are very imperfect, what you have heard must consequently be so too. You should have had more early accounts of it, but every officer whose business it was to have informed you was either killed or wounded, and our distressful situation put it out of our power to attend to it so much as we would otherwise have done.

"The 9th instant we passed and repassed the Mononghahela, by advancing first a party of 300 men, which was immediately followed by another of 200: the General with the column of artillery, baggage, and the main body of the army, passed the river the last time about one o'clock. As soon as the whole had got over to the fort side of the Mononghahela, we heard a very heavy and quick fire in our front; we immediately advanced in order to sustain them, but the detachment of the 200 and 300 men gave way and fell back upon us, which caused such confusion, and struck so great a panic among our men, that afterwards no military expedient could be made use of that had any effect upon them. The men were so extremely deaf to the exhortations of the General and the officers, that they fired away in the most irregular manner all their ammunition, and then ran off, leaving to the enemy the artillery, ammunition, provisions and baggage; nor could they be persuaded to stop till they got as far as Gist's Plantation, nor there only in part, many of them proceeding as far as Colonel Dunbar's party, who lay six miles on this side.

"The officers were absolutely sacrificed by their unparalleled good behaviour, advancing sometimes in bodies, and sometimes separately, hoping by such example to engage the soldiers to follow them, but to no purpose.

"The General had five horses killed under him, and at last received a wound through the right arm into his lungs, of which he died the 13th instant. Poor Shirley was shot through the head; Captain Morris wounded.

FLIGHT OF THE TROOPS.

their advantage, spread themselves in every direction, both in front and flank, pouring destruction upon the retreating mass, and creating such dismay by their incessant firing and yelling, that the bewildered troops at length took to flight, abandoning all the waggons, the artillery, the ammunition, the military chest, and provisions, with all the General's public and private papers containing his instructions. The unfortunate commander and several of the wounded officers, who had been safely conducted to the other side of the river, were obliged

Mr. Washington had two horses shot under him, and his clothes shot through in several places, behaving the whole time with the greatest courage and resolution. Sir Peter Halkett was killed upon the spot; Colonel Burton and Sir John St. Clair wounded. And inclosed I send you a list of killed and wounded, according to as exact an account as we are yet able to get.

"Upon our proceeding with the whole convoy to the Little Meadows, it was found impracticable to advance in that manner: the General, therefore, advanced with 1200 men, with the necessary artillery, ammunition, and provisions, leaving the main body of the convoy under the command of Colonel Dunbar, with orders to join him as soon as possible. In this manner we proceeded with safety and expedition till the fatal day I have just related; and happy it was that this disposition was made, otherwise the whole must have starved or fallen into the hands of the enemy, as numbers would have been of no service, and our provision was all lost.

"As our number of horses was so much reduced, and those extremely weak, and many carriages being wanted for the wounded men, it occasioned our destroying the ammunition and superfluous provisions left in Colonel Dunbar's convoy, to prevent it falling into the hands of the enemy.

"As the whole of the artillery is lost, and the troops are so extremely weakened by deaths, wounds, and sickness, it was judged impossible to make any further attempts; therefore Colonel Dunbar is returning to Fort Cumberland with everything he is able to bring up with him.

"I propose remaining here till my wound will suffer me to remove to Philadelphia; from thence shall proceed to England Whatsoever commands you may have for me, you will do me the favour to direct to me here.

"By the particular disposition of the French and Indians, it was impossible to judge of the numbers they had that day in the field.

"I am, dear Sir,
"Your most obedient and humble servant,
"ROBERT ORME."

to be instantly sent on; for so great was the terror of the flying soldiers, that they could not be rallied even when they had crossed the ford, continuing, with few exceptions, their flight through the woods, a distance of thirty-five miles, until they reached Colonel Dunbar, who was advancing to support the main body. Upwards of seven hundred officers and men were killed and wounded in this disastrous affair. The greater part of the officers engaged were either killed or wounded; not one of them being taken prisoner. The General lingered until the fourth day after he had received his wound, when he died.

Colonel Dunbar now found himself with a force consisting of about fifteen hundred men, infected with a constant fear of an approaching enemy, but without artillery. He might have entrenched himself and waited for reinforcements, but the panic had seized his own detachment; having also many wounded officers and men to take care of, the determination was taken to abandon the undertaking, and fall back upon Fort Cumberland. All the ammunition and provisions, therefore, except what was deemed necessary to subsist them to the fort, were destroyed, and they turned their backs upon an unpursuing foe.

No one was probably more surprised at this signal discomfiture than the commandant of the French garrison at Fort Duquesne. He had been expecting reinforcements, but they had not arrived. The whole force he could muster, when Braddock was drawing nigh to the Mononghahela, has been supposed not to have exceeded four hundred, comprising both French and Indians. His scouts had brought him intelligence that the English would cross the river on the morning of the 9th, and he had lost no time in planting those ambuscades, to embarrass and delay its march, without the slightest idea of effecting any other advantage. Finding his enemy overthrown, and all his *matériel* in his power, he did not attempt to pursue his success; and perhaps was unable to do so, for, as soon as the last of the English troops had crossed the river, the Indians and Canadians began to plunder the waggons containing the baggage and military chest; and when darkness had set in, and the terror-stricken invaders were still continuing their flight, the victors, according to their custom, were already furiously drunk with the rum found amongst the stores, and wallowing upon the field of battle.

CHAPTER VII.

THE INFLUENCE WHICH THAT DEFEAT HAD IN PRODUCING THE REVOLT OF THE BRITISH COLONIES IN 1776.

BRADDOCK's defeat may, independent of the exultation and increased confidence of the French, and the corresponding gloom and depression which it produced in the British colonies, be considered as an event more deserving of attention than any other which occurred at that period. To military men it furnishes a most impressive lesson, showing how dangerous it is to undervalue and neglect advice, appropriate to local circumstances, lest its adoption should appear to detract from the dignity of military etiquette; for in martial campaigns it would seem to be as important to every enlightened commander to consider a battle as well in relation to the political consequences which it may be followed by, as to the immediate advantages and glory to be derived from it. In the brave General Braddock military pride was a fault which proved the ruin of his army, caused the loss of his own valuable life, and produced a fatal example of misconduct in his troops, which signally assisted to bring about unforeseen events that have more or less affected the whole structure of civilized society. From not using those ordinary precautions, without the observance of which he was always exposed to a defeat, he not only deprived himself of a sure victory, but planted the seeds of much future humiliation to his country, and probably of misery to mankind.

It is the particular glory of Wellington, that, like Nelson, he appears always to have been superior to selfish considerations, and to have made every feeling subordinate to his country's welfare and glory; and it may be inferred, from the uniform success which has accompanied him in all his glorious undertakings, that during his military, as in his civil career, prudence has prevailed over all his deliberations.

Had Braddock been prudent, it is far from being improbable that the British colonies would not have revolted in 1776; and in that contingency it is equally probable that the French Revolution might have taken a much milder character, the success of the colonists, and their establishment of a republic, having exceedingly added to its asperity. That Braddock's defeat made a deep impression upon the minds of the colonists, there is no room to doubt. Colonel Washington, who witnessed the rout, wrote to his mother that nothing could be more dastardly than the conduct of the troops. For a long time afterwards their cowardice was the engrossing topic in the colonies; and many letters are extant, written by leading colonial gentlemen at the time, expressing an opinion that English soldiers could not be depended on, except in battalion in the open field. During the consultations also held amongst the leading colonists in 1774, as to the ability of the colonies to resist the power of the Crown, Braddock's defeat was always quoted as a proof that regular troops could never succeed in America against provincial riflemen. Even Dr. Franklin, in his Autobiography, speaking of it, says, "This whole transaction gave us Americans *the first suspicion* that our exalted ideas of the prowess of British regular troops had not been well founded."* And I have heard several of Washington's nearest relatives say that he also entertained that opinion! When we reflect, therefore, that it was the very man who had witnessed the disgrace of the British arms, who was afterwards selected to command the troops of the insurgent colonies, it becomes very probable, that, if Braddock had been more cautious, he would have captured Fort Duquesne, and that the minds of the leading colonists would have, in that event, taken a different direction, and have been rather disposed to contemplate the gallant achievement of the immortal Wolfe on the plains of Abram, than to have found encouragement in the inglorious discomfiture of Braddock on the banks of the Mononghahela.

The scene of that melancholy disaster, when I was there, was principally laid out in fields inclosed with rail fences; the forest trees had been cut down, and a country road ran along the terrace. In an adjacent hut I found a talkative old soldier—the Cicerone of the place—named Dean, who had served in the revolutionary war, and who had been wounded five times at the battle of the Miami in 1791, when the Indians defeated General St. Clair. This worthy informed me that he had lived twenty years neighbour to another old soldier, who had served in Washington's rifle corps in Braddock's affair, and that he had heard him tell the story so often, and with so much detail, that he could almost fancy he had been there himself, now that he had become acquainted with the ground. Old and lame as he was, he got over the high rail fences with surprising activity, conducting me successively to

---

* Memoirs of Benjamin Franklin, vol. i. p. 220.

all the most interesting points of the eventful day, from the landing-place at the Ripple, to the furthest point to which Lieut.-Colonel Gage had advanced. With a melancholy interest I entered the ravines, and endeavoured to realise in my imagination the terrible activity of the Indians, and the astonishment and affright of the soldiers. From the stump of the tree where the wounded General had been placed, I made a sketch of the scene, continually interrupted by the loquacity of my guide, who wanted me to put every thing in it that he had told me. He was constantly saying, " I tell you, it ain't just nothing if you don't put the Indians in !" The garrulity of this veteran was unceasing; he got on so fast that it was impossible to follow him; and I was constantly obliged to interrupt him, to accommodate his narrative to the locality.

Before I left the ground, the old man, who had been walking about with me a long time, became fatigued, and sat down to rest himself; and being rather tired of his company, I left him, to measure the distance betwixt the ravines. Whilst thus occupied, a stranger from Pittsburg, who had, perhaps, also come to visit the locality, joined him; and there I could see him gesticulating with animation, and his companion listening with avidity, his powers of talking not appearing to be at all impaired. When I had measured over the ground, I went to them, and found that the old man was giving the stranger an account of some of his own feats, and was describing to him the incidents of St. Clair's defeat at the Miami; and this he did in such a spirited way that I prevailed upon him to tell me the whole story, of which he certainly made a very thrilling narration. As to the stranger, he mounted his horse as soon as the story was over, and rode off, probably supposing that the old soldier had been talking about Braddock's Field all the time; for he was a silent man, not very intelligent apparently in historical matters, and one story seemed to suit him quite as well as another. I have reason to believe this to be the fact; for the old man told me that the stranger had commenced the conversation by asking him the cause of his lameness, which had led him to talk of himself, and that he had not adverted at all to Braddock's affair until I joined them. If he should hereafter write an account of Braddock's Field, it will be an admirable *pasticcio*.

BRADDOCK'S FIELD.

Old Mr. Dean told me that he had found the greatest number of bones at the point marked No. 6, which, no doubt, was where the ineffectual attempt was made to cover the waggons. He also shewed me a place where he said he had buried "a great many bushels of them." I saw numerous canister-shot, broken musket-barrels, and musket-balls, that had been found when the field was ploughed; and, of course, every stranger carries away some relic with him. A gentleman of Pittsburg afterwards informed me that a skeleton had been found some distance from the field of battle on the Alleghany river, with military buttons and several guineas coined in the reign of Queen Anne beneath it,— the remains probably of some wounded officer, who had crawled from the field to avoid the scalping-knife, and had died from exhaustion. I was told, also, that a farmer some time ago found an entire musket-barrel, and taking it home, put it in the fire one day to use as a poker, when it went off, and lodged a ball in one of the logs of his hut.

On leaving Braddock's Field I called to see a Mr. Oliver, who lives in the vicinity: he accompanied Mr. Morris Birbeck when he emigrated from England to America, and seems to have finished his Transatlantic adventures by opening a seminary for young ladies here, which is very usefully and respectably conducted by his wife and himself. From thence I returned to Pittsburg along the banks of the Mononghahela through a charming country, and amused myself collecting freshwater and land shells, some of the last of very great beauty, with fine specimens of encrinital limestone, the beds of which are in some places well exposed in the banks of the river.

CHAPTER VIII.

VISIT TO THE GERMAN SOCIETY OF ECONOMY.—ITS ORIGIN.

Having remained longer in this very dngy town of Pittsburg than was quite agreeable, and having visited the principal coal localities in its immediate neighbourhood, I determined, before I left the Ohio, to pay a visit to the celebrated George Rapp, at his colony of Economy, about eighteen miles below. I embarked, therefore, early one fine morning, in the steam-boat Beaver, which was going down the river. The view of Pittsburg and the junction of the Alleghany and Mononghahela, at some little distance from the town, is very peculiar and pleasing; and the banks of the Ohio, which are frequently 300 or 400 feet high, with veins of coal in the rocky ledges far above the level of the river, and beautiful slopes coming gently down to the alluvial bottoms, bearing heavy crops of grain, present a succession of engaging objects to the traveller, amongst which the fertile islands that are rapidly passed are not the least interesting.

We soon reached the landing-place, at which there were no symptoms of a town, not even a jetty for the steamer to lie alongside; so, scrambling up the bank, I followed a road for a short distance, and passing a manufactory with thick coal-smoke reeking from it, at length entered a street about eighty feet wide, containing a great many good houses, the greater part of which were built of brick; the rest were neat wooden buildings, carefully painted, an excellent garden being attached to each of the dwellings, the doors of which, to avoid publicity, rarely opened into the street, but into the garden, from which, by a small gate, the inhabitants communicated with the thoroughfares. It was impossible for families residing in a town to enjoy a more perfect retirement; and I soon perceived that this was an important consideration, not only in the peculiar arrangement of the place, but in planting the settlement so distant from the river. In all other American villages on the banks of rivers publicity is considered the most essential of all advantages: a jetty is run out, to facilitate the landing of passengers as well as commercial intercourse; and immediately at the end, next to the shore, taverns, redolent of new-made whisky, vie with each other in every direction in offering their attractions to that class of thirsty wayfarers that never passes their alluring thresholds without refreshing the burning palate with a cool half-pint of "half-and-half."* Mr. Rapp, desirous of not exposing his colonists to the inconveniences of too many visitors, has prudently placed them in a situation where he has supposed no one will seek them without a reasonable motive.

As I walked through the streets, so perfect was the silence, that the town appeared to be deserted; but, as I advanced, I occasionally saw a female clad in the simplest manner in dark blue homespun garments, white cotton stockings, a blue neckerchief, and a peaked cap,

* "Half whisky, half cider-brandy, and no *mistake*," a word which in the preparation of this libation represents water.

standing for about six inches stiffly up behind, made of dark blue cotton stuff, the costume being precisely that of the lower order of females in the vicinity of Stutgard in Germany. I asked one of them where the *gasthaus* was, and she very obligingly gave me the proper directions; and as I proceeded, I espied a young and rather attractive girl up a tree gathering ripe cherries. Upon asking her whether she was gathering them to sell or to preserve, she descended very nimbly, and coming close to the gate, not only gave me an excellent opportunity of looking at her cherries, but at her cherry cheeks, very kindly offering me some of the fruit. I was rather glad, upon the whole, that Mr. Rapp was not present, though nothing was said inconsistent with the modesty of a *mädchen* quite conscious of her attractions. Afraid of compromising my young friend with any of the formidable caps, some of which were sure to be pricking their ears, I thanked her in a very kind manner, and declining her offer, proceeded to the *gasthaus*, or tavern, a very commodious house in the main street.

On entering the house I learnt that it belonged to the society, and was kept for the purpose of entertaining strangers who visited the place. Informing them, therefore, that I had introductions to Mr. Rapp, and was come to see the colony, I was shewn into a nice clean bed-room, and soon discovered, from the general neatness around, that I was likely to be very comfortable. Having refreshed myself with nice cool water and snow-white towels, very different from the coal-stained patches of linen in use at the hotel at Pittsburg, I sallied out and made myself familiar with the topography of the place; after which I went to the public store or warehouse, to inquire for Mr. Baker, the factotum of George Rapp, the name he went by in every person's mouth. I had a letter of introduction to Mr. Baker also: he was a plain man, about thirty-six years old, with intelligent and pleasing features; and putting my letter into his hands, he read it very slowly, and then received me in a frank and engaging manner. I told him that I had but one day to stay there; that I was exceedingly desirous of seeing, with my own eyes, what the success of Mr. Rapp's project had been; and that I was, above all things, anxious to see Mr. Rapp, and have some conversation with him. Mr. Baker did not seem very much afflicted that I was only going to stay one day;* he said he was very much engaged at that moment, but that he would call on me at 1 P. M., and that, if I would give him my letters to George Rapp, he would endeavour to procure me an interview. I was glad to hear him say so, being aware that some recent circumstances had made their head very indifferent about any one who did not belong to his society, which made it somewhat doubtful whether he would receive me.

I now returned to the inn, and was told dinner would be punctually ready at twelve o'clock: this was rather too early an hour for one who always dines late, and never takes luncheon; so, informing them that I had no appe-

* It is not agreeable to these societies to have strangers about them long. I paid a visit in 1808 to the Moravians, at their colony of Bethlehem, in Pennsylvania, and being very much attracted by the tranquillity and order of their life, and desirous of gathering what information I could respecting those Indian tribes they had been such benevolent friends to amidst the cruellest persecutions, I remained at the society's tavern a whole week; and, although I was treated in the kindest manner by the bishop and the leading members, and admitted in the evenings to their social musical concerts, I was politely informed, at the end of the week, that it was contrary to their rules to entertain me any longer.

VOL. I. F

tite, and would take something at a later hour, they told me there would be nothing more provided until half-past six o'clock. As this was the most convenient hour imaginable to myself, I strolled to the hills which bound the rich alluvial lands—once the ancient bottom of the river—to the north, from whence I had a fine view of the immense fields of grain and maize belonging to the society. The wheat-fields, containing about 150 acres, were already cut and in sheaf; the shocks standing in straight lines, and all of them well capped to protect them from the rain. There were also about 150 acres of maize, bearing at least 50 bushels to the acre. The oats were surprisingly stout, and covered a great deal of ground; and the meadows, the grass of which was nearly secured, were of the very first quality, appearing to me to average two tons to the acre. Mr. Rapp afterwards informed me that the society owned 3000 acres of this rich soil, of which one-half was under cultivation. The land is exceedingly fertile and productive, and quite capable of supporting a numerous and industrious community. Near to all this agricultural luxuriance stood the neat compact town; nor have I ever seen, from any eminence in America, such an admirable specimen of the results of human industry, comprehending the fields, the meadows, the town and its gardens, as is presented from the hills which look down upon this rich scene, where one solitary simple wooden steeple raises itself above the roofs of the adjacent houses, to announce the presence of the temple, for freedom of worship in which they have abandoned their cherished Vaterland.

At the appointed hour Mr. Baker called and took me to the manufactories, where the people seemed very industriously employed in fabricating blankets, coarse cloths, and cottons, the superfluities of which meet with a ready sale at Pittsburg, all of them being well made and excellent of their kind.

Mr. Baker, being called off to transact some business, deputed a very intelligent and interesting young man, of an extreme simplicity and gentleness of character, to attend me until he was at liberty. This young man, who was named Jacob, was an assistant at the public store; he spoke very good English, and under his guidance I completed the observations I had to make. But what attracted me more than anything else was the conversation of Jacob himself, who was filled with religious feeling of the purest kind, and the most enthusiastic devotion to his beloved chief, George Rapp, and to the society of which he was a member. Finding this amiable and, as I believe, very sincere man disposed to satisfy my inquiries respecting their history, and their religious and economical policy, I proposed to him to leave on one side for the present those wonder-working contrivances of the calico period, the shuttles, with their kindred rattle-traps of the manufactories, and adjourn to the church; to which he assenting, we bent our way thither. It was a spacious, but plain wooden building, with benches, having backs, for the congregation, in separate compartments for the men and women. In front was a small platform or daïs, somewhat raised from the floor, with a plain table, and a chair appropriated to Mr. Rapp, who officiates as their spiritual instructor. After they have united in singing, he reads to them in the Bible, and then delivers to them an extempore discourse. There is a gallery in the church, in which, upon festival days, instrumental music is introduced.

From the steeple of the church I had an excellent view of the adjacent country, and a close view of the plan of the town: the streets were all laid out at right angles, and the most retired of them had still the sward growing there, though closely kept down. The spacious gardens were filled with a profusion of fine vegetables, cabbages, beans, peas, potatoes, carrots, onions, beets, and *kohl-rabi:* these are for the family use until winter sets in, for which season large fields of potatoes are cultivated, which, when gathered, are divided amongst the families *per capita.* The gardens were also well stocked with fruit-trees loaded with fruit, apples, pears, peaches, cherries, plums, currants, and gooseberries. The gable-ends of the houses, too, were covered with vines, bearing great numbers of healthy-looking grapes, this being a fine bearing year. I never saw a more satisfactory picture of abundance; it reminded me continually of the gardens of the farmers in Tuscany and Lombardy, and was the more striking from the contrast it presented to the wretched inclosures which the greater number of American settlers are contented with for gardens, where nothing is to be seen but a few potatoes and cabbages, choked up with weeds. On descending into the body of the church we sat down, and Jacob gave me a most interesting account of the society; which was afterwards confirmed to me by Mr. Baker, and partly by Mr. Rapp himself. It made a deep impression upon me. Every thing that I had seen bore the impress of a powerful and persevering mind, moved by an impulse of the loftiest kind; and in nothing was it more conspicuous than in the affectionate and most completely obedient deference that the colonists delight to pay to their extraordinary head. Before I relate the interview which I had with him, I shall hope to do an acceptable thing to my readers, by sketching out the history of this society and its venerable patriarch.

HISTORY OF THE SETTLEMENT.

About the year 1803, a number of respectable farmers in the neighbourhood of Stutgard conceived that the rule of Scripture was not lived up to with sufficient simplicity, and, without any immediate concert with each other, began to absent themselves from the churches, and to worship at home in conformity with their own opinions. This, in the end, produced persecutions from the authorities, and a closer union amongst themselves. At length, becoming exceedingly dissatisfied, they turned their attention to emigration; and George Rapp, whose energy of character seemed by consent to fit him to become their leader, left Germany for the United States, to select a situation suited to their views and means, and where they could live in the tranquil enjoyment of their opinions. His first purchase was in Pennsylvania, in the neighbourhood of the river Ohio, not very far distant from where they now are. Having made his friends acquainted with his proceedings, they soon after joined him to the number of one thousand souls, who, ere they had been long in the country, resolved themselves into a community, called the "Harmony Society;" and each individual throwing his property into a common stock, they resolved hereafter to form only one family, to hold every thing in common, and to labour for the common advantage. Subsequently they left their first settlement, and purchased some rich bottoms on the Wabash, in the state of Indiana, giving to this establishment the name of "New Harmony." Here they continued to reside until about the year 1824; but the situation being found unhealthy, and inconvenient as respected markets, Mr. Rapp privately purchased for the use of the society 3000 acres of land, comprehending the rich bottoms they now occupy.

CHAPTER IX.

COUNT ST. LEON, A SINGULAR ADVENTURER.—SOWS DISSENSION IN THE SOCIETY, WITH THE INTENTION OF PLUNDERING IT.

ABOUT this time, Mr. Robert Owen, of Lanark, now known as the leader of the Socialists, purchased New Harmony of Mr. Rapp; whereupon the society went vigorously to work to put their new acquisition into a state for cultivation, erected log huts for their accommodation, and called the place "Economy." The society had now removed into a healthy situation, in the vicinity of one of the best markets in the western country, and upon the banks of a river by which they could communicate readily with every part of the world. Their prosperity soon became great, they built their town and their manufactories, every thing flourished, and by their industry and punctuality they soon acquired universal respect and confidence.

In consequence of the great emigration from other parts of Germany to the United States, vast numbers of Germans had found their way to this new colony of their nation; many of whom, from various benevolent considerations, had been received into the society, and who, without being disciplined in its ways and customs, or cordially entertaining its religious opinions, ostensibly conformed to them. In this state of things, Mr. Rapp, in the year 1829, received a communication from a Dr.

Guentgen, on the part of a number of persons living near Frankfort in Germany, giving an account of the political and religious state of that part of the country, and expressing in a marked manner their dissatisfaction with it. The letter was ably drawn up, contained a great many sound views, spoke of the United States as a country which was the open asylum of the oppressed, and of Mr. Rapp's society as the liberal refuge of conscientious Germans. Direct allusion was made in the letter to a person of great eminence, personal character, and wealth, who proposed conducting a colony from Germany to join the society at Economy; and Mr. Rapp was requested to return a frank and detailed account of its situation.

This communication received the most friendly consideration, and Mr. Rapp returned a liberal and circumstantial answer to it, without, however, giving any direct invitation to the parties to join his society. No further correspondence took place, but about two years afterwards, a letter was received from the same Dr. Guentgen, apprising Mr. Rapp that he had arrived at New York with a party, and should soon proceed to Pittsburg to communicate with him. Soon after another letter was received, announcing their arrival at Pittsburg; upon which, Mr. Frederick Rapp, the adopted son of George, a person of great worth, and, next to himself, the most efficient member of the society, was sent to Pittsburg, to confer with Dr. Guentgen. There he was with much form presented to a Count St. Leon, as the eminent and opulent person who had been spoken of in the letter from Frankfort, and remained some time conferring with them as to their plans and opinions.

On Frederick Rapp's return to Economy, he openly expressed his opinion, that he had seen and heard enough of them to come to the conclusion, that the new-comers would never become incorporated with their society. They, however, came to the place, were lodged for a while at the inn, and for the ensuing winter had some dwelling-houses assigned to them. It appears, however, to have been early determined by George Rapp, and the elders of the colony, not to connect themselves with this party; but only to extend the rites of hospitality to them during the ensuing winter, and then let them depart to pursue their own plans.

They had not long been in the place, before it was discovered that they were in the habit of drawing some members of the society who had joined it in America, and some young persons of the old stock, secretly to their houses, with an intent to persuade them that Count St. Leon was gifted with prophecy, that he had predicted several great events which had been accomplished, and that the cold winter which had destroyed the French army in Russia had been foretold by him. In announcing this his prophetic character, an intimation was not omitted, that he had the power to punish those who would venture to disregard its importance. Occasionally they were told also that he had the faculty of discovering hidden treasures, and of producing gold by transmutation, that he was excessively rich, and was sent by God to carry the society to a greater degree of happiness than it could ever attain without his assistance.

By exciting their discontent with those regulations of the society which placed restraint on their passions, by flattering their weaknesses and prejudices, and amusing their ignorance, they had at last formed a party devoted to St. Leon, and disposed to depose George Rapp, and place St. Leon at the head of the society. Amongst those regulations was one which committed all important affairs relating to the moral conduct and government of the community to George Rapp and the elders; and, amongst other things, no marriages could be contracted and solemnized without their consent. The new party was told, that, as soon as Count St. Leon was placed at the head of affairs, marriages would be permitted as in other communities, and that the young men should have a vote, as well as the elders. The reformers, having augmented their number by an accession of betwixt two and three hundred thus seduced from the society, now proposed to the society to establish St. Leon as their head, as a person sent by God with supernatural powers, for the purpose of leading them to the highest point of human happiness; but they found a large majority immoveable in their attachment to George Rapp and their old customs, and were not slow in perceiving that the men of sense and experience in the society had had their eyes open from the first, and that they considered St. Leon and his Frankfort associates as a set of adventurers who wanted to delude a majority in order to get possession of the common property.

The dissensions now became violent. Every day produced its rumour of some one having gone over to St. Leon; who, to give a bolder character to his enterprise, marched his followers to the hills which overlook the settlement, and declared to them that God had shewed it to him in a vision. The devotion which the new party shewed for him was so great, that upon an occasion when some goods were about to be sent to Pittsburg for sale, they went down to the river to prevent their being shipped, and declaring that they had a common interest in all the property of the society, announced that no business should be transacted without their consent.

During the painful progress of this revolt of the weakest heads of the community, Mr. Rapp conducted himself with great wisdom, moderating the zeal of his friends, who upon several occasions were almost provoked to hostilities, and calming as much as lay in his power the enthusiasts whom these adventurers had deluded; but when he saw that nothing would satisfy them short of delivering the public property into the possession of St. Leon, he took legal advice, and caused process of legal ejectment to be served against St. Leon and his party. Under this they would ultimately have been dispossessed of their dwellings; but the adverse lawyers, whom Dr. Guentgen — the brother-in-law of St. Leon, and the most astute person of the party — employed, contrived so to procrastinate the suit, that a year would probably have elapsed before the parties could have been ejected. Under this view of his affairs, and perceiving how improbable it was the minority would ever come again into a voluntary and cordial union with his friends and himself, he determined in concert with them to offer to the discontented party a sum of money as an equivalent for the interest they had in the property of the society, which, after some discussion, was accepted.

This was transferred into the possession of St. Leon, who then purchased eight hundred acres of land about twelve miles lower down the river, where a small village called Philipsburg already existed. Here his party settled, encouraged by the assurances of St. Leon that they were to be the most prosperous and favoured people of God. To strengthen their confidence in him, he now began to collect great quantities of sandstone from the hills, caused it to be ground into powder, erected furnaces, and commenced the attempt of transmuting it into gold. After expending about 10,000 dollars in vain experiments, he discontinued them, assuring the society that the rocks (which belonged to the old carboniferous series) were not mature enough by forty years, at the accomplishment of which period he announced that they would be in a proper state for transmutation. By this ingenious device he satisfied his disappointed followers for the moment, and assigned a convenient time for the delay equal to the probable duration of his own life, as he was now entering the middle period. At length his money was expended, and his debts at Pittsburg and other places having greatly accumulated, he found himself unable to pay either principal or interest, and became a bankrupt. The reaction of opinion in his party now commenced; they began to perceive how great his knavery and their credulity had been, and, throwing off all reverence for their prophet, proceeded to sell his plate, his pictures, and personal property, to discharge the debts he had contracted in the name of the community. Having at length sunk down to his true character of an impostor, he, in company with his knavish brother-in-law Guentgen, set out in quest of new adventures, and, after wandering about the continent, died under circumstances of great distress in the vicinity of Alexandria, on Red River.

As he had been announced on his first arrival at New York from Germany as a nobleman of illustrious family, some individuals, during the most turbulent part of the proceedings at Economy, wrote to Frankfort for information respecting him. Accounts subsequently arrived that he had at one time passed under the name of Müller, but that his true name was Prole; and, as to his illustrious descent, it unfortunately turned out that he had been a tailor's boy, and half rogue, half enthusiast, had travelled over Europe, learning various languages in an imperfect way, and acquiring a smattering of various branches of knowledge, sufficient to give him importance in the eyes of the credulous and the illiterate. Guentgen, however, was the more accomplished knave of the two, being a *Dousterswiller* of some notoriety; and the plan they had concocted was to draw Mr. Rapp, whose great success as a colonist was publicly known in Germany, into a correspondence, and then to give a construction to it as if they had undertaken the voyage to America by Mr. Rapp's invitation.

On the voyage out, Guentgen one day unexpectedly announced to the rest of the party, that their companion Müller was henceforward to be called Count St. Leon, a descendant of the house of Este, and that he should land at New York under that title. Being thus announced in the American papers, he immediately got into circulation as a nobleman of the most illustrious descent, who was proceeding to extend the well-known colony founded by George Rapp. What, however, gave him the greatest importance in the eyes of the New-Yorkers and Pennsylvanians, was the statement that he had brought several millions of dollars with him. Having thus laid a broad foundation for the most favourable reception by Rapp's community, he added on his arrival there the loftier attributes of prophet and alchymist. Finding that the watchful judgment of George Rapp never slumbered, and that it was not practicable to draw him into the snare they had laid, these adventurers adopted the base and unprincipled expedient of sowing dissension in the society in order to plunder it, and an animosity between children and their parents which has been seldom exceeded.

Relieved as the society felt itself by a separation from that portion which had thrown off all brotherly affection and friendly courtesy towards them, yet the moment of parting was a painful one, for many husbands were separated from their wives, and children from their parents. On the bankruptcy of De Leon taking place, a great number of his followers came to Economy, with the intention of compelling George Rapp to give them more money, and behaved very turbulently; but acting with great energy, and causing them to be bound over to keep the peace, they returned without effecting anything. Since that time they have dissolved their community, and have divided the land, each man living upon his own resources. Many of them have applied to re-unite themselves to Mr. Rapp and his people, but they have been uniformly refused. The separation has been a real blessing to the old colony, and is regarded by them as a providential purification from all the light and unquiet members of their society, without the pain of discarding them. The most perfect harmony appears now to reign; the reverential deference which is paid to Mr. Rapp seems common to them all, and to be sincerely felt: his great prudence and devotion to their interests have been so unceasing, that they are convinced he entertains no views respecting them inconsistent with those of a parent to his children; and so entire is their confidence in him, that, upon the death of Frederick Rapp, they insisted that all their transactions should be conducted in his name alone, so that, in virtue of the unbounded trust reposed in him, George Rapp is the nominal proprietor of all the property of the society.

CHAPTER X.

PROSPEROUS STATE OF THE SOCIETY.—INTERVIEW WITH ITS HEAD, GEORGE RAPP.

CONSIDERING the perfect success which has attended his exertions, and the undeviating simplicity of his personal character, this pleasing instance of generous and affectionate feeling is not very surprising; for after the persecutions, troubles, and changes they have gone through, the society, consisting of about five hundred persons, now finds itself in possession of a rich domain, and of a great deal of superfluous wealth: each family has its comfortable dwelling-house, with the best of all appendages, a well-stocked fruit and vegetable garden. If any one wants a hat, he goes to the superintendent of that branch, and is supplied; if he wants clothes, he goes to the tailor. At the public store, tea, coffee, sugar, spices, knives and forks, and all other articles of domestic use, are delivered upon application. In all this, however, a prudent administration of the public property is observed; and when the superintendent of any branch perceives that some individuals are less economical than others, and require to be supplied beyond their just wants, it is his duty to check this tendency to waste, generally the effect of inadvertence or inexperience. Few individuals, I was told, require to be admonished twice.

About one-third of the whole number of adults are

agriculturists, the rest manufacturers and artizans. There is a market, to which, when animals are slaughtered, each family sends for its proportional share of meat. Each family also keeps a cow, and milks and takes care of her, but the milk, when strained, is all put into a common stock, and divided *pro rata*, as everything else is; so that, when the cow of any particular family is dry for a time, they are not without milk on that account. It is in fact a family upon a large scale, for the support of which every individual contributes his assistance, with an unceasing and willing industry, producing everything within itself, and dividing everything in an equitable manner and according to their just wants.

There is also an excellent school for the children, where they are instructed in reading, writing, arithmetic, &c.; and for those who have a talent for other acquirements, they have a library of useful books and a museum of natural history. Music also is cultivated, and upon festival days they freely indulge in this their happy national taste. When they first arrived in America, in common with all their countrymen, they smoked a great deal of tobacco, and drank ardent spirits, though in moderation; even Mr. Rapp used these indulgences: but he soon took a right view of those artificial wants, which often allure men into an excessive gratification, and discontinued the use of them. At present no one in the society uses either ardent spirits or tobacco in any form. When the elders recommended to the society the disuse of ardent spirits, Mr. Baker informed me, that all the families returned to the public store the stock they had on hand both of tobacco and spirits, simply saying, "The society is not going to use these things any more and therefore we return them."

I paid a visit to the doctor, a clever little man, named Feucht. His apothecary's shop was small, but very neat, and well supplied with drugs: he told me that he gave out very little medicine, and that of the simplest kind. The bell rings for breakfast at half-past six A. M.: at seven they all go to their various avocations, and at twelve they are summoned to dinner. At one they resume their work, and at half-past three beer and cake are served to refresh them. In harvest-time currant or other home-made wine is given to the women, and men also if they desire it. At seven P. M. the labours of the day cease, and all retire to their homes to supper, each family having a proportional number of unmarried persons living with them.

Mr. Rapp's only son John died about twenty years of age, and left an only daughter called Gertrude. I had heard her frequently spoken of as a person of great merit: she had successfully introduced the culture of the silk-worm and the manufacture of silk at Economy, and I was very anxious to see her. My friend Jacob, after leaving the church, took me to a building where in a small room were a few females cleaning damaged cocoons. One of these, who appeared somewhat turned of thirty, had a very pleasing countenance, with more character in it than the rest, but in her dress and manner did not differ from them. Jacob conversed with her more than with the others; but whilst I was in the room, I never suspected her to be Miss Gertrude. The idea I had formed of her was that of a maiden to be seen rather in the spacious dwelling-house of her grandfather, than of a woman dressed in a plain blue garment, with her hands in hot water, picking cocoons in a steam-house. I was therefore not a little surprised when Jacob told me it was Miss Gertrude he had been talking to, and who had been giving him such a cheerful and encouraging account of her branch of industry. In the evening, whilst I was standing, about seven o'clock, at the door of the inn during a heavy shower, I saw her come from the workshop with her blue gown turned over her head and drenched in the rain, shewing the great interest she took in her silk establishment by remaining there to the latest moment.

The introduction of the cultivation and manufacture of silk at this place is entirely due to her: she procured a few worms for her amusement only in the first instance, and, having enlarged her stock, set up a loom, where they now weave silk handkerchiefs and waistcoat patterns. It is quite probable, that, when their mulberry-trees are old and plentiful enough, the manufacture of silk will become an important branch with them, as no labour can be afforded so cheap as theirs, especially such willing and intelligent labour.

Finding Jacob on such pleasant terms with Miss Gertrude, I asked him what the real objection was to countenancing marriage at Economy. He answered me frankly but ingeniously, that it was not discountenanced for political reasons, and that their conduct was the simple result of religious feeling. Upon this I ventured to say to him, "It cannot have escaped the attention of your society, which is opposed to all irregularities, that if marriages were not solemnized amongst Christian communities, your principles would lead to the extinction of all society." He answered modestly, but with a gravity a little lighted up with enthusiasm, "If men, by subduing their passions, which are the cause of so much trouble in life, could accomplish an eternal life of innocence, perhaps it would suit God's design, if we knew enough of it, that our race should become extinct. We certainly can comprehend that an existence in Heaven is infinitely more worthy of our attention than an existence on earth." This answer was so far beyond my expectation, somewhat prejudiced as I was by the accounts I had heard of Mr. Rapp's endeavouring to keep down their intellect as low as possible, that I could not but perceive that a deep religious feeling was the true bond of this society; and I began to look upon Mr. Rapp as a very superior being, as any man certainly is, who can infuse into the hearts of mechanics aspirations so lofty as to raise them beyond all the other conditions and temptations of life.

Upon another occasion, when I observed, "The death of Frederick Rapp must have distressed you all greatly," "We missed him," he replied, "for a while; but we cannot be made unhappy by the death of one, when we have so many brothers and sisters left." The only death, probably, that would greatly afflict them, would be that of Mr. Rapp himself, to whom they bear the love of children, always calling him "Father," when they speak to him. "We never talk of that," said Jacob; "we live as if he was always to be with us; and then he is so fresh and strong, that we are never afraid."

In the many independent communities that I have had opportunities of observing in various countries, it has always appeared to me that there was, more or less, some conspicuous failing of humanity to be discerned, and which could not be kept down, however excellent and meritorious their other faculties : there seemed to me to be always some touch of pride, conceit, self-righteousness, or self-interest, for the sake of which the semblance of a virtuous simplicity was assumed : but here I saw nothing of these weaknesses; and having satisfied myself that this was a most remarkable community for effecting the progress through life under rational and pure views, and consistent and pure conduct, and having witnessed the abundance, the peace, and the happiness which a large family enjoyed through the wisdom of their head, I became very desirous of seeing him as soon as possible. Jacob, therefore, about 6 P. M., conducted me to the spacious garden attached to Mr. Rapp's premises. This, which contained more than half an acre of ground, was laid out in very narrow walks, separating beds crowded with vegetables, and was filled to repletion with fruit-trees of every kind—peaches, plums, apples on trellises, numerous varieties of pears, figs, and cherries, with raspberries in the greatest profusion. There was also a good, but unpretending conservatory, with oranges and lemons of a large size pendent from many of the trees, and various green-house plants in good order. In the centre of the garden was a small temple, with pillars, surrounded with water, and a neat bridge thrown across it. I felt quite sure that Miss Gertrude was the presiding genius in all these elegances, and Jacob informed me it was so. This exceedingly fruitful though rather too umbrageous garden was the only marked aristocratic feature about Mr. Rapp's premises : there was a general air about it which announced that it was not common property; but then every dwelling-house had its private garden, so probably its superior condition was as well the fruit of their attachment to him, as of his own taste and inclination. If I had not been afraid of appearing too inquisitive, I should have informed myself as to that point, although I have no doubt but that the society would be desirous of conferring every distinction upon him, and every embellishment upon his private life, that he would consent to receive at their hands.

After taking a look at everything, Jacob left me, to announce, as I suppose, my arrival, and soon after returned. We were walking slowly in the direction of the house, and admiring the clustered abundance of this labyrinth of Pomona, when, at a moment when I was least thinking of such a vision,

> Vidi presso di me un veglio solo,
> Degno di tanta reverentia in vista,
> Che più non dé à padre alcun figluolo.
> Lunga la barba, e di pel bianco mista,
> Portava à suoi capelli simigliante;
> Di quai cadeva al petto doppia lista.*
> *Purgatorio*, Canto I.

This venerable figure turned into our walk, and approached us with a firm step, bearing a walking-stick in his right hand, which seemed to go to the ground with an air of authority. His athletic frame was covered with a blue frock-coat, of light home-spun cloth: his face, which was tempered with a cheerful benevolence, was broad and ruddy; and a remarkable bushy white beard, of great volume, hung from his face from ear to ear. He stopped

---

* Alone, and near unto me stood, an ancient form,
Whose aspect might awaken reverend thoughts,
Such as a son may cherish for his sire.
His ample beard fell down upon his breast,
Which, like his head, with hoary whiteness crowne
Reposed between his venerable locks.

and smiled, as much as to say, "I am George Rapp, whom you desire to see." I was very much struck by his appearance; and being naturally of a reverential turn of mind, instantly uncovered my head in the most respectful manner; and after apologizing as well as I could in German for not speaking his language fluently enough, requested permission to converse with him through Jacob, as I was informed he did not speak English. Having expressed his satisfaction to me, I desired Jacob to say in complimentary terms how much I had been gratified with what I had seen at Economy, that it appeared to me he had been successful in the execution of a wise and benevolent plan, and that I congratulated him on being permitted to be the dispenser of so much happiness; that I sincerely thought him entitled to be considered a great benefactor to his countrymen, and esteemed myself happy in being able to say that I had shaken hands with him. When Jacob had interpreted this to him, he struck his hand into mine with a friendly smile; and in a jocular tone said in broken English, "Very gut, very gut." We now began to talk about the place, and he related to me how, near eleven years ago, he had found it an unreclaimed wilderness, and the steps he had taken to improve it. He said it combined more advantages than any situation he had seen, and expressed a hope that it would be the abiding-place of his people.

Having turned the conversation to their old establishment, New Harmony, on the Wabash, I asked his opinion as to the probable success of Mr. Robert Owen, with whom I was acquainted, and who, like himself, was engaged in the attempt to establish independent social communities. He replied, that, judging from what he had seen of Mr. Owen, he thought he was a man of benevolent intentions; but that it appeared to him that Mr. Owen and himself had no principles in common, and were not to be considered as walking in the same path. That he and his countrymen had undergone a great trial in abandoning their Vaterland, and aimed at nothing now but to lead a peaceful and contented life, being well disposed to obey the laws of the country they lived in, and having no inclination to interfere with the opinions or pursuits of anybody else; whilst Mr. Owen's object did not seem to be peace and comfort, so much as to persuade all the world that they were in error on the score of religion, morals, laws, and manners. Stopping for a moment, he put his hand on my shoulder, and looking me in the face, said, in German, "My friend, old George Rapp thinks that whoever attempts to bend men into a community of interests upon any other grounds but a strong religious feeling, will not succeed. It is religion gives peace here, (putting his hand to his heart,) and keeps the mind clear and steady. Men that are not religious are always uneasy; far from making sacrifices, they are always wanting something; but religious men are contented to make sacrifices in this life, because they consider them as seeds sown to fruit hereafter in the life to come."

As we advanced along the walks of the garden, holding this very interesting conversation, the old patriarch, who seemed disposed to continue it, would frequently stoop and pick the finest bunches of currants for me, and would occasionally give me the history of his grape-vines and espalier-trees, of which there were many fine ones. At length we adjourned to the house, a spacious brick building, and introducing me into a room, where there was a large copy of West's picture of "Christ healing the Sick," he desired me to take a seat, and apologizing for leaving me a moment, went out, and returned with two bottles of wine. One of them was forthwith uncorked, and wine-glasses, with some cakes, being there ready on the table, Mr. Rapp telling me it was *keimgemacht*, or home-made, poured some out, and invited me to drink it. It was a light, sweetish wine; and after I had commended it, he rose, and with an air of importance uncorked the other bottle, saying, "You shall now drink of some *heimgemacht* I made fourteen years ago of the wild grape on the Wabash river." I carried the glass to my mouth with great reverence, shook my head sagely, and observed that "few persons could boast of having drunk wine of that kind." I had scarce tasted it, however, before I hastily set the glass down, not a little apprehensive that the old patriarch had made a mistake, and uncorked a bottle of physic. Such a murky and distressing cordial I certainly never tasted before; but as it had been so long in bottle, and I could not find it in my heart to act unkindly to anything belonging to my venerable host, I made a grand effort, and bolting it to the last drop, declared, with my teeth on edge, that I had drunk a great many delicious wines in various parts of the world, but that I had not supposed there was anything exactly like that in America. Touched with my eulogium, the old gentleman grasped the bottle, and said, "Mein lieber Kind, du wirst ein anderes Glas haben!" and instantly poured me out a second, which he insisted upon me swallowing.

In the course of our interview, I asked him his age, and he informed me that he was in his seventy-ninth year. I said, "You look like a healthy man of sixty-five, and on more."—"Oh!" said he, with a smile, and looking to Jacob, "that is because I am so much wanted for these children;" meaning, that Providence preserved his life, that he might be useful to the society. Perhaps, knowing the weakness of men, he is apprehensive that the harmony which now exists is, in a great measure, an effect of the general reverence and affection for his person; yet, I trust, some one will at the proper time be found worthy to succeed him in the society.

The supper-hour at the hotel being now arrived, and having eaten nothing since 7 A. M., I took leave of this interesting and distinguished man: he gave me his blessing at parting, which I received most gratefully. No interview that I ever had with any individual gave me greater satisfaction; and I left him, impressed with the most respectful feelings.

CHAPTER XI.

REACH RAVENNA, THE SUMMIT LEVEL OF THE COUNTRY.—CROSS THE LAKE RIDGES, AND REACH CLEVELAND ON LAKE ERIE.—REACH DETROIT.

AFTER a comfortable night's rest in a clean bed, and a good breakfast, I got into a carriage, which they obligingly engaged for me, and left this peaceful abode, passing two or three miles along its rich harvest fields. It was very easy to perceive when I had passed beyond the territory of the society, the contrast was so great: every settler's house gave abundant evidence of the slovenly manner in which the individual system is carried on by their neighbours. One would have thought that so much system, and the comfort it produced, would have inspired an universal emulation; but it seemed to have produced an opposite effect, as if they were determined to proclaim, that one of their privileges was to set all comfort at defiance—badly built houses, windows without glass, dirty children, lean mongrel cows, barns in ruins, patches representing gardens, with nothing but potatoes and cabbages, choked up with weeds, and every appearance of discomfort about the persons of the indolent occupants of the tenements. I stopped to speak to a few of them, and found them all entertaining a strong antipathy to Mr. Rapp's people, probably because they avoided any connexion with them.

The drive, however, was through a pretty country; and having made ten miles, we arrived at Big Beaver, a large tributary of the Ohio. Here a trick was played upon me, of an unusually shabby character, by the landlord of a house at which I stopped, near the bridge. Being desirous of pursuing my journey through the state of Ohio to a town called Poland, he informed me that I ought to lose no time in going a short distance further, to a village where the stage-coach was. Having dismissed the carriage which brought me from Economy, it became necessary, therefore, to engage another belonging to himself: this I accordingly did; and having paid him for it beforehand, which he required me to do, and directed my luggage to be put into it as soon as it was ready, I set off on foot as quick as I could, to catch the stage-coach before it left the village, which I succeeded in doing; and my luggage coming up, I now took my place in the stage, and off we started. To my great surprise, we stopped, in less than an hour from the time I had left it, at the landlord's door at the bridge again; and, perceiving the fraud he had practised upon me, I sent for him—for he was evidently keeping out of the way—and demanded of him the reason why he had so misled me. He shuffled out an excuse, that the stage did not come every day past his door, which the driver contradicted immediately. I told him it would be good policy in him to behave with more kindness and justice to travellers in future, for this transaction was enough to ruin his character all round the country. I have no doubt he was sorry for what he had done; for several persons were round the door, and all seemed to concur in reprobating his conduct. Generally speaking, the American landlords are a very obliging set of men, and, being in the unsettled parts of the country much greater men than their guests, consider them as being under their protection. I have received many acts of kindness from some of them: this fellow probably was a rogue in grain, and would have acted in the same manner in any other country, if he had been born there.

For the first few miles the road ran in the valley of the Big Beaver, near the stream, and was very beautiful. We could see bituminous coal amidst the ledges of the opposite bank very distinctly. There is a canal here, which extends to Newcastle; and they are now projecting a junction from thence into the Ohio Canal. We soon rose upon the table-land of the country, about 800 feet above the level of the navigable streams, in a rather fertile, but very monotonous country, abounding in sordid and filthy taverns, where dram-drinking seems to be the principal branch of business. The distance to Poland was thirty miles, and we reached it before sunset: and, the country not being attractive, I continued my journey all night in the stage, and in the morning reached Ravenna, a large village in Ohio; a point which is almost the summit level of the country, at an elevation of 1140 feet above tide-water. Here I breakfasted, and then continued my journey sixty-four miles to Cleveland, on Lake Erie; the country sloping the whole distance, and containing vast quantities of boulders of primary rocks strewed upon the surface, which appear to have been transported there when the waters of the western lakes extended to the neighbourhood of Ravenna. The land appeared very fertile; new villages were springing up in various places, each one with its neat meeting-house; and evidences abounded of a resolute, industrious, and orderly population.

For some miles before reaching Cleveland we crossed what are called the Lake Ridges, formed of gravel and sand, which in their structure and parallelism resemble other ridges near the western lakes, and conceived by some to have been ancient beaches. The last three miles of the country was a dead alluvial flat, the most recent margin from which Lake Erie had receded. I saw many good vegetable gardens, and extensive nurseries full of thrifty plants, betokening the vicinity of a flourishing town. Cleveland, like all the river and lake towns, has one wide busy street, parallel with the lake shore, thronged with people and shops; whilst in the new streets, running at right angles to it, scattered houses are being rapidly erected in various directions. Although it was late in the night when I arrived, I hastened, as soon as I had secured a bed at the hotel, to the shore, from whence I obscurely saw the magnificent Lake Erie, expanding its ample bosom beneath the star-lit canopy. Everything was still; and, my mind filled with various reflections, I continued wandering on the solitary shore, the banks of which appeared to be from 60 to 70 feet above the level of the lake.* Just as I was thinking of returning to the hotel, to get something to eat, which I had not done since I left Ravenna, the lights of a steamer appeared upon the lake, and approaching nearer and nearer, it was evident she was bound to Cleveland. I waited on the bank until I could hear music on board, and then, being quite sure she was coming in, I hastened back, and had scarce finished a slight repast, when information was brought that it was a steamer of the first class, called the Munroe, from Buffaloe, and would depart immediately for Detroit. Nothing could be more agreeable, so I immediately transferred myself on board; and being fortunate enough to secure a separate cabin, called a state-room, I remained

* The lake here washes the lower beds of the Devonian series.

on deck until midnight, when we left Cleveland, and were soon steaming away on Lake Erie, out of sight of land. I was awaked in the night by a little bustle on board; and finding that the steamer was not under way, I hastily dressed, and going on deck, found we had stopped for a short time at Sandusky. Here I stepped ashore, merely to look at the limestone ledges, which I knew were here in horizontal beds, and, returning on board, was a second time awaked by the broad light of day. I now made my *toilette*, and going upon deck found we were near the Ohio shore. It was a beautiful morning, and the lake was most placid. Having passed Sister's Island, we stood into the bay at the mouth of the river Raisin, to land some passengers.

I had now an opportunity of examining the steamer, which was about 150 feet long, and 40 feet wide; the cabin was spacious, and when new must have been a handsome room; the berths were neatly arranged; and commodious and wide ottomans were placed at the stern. I should have exceedingly liked to repose on one of them with my book; but they were filled with nasty stinking-looking fellows, with dirty boots on, spitting about at random, without caring for the disgust their practices excited in the more respectable passengers. These are the cherished privileges of the levelling system. If the captain of one of these steamers is a vulgar fellow himself, a few blackguards on board can effectually destroy the comfort of respectable travellers; for he makes those his companions, and has no sympathy with these. The monstrous and striking inconsistency too often connected with public travelling in this country is, that the arrangements in the first instance, especially in the steamers, being excellent,—the furniture always handsome, and often superfluously and gaudily so,—every thing announces preparation for well-

DEMOCRACY AND DIRT.

bred and refined travellers. This is the theory of the thing. Then comes practice, and the unremitting efforts of the dirty portion of the travelling world to bring every thing down to their own level, which is soon done by chewing, smoking, spitting, and drinking. They have the same right to be dirty that others have to be clean, and maintain their rights in that particular with as much pertinacity as they would in any other. Democracy and dirt have a great regard for each other; and where the first has the upper hand, the second never fails to assert its authority. Time will hereafter more fully show the effect of this.

July 30.—About 3 P. M. we were opposite to Grosse Isle, and having left the lake behind, passed sufficiently near to the Canadian shore to see the sentinels at Fort Malden in their scarlet coats. Amherstburg appeared to be a neat little place. The strait* here seemed to be about a mile and a half wide; the banks clay and sand, the country extremely flat, and the water a dull blue colour. The farms on the British side, following the Canadian custom, go back some distance into the country, with a narrow frontage on the river; the houses are usually plain framed buildings, and sometimes constructed with squared logs. On the American side no buildings were visible. The country was a dead flat, presenting nothing but a low sedgy shore. The banks of the strait did not appear to be more than 30 feet above the water; and the adjacent lands, as far as the eye could reach, announced an ancient lacustrine deposit, without visible elevation upon it.

As we approached the town of Detroit, the river narrowed to about 1500 yards, and a scene of some anima-

* This strait, or river of Detroit, as the French call it, connects Lake Erie with Lake Huron.

tion appeared. I could see half-a-dozen church steeples, with numerous buildings in the distance, and several very neat-looking painted cottages on the American side. On the British side there was Sandwich, not a very neat-looking village, with a small Episcopal church, and a larger wooden edifice, but still unpainted, of an antiquated structure, for the Roman Catholics. In North America, where there are so few localities to which any historical interest attaches, Detroit is conspicuous, for the military incidents connected with it have more than once been rather of a thrilling character; and I landed here for the first time, delighted at having an opportunity of examining a place about which I had read and heard so much.

On reaching a large hotel called the Michigan Exchange, I was so fortunate as to obtain a spacious private room with a clean bed; and having made my arrangements, and enough of daylight remaining to take a look at the place, I wandered about for a couple of hours. What would have pleased many, exceedingly disappointed me. With enthusiastic predilections for the scenes made almost illustrious by the exploits of the early French, the audacious daring of the crafty Indian chief Pondiac, and the inflexible resolution of our own gallant Brock,—scenes than which few places can boast of so exciting and various a character, I could not view without distaste the long street, 80 feet broad, filled with Yankee stores, lawyers' offices, doctors' shops, dens where vulgar justices of the peace hide themselves, and an assemblage of long eager visages eternally talking about dollars and business. In the morning I hastened to look for some vestiges of the ancient fort that Pondiac had beleaguered; but, alas! every thing was razed to the ground; and, indeed, not a vestige was even left of the modern fortification that General Hull so hastily surrendered in 1812 to the resolute Brock, except the house of the commanding officer, that was *too good* to pull down. The settlements of the United States are spreading so rapidly, and the passion for making money is so absorbing, that there will soon not be a stone or a stick standing where a fort once stood, or a battle was fought. This is deeply to be regretted, as historical monuments assist greatly to elevate the character of a people.

On my return from my walk, Colonel W., a very gentlemanly person, and an officer of great merit in the service of the United States, called upon me, and engaged me to dine with him the next day. I was delighted with this incident, because I had known his lady a great many years before, and because I was sure to receive a great deal of information from so intelligent an officer.

July 31.—Having passed the morning in making observations, at 2 P. M. I dressed for my engagement, and went to Colonel W.'s. We had a very pleasant dinner. Mrs. W. is a lively, well-bred gentlewoman, and received me cordially. There was also a Miss R. and her father, whom I had formerly known, both of them agreeable persons, who resided at Grosse Isle. What a charm agreeable women infuse into society, and what an immense difference education makes in them. The same morning, at the public breakfast table at the hotel, there was a very pretty woman, who, apparently, had not had many of its advantages, stuffing in onions and an immense quantity of nasty-looking trash for her breakfast. I thought I would rather be married to a she codfish, as there would be some chance of her being caught. I found my host, Colonel W., a person of various attainments : he had cultivated letters with success, and would have been considered a most agreeable companion in any society. Besides his other advantages, he possessed some exceedingly fine *Château Margeaux* of one of the best vintages, a merit that few field officers I had lately seen could boast of.

In the evening the Colonel drove me to Spring Wells, a place about three miles from Detroit, where General Brock effected his landing, on the 16th of August, 1812. From the account which his own countrymen give of the American General Hull, it appears that he was totally without soldierly qualities. He had commenced hostilities on the declaration of war by invading Canada, with a vapouring proclamation announcing that he would not stop until he had taken Quebec; but advancing no further than the opposite shore, he made an inglorious retreat to Detroit in less than a month, permitting General Brock, with less than one thousand men, principally composed of Indians and militia-men, to invade him in turn without opposition; and although in a strong fort sufficiently garrisoned, and assisted by able and spirited officers, he became so intimidated by the exaggerated view he took of the excesses that the Indians under the British flag might commit if victorious, that he not only withdrew the cannon that could have raked the whole line of approach of the British troops, but neglected to line the fences of the farms, that were on the line by which they were advancing, with troops that could from their cover have cut off almost every man that appeared in sight; so that General Brock, after making this bold dash, had very little trouble after touching the American shore, beyond receiving the capitulation of his enemy upon the very day that he landed. In fact, he never approached nearer to Detroit than a mile, and negotiated the capitulation of Hull and his troops from a house where he stopped to breakfast. Everything was signed before he left this house, so extremely eager was Hull to shelter himself and his friends from the dangers his apprehensions had created. It is to the credit of the officers under his command that he never consulted them, and turned a deaf ear to the suggestions they ventured to their commander, to save themselves and their country's flag from dishonour.

This being the last town on the Indian frontier, and the only place where I was likely to find any mechanics, I directed a comfortable tent to be made, and procured a variety of objects that were likely to be useful to me in my projected excursion into the Indian country. It is much better to provide these things at the frontier towns; the tradesmen there are more familiar with the wants of one who is about to travel in the Indian countries; and Detroit is a place full of resources, and much frequented by straggling Indians. I called to give some directions one morning at a boot-maker's, and found an elderly-looking Ojibway Indian there, in company with what I took to be a young-looking squaw, of a fine character of countenance. She was trying a pair of shoes on, which I was rather surprised at, as the squaws always wear mocassins. I asked the tradesman if she was the Indian's daughter or his wife, and understood him to say that she was his wife, and that he had another who was older. The Indian understood English a little, and having been a great deal amongst the Canadians, spoke French tolerably well, as the tradesman told me. I therefore spoke to him in French, and asked him if she had brought him any children, but he would give me no answer, saying something in Indian to his companions; upon which they gave a mortal grunt of dissatisfaction. I saw that they were offended at something, but could not imagine what it was. Whilst she was drawing on one of the shoes, her robe got a little a-side, and her naked thighs were rather too plainly seen; upon which a bystander remarked, that for a young squaw she was not very modest. Just at this time a person happened to come in who knew them, and said we were all under a mistake, that it was a young man of eighteen, and not a squaw. We were all exceedingly surprised, and had a very good laugh; the smooth chin, feminine face, and peculiar dress of this handsome youth having completely deceived us. Female Indians, however, of the common class, are so ugly, that a youth dressed as this one was is easily mistaken for a female; indeed, I have often found it as difficult to conjecture what sex individuals of this race were, by merely looking at their faces, as I should be on looking at the faces of animals.

Having before left my card at the quarters of General B., the commanding officer of this district, I called upon him again, in company with Colonel W., and found him at home. He was not particularly polite, and quite ungrammatical enough to make me believe what I had already learnt, that he was an uneducated frontier soldier of great merit in his line, but not remarkably disposed to be useful to a traveller.

CHAPTER XII.

AGREEABLE AMERICAN SOCIETY.—MANNERS OF THE FRENCH CANADIANS RESIDING AT DETROIT.

A SUNDAY intervening during my stay, I went to the Catholic Church about 6 A.M., that I might have an opportunity of forming an opinion of the Canadian population here. Very few persons were present, and I returned again after breakfast to the morning service. The congregation was chiefly composed of the humbler class of French Canadians, dressed in coarse home-spun clothes. With few exceptions, neither men nor women looked much better than Indians, and most of them seemed to have Indian blood in their veins. A few persons of a superior degree, in dress and manners, were present, but very few. The music was good, and the organist was an excellent performer. The Curé was a venerable-looking man with grey hair; and a Bishop, a native of Tyrol, whose name I have forgotten, delivered an admirable sermon: he was a very short, odd-looking little man, but full of talent. As soon as the service was over, the Bishop, with his Curé and his *cortège*, six in number, made a very episcopal exit into the vestry-room. I was exceedingly pleased with the whole service, and the devout conduct of the congregation. At the door of the church I found several *charettes*, or little waggons, belonging to the inhabitants of the vicinity, each of them drawn by one horse, and all without seats. In some of them half-a-dozen respectably dressed females squatted themselves down with their children, a male in front driving the "*marche donc.*" * Colonel W. told me that the streets of Detroit, not being paved, were sometimes, on the approach of winter and in spring, excessively muddy; but being the season when the Canadian families kept up their *bals de société,* each of them had one of these machines to go to their parties in, and that it was not unusual to see ladies upon these occasions, dressed in grand toilet, squatted down in them.

As soon as the Roman Catholic service was over, I crossed the river in the ferry-boat to Sandwich, on the British side, intending to go to the Episcopal Church there, and had an agreeable walk of about a mile and a half along the bank of the river. At the court-house I got into conversation with the person who had charge of the church as well as the gaol, a respectable old English soldier, who had been near half a century in Canada. This interesting man had preserved his loyalty to his sovereign and native country amidst all the changes and temptations he had been exposed to. He conversed with me freely about the state of that part of the country, and observed that it was gradually settling with respectable English families; that demagogues and agitators were not much countenanced by them, and that the whole population, with few exceptions, promised to be as loyal as it was industrious. He said their American neighbours were a very industrious and active race of people, and that they lived upon good terms with them. I was struck with this pleasing instance of two people, only divided by a river 1500 yards wide, each living happily under two such different forms of government, in a sincere attachment to each of which they have been respectively brought up.

* A soubriquet generally given to their horses.

After dinner Colonel W. called upon me, and we took a drive by the river side, along the ancient road to Bloody Bridge, where Major Dalyell's detachment was defeated by Pondiac in 1763, and himself killed. It consists of a few planks laid across a small brook, which here empties itself into the Detroit: the bridge is not more than 5 yards from the river, and there is not a space of more than 6 inches from the under-side of the bridge to the brook; yet the author of "Wacousta," one of the most stirring romances I have ever read, has made it wide enough to conceal a company of soldiers beneath, and to permit a canoe to pass under. Whether that agreeable writer has ever been in the country he describes, I know not; but he has exceedingly distorted probabilities, and misrepresented distances and localities. He makes a schooner perform the distance from old Michilimackinac to the southern extremity of Lake Huron, now Fort Gratiot, which is a distance of 240 miles, betwixt sunrise and sunset, and without a breath of wind; and transforms the Detroit river, which is a magnificent stream 1500 yards wide in the narrowest part, and often a mile and a half, into a confined meandering stream, across which a fallen tree could rest upon both banks, and from the channel of which the yards of the schooner could rake the branches of the trees growing on each side. Such egregious exaggerations in an historical romance more than counterbalance its merit in the eyes of the traveller, for with him the absurdities become the most conspicuous features of the work; and nothing would have been more easy than to have avoided them.

As Detroit is a point on the water communications of this part of North America, by which the first French explorers advanced from Quebec to the discovery of the

Mississippi river, and became consequently more conspicuous in the variety of its historical incidents than perhaps any other locality in North America ; and as the tour which I am about to narrate is precisely upon the line of advance of the first French adventurers to the extreme points to which they penetrated, and much beyond them; I hope to do an acceptable thing to the reader in suspending for a while the narrative of my journey, in order to make it more interesting and intelligible by a rapid sketch of the history of this part of the country since it was first visited by Europeans.

CHAPTER XIII.

DOMESTIC CONNEXION OF THE FRENCH WITH THE ABORIGINES. — THEIR EARLY EXPLORATIONS OF THE WEST. — PONDICA, A CELEBRATED OTTAWAY CHIEF. — MASSACRE OF THE ENGLISH GARRISONS. — DEATH OF MAJOR DALYELL.

THE French preceded the English in their settlement in North America by about fifty years, their first fort being built by Jacques Cartier on the St. Lawrence, in 1535. From this moment, tempted by the fur trade, they extended themselves further up the St. Lawrence, exploring the haunts of the Indians, forming domestic connexions with them, and often adopting their manners and customs. In whatever wilderness the French race is planted, the greatest of all the wants experienced is that of society: a Frenchman must have somebody to talk to every hour of the day: when he leaves his home no one thinks himself so miserable as he does; but he soon consoles himself for the loss of his earliest friends, if he can only find bipeds of any other branch of the human family, *se faufiler avec.* Volney, in his account of the United States of America,* observes, that "Visiting and talking are so indispensably necessary to a Frenchman from habit, that throughout the whole frontier of Canada and Louisiana, there is not one settler of that nation to be found whose house is not within reach or within sight of some other."

* Appendix iv.

It is a result of that habit, that Canadian Frenchmen have been at all times, since the middle of the sixteenth century, domesticated with almost all the Indian tribes in the far western country; and hence, in the contests which prevailed between Great Britain and France on the American continent before the peace of 1763, a majority of the Indians adhered with steadiness to the French. It is true this attachment on their part had been greatly cemented by the conduct of many of the French missionaries of the Roman Catholic Church, men of unquestionable piety and simplicity of life, who, abandoning all the comforts of civilized society, endeavoured, by a self-devotion which excites our respect and admiration, to restrain the ferocious propensities of the savage aborigines, and to introduce to their knowledge the saving truths of the Gospel.

The Aborigines, at the period when the French first began to penetrate into the interior of that country which is now called Canada, were subdivided into various tribes, each of them occupying distinct districts of the country, subsisting themselves upon the products of the chase and the waters, and clothing themselves with the skins of the animals inhabiting the dense forests which covered all the country betwixt the Atlantic Ocean and the great western prairies. The tumultuous enjoyments which the males there found in the chase, and the impossibility of restraining the youth of the conterminous tribes from intruding upon each other's districts, would naturally lead to the fiercer excitements of war amongst the tribes and bands into which the aborigines had been separated for the convenience of subsisting themselves. On the arrival of the whites in the country, they found feuds established between all the great tribes, and war carried on with a rancour as inveterate as ever animated neighbouring nations in the Old World, and a ferocity unknown to it; for the American Indian, trained up in the woods as a butcher of animals, is, when a warrior, but a hunter of men, taking the scalp from his fallen enemy, as he strips the skin from the animal he has slain. This was the state of things which existed almost in every part of the American continent when the Europeans first landed there. War and the chase were the only occupations of the men, who, resigning themselves at all other moments of their existence to a haughty indolence, abandoned every kind of domestic drudgery to their women.

The names which the early French writers gave to the nations they entertained friendly or hostile relations with, have very little resemblance to the words in the Indian languages they were intended to be the representatives of. This has been at all times a fault with French travellers; for, entertaining an exalted opinion of the paramount capacity of their own admirable language to be the universal interpreter and measure of everything difficult in prosody, they have been too often contented with seizing the shadow of a sound, and then, thinking it sufficient to clothe it in characters representing sounds familiar to their own organs of speech, have not hesitated to put proper names relating to foreign countries often beyond the reach of legitimate etymology or rational analysis. To this day even we do not find a term in any of the northern languages of America to which we can assign the word "Canada," the name which the French discoverers gave to that important province.

In this manner we find, in all the early accounts of the French, the term *Algonquin* applied to the tribes inhabiting the Atlantic frontier of North America, and *Iroquois* applied to the Mengway, or " Six Nations," occupying the districts south of the St. Lawrence ; but whence the term Algonquin has been derived I have never been able to discover ; and, indeed, the obscurity in which the origin of the word Iroquois is buried is, perhaps, equally great. The same Algonquins, whose true national name was *Lenni Lenape*, or " Original or Unmixed People," were known to other tribes lying further to the east by the designation of *Wapanachki*, or " People at the Rising of the Sun :" of this term the French made *Abenaquis*, a people who figure very much in the accounts of the early French writers. The *Ahwāndate* (Wyandots) by some process became, with the French, *Hurons*. La Hontan, who to be sure is extremely superficial, says there are but two distinct tongues east of the Mississippi, the *Huron* and the *Algonquin*, each of which we now know is an imaginary term. If, in their progress to the west, a strange Indian was met, and asked what nation he belonged to, his answer perhaps would be " W'tassone," with a sort of whistling sound, meaning " I am one of the Pipe-Makers." He would be immediately set down as a *Mitassin*, and this new nation added to the list. Now " W'tassone," or " Stone Pipe-Maker," was a designation given by the Lenape to whoever was skilful in that art, and they called the Oneidas so, one of the Mengway tribes. The process was about the same as if a Frenchman meeting a Manchester man abroad, on being told he was a calico-printer, was to dub him in his travels as belonging to the nation of *Calco Prins*. Even the philosophic Volney fell into the practice of adapting the pronunciation of proper names of other countries to characters most familiar to French organs : he writes

EARLY PROGRESS OF THE WHITES. 109

ouait for white, *grine* for green ; and seems to think it of sufficient importance to remark that the English do not understand the French when they write " Vazingueton" for *Washington*.

But "non ego paucis offendar maculis ; " and this superficial way of dealing with the languages of foreign countries, although it sometimes becomes a source of much perplexity to philologists, is more than compensated to the traveller who knows how to appreciate those exertions and high qualities which distinguish the first intrepid and enterprising French adventurers in North America. Soon after Quebec was established as a French port, the missionaries succeeded in reaching Lake Huron, accompanying the Wyandots, whom the Six Nations had driven to the countries north of the St. Lawrence, and there sharing the sufferings of this people, whose conversion to Christianity they were endeavouring to accomplish, and yielding up their lives to the tomahawk, the scalping-knife, and burning stakes of the ferocious Mengway, who were determined upon the extermination of the Wyandots.

The first advances of the French traders to the upper lakes were made by the Otta-wa river, (from W'tāwháy, "he trades,") and not by the line of Lake Ontario, Lake Erie, and Detroit. Trading posts were established at the Sault St. Marie, near the entrance to Lake Superior, at Old Michilimackinac, at the southern termination of Green Bay, and at Chicago, on Lake Michigan. At the post at Green Bay they got into communication with Indians who frequented the more distant western country, and were informed of the existence of a great river, which, further to the west, traversed the whole country. This was the Mississippi ; and Father Marquette, proceeding

110   LA SALE REACHES THE GULF OF MEXICO.

from Green Bay by the way of Fox River, and the water communications and *portage* to the river now called Wisconsin, descended that broad stream to its mouth, and entered the Mississippi in June, 1673. Pursuing the southern course of this mighty flood, as low down as the mouth of the river Arkansa, he found himself unable to advance any further; and leaving the problem of what sea it discharged itself into to a more distant period, he returned in his canoe by the river Illinois, and from thence passed into Lake Michigan. Six years afterwards, La Sale, one of the most adventurous men of his period, caused a small vessel to be constructed on Lake Erie, the first that ever navigated upon the American lakes; and leaving his craft at Michilimackinac, made his way to the Mississippi; and amidst difficulties that would have deterred an ordinary man, followed the Missisippi to its mouth, which he reached in 1679. The agents of the French government had now traced a line from the mouth of the St. Lawrence to the mouth of the Mississippi, in the Gulf of Mexico, and an immense field was open to the enterprise of its subjects and to its own ambition, in the attempt to accomplish the objects of which the various incidents which have made Detroit so conspicuous in the history of this part of the country successively arose.

Whilst the French were thus laying, as they supposed, the foundations of a great colonial empire in North America, the English had also planted their colonies upon a great scale betwixt the Atlantic Ocean and the extensive line which the former had penetrated through; and the rivalry of trade, and the then existing antipathy betwixt the two races, not only frequently brought them into collision, but ultimately made the French possessions to the north the seat of contests, which sooner or later threatened to be fatal to the ascendancy of one of the parties.

About the close of the seventeenth century the English trading expeditions began to visit Lake Huron, passing into it by the strait which communicates betwixt Lake Erie and that lake. At this intrusion into their best fur-trading district, the French took alarm, and sent M. La Motte Cadillac with a party, in 1701, to establish a stockaded fort on the strait, not only for the purpose of shutting up an avenue which they had so long left open to their rivals, but of facilitating the fur trade, and curbing the hostile Indians, amongst whom the Ottogamies, or Foxes, were for a long period their inveterate enemies. This post was called, from its locality, Le Detroit, a name still retained by the flourishing town of Detroit, the present capital of the state of Michigan. At this period the country was remarkably well stocked with game, and herds of buffaloes roamed on the western shores of Lake Erie, as they do now on the Platte and Arkansas, a circumstance which accounts for the numerous population of aborigines in that part of the lake country.

With the exception of the fierce war which raged betwixt the French and the Ottogamies in the early part of the eighteenth century, and the defeat of General Braddock in 1755, at which some of the French inhabitants of Detroit assisted, no great event took place in the western Indian country until the year 1760, when a remarkable Ottaway chief, named Pondiac (or Pontiac, as his name frequently appears), began to attract universal attention, both from the Europeans and Indians. He had fought on the side of the French in 1746, in the war that preceded the peace of Aix la Chapelle, and had evinced at that time a rare capacity, both in the field and in council. As a successful warrior he was without a rival amongst the Indians, a circumstance which alone would have made them defer to him in all their enterprises. To his courage and ferocity, he added an attentive observation of the arts which enabled Europeans to excel his countrymen; and was at all times ready to practise the most refined cunning, and the basest treachery, to obtain his objects, when they were otherwise beyond the reach of the rude resources of the Indians.

Up to this period nothing had seemed to oppose the steady advances which the French were making in the western country to monopolize the whole fur trade, and establish such an influence amongst the aboriginal tribes as would effectually exclude the English from the advantages of that trade, and secure the alliance and co-operation of the Indians in all their warlike operations. From New Orleans to the Illinois river, and from thence by the way of Detroit to Quebec, they had a line of posts, and various settlements for the protection of their traders, most of whom had formed domestic connexions with the natives, and all of whom, except the Five Nations and others who traded with the British colonists, considered the French as brothers, and called the King of France their father.

Great was the shock, therefore, when intelligence was circulated through the western country of the brilliant victory which the renowned Wolfe obtained on the plains of Abram, on the 13th of September, 1759, of the surrender of Quebec, and the subsequent capitulation of Montreal, by which Detroit, and all the French posts in the upper country, were ceded to the British flag. The

French traders, who perceived what a mortal blow this was to them, for a long time deluded the Indians with information that the King of France was about to send a fleet and army to drive the English out of their conquests,—a vain hope, that was only dissipated by the appearance of Major Rogers, with a detachment, in 1760, to take possession of Detroit. It was upon this occasion that Pondiac, accompanied by a retinue of his chiefs, and assuming all the barbarian authority he was capable of, met the British officer, and inquired how he dared to enter into a country which belonged to him. Major Rogers informed him that he came not to take the country from the Indians, but to remove the French from it, who had prevented the English trading with them. Friendly belts were interchanged, and the British commander having acted in a judicious manner, and Pondiac perceiving that the French were conquered, and would be supplanted by the English, declared his intention to acknowledge the King of England for his father, and to live in peace with the English.

During this period of tranquillity the English took possession of the French posts of Niagara, Michilimackinac, St. Joseph, Sandusky, Miami, Presque Isle, Fort Duquesne, the name of which had been changed to Fort Pitt, Fort Chartres, on the Mississippi, and others, amounting to twelve in number; and the English traders began under their protection to exchange commodities with the Indians. Their rivals, the French traders, now exerted themselves strenuously to maintain their ground; and perceiving that without some great revolution in the political state of the country this could not be accomplished, they availed themselves of their connexions and influence with the Indians, to excite the greatest possible degree of distrust in their minds against the English, representing to them that it was their intention to take the country from them, as they had taken it from the French; that the English were few in number, and could be easily driven out of the country, if the Indians would unite together for that purpose.

On the other hand the English garrisons took no pains to conciliate the Indians, contenting themselves with keeping the country in as tranquil a state as they could for the short period they supposed they would have to remain there, it being generally supposed that the country, to a certain extent, would be restored to the French at the peace. In this state of things, Pondiac, finding himself neglected by the British authorities, and urged by the French traders to take some step towards the expulsion of the English, conceived the bold plan of simultaneously surprising all the British posts. Indians under friendly pretences were to introduce themselves into the forts; and when the officers were off their guard, were to massacre them and the garrisons. If success crowned their treacherous schemes, Pondiac was to unite all the Indian tribes into a confederacy, and make a stand against the English who might be sent to oppose them, until the King of France could send assistance to him. It does not appear, from the various official accounts of these transactions (which I have had an ample opportunity of examining), that the officers in the service of the King of France had assisted Pondiac in these plans; but there is abundant evidence that the French traders, and a great portion of the French inhabitants of Detroit, had a perfect knowledge of them.

This infernal piece of treachery, which was to sweep over a line of 1000 miles, was the conception of a strong mind;

MASSACRE AT MICHILIMACKINAC. 115

and its diabolical execution upon three-fourths of these doomed posts evinces a degree of calculation, and power of combination, which many writers have denied to the uncivilized denizens of the wilderness.

So great was the security of the different garrisons, that up to the very moment when the perfidy of the savages burst upon them, they had not the least suspicion of their intentions; for, although the Indians had assembled in great numbers at some of the posts, their dissimulation was so perfect, that every facility seems to have been given to them to immolate the garrisons. The particulars of the surprise and massacre of Fort Michilimackinac have been recorded upon other occasions with more or less accuracy; but the official letter of the commanding officer, Captain Etherington, to Major Gladwin, the senior officer then in command at Detroit, gives the true story, and a sorrowful one it is. It was the Ojibways, and not the Ottaways, as has been represented, who performed that sanguinary and audacious act. By the extract below,* it will be seen that the Indian women

---

* "Michilimackinac, 12 June, 1763.

"SIR,—Notwithstanding what I wrote you in my last, that all the savages were arrived, and that everything seemed in perfect tranquillity, yet, on the 2nd inst., the Chippaways, who live on a plain near this fort, assembled to play ball, as they had done almost every day since their arrival : they played from morning till noon; then throwing their ball close to the gate, and observing Lieutenant Leslie and me a few paces out of it, they came behind us, seized and carried us into the woods.

"In the meantime the rest rushed into the fort, where they found their squaws, whom they had previously planted there, *with their hatchets hid under their blankets*, which they took, and in an instant killed Lieut. Jamet, and fifteen rank and file, and a trader named Tracy. They wounded two, and took the rest of the garrison prisoners, five of which they have since killed. They made prisoners all the English traders, and robbed them of everything they had, but they offered no violence to the persons or properties of any of the Frenchmen."

assisted in the execution of the plan, having entered the fort whilst the men were pretending to be engaged in their favourite ball-play, with tomahawks concealed under their blankets.

The capture of Sandusky is thus described, in an official letter from Major Gladwin to Sir Jeffery Amhurst:— "On the 16th of May, Ensign Paulli, who commanded at Sandusky, was informed by his sentry at the gate, that there were Indians come who wanted to speak to him; upon which he went to see who they were, and finding them *to be some of his own Indians*,* who received him very friendly, he permitted *seven* of them to come in, and gave them a little tobacco to smoke. In a short time after, one of them raised up his head, which is supposed to have been a signal; upon which the two that sat next Ensign Paulli seized and tied him, without saying a word, and carried him out of his room, where he found his sentry dead in the gateway, with the rest of the garrison,—one here, one there,—*all massacred*, and the fort surrounded with Indians. His serjeant, who had been planting something in the garden, was killed there. The merchants were all killed, and every thing they had plundered."

At St. Joseph's the garrison was massacred by a similar stratagem, executed by the Potowattamies. At the fort of the Miami, Ensign Holmes, the officer in command, was decoyed out of the fort by a squaw, who lived with him, and who asked him to go and bleed another squaw, in a cabin about 300 yards from the fort. There he was butchered by some Indians.

But the post which Pondiac was most anxious to make himself master of at this juncture was Detroit, and he

---

* Indians to whom he distributed rations.

determined to make the attempt in person. He could not venture to move either to Niagara or to Fort Pitt, and leave Detroit behind him, which was in the heart of the Indian country, and had a garrison of 120 men, eight officers, and a number of enterprising traders, who, with a few influential French families within the pickets of the town, would, he was well assured, oppose all his designs. His first attempt, therefore, upon the place was as bold as it was treacherous, and, although not accompanied by all the incidents with which some writers have embellished it, is a remarkable instance of coolness whilst engaged in an act of great daring. The following passage is extracted from one of Major Gladwin's official letters to Sir Jeffery Amhurst, which, I believe, has not yet been published:—

"Detroit, May 14, 1763.

"SIR,—On the 1st instant, Pontiac, the chief of the Ottaway nation, came here with about fifty of his men, and told me that in a few days, when the rest of his nation came in, he intended to pay me a formal visit. The 7th, he came; but I was luckily informed[*] the night before that he was coming with an intention to surprise us; upon which I took such precautions, that when they entered the fort, (though they were by the best accounts about 300, and armed with knives, tomahawks, and a great many with *guns cut short, and hid under their blankets*,) they were so much surprised to see our disposition, that they would scarcely sit down to council. However, in about half an hour after they saw their designs were discovered, they sat down and made several speeches, which I answered calmly, without intimating my suspicion of their intentions; and after receiving some

[*] By the Messrs Baby, respectable inhabitants of the place.

trifling presents, they went away to their camp. The 8th, Pontiac came with a pipe of peace, in order to ask leave to come next day *with his whole nation* to renew his friendship. This I refused, but I told him he might come with the rest of his chiefs."

Finding himself excluded from every opportunity of carrying his treacherous intentions into effect, he determined to invest the fort, knowing it to be but scantily provisioned, and relying upon the French party in the town to give him information of what was passing in the garrison. All the prominent points of Pondiac's character were well developed upon this occasion. He had from 700 to 1000 Indians to subsist, and sometimes a greater number, and had no means of procuring provisions but by purchasing them: he therefore imitated a practice he had observed in use amongst the white men, and issued not paper, but bark money, being slips of birch bark, with the object he wanted in exchange for it rudely scratched upon the bark, and his *totem*, or coat of arms, which was an otter, drawn beneath. These, which were paid over to persons attached to the French interest, were all honourably redeemed by payments in peltry after the war.

A remarkable instance of this chief's sagacity and caution is recorded by General Gage, in a letter to the Earl of Halifax, from which the following is an extract:—
"From a paragraph of Mons. d'Abadies' letter, there is reason to judge of Pondiac, not only as a savage possessed of the most refined cunning and treachery natural to the Indians, but as a person of extraordinary abilities. He says that Pondiac keeps two secretaries, one to write for him, and the other to read the letters he receives, and he manages them so as to keep each of them ignorant of what is transacted by the other."

But his cold-blooded ferocity threw a shade over his great qualities, and made him an object of detestation to all persons in the British interest. The very day that he came to the fort he had already commenced hostilities by putting to death Lieut. Robertson, Sir Robert Danvers, and a whole boat's crew, who, unconscious of danger, were surveying in the river, and had been brought in by some Indians. This atrocity was well known to some of the French inhabitants in Pondiac's interest, but they concealed it from Major Gladwin, until Pondiac had failed to surprise the garrison; and on leaving the fort the day that he went to it with the pipe of peace, he caused the people that took care of the cattle belonging to the garrison to be tomahawked, and put to death all the members of two poor English families that had settled outside of the fort. Captain Campbell also was put to death whilst with Pondiac as a hostage.

Having surrounded the fort, he harassed the garrison in every possible manner, intercepted the supplies that were sent to it from Niagara, and but for the friendly services of M. Navarre, the two Baby's, and Major Gladwin's interpreters, St. Martin and La Bute, whom he mentions as having furnished him "with provisions at the utmost peril of their lives," the post could not have been maintained. In the meantime the greatest exertions were making at Fort Niagara to relieve the garrison; and Captain Dalyell, with a reinforcement of about 300 men, and supplies, was dispatched for that purpose. Most fortunately they reached the mouth of Detroit river on the evening of the 28th of July, and proceeding under cover of the night, escaped the vigilance of the Indians, and to the great joy of the garrison, appeared in sight close to Detroit, on the morning of the 29th, at daybreak.

Captain Dalyell, who was full of ardour to distinguish himself, on being made acquainted with the situation of Pondiac's camp, which was up the river some distance from what is now called Bloody Bridge, requested Major Gladwin, in the most urgent manner, to place a detachment under his command for the purpose of surprising the savages. Major Gladwin, in his official letter, says, that he consented with great reluctance to the proposition. The rest of the day passed in preparations, and an hour before day-break, on the 30th, Captain Dalyell left the fort at the head of a detachment of 247 men. But Pondiac's friends in town had already apprised him of what was going on, and that astute chief rapidly made arrangements to turn the tables upon the unfortunate detachment. Warriors furnished with fire-arms were posted behind the pickets, and in every advantageous position, so that when the troops were silently crossing the bridge, before even the twilight broke, preparatory to their advance upon the Indian camp, in the full belief that they should fall upon them unawares, they were fired upon from every quarter; and the confusion being increased by the yells and screams of the Indians, the whole detachment was in great danger of perishing. In a letter from Sir Jeffery Amhurst to the Earl of Egremont, it appears that the gallant Captain Dalyell was slain in the attempt " to bring off some wounded men from the hands of the savages," and that eighteen men and three officers were killed, and thirty-eight men wounded. By the presence of mind of Captain Grant, who succeeded to the command, some order was restored: charging the Indians successively with the bayonet, at the head of some brave fellows, he drove them back, and collecting his wounded, marched with the detachment back to the fort, a distance of about two miles.

PONDIAC KILLED. 121

This was the last incident of any importance in Pondiac's career. As soon as intelligence reached the western country, of the establishment of peace betwixt England and France, and the entire cession of Canada in full sovereignty to the King of Great Britain, the hostile French settlers began to relax in their intrigues, many of them abandoning their settlements, and crossing the Mississippi to find new homes. The Indian tribes also almost universally separated themselves from Pondiac, who retired to the Illinois country. He appears to have acted in a friendly manner to an English officer, Lieutenant Fraser, of the 78th regiment, who was sent on a mission to Kaskaskias in 1765, and who, at the instigation of some French Canadians, had been ill-treated by some Indians. Soon after this he is said to have been killed by an Indian in that country.

CHAPTER XIV.

EMBARK FOR LAKE HURON.—INTELLIGENCE IN PIGS.—GREAT LACUSTRINE DEPOSIT.—CHRISTIAN INDIANS.—EMBARK ON LAKE HURON.

HAVING examined the interesting locality where Captain Dalyell met with his untimely death, and visited the place where Pondiac was encamped, I returned to Detroit with Major W., and having made all my arrangements, and bade adieu to the amiable friends who had made my stay there so agreeable, I embarked on the 4th of August, in the steamer "General Gratiot," for Fort Gratiot, at the south end of Lake Huron, distant from Detroit about seventy-five miles. On board the steamer was a singular, hairy, wild-looking, ascetic person, who wandered about the frontier part of the country, affecting to live after the manner of St. John, upon milk and honey,—two very good things, by-the-by, especially when there is plenty of good bread to eat with them. The oddity of this man's career consisted in his pretending that conscience compelled him to eat nothing else, and in the facility with which the good-tempered and hospitable wives of the settlers permitted themselves to be imposed upon by his pretended sanctity, bustling about, as I was informed, to procure him what he wanted, sometimes at great inconvenience to themselves. This Yankee dervish, who was stated to be born in Connecticut, had evidently cut his eye-teeth. He was very shy of conversation, seldom addressing himself to his own sex.

We were soon in Lake St. Clair, a sheet of water about thirty miles wide, midway betwixt Lake Erie and Lake Huron. Being in a very flat country, it has the appearance, from the centre, of a huge basin of water, with a dark low rim of trees round it. The passage from this lake to Lake Huron is called St. Clair River, the approach to which is extremely shallow, strong beds of sedges and rushes appearing in every direction. There are various channels through the muddy bottom, and the land to the right and left is singularly low and flat, a few indifferent cottages of Canadian peasants appearing now and then amongst the trees. Higher up the St. Clair is a fine stream about 1000 yards broad, with settlements here and there. On the British side there were many modern comfortable-looking houses, but not one on the other. The orchards appeared to be prosperous. These were, however, mere patches of civilization on the river's bank, the country back being an unreclaimed wilderness. When our steamer had advanced about fifteen miles up the St. Clair, the banks of the river became a few feet higher, and the west bank shewed several good American farms with fine crops growing on them. These settlements, as usual, had a fair proportion of small taverns amongst them, one of which, called the St. Clair Hotel, was rather a neat-looking place.

About seventeen miles from Black River we stopped a short time at a good farm on the American side, belonging to a Mr. Ward, a man of some property. At this place there was a vessel building of 100 tons burthen, and great appearance of industry in every direction. On entering the house I was exceedingly distressed with a sad spectacle that met my eyes; this was his only son, a fine-looking youth, deprived of reason and chained to the floor, being too strong and vicious to be permitted to go loose.

Just as we passed Black River we met some canoes with Ojibway Indians in them; one of them, in which was a man, his squaw and four children, came so near the steamer that the engineer let a quantity of steam off upon them, which seemed to amuse them very much. The banks of the river now rose to a height of fifteen feet, which I was glad to see, as they promised to furnish me with a favourable opportunity of examining them, which I had been precluded from doing hitherto by the surface of the ground being so near the water.

This very beautiful flat country requires to be seen only once to produce the conviction, that at no very remote geological period an immense area of country in this part of the world, including part of the shores of the Niagara river, Lake Erie, Lake Huron, Lake Michigan, with all the flat territory adjacent to them, was covered by one vast body of fresh water, and that the fertile soil now above the level of these waters is a deposit from that ancient lacustrine state of things. In passing up from Detroit here, I have had two or three opportunities of examining the earth brought up from fifteen to twenty feet below, where they were constructing wells, and in each case it was mixed up with shelly matter, but so decayed and broken that it was very difficult to identify the species. There was now a good prospect of finding a natural section, where the shells might be taken out in an undisturbed state, and of settling the point whether they belong to the same families that live in the lake waters at present.

As we approached a farm on the American side of the St. Clair river, belonging to the captain of our steamer, a curious fact fell under my observation: the pigs belonging to the farm came squealing down to the water-side, a thing which the persons at the farm assured me they never did when other steamers passed. The captain explained this singular recognition on the part of the pigs, by stating that the swill of his steamer was always preserved for them; and that on reaching the landing-place, it was immediately put on shore to feed them. The animals having been accustomed to this valuable importation during the whole summer months, had learnt to distinguish the peculiar sound which the steam made in rushing through the pipe of the steamer; and as they could do this at the distance of half a mile, they immediately upon hearing it hastened down to the river, whilst the noise made by other steamers was disregarded. This is a curious instance of the possibility of sharpening the faculties of the lower animals by an appeal to their appetites; and a conclusive proof, that the readiest way to make all swinish animals reasonable, is to provide plenty of swill for them.

From this place I was glad to see that the country continued to rise until we reached Fort Gratiot, a garrisoned post of the United States, near to the entrance of Lake Huron, and where we arrived at 8 P. M., after a most agreeable trip through an interesting country. Here I left the steamer, and went to the fort, where I was most kindly received by Major H., the commandant, and the other officers: a bed was provided for me at the quarters of a young officer, whose father, Colonel B., the head of the ordnance department in the United States service, I had been long acquainted with; and nothing loth, I prepared to share the society of these gentlemanly and obliging hosts until I could get on board some vessel that was passing into Lake Huron.

August 5.—I rose at break of day in the morning, and walked through the woods to Black River: the stream was excessively dark, owing to the decomposed vegetable matter at the bottom, and ran through a broad area of the lacustrine deposit, of which the right, or American bank of the St. Clair, forms a part. The top of the bank was about thirty feet from the water; clay, sand, and vegetable matter composed the bank, down to the water's edge. Having made this *reconnaissance*, I retraced my steps to the garrison, and breakfasted; and having provided myself with assistance and tools, returned to that part of the bank of the St. Clair where it was highest, and commenced some excavations where the bank was nearly on a level with the river. I found great quantities of unios and anadontas at a depth of nearly thirty feet, but so decomposed and pulpy, that they required to be removed with great care, and to be left to dry a few hours, before they could be put away in a condition proper to preserve them. They were all colourless; but many of them were identical with the bivalves now found in great abundance in Lake Huron. Nearer to the surface of the ground I found occasional patches of univalves, paludina, lymnea, and planorbis, as though they had lived in limited spots of stagnant water, as they are frequently found at present. The morning's work furnished the fullest proof of the ancient lacustrine state of the country.

Having conveyed my collections to the fort, I walked on the beach of Lake Huron to the Light-house. The lake had every appearance of a calm sea; and the gravel on the beach was composed of a mixture of fragments of primary rocks and fossiliferous limestone, with immense quantities of dead valves of unios and anadontas, thrown up by the lake when its waters were agitated by storms, which, I was told, frequently occur of a terrific character.

On my return I dined with the commandant, and passed a couple of hours very agreeably. The attentions which a traveller receives at these frontier forts are always most grateful to him : he is not only restored to the comforts of society, but acquires a great deal of useful information respecting those more distant points which he purposes visiting. The American officers, who are always enterprising men, are very often extremely intelligent; and some of them are kept so many years on the frontiers, that they come at length to take as lively an interest in the affairs of the Indian country, as in that of their youth, whence absence and death often weans them to a great extent. Unfortunately, however, some of them, for want of occupation at these frontier posts, fall into a listless and indolent way of life ; and instead of exerting themselves to contribute to the general stock of knowledge, fly to tobacco, whisky, and cards, to get over the tedious hours ; so that when they return to society, they fall naturally into the sottish classes,—some melancholy instances of which I have had occasion to observe. When they are fond of science and literature, as in the instance of Colonel W. of Detroit, and many others I have had the advantage of knowing, they become accomplished and valuable men, that would be admired and esteemed in any country.

This day (*August* 6) the weather became unexpectedly very cold, and I remained all the morning in my quarters, bringing up my Journal and writing letters. I dined with a Mr. Eaton and his family, a very modest and intelligent officer, the son of Mr. Amos Eaton, of the state of New York, well known as being one of the earliest labourers in America in the cause of geology. This family were exceedingly religious, after the manner of those persons who call themselves evangelical, a class which, I believe, admits of no coquetry with anything approaching to worldly vanities. I was sincerely disposed to respect everything that I saw upon this occasion: there was an impress of sincerity in the studious observance of a rigorous temperance, and the constant recurrence to prayer. It seemed to be a happy family; and their example led me to think that the composure of mind which may be attained through what the world calls self-denial, perhaps has a steadier effect in promoting purity of life, than can be reached by those excitements which lead to what the less austere part of the world supposes to be happiness. In various garrisons of the United States that I have visited, I have seen persons claiming to belong to this class, in whom I have not placed so much confidence; for they appeared to practise temperance for the purpose of making a parade of it, never permitting it to deviate beyond the excesses of the tea-pot; and indulging in such frequent effusions of prayer, as if they had not much faith in those that had preceded the last. Temperance in tobacco they do not seem to count amongst their virtues; and although they profess to have drawn a line betwixt themselves and the sinful part of mankind, yet in this particular, as well as in that of choosing young and pretty wives, they still seem to have carried out the line of demarcation imperfectly. I have observed that this last commendable practice seems peculiarly to belong to missionaries and saintly-disposed persons.

August 7.—After breakfast I crossed the river into

the British territories, and rambled about the greater part of the day. Advancing some distance into the woods, I came upon a nice little sequestered pond or lake, where I found an immense number of fine large anadontas alive, with some large lymnea and planorbis adhering to tall reeds. Having waded through this pond for two or three hours, and made an ample collection of shells, I placed my bag on my back, and setting my compass, made for the shore of Lake Huron, which I soon gained. It was strewed with the valves of dead anodontas, some of which contained a portion of the mollusk, left by the musk rats, which feed upon them, and which always resort to the shores after a gale of wind. It was late in the evening when I got to the boat in which I crossed over; and having drank tea with Dr. W. and his lady, and passed a pleasant evening, I was informed that my quarters were transferred to Mr. Eaton's, as it had been discovered that I occupied the only bed belonging to my host, Lieutenant B. I was very sorry to learn this, for although it is very satisfactory to be in good quarters, yet the pleasure is very much diminished by the discovery that it is at the expense of those who have a much better right than yourself to be there. Fortunately for me, Mrs. Eaton had a small room and a bed unoccupied, so that I went to rest without any care upon my mind on that score. I was determined, however, in the morning to have my own tent pitched, and my mattress spread out in it, not only to see if everything was right about them, but that I might have a domicile of my own to resort to in case of need.

August 8.—This morning I had my tent pitched, and found that it would answer my purpose perfectly well: leaving it standing, I recrossed the river to the British side, and paid a visit to Mr. Evans, a Methodist missionary established amongst a band of Ojibways living there. The success of this excellent person appeared to have been perfect. He had induced a great many Indian families to renounce their Pagan practices, and to deliver up to him all their medicine-bags, with the rest of their conjuring apparatus, drums, &c.; and had formed them into a regular Christian community, where they appeared to be happy and to show no desire to relapse. Mr. Evans informed me, that, when any of the Indians had determined to join his congregation, they always came quietly to his house, and deposited unobserved all their bags, made of the skins of animals, their conjurors' drums, with everything that appertained to their superstitions, upon a table in the hall of his house; so that when he returned from his walks he often found a great many of these things, and thereby knew that his congregation was going to be increased. He presented me with several of these medicine-bags and instruments belonging to their conjurors. I was so much pleased with Mr. Evans's little community, that I conceived the idea of removing my quarters to his settlement for a short time. I had seen every object of natural history that was accessible to me in this flat country, and as it might be some days before a vessel appeared to take me to Michilimackinac, I might employ my time more usefully in studying the Ojibway language, than in remaining at the garrison; besides, the weather had become exceedingly hot again, and there was very little temptation to walk out.

August 9.— This being Sunday, I crossed the river again, and went to Mr. Evans's mission, to be present at his church service. The congregation was entirely composed of Indians,—men, women, and children,—all decently dressed, and conducting themselves in a manner that would have been creditable to any class of Christians. Mr. Evans gave out a hymn, and the interpreter having repeated it in the Ojibway tongue, the Indians united in singing to the words in a very agreeable manner. A prayer followed, and afterwards a sermon. At every phrase the missionary stopped a moment, and the interpreter rendered it audibly into the Ojibway, the whole congregation paying the most serious attention to what was said. The service concluded by another hymn, when the congregation being dismissed, departed with as much order as any other congregation would have done, falling into little groups and conversing in a cheerful manner together. It was quite evident to me that those who proclaim the aborigines to be an irreclaimable and incorrigible people, are mistaken: by proper management on the part of zealous missionaries, *living amongst them*, and devoting their lives to their instruction and welfare, we see that they can be reclaimed from their superstitions and their wild state, and become a good Christian agricultural people. The Moravians had proved this before, and would have reclaimed many tribes long before this, if the cupidity of the whites, greedy of their lands, had not murdered and persecuted them, till, in despair, they struck a last vindictive blow before they were exterminated.

The more the aborigines see of the white people, their cupidity and vices, the less are they disposed to attribute any virtue to whatever they may teach: but where missionaries, in the holiest sense of the word, have virtue enough to bring themselves down to a level with them in the simplicity of their modes of life, and self-devotion enough to consecrate their lives to diffusing the truths of the Gospel, the Indians, whose hearts, like our own, obey all the natural impulses, are as liable to be touched with the excellence of those truths as other people have been, and as the earliest members of the Christian Church were, when they were unostentatiously taught by the humble Apostles. Before confidence can be created in the breasts of the simplest class of the human family, whether Indians or white men, the connexion betwixt the teacher and the taught must be an intimate one, and they must not be separated from each other by a vast chasm between worldly advantages on the one side, and simple and ignorant aspirations for the peace of the soul on the other. Before society in any part of Christendom is placed upon the securest foundations, this truth will have to be recognized and acted upon, and until then it will continue to be agitated by a spurious Christianity, too much distinguished by want of charity and brotherly love.

Exceedingly gratified with what I had witnessed at this mission, I returned to Fort Gratiot to consider my project of removing to Mr. Evans's mission over a little; but whilst at dinner with the officers the schooner Marengo hove in sight, bound to Michilimackinac. I should have been better pleased if it had been a steamer, for lake voyages in small schooners are frequently, as experience had taught me, tedious and disagreeable undertakings: however, if the very long journey I had still before me was to be accomplished, time was very precious; so I determined not to neglect the opportunity, and bidding a hearty adieu to my hospitable friends, got at once on board the schooner. The captain's name was Dingle, who, with his wife and an unmarried female friend of her's, of about thirty-six, were the only persons on board except the crew. He said he had room for me in his very, very small cabin, where we all were to sleep, so I determined to make myself as comfortable as I could. The breeze was favourable, and carried us without difficulty over the strong current which sets in from the lake where the river channel commences.

CHAPTER XV.

CAPTAIN AND MRS. DINGLE, AND CO.—REACH MICHILIMACKINAC.—
FINE SALMON-TROUT.—VORACITY OF FISH.

A FEW minutes sufficed to convince me that I should not get much agreeable society from the Dingle party. I was asked to drink tea with them in the cabin, but as I found nothing there very tempting, I hastened upon deck, where I remained to a late hour in the night, the schooner gliding over the glassy surface of the lake with a gentle breeze in the most agreeable manner, and only retiring to my berth when I could scarce keep my eyes open. I was soon asleep, but unfortunately the inferior extremity of my berth abutting upon the same end of the adjoining one, where Mrs. Dingle's female friend stretched her proportions, she took to kicking every now and then as if she had the *diable au corps*, which perhaps she had, or the cramp, which is only another name for it. She awoke me several times, but happily I got at last so soundly asleep as to withstand all the efforts of her troubled spirit. I awoke early in the morning, almost suffocated by the confined hot air of the cabin. The Dingles were snoring most joyously, the kicking lady seemed to be exorcised, and staying as short a time as possible to witness their happiness, I soon established myself upon deck, where, with a tub and a *quantum suff.* of lake water, I contrived to refresh myself very well, and made

AN ERRONEOUS MAP.

my *toilette* very much to my satisfaction, having the whole portion of the deck which was not encumbered with freight to myself.

The breeze had continued through the night, and we were making very pretty progress. In about an hour and a half Captain Dingle reluctantly left the couch of his *cara sposa*, which was about two feet wide, and made his appearance on deck. I found my large map of Lake Huron very erroneous, the localities being often apparently noted at random : *Presque Isle* was put down a great deal too near Michilimackinac, and *Middle Island* was placed where *Thunder Island* ought to be. I was glad, therefore, of an opportunity to obtain some correct information from one who had navigated the lake several years, and, with the assistance of Captain Dingle, made some important corrections on the map, and established the following distances :—

From Fort Gratiot to Pointe aux Barques, the most easterly point on the American side	70 miles.
Thence to Thunder Island	70
,, to Middle Island	12
,, to Presque Isle	18
,, to Boisblanc (called by the Americans, Bobelo)	55
,, to Michilimackinac	10

making in the whole 235 miles from Fort Gratiot to Mackinau, as it is familiarly called.

The breakfast was a very so-so affair, and the dinner was ten times worse, quite in keeping with Captain and Mrs. Dingle, as rude and vulgar a pair as ever were matched. Happily there was the deck to go to, and the beautiful lake and the shore to look at.

In crossing Saginaw Bay there was a good deal of motion, which I withstood most manfully for some time, but all in vain, being obliged, as I always am where there is the least motion in a vessel, to render up all my delicacies without reserve. This made me an object of great compassion to the captain and the ladies. Being an incessant chewer and smoker of tobacco, he advised me to follow his example, saying, " Tobacco was a particular curous thing for stopping that kind of sickness." This I had never heard of before; but I was not disposed to try his remedy, for, although I have crossed the Atlantic on errands of duty many a time and oft, and have passed the greater portion of my life in smoking and chewing countries, there are no two roads to happiness I avoid with more care, than making one of a nice party of pleasure at sea, or of any party where a delightful cigar is to be of the number. Mrs. Dingle, perhaps with more judgment, advised a *leetle* brandy and water: she said it always did her good, and I verily believe she thought so, from what I saw of her performances in that line at dinner. Her fair friend advised my sucking some uncooked salt fish. However, I took none of their remedies, but had recourse to my invariable plan of lying down on my back, and giving my attention to a book, in such a manner as to abstract myself if possible from all disagreeable thoughts. Night came, and about ten o'clock the lake became quite calm again,—a delightful relief; so, remaining on deck until I was ready to drop asleep, I went again to the close cabin, and lay down as quickly as possible. Here the kicking was renewed, but at more distant intervals than the night before, so that I supposed I had come to the performance at half-play. Whether it was owing to the quantity of salt fish she ate at dinner (we had nothing else), or to some other cause, I know not, but it is certain, that, if the poor lady went to bed with spurs on, she would be sometimes reminded rather painfully of her calcitrating propensity.

In the morning I arose at break of day, delighted to feel, by the steady hitch of the little schooner, that we were sailing on with a gentle and favourable breeze. Fortunately there was no swell; would that there had been no smell! but in the wretched confined little cabin, what with Mr. and Mrs. Dingle and Co., a parcel of salt fish, and frowzy old garments, it was almost intolerable. Having made my ablutions and fortified my unhappy stomach with some bad tea, dirty brown sugar, and stale bread, I betook myself again to the deck, determined to endure a little starvation rather than come within the atmosphere of the salt fish again. In the night we came up with the light-house at Boisblanc, or Bobelo, and I wrapped myself up with the intention of remaining on deck until we reached Mackinau : but the wind unluckily fell again, so that I was obliged to retreat once more to my birth.

Happily the breeze revived before morning, and I was awoke soon after day by hearing some one hail the schooner, and hurrying on deck I found we were arrived at Mackinau; so, bidding an everlasting adieu to the schooner, I got a boat, and went ashore to seek for a lodging. After a short time I found and engaged a small but neat and sweet bed-room to myself, at a house of entertainment. Finding myself once more on *terra firma*, and revived by the fresh land breeze, I was seized with a prodigious inclination to make amends for the vile life I had led on board the schooner, and making inquiries about breakfast as soon as I had made my *toilette*, I was told it would be ready in five minutes. What was my satisfaction on entering the breakfast-room, at seeing a clean table very respectably set out with tea, coffee, hot and cold bread, very nice milk and butter, and at the head of the table a most magnificent salmon trout, weighing at least 30 lb.! We were only four of us to this superb repast; and though I had not any very great love for them, I could not help wishing that the Dingle family had been there to partake of it, not only that they might enjoy the comfort of a good breakfast, but that they might be encouraged to try whether they could not do better than live upon brandy, tobacco, and salt-fish. Everything was good, and I passed at least an hour most satisfactorily, returning to the delicious salmon trout repeatedly, and retiring from it with regret.

Having now got into good train again, I called upon Mr. Schoolcraft, the Indian agent for the United States, whom I had formerly known, and found him residing in a very pleasant house, with a garden attached to it, in front of the lake. He received me very kindly, and introduced me to his wife, a half-breed, who had received her education in England, and whom I found a very pious, respectable young woman. She had one of her sisters staying with her, also a half-breed, and quite an agreeable person. From their house I strolled to an encampment of Ojibway Indians, on the shore of the lake, and amused myself for a while endeavouring to converse with them.

This island, which is the most enchanting little place of the kind I have ever visited, is a geological outlier in the lake, about 1100 feet high; and when approaching it from a distance, somewhat resembles a huge turtle: the Indians therefore have named it *Mitchili Mackinac*, or the Great Turtle. Nothing can be more pleasing than

DESCRIPTION OF THE ISLAND.

its appearance from the lake : the beautiful bay, with the neat little town at the edge of the water; the respectable-looking fort, rising above the town on an escarpment of rocks; and the conspicuous remains of the old French fort, at a greater distance inland. All these pleasing features were accompanied by another, that always has great attractions for me, an encampment of Indian wigwams. Amongst other objects, Mr. Schoolcraft's very comfortable house makes a conspicuous figure, being well situated at the foot of the hill, with a good garden in front, and the fort, of a dazzling white, rising behind it a little to the west.

Michilimackinac is composed of a curious brecciated limestone, resembling, in some parts, a conglomerate; but it is only a very porous calcareous rock, the parietes of which being frequently crushed, the mass has taken the appearance of a breccia. This brecciated state of the rock appears to have been in a great measure induced by a violent movement; for there are beds of the limestone amidst the breccia, both vertical and horizontal, and large honeycombed masses are fished up in distant parts of the bay, shewing that the island has once been much more extensive.

Amongst the natural curiosities of this island, is one called the *Sugar-loaf*, and the other the Arched Rock. The first is a sort of pinnacle, rising to a considerable height above the general level, having resisted the general wearing away of the strata : like other portions of the island, it has quite a conglomerated appearance, and contains what I saw in no other part, a few rolled pebbles. The arch has been excavated by natural causes, and leads to an escarpment, where the rock can be conveniently examined. Owing to the extreme thinness of the parietes of these very porous strata, and to their having given way so frequently, the surface of the island consists of innumerable knobs and depressions, which makes it embarrassing to travel either on foot or horseback, and in a carriage the jolting is perpetual. The island, however, is an exceedingly interesting place; and through the kindness of Mr. Schoolcraft, who drove me to various accessible parts of it, I had a good opportunity of examining it.

On our return, I was present at a speech delivered to him as American Indian agent, on the part of a band of Indians from White River, on Lake Michigan. The chief, who performed the part of their orator, was a fine-looking fellow, named *Makooshwayan*, or Little Bearskin. He delivered his speech in the usual manner, by phrases, which the interpreter rendered into English from time to time. It consisted of a statement of their wants, and was very artfully contrived to accomplish their object, which was to procure blankets, tobacco, ammunition, &c. Mr. Schoolcraft made him a cautious answer, which was in like manner interpreted by phrases; giving him to understand, without telling him so in direct terms, that he did not think him very deserving of assistance. The Indians were all squatted down on the floor with their pipes, and at the interpretation of every phrase of the answer gave a sort of dissatisfied grunt, which even I understood to mean, "It was not worth our while to come to hear this;" but when the interpreter concluded, by saying, that, " Since they had come from such a great distance, the agent had determined to give them some tobacco," they gave an unanimous grunt expressive of their satisfaction, and arose and departed.

The fact was, that these fellows had been begging of

the British agent in Upper Canada, who had liberally supplied them; and were now trying, by professions of attachment to the United States, to cajole their agent. It is probable that the agents of the two governments keep each other informed of the movements and proceedings of the different wandering bands, for Mr. Schoolcraft knew where these men had been, and what they had obtained. Upon such occasions they take care never to offend them, but dismiss them with some little present. The poor pagan Indian, since he has been compelled to lay down the character of a warrior, and to be dependent upon the white man for his wants, has become a very degraded animal. The interpreter, upon this occasion, was one of Mr. Schoolcraft's brothers, a very worthy and intelligent man.

I dined and passed the rest of the day very pleasantly with this excellent family. Professing temperance and a strict piety, they were, nevertheless, very cheerful and communicative. The ladies took a great deal of pains to give me information respecting the moral condition of the Indians of this district; and Mr. Schoolcraft's intimate knowledge of the Ojibway tongue and of the Indian country, made him a most agreeable companion.

The next morning, an officer of the United States garrison called, and most obligingly offered to take me round the island in a boat which he had: as no proposition could be more agreeable, I accepted it immediately, and we made the tour of the island, landing at various points to examine the rocks, and taking sketches on the way. We stopped at the Arched Rock, and inspected it from below: in the lower part, near to the water, I observed several rounded pebbles imbedded in it, which, if I had seen no other part of the island, would have induced me to consider it a conglomerate; but it can only be considered an imperfect one, since, as has been stated before, there are calcareous beds lying undisturbed, and others which are vertical. Having examined all the escarpments, we prolonged our excursion, and made the circuit of *Round Island*, another outlier. At this place we landed to examine an ancient Indian settlement, near a pleasant well-sheltered bay, and which had been abandoned in 1763 by a tribe of Indians that had been connected with the surprise and massacre of the garrison of Fort Michilimackinac. There were a great number of graves, several of which, I am sorry to say, we disturbed. One violation ought to have satisfied us, for each of them contained nothing but bones and a few Indian trinkets, carefully wrapped up in a kind of cerement. If a party of Frenchmen had landed on the English coast, and had amused themselves by opening the graves in the church-yard, whilst the villagers were engaged in their harvest-fields, their conduct would not have been more absurd and irrational than ours.

For my portion of this body-snatching entertainment I selected a very antique-looking mound, standing on a steep bank immediately above the lake: the bank had already partly crumbled away into the water, so that my excavations were partly made to my hands. Having, with a little assistance, sufficiently opened the mound, we proceeded to plunder it, and I obtained for my share a noble skull with a remarkably fine set of teeth, without any marks of a pipe on them. This I destined for some learned craniologist; but if I had sufficiently counted the cost of all this desecration before I had engaged in it, it would have been more prudent; for in my anxiety to secure a number of Indian relics, that some of the party presented me out of their spoils, I put them into my pockets, and the skull into my pocket-handkerchief; on reaching my lodgings, however, and disencumbering my pockets hastily, to go to a dinner, which was to conclude the day, I found my hands and my clothes so infected with charnel-house nastiness, that I could not endure myself; so, throwing off all my clothes, and sending them immediately to be washed, I spent more than half an hour scrubbing my hands in vain to purify them: the horrid stench was in my nostrils all the evening; everything smelt of a dissection-room; and I must say that I never was more uncomfortable in my life. As to my bones and relics, I had them all put, on my return to my lodgings, into a bag, and sent them to one of the party, who seemed to value them very highly; for if I had packed them up to take along with me, I should have passed for a resurrection-man wherever I went.

On awaking in the morning, the first thing I was conscious of was the infernal smell of my disgusting plunder; so I jumped out of bed, and armed with brushes and soap, and a bottle of eau de Cologne, went to the lake, where I exercised myself most vigorously for half an hour, and having got myself into a more comfortable state, returned to my hotel to breakfast; after which, I determined to give myself an airing alone on the summit of the island. It usually happens to a stranger, when he falls into the hands of a Cicerone, to be taken to see objects, and to hear a great deal about them, not very interesting to him. His friend is not disposed to forego the opportunity of patronising his intellects, and furnishing him with a set of opinions about everything he thinks it worth while to shew him. It is therefore always advisable for the traveller, when he has gone through this ceremony in an interesting locality, to take a review of what he has seen alone, unembarrassed by another's opinions, and free to look for objects that another may not think it worth his while to pay any attention to. I have generally followed this plan, and not unusually without being satisfied with having done so. Wandering about at random in every part of the island, I passed the morning most delightfully, refreshing myself from time to time with wild raspberries, wild strawberries, and whortleberries, of which I found a great many quite ripe, though the strawberry season was nearly passed. Towards the west end of the island I found, near the farm of the Mission, a lacustrine deposit, containing immense quantities of planorbis. The island at this end slopes gradually to the lake, whilst at the eastern end the shore is precipitous, the bluffs being generally from 100 to 150 feet high.

On returning to my lodgings, I found another immense salmon trout waiting for my dinner, of which I made an excellent repast. These fish abound so much in the lake waters, that a profitable fishery has already been commenced of them, the produce of which is put into barrels and sent to the cities on the Atlantic. A Mr. Biddle related to me a curious fact respecting the large trout of this lake. Upon one occasion he caught one weighing 72 lb., which, when it was drawn up, had a large white fish (*Corregonus albus*) in its throat, with its tail sticking out of the trout's mouth, whilst inside of the salmon were two more white fish, each weighing about 10 lb.: both of these fishes were lying with their heads downwards, and in this manner he had invariably found them when inside of a salmon trout. The voracity of this animal must be great, if, not satisfied with three large fishes, he must dash also at the bait of the angler. Propensities of this kind sometimes lead others, who are not fishes, a little too far. An Indian, who was a very experienced fisherman, explained to my informant the probable reason why the white fish are found with their heads downwards. He said he had frequently seen from his canoe, when in still water, the salmon trout chase the white fish; and that whenever they perceived he was near them, they invariably turned round as if to look their danger in the face, and making no resistance, were taken head foremost into the jaws of their enemy. A curious provision of nature, unnerving the weak to feed the strong.

In the winter season the Indians cut holes in the ice where it is transparent, and contrive to drag their nets beneath it. They also spear the trout, using upon such occasions a painted fish as a decoy, which attracts the minnows. The voracious trout, perceiving that something is going on, now gets in motion, and the minnows, aware of his approach by the movement of the water, run off in a contrary direction; which apprizing the Indian of the quarter from whence he is making his approach, he adjusts his spear and transfixes him as he comes up. These large trout look very much like cod-fish; but in their huge gaping mouths are rows of excessively sharp teeth, indicative of their voracious nature. The white fish is a sucker, and is not, I think, as pleasant to eat as the trout. This last fish is very firm, and but faintly resembles the salmon both in colour and flavour; neither is it as rich, but it is very good, and is a blessed sight to set before a hungry traveller. The white fish, however, is preferred by the inhabitants of Michilimackinac, who almost live upon it when it is in season.

Having visited all the objects which appeared to merit particular attention at this charming sequestered island, I devoted the remainder of my stay here to the acquisition of information respecting the Ojibway language. Having possessed myself of ample vocabularies, an excellent opportunity presented itself of acquiring from the natives the correct pronunciation of the words, and noting it in a permanent manner. I found Mr. Schoolcraft an invaluable assistant in this difficult inquiry, and always had recourse to him when I met with any embarrassment. The grammatical inflexions of the Ojibway, like those of all the Indian tongues I had had an insight into, are very curious and exceedingly complicated. It not only resembles the Hebrew and other Semitic tongues in the adoption of prefixes and suffixes, to express modifications of the verb by using one word instead of two, but goes further, by applying the inflective process to nouns, adjectives, and all the parts of speech, so as, in fact, to inclose the compound idea we express by many words into one syllabic frame or word, after the manner of written Chinese characters; a mode of communication which is neither more nor less than the forming of one united picture or character from a great many pictures, or fragments or representatives of them. And this pictorial arrangement of the Chinese no doubt produces, from long habit, as instructive and pleasing an effect upon the Chinese eye, as the eupho-syllabic arrangement of sounds does to the Indian ear. Perhaps it will be seen hereafter that this structure of the Indian tongues comes naturally to a barbarous people, and is not, as has been supposed by some, the grammatical result of an ancient civilization, of which the Indians, who have no records but the limited traditions commemorated by their wampum belts, have preserved no other remembrance.

FORT MICHILIMACKINAC.

CHAPTER XVI.

EMBARK FOR LAKE MICHIGAN.— VIOLENT STORM — REACH NARAVINO.— FLUX AND REFLUX OF THE WATERS OF GREEN BAY.— FORT HOWARD.— PURCHASE A BARK CANOE AND ENGAGE A COMPANY OF VOYAGEURS.

ON the 17th I was awoke early with the intelligence that the steamer Monroe had arrived in the night from Sault St. Marie, and was bound to Green Bay. Nothing could be so opportune for my plans; so sending my luggage on board, I hastily breakfasted, and going on board, had the pleasure of finding Mr. Schoolcraft there, who had also determined upon the trip. As we stood out of the bay, I was struck with the great beauty of the scene; the lofty island, the old French fort conspicuous in the distance, the American fort, of a dazzling whiteness, just above the town, which is partly built upon the sloping bank of detritus at the foot of the escarpments, and numerous groups of Indians standing near their lodges to view the departure of the steamer, which moved on in gallant style with four Kentish bugles playing a lively air, concurred to produce one of those rare effects which a traveller sometimes witnesses.

We soon passed the site of old Fort Michilimackinac, upon a lofty bank of the continent to our left, celebrated for the treacherous ball-play and the massacre of the English garrison in 1763. Next we passed Wagushance, or little Fox Island, then Great Beaver Island, on the right. The Fox Islands further to the south presented themselves very beautifully, the southernmost having lofty cliffs, apparently of a light-coloured sandstone. Nothing could be more pleasant than our voyage hitherto, but at the close of the day one of the most fearful-looking storms I ever was in broke over the vessel. The clouds became gradually as black as night, and constantly gave out such vivid lightning, accompanied with astounding claps of thunder, that it appeared almost certain to many of us that the steamer would be struck. At length it became so dark that it was impossible to discern anything out of the vessel, and the rain came down in those incredible torrents which sometimes are poured from the terrible summer storms of North America, of which this was one of the first class. Our captain was an active and wary man; he said nothing to any of the passengers, but we observed his great anxiety; indeed, there seemed to be no inclination for conversation on either side, for whilst we were in the midst of the worst part of the hurricane, we seemed all to feel as if the next crash would decide our fate. It was a fearful scene; the impenetrable darkness, which at frequent but irregular intervals was interrupted by corruscations that seemed to have set the world on fire, bringing to my remembrance Milton's fine line,

> "The sudden blaze far round illumined Hell,"

and our too close propinquity to the sharp, loud, and angry cracks of thunder, appeared to have combined to prepare for us an exit of the most sublime character.

Suddenly the steamer was in a bustle: we were not very far distant from the strait which leads from Lake Michigan into Green Bay, in which there were some islands; and the captain, not deeming it prudent to attempt the strait in such a state of things, put the steamer about. This withdrew our attention in some degree from the storm, upon which all our nervous energies had been concentrated to the exclusion of every other influence; but the moment we relaxed sufficiently to feel the movement of the steamer in the immense swell that was upon the lake, we all became dreadfully sick; as to myself, cold, wet, and a perfect victim to the detestable motion of the vessel, I lay down on the deck, losing all apprehension of the elements, and feeling, as I have often felt before, that any change in my condition, however serious, would not be quite such a bad thing.

At daylight, the storm having abated, we got into Green Bay, keeping close to the east shore; and the water having become smooth again, the poor passengers, whose fine spirits of the preceding morning had long ago evaporated, made haste to adjust themselves a little.

The extended woody shores of this large bay — in itself a lake of no small dimensions—present a singularly verdant appearance, which has probably suggested the original name of "La Baie Verte." There is an uninterrupted line of trees growing from a fertile soil incumbent upon beds of horizontal silurian limestone, and the shore, as well as the islands in the bay, present strong bluffs of the rock. Towards the south end the bay becomes very shallow, and the channel, which is serpentine, meanders through low marshy grounds. At length we reached the southern termination of the bay, and stopped at a new American settlement called Navarino, separated from which by the Fox River, which empties itself into Green Bay, is a post of the United States, called Fort Howard. The best tavern at the place being full of guests, I got very indifferent lodgings at an inferior one.

Having transferred my luggage to my quarters, I sallied out to make some observations respecting a phenomenon which was observed as early as the time of Charlevoix. This was a flux and reflux of the waters of the bay, somewhat resembling the tidal action of the sea, although so extremely irregular as not to be explained in any manner by lunar influence. I had observed evidences, when at Fort Gratiot, of a varying level of the waters of Lake Huron; but as they did not differ from those which are frequently to be observed in large bodies of fresh water, I attributed them to the influence of winds on the surface of the water. Here, however, the change of level more resembled tidal action. I therefore placed some sticks at the edge of the water at 6 P.M., with the intention of visiting them during my stay, in order to acquire some accurate idea of the amount of change to be observed. Wandering about until night, I returned to the inn, where some fellows by their dancing and orgies kept me awake until a late hour in the morning. But this was not the first time I had reached the extreme frontier of civilization, where man reverts without pain to his natural condition, which is to be a little above the beast of the field, and not much more.

Having breakfasted and called to see a trader, to whom I had been addressed as a person who would be useful in equipping me for the long journey that lay now before me into the Indian country, I visited my sticks at 11 A. M. The water had receded from them twenty-four feet since 6 P. M. of yesterday, which was equal to a little more than one foot in height in that distance. Various persons with whom I conversed about the phenomenon, said that it occurred every day, but not at the same hour. It was also said that the same thing takes place at Chicago, at the foot of Lake Michigan, and at Saginau. This is very probable, as any sensible change in the level of the waters here must be felt at other places on the lake. It is probably caused by local winds, that pack the waters up into Green Bay, the reflux taking place when the action ceases. A series of observations made at various places, accompanied by a contemporaneous state of the winds, would soon explain the subject. I had observed with regret that the American officers at their advanced posts seldom engaged in scientific pursuits, although I believe they have been much encouraged to do so by the superior authorities at Washington.

By a reference to the map, it will be seen that Green Bay is an arm of Lake Michigan, running nearly parallel to it, and about one-fourth of its length. Governor Cass,

INVITATION TO FORT HOWARD. 153

who made observations upon this phenomenon in 1828, supposes that when the northerly winds are packing up the waters at the mouth of Fox River, the same wind tide will keep driving on to Chicago, and make high water at both places, though not at the same time. The level of the mouth of Green Bay, where it joins Lake Michigan, being thus lowered, an ebb will be produced from the bay into the lake, which will soon be felt at Fox River, even during the continuance of the wind that had caused high water there. And this would explain the reason of Charlevoix's surprise at seeing his canoe float off against the wind.

General Brooke, the commandant at Fort Howard, called upon me during the morning, and invited me to accompany him to his quarters at the fort. I therefore crossed Fox River to the garrison in his barge. Fort Howard is built on a very flat piece of land, of exceeding fertility, being a darkish-coloured sandy loam, composed of sand, vegetable matter, and comminuted shells. The extensive gardens attached to the fort are surprisingly good, and are filled with excellent vegetables. I never saw things grow more luxuriantly. The tomatoes were led over trellises, upon which they ran upwards of six feet high, and the plant being thus kept dry and exposed to the sun and air, produced fruit of a remarkably fine quality. All the other vegetables attained great perfection, and the profusion of them was so great, that the quantity was at least three times as great as the wants of the garrison required. Every thing that I saw at the fort convinced me that General Brooke was exceedingly attentive to the welfare of those under his command. Having a passion for horticulture, he had laid out extensive gardens, and turning his men into gardeners when they were not on duty, had not only taught them a valuable art, but had enabled them to provide amply for their own subsistence.

I learnt at the fort that Fox River was affected to a certain distance by the rise and fall of the lake, and that in winter the river near to the banks froze to the bottom, being very shallow there, (tall grass was now growing in those places, covered with innumerable quantities of beautiful lymneas,) whilst there was always water under the ice in the middle of the river. When the wave of the lake, therefore, at that season, is put in motion and enters the river, it lifts up the ice and arches it, and when it retires the ice sinks down as the water recedes.

Having collected a good deal of information respecting what it would be expedient for me to do to procure the safe means of advancing into the Indian country, of carrying supplies with me, and making a secure return before the winter should set in, I found it would be necessary to procure a substantial canoe, and a crew of experienced *voyageurs*. This plan, therefore, I determined to adopt, and instructed Mr. Whitney, the trader, to inquire for a set of men deserving of confidence, and to send them to me with his recommendation. Meanwhile I lost no time in providing supplies of every kind — pork, biscuits, tobacco, blankets, tea, sugar, tin-ware, pots and kettles, knives and forks, and, above all, presents for the Indians. These things I was able to obtain at the different stores, but it cost me a great deal of trouble. An old Canadian, of whom I inquired for something which he had not, replied, "Non monsieur, nous n'avons rien ici. Nous sommes pauvres diables, nous autres; en effet, nous ne sommes que des enfans de la nature!" These *enfans de la nature*, however, knew how to ask quite enough for their commodities, and a prodigious deal of trouble I had to *marchander* with them, the which if I had not done, I should have changed places with them, and become a *pauvre diable* in the most serious sense of the words.

Having provided myself with supplies, I next walked over to a small *bourgade*, a short distance from Navarino, called by the Americans *Shantytown*, principally inhabited by a few *anciens voyageurs*, who, having learnt the art of constructing birch-bark canoes of the Ojibway Indians, followed it now as an occupation. Here I found a *vieux habitant*, who had precisely what I wanted, both birch-bark canoes for sale, and a vast deal of curious information, being a *voyageur* of great experience. I remained listening to the yarns of this entertaining old man a long time; and he was so grateful to me for my patient attention, that I believe he let me have the canoe *au juste prix*. It was perfectly new, would carry eight people commodiously, besides a ton and a half of provisions and baggage, and he only asked me fifteen dollars for it, when I should, without hesitation, have given him thirty. I paid him the money down in hard silver dollars; and being thus become the proprietor of a canoe, had already half taken upon myself the *métier* of a *voyageur*. The last piece of counsel which the *ancien* gave me was respecting the management of the crew that were to navigate it. "Quand vous aurez engagé vos b——, tenez toujours une main de maître sur eux. La loi du bourgeois* dans un canot est la loi du pays; et surtout ne les donnez pas à boire." Thanking him heartily for his advice, I walked slowly back to my quarters. The banks of the river at this little settle-

---

* The trader or principal person in a canoe is always called "le bourgeois."

ment were about forty feet above the water, and were composed of sand and black earth; large primitive boulders were strewed about on the shore, probably derived from the country to the north-west.

After dinner I procured a horse, and rode about ten miles in a north-east direction, to examine the limestone bluffs and a ridge I had observed from the steamer. On reaching that part of the country, I found two terraces, evidently of old shores, analogous to those near Lake Ontario. This state of things exists in every part of the western country which I had yet visited, and is so obvious and general, as to mark two distinct epochs when the waters of this continent have retired to lower levels. All the lakes have extensive shallow shores, and the same may be said of the rivers, so that, when at any period the waters were let off either by a partial subsidence of the bottom of the ocean, or the elevation of the land, the part abandoned by the water would have the appearance of a terrace. These terraces perfectly explain an action of this kind.

Having tied up my horse, I rambled a long time about the neighbourhood, where were many strong horizontal beds of limestone, containing orthocera and other fossils characteristic of the lower silurian limestone. Between the ledges of limestone and the shore of the bay I saw other indubitable evidences of the ancient recession of its waters. Near to the water were immense quantities of valves of anadontas and unios, that had been the food of musk rats; and having collected some good specimens of these, I remounted my horse and returned to Navarino.

The succeeding morning found me with plenty of business on my hands, a great number of *voyageurs*, who had heard of my projected expedition, presenting themselves to make part of my equipage. I had observed so much beastly drunkenness in the place, both amongst the men of this class and the wretched debauched Indians, both male and female, who had given themselves up to every vice practised by the whites, that I was determined to be very particular before I formed an engagement with any of them. Many of them were represented to me as "*mauvais;*" and a *mauvais voyageur* means a fellow who solemnly promises never to touch a drop of ardent spirits during his engagement, but who, unable to resist his propensity, will, when near a post where rum or whisky are to be obtained, abandon you without remorse, and remain beastly drunk from morn till night, as long as he can get anything to drink, parting with his cap and his clothes to the last rag.

There was another great difficulty to be met : all the *voyageurs, without exception,* were in debt to the *petits magazins,* for tobacco, liquor, clothes, &c.; and when going upon a new expedition, it was the established custom for a *bourgeois* to advance each of them money enough to satisfy their creditors, without which they were not permitted to go. Besides this, the *bourgeois* must leave authority with some one to advance a portion of their wages for the use of the families of those who were married, the amount to be deducted from their wages on their return. It would have been impossible for me to have made, without assistance, a fortunate selection out of such a set, and, if I had attempted to do so, I should most probably have been compelled to turn back. I therefore determined to do nothing without the sanction of Mr. Whitney, the trader, or rather to get him to select such men as he would have been willing to risk himself with, as he knew them all pretty well, and the chances there were of my being able to control them.

Through his means I at length engaged five French Canadian *voyageurs*, all of them guaranteed to me as men of great experience in matters connected with Indian life, and trustworthy in everything except the abuse of ardent spirits, a point in which they were stated to me to have no control over themselves, and about which I must exercise a perpetual vigilance. For my first lieutenant I engaged *Louis Beau Pré*, a married man, with a family: he was to steer the canoe, and be responsible to me for the conduct of the men when I was not with them, and was to be paid accordingly. The rest were *Louis l'Amirant*, a dreadful drunkard, but when sober a resolute and useful fellow; *Jean Champagne*, a fellow as lively as his name; *Joseph Dumont*, a married man with a little reputation for steadiness; and *Germain Garde Paix*, a taciturn and rather heavy-looking man for a Frenchman, who turned out better than he looked. Amongst their other qualifications, I had required that those who were to accompany me should be well acquainted with the popular Canadian airs, and be able to sing them after the old approved fashion of keeping time with their paddles. This they all professed to be both able and willing to do. The next step was to authorize Mr. Whitney to become responsible to their creditors for a certain amount, and to furnish them with a limited quantity of rum, to be drunk by themselves and their friends before departure. The day before my departure, with a view to keeping my people as sober as I could during our stay, I directed Beau Pré to have the canoe put in order for the voyage, and to be ready with the men to take me over to the fort, where I was engaged to dine with General Brooke. I was glad to see them all at the appointed time tolerably sober ; and after making a grand flourish along the river side with their paddles, they worked the canoe across to the fort in admirable style, to the very popular air of "Et en revenant du boulanger," from which Mr. Moore took the idea of his Canadian boat-song of "Faintly as tolls the evening chime," After passing the day very agreeably at the fort, and taking leave of the officers, I returned in the evening to Navarino, giving orders for the canoe and men to be all in readiness the next morning to receive the lading and take our departure.

CHAPTER XVII.

ASCEND FOX RIVER. — VORACITY OF THE VOYAGEURS. — DRUNKEN WINNE-BAGOES. — EXPLANATION OF THE ARRANGEMENTS FOR A CANOE VOYAGE. — LAKE WINNEBAGO.

ON the morning of the 22nd I rose with the break of day, and arranged everything for my departure. It appeared to me as if it would be impossible to stow away in such a small vessel the immense quantity of things I had from time to time purchased. I had been told that I should find my crew voracious eaters, and having had before some experience of men of their class, had provided accordingly. I had purchased a barrel of pork, two barrels of biscuit, two large bags containing hams, two containing potatoes, one bag of flour, boxes with rice, sugar, candles, tobacco, axes, powder and shot, and a variety of other articles, consisting of pots, kettles, frying-pans, tin-ware, plates, knives and forks, &c. In addition to all these necessary articles, were the tent, my luggage, and a case of books, and a small service fitted for my own use for breakfast and dinner. As the hour approached for the canoe to arrive, I became very much concerned which of these multifarious objects I should determine to leave behind, for it appeared to me impossible to take them all.

When Beau Pré made his appearance I communicated my fears to him, and was glad to find he did not enter into them. "Le porc, Bourgeois," said he, "se mangera bien vite; ces gaillards là n'en ont pas goûté depuis longtems : et pour les biscuits, ne craignez rien. Vous verrez comme les patates disparaitront; on ne s'arretera pas à les compter, j'en reponds." A little after seven the men all made their appearance, and to my great surprise they did manage to stow every thing away in the boat, so that we were not obliged to leave anything behind. They contrived, too, to arrange plenty of room for the *bourgeois* in front of the steersman; so that I could either sit with my back to the trunks, that were covered with a large bear-skin I had purchased, or recline on a sort of sofa made of blankets. My books and portfolio were near me, and a commodious and handy place for my compass, telescope, and gun. When the last man stepped into the canoe, the water was within a few inches of the gunwale, and everything being ready, we pushed off from the bank amidst the salutations and good wishes of our friends; and my men, striking into a Canadian barcarole and chorus, plied their paddles lustily up the Fox River. In half an hour I had got accustomed to my situation, and was perfectly delighted at commencing my adventures under such promising circumstances.

The Fox River is about 1500 feet wide, with gentle sloping banks, which became higher as we advanced. Coming to a rapid, we all got out to lighten the canoe, the men walking in the water and conducting it by their hands through the most rocky parts. Near the banks I found unios in great abundance, especially those species inhabiting the waters which run to the Atlantic, all of them plain unpretending shells, without that brilliancy and beautiful nacre which distinguishes the unios dwelling in the streams which discharge themselves into the Gulf of Mexico. At fifteen miles from Navarino we came to a still more severe rapid, and again had to lighten the canoe. At the head of the rapid we met some officers of the United States army, with a party of men, making a military road. At 12 P.M. I made the signal, and the canoe was paddled to a convenient place on the shore for the men to cook their dinner. They soon had their pot of pork and potatos placed on a good fire, and leaving them to enjoy their meal, I wandered about in search of plants and land shells. On my return, an hour afterwards, I found them all enjoying their pipes and chattering away at a great rate; and proceeding to the canoe they all followed me, and having stowed away their *batterie de cuisine*, we again started.

As we advanced the river widened, and the country became strikingly beautiful, the banks, with fine trees here and there interspersed, sloping gracefully down on each side, as if the river was gliding through an amphitheatre. Further on the amenity of these slopes became strongly contrasted with the foaming of the most formidable of all the rapids on this river, called in the Menomminie tongue Kāwkāwnin, literally "can't get up." The rocks here are in such amazing numbers, and are so piled up, and the rapid is so strong, the fall being equal to about twenty feet per mile, that it is impossible to get canoes up it. The Canadian *voyageurs*, who ruin every Indian word they meet with, have called this place, whose Indian name is so significant, *Cocolo*, by which name it is universally known amongst them. Here, then, we stopped at the eastern end of the *portage*, it being necessary to unload the canoe and carry it and all our lading to the other end of the *portage*. Some drunken Winnebago Indians haunt this place for the fish that frequent the rapids, and to assist in carrying heavy loads, expending what they earn in rum and whisky at a low dram-shop, which the traveller is sure to find at all such places where there are white men. The *portage* lay over a rich black soil lying on the horizontal limestone extending over this part of the country; and taking my gun and portfolio, I left Beau Pré in charge of everything, and directed him to watch the Indians whom he should employ to carry the *butin* across very closely, for I had always found in my travels that good luck and good lookout were very intimately connected together. This word *butin* seems to be a remnant of buccaneering times, and to have been applied to luggage and personal property of every sort from the time of the first French *flibustiers* or freebooters, and to have come from the Gulf of Mexico, up the Missisippi, the Ohio, and all the great water communications, for the Kentuckians and generally the Americans in the southern parts of the Republic have literally translated the word into *plunder*. I well remember my extreme astonishment, the first time I was asked by a stage driver, in one of the Southern states, " How much plunder have you got, mister ?" as though my luggage had been stolen from some other person.

As I was proceeding across the *portage*, I met with three dirty ferocious-looking Winnebagoes, more than half-drunk, one of whom, called " the Blacksmith " by the whites, on account of his muscular frame, came and offered me his hand, which when I had taken he endeavoured with a jerk to drag me to the ground, not with an intention to do me any harm, but to show his strength. Seeing, however, by his drunken eye, that he meditated some trick, I was upon my guard, and shutting my fist instead of giving him my open hand, I slipped it out and gave him a knowing sort of a nod, which was perfectly comprehended, and his companions laughed heartily at him. Nothing can be more deplorable than the state to which these poor Indians, once lords and masters of these forests, have been reduced by the drunkenness which they have been taught by the whites.

As soon as we had got our *butin* and canoe to a dry clean place at the west end of the *portage*, I had my comfortable tent pitched, all our lading placed inside, and a good fire made in front of the entrance. The next thing was to prepare my dinner, and having appointed one of the Canadians my cook, I stood over him at the fire, to see that he attended to his duty in a proper and cleanly manner. My dinner consisted of fried ham and slices of boiled potatos fried along with it, and browned in the most satisfactory and savoury manner. To this I added excellent black tea, bread and butter, and some milk from a bottle with which I had provided myself, and I certainly never made a more hearty meal upon any occasion.

After a good deal of experience in travelling in Indian countries, I find that, with system, you can lay the foundation for a great deal of comfort, quite as much as that mode of life admits of. My rule always is, to make a hearty breakfast after travelling ten or fifteen miles, stopping at the most eligible place for that purpose, where wood and water and shade—if it is wanted—unite in inviting you. The moment breakfast is over, all re-embark, since that is not the time of day for *commerage*. The *bourgeois* is the supreme head; the men look upon his word as their law; they obey his orders, and never question his reasons. If he wishes to go ashore, he informs the man behind him who steers; and when he requires them to wait for him at the place where he lands, they know that their business is to wait as long as their provisions last ; for they have nothing to do but eat and drink, and obey him, and have not the least objection to pass a few days at any one place in idleness. About three-quarters of an hour before night, on the order being given to land and encamp, as soon as the canoe reaches the shore, two of the men, selected for that duty, take out the tent and pitch it : the steersman's business is to see that everything is taken out of the canoe, and placed under the tent. Last of all, the canoe is taken out of the water, placed on its edge on a level piece of ground, and, being supported by poles, forms a canopy for the men to sleep under. Then comes the important business of preparing the *bourgeois'* dinner (I never eat but twice in the day) and their own. As soon as his tent is pitched, the two men whose duty it is to attend it cover the ground within with tender branches of the spruce fir tree, putting a double quantity where he is to sleep, over which is placed an oil-skin, and a bearskin over that, with a blanket or two for covering. The rest collect fire-wood, and build immense fires—one before the *bourgeois'* tent, and the other before their own quarters, which they replenish during the night if it is cold.

Nothing can be more agreeable than this sort of life, if the people behave well ; and when they do not, the best way is to be firm, and even arbitrary, especially with Canadians. Kindness, however, is not thrown away upon them, and very long journeys may be prosperously made with their assistance, by the aid of a little quiet management, encouraging them to sing, and joining with them in their choruses. They are, like the Indians, voracious eaters, and have so little foresight, that they really seem impatient to eat up all the provisions as fast as possible. Fat salt pork is their delight: they do not get it when at home, where vegetables form their principal diet; and they like it so much, that they absolutely appear unhappy when they can eat no more. After stuffing to the greatest extent, they cover their heads and every part of their bodies with their blankets, and lie down with their feet to the fire, snoring away, as I have often seen them, with the rain pouring down upon them, and the steam reeking from their bodies.

This night, as soon as my evening's repast was over, I made the entrance to my tent fast, and, with my stores and luggage around me, lay down to sleep. A troop of drunken demon-looking Winnebagoes were bellowing around me till near midnight, but they could not get into the tent, and went to my men's bivouac; finding they could get nothing there, they at last retired, and we all got a few hours' refreshing sleep.

I rose at daybreak, and after making my *toilette*, went to an eminence, a little north-west from my camp, from whence I had a fine view of the river and surrounding country. It divides here, and forms a channel on each side of an island, which is almost round.

A group of wretched-looking Winnebagoes were lying about some nearly extinguished embers in the open air, not far from the bank of the river; one of them was quite naked, except his breech-clout; but being accustomed to this mode of life, they appear insensible to its inconveniences. Observing one of the squaws with a papoose, or child, about eighteen months old, I went to my tent, and taking a biscuit, gave it to her, telling her it was for the child. She smiled, and seemed very much pleased, but the papoose seemed not to care much about it, for I saw the mother a short time afterwards eating it. Most of the Winnebagoes, who had been so drunk the preceding evening, were lying about, some of them without any fire : they all appeared very much dejected, and nothing could be imagined more miserable than they looked, for the dew had fallen in a remarkable manner during the night.

Finding there were more rapids ahead, I proceeded on foot by the bank of the river, after seeing the men off with the canoe, and walked in the long grass about six miles ; but I was so thoroughly wet with the heavy dew upon it, that, after gaining the head of the rapid, I collected some wood and made a fire, which I found very comfortable, and had time to dry myself before the canoe came up, which was about 10 A.M. We breakfasted at this place ; and feeling myself perfectly refreshed, I walked to some Winnebago huts, where there was a flag flying, built upon a hill, at no great distance : they were six in number, and one of them was twenty-four feet long. This was a settlement of Indians, that had been formed by the Canadian priests, and professed the Roman Catholic religion. It was a flag of the United States which was flying, with a cross in the centre. There was abundance of corn and pumpkins in the wigwams.

Nothing can be more filthy than these Indians in their persons : the wandering part of the nation live principally upon fish ; and, as they neither wash their food nor themselves, are necessarily a frowsy odoriferous race. The French, who found them with the same manners and customs they have at present, game them the name of *Puants*, a soubriquet they well deserve now. How they got the name of Winnebagoes I know not—they do not know the word. It seems to resemble Winnipec, the name of the lake into which Red River flows; but whether derived from it or not, it is certain that it has been given to them by others, and is another instance of the folly of distinguishing the Indian tribes by any but national names. Every one of them that I conversed with stated the name of the nation to be *Howchungerah*, from *howrah*, fish, and *wungerah*, man; they being a fish-eating tribe of the great Nacotah nation, further to the west, a dialect of whose tongue they speak, and having separated from whom, they settled in a lake country abounding in fish, which thus became their principal diet.

Making use of every opportunity to increase my vocabulary, I succeeded in getting more words than phrases. Beau Pré, my pilot, who had been a great deal amongst them, and knew many of their customs, encouraged me to suppose he could interpret for me; but he knew nothing beyond a few words, and these he pronounced very improperly. Whenever I desired him to ask questions of them, with a view to obtain their answer, and they did not comprehend him, he always laid the blame upon the Indians, and said, " Que voulez-vous Monsieur ? Ce ne sont que des pauvres diables de Puants !"

From this village we had good paddling water for three miles, when I got out of the canoe again, and walked a mile and a half to *La grande Chûte*, a fall, where the river comes over a ledge of limestone rocks six feet high. Above this the stream became exceedingly beautiful; the banks of the river presenting on each side broad and gentle slopes; the trees growing park-like, and the wild grass being very high. Nothing could exceed the fertility of the soil, which is a black vegetable mould upon a deep red loam.

At a place called *La petite Butte des Morts* the river widened into a small lake. Here Mr. Whitney told me he had an agent, a Mr. Cottrell, to whom he had requested me to deliver a message: accordingly I left the canoe, and walked through the forest to his house. On approaching it, I perceived several Canadians and Indians in and about it most uproariously drunk, and very much disposed to be too familiar with me — some of them trying to take my gun away. After a long attempt to get an interview with Mr. Cottrell, he at length made his appearance, but intoxicated in so beastly a manner, that I was excessively disgusted. At first he insisted upon my stopping with him and " taking a drink," as he called it; but when he heard me say, that, " being a friend of Mr. Whitney's, I had promised to call and see how he was going on," he seemed quite as anxious to get rid of me.

I now hastened back to the canoe, lest these drunken fellows should get into communication with my own people, but I was too late; they had found them out, and were already pulling them ashore, to carry them off to the house to drink. I saw at once that my men desired nothing better, and that, if I permitted it, I should lose all command over them; so, entering the canoe, I ordered them to come on board, and said that I would leave every man behind who did not immediately obey me. Beau Pré behaved very well upon the occasion, and seconded me: all but L'Amirant sulkily got into the canoe, and I pushed off into the stream. Seeing that I was in earnest, L'Amirant, knowing that we should soon be out of sight, left his drunken companions, and taking a short cut through the woods, came to the waterside to get on board. I directed Beau Pré to steer the canoe sufficiently near to the shore to speak to him, and told him I did not want a fellow that preferred being drunk ashore to doing his duty with his comrades ; that I knew Cottrell would not dare to keep him there, but would turn him out of doors ; and that when he got back to Navarino, Mr. Whitney would put him in prison for breaking his engagement. He now was very much frightened, and began to entreat me in the most piteous manner to take him on board ; and Beau Pré and the men uniting with him, I consented as a matter of favour to them, though I was quite as anxious to have him back as he was to come, for he was a resolute *bon enfant*, and drinking was his only fault. I therefore took him on board, satisfied with the opportunity the incident had given me of convincing them that I was determined to be obeyed.

We now proceeded a mile and a half further to the foot of Lake Winnebago, a very extensive sheet of water, running north and south ; and the day drawing to a close, I thought it not advisable to enter upon the navigation of the lake until morning : we accordingly made for a rich prairie flat on the right bank of the lake, where there were a few Indian wigwams, and there I directed the tent to be pitched. Beau Pré advised me to encamp nearer to the woods, on account of the fuel ; but being desirous of talking to the Indians, and getting a few phrases from them, I overruled him, and committed, as I soon found, an error ; for in the first place the men had to do three times the work to collect fuel for the night ; and next, having gone to talk to the Indians after I had seen the canoe brought ashore, I found upon my return that the men had pitched my tent in a place where it was impossible for me to permit it to remain ; the fact being, that these poor Indians, who had been a long time encamped here, had shifted their bivouac from time to time, to escape the inconvenience of a practice which places them upon a level with the beasts of the field; and it had been my bad luck to get my tent pitched in one of their old nests, which I was not long in detecting. Dark as it was, with the aid of torches I selected a clean place, and immediately had the encampment removed, so that it was late in the night before we got settled: but the men behaved very well; and by the alacrity with which they completed all the arrangements, seemed to wish to compensate for their previous misconduct.

Almost all the night we heard a horrid yelling, kept up by the drunken party we had escaped from on the other side of the lake; and great was the satisfaction I felt at having extricated my party from them. Rivers, lakes, woods, and prairies, embellished and made attractive as they are by nature, would be sources of the most perfect comfort and the purest pleasures at all times, if it were not for man,—drunken and brutal man,—who sometimes comes and disturbs these enjoyments.

CHAPTER XVIII.

DROLL DISASTER OF AN INDIAN CHIEF.—BUTTE DES MORTS —REMEDY AGAINST MUSQUITOES.—IMMENSE FIELDS OF WILD RICE.

I AROSE at sunrise, and seeing the Indians stirring, went to them. The squaws were bringing in wood on their backs for fuel, whilst the men were squatted down on the ground with a dirty blanket thrown over their shoulders, grinning hideously, and looking as if the muscles of their faces had been trained to nothing but to express suffering. The women appeared to be resigned slaves, and the men clearly intended to keep them so. Such is man in the state of nature, or the point where civilization has not begun ; worse than the brute animals, in putting all the burthens upon the woman, for I have often seen the cock,—who ranks amongst the brutes,—when he comes from his roost in the early morning, picking up the matutinal delicacies, and laying them in the most graceful and gentlemanly manner at the feet of the hen.

The canoes of these Indians were in the water, close to their encampment, and I was desirous of engaging one of them to take me out upon the lake, and show me their manner of fishing ; but I found the man whom I had engaged, and the canoe also when I had entered it, so indescribably filthy, and the stench so intolerable, that I am sure, if I had gone upon the lake, I should have jumped overboard and swam ashore, so I gave it up ; and as soon as my own canoe was ready, got into it, and pushed off into the lake to a small island about ten miles off, opposite to a Winnebago village. The west shore of the lake, as we coasted it, was low, and very fertile, as I could perceive by the fine trees growing there, with occasional lodges of Indians, all of them fishermen. We had no sooner reached the island, which was very commodious for our purpose of breakfasting, than the Indians began to cross over, bringing with them potatos and Indian corn, which we exchanged for a little pork, more for the purpose of keeping on friendly terms with them, than because we wanted them. And here a rather droll incident occurred. My tea-kettle was boiling at the men's fire, and the tea being already in my tea-pot, as soon as the kettle began to boil I took it from the fire, and hastening to a nice shady place where the oil-cloth was laid, upon which my breakfast things were placed, I tripped, the lid of the kettle came off, and I scalded my hand. But the joke came from another quarter. A fat, lazy old Indian, one of their chiefs, after very minutely inspecting my preparations for breakfast, had dignifiedly laid himself down with his face next to the grass, close to my oil-skin, and the boiling hot water — a considerable quantity of which came out of the kettle when I tripped—fell upon his nobler parts. Prince Bare-behind, who could not have the slightest idea that I was near him with such a thing as a boiling tea-kettle, and was probably half asleep, immediately took to grinning, kicking, and roaring, as if a set of angry bees had alighted upon his *sequitur*, and jumping up, saw the fatal cause of his mishap in my hand. As I was not master enough of his language to explain how the accident had happened, it struck me that he might think I was a sort of hot water Baptist preacher, and had done it on purpose; and as that was not the fact, and I wished to avoid a quarrel, I immediately took to kicking and grinning, and wringing my hand as if I had been injured as much as himself, though I had a great deal to do to suppress my laughter. Misery certainly loves company, for after he had made up his mind to believe that he had a fellow-sufferer, he called to one of the squaws, and giving some lamenting grunts, got into a canoe, and crossed over to his village. I called this place in my Journal "Hotwater Island."

Resuming our voyage, we made ten miles more by noon, to the reach which leads to Pawmāygun, an Ojibway word for Wolf River, about half-way down the lake, where upper Fox River comes into it. Immense quantities of *Zizania aquatica*, or wild rice, were growing here, which the French call *folle avoine*. The Indians who frequent the localities which produce this grain are called *Menominies*, or "Wild Rice-eaters," a tribe whose language appears to have an affinity with that of the Miamis and other Illinois tribes. The Canadians, when speaking of these Indians, call them *Les Folles*.

At 1 P. M. we landed for the men to dine, opposite to the *portage* of the Fond du Lac, where there is an Indian mound, and proceeded as soon as that ceremony was over. Lake Menominey is a small expansion of the river, about a mile in breadth, on the borders of which great quantities of the wild rice were growing: it terminated in a serpentine channel, running between lofty plants of zizania, 10 feet high, bearing a great crop of seed, not yet quite ripe.

After paddling a short distance, we came to *Butte des*

Morts, an eminence without any trees upon it. The stream here is so narrow as to bring the banks within rifle-shot. In the early part of the eighteenth century, when the Ottogamies were carrying on a desperate war with the French, they occupied this position, and fortifying it, embarrassed their communication so much with the Mississippi, that the French formally invested it. But the occasion when the place received the name of Butte des Morts was, as I have been informed, as follows. Some Indians, in the old French times, established themselves here, and frequently prevented the French passing with their merchandize to the Mississippi, unless they surrendered a share of it to them. To remove this impediment to the communication, a French officer concealed a number of men in his boat under tarpaulins; and when the Indians rushed down to stop the boat, the men rose, and firing upon them, destroyed so many, that it then received the name it now bears. I have seen other places named Butte des Morts, or "Hill of the Dead."

As we passed on from this place, we met several canoes, with Menominey Indians in them, all the men having their faces entirely blackened over with charcoal, which is their mourning for the death of a relative. They would not have been ill-placed in "Dante's Inferno." Where Wolf River comes into upper Fox River, there was a very broad area of zizania. Just beyond the junction we had a very tight canoe race, with a canoe containing three Menominies and two of their squaws. They paddled with all their might for some time, both men and women; but after a protracted struggle my men left them behind, inspirited by one of their most lively *chansons*, at quick time with their paddles. Our men having shewn the Indians they could beat them, let them come up with us again, and we got into conversation with them. The men had very good teeth, and the women wore their coarse black hair in long, thick queues, such as some sailors were formerly seen to have, only that these were wound around with strings of white beads.

The river now became very serpentine, our course being sometimes W.N.W., and at others S. by W. A black-looking storm was gathering in the west of a serious character; and fearing lest it should continue into the night, and prevent my selecting a good encampment, in a country where the banks of the river were generally low and sedgy, I landed in the best place we could find, but where the wild grass and zizania, mixed up together, were 8 and 10 feet high : this we had to cut down to the ground as close as we could, to make a tolerably even floor; and in doing this we dislodged such myriads of enormous-sized *marengues* (mosquitoes), as the Canadians call them, that there were one or two moments when they were near overpowering us, getting into our ears, our nostrils, and eyes, in a manner to render us unable to do anything. I was obliged to cover myself up, whilst the men built a damp fire to windward, and working away in the smoke, which is the only thing that conquers these insects, at last succeeded in pitching the tent, and collecting wood enough to cook our evening repast.

They had just handed me the boiling tea-kettle into the tent, when the storm came up with us in the most furious style of a truly American hurricane ; but the tent being well pegged down, stood it bravely, and resisted all the attempts of the wind to get in. We had put the *butin* on the ground to windward, close to the edge of the tent, in the inside, to prevent the catastrophe that such an innovation would have occasioned; for if the furious wind had made an entry, we should probably have never seen the tent again, or many other things that were in it, as they would have been blown into the river close by. Soon the rain came down in torrents, accompanied from time to time with such peals of thunder as are rarely heard in Europe. I heard my Canadians *sacré-*ing and grumbling occasionally; but how they had disposed of themselves during this demonstration of the elements, I was at a loss to conceive, for they had not had time to get the canoe out of the water to shelter themselves under. In the meantime, having made a not very comfortable dinner, of mere tea and biscuits, and the storm beginning to abate, I prepared to lie down, and had nearly completed my arrangements, when I discovered that I was not alone in the tent by many millions, the inside of it being literally covered with the mosquitoes which we had disturbed, and which had got in whilst the men were tightening the pegs. There they were, quietly remaining on the canvas as long as the light was burning, but with the intention to regale themselves out of my veins, with that liquid animal food they are so fond of, as soon as it was dark. I had had long experience of these persevering and persecuting little creatures, and knew that as soon as the light was out they would all wing their flight to my face, trumpeting forth their triumph on the way. Perhaps there is no greater annoyance to a traveller, than when, preparing to sink to sleep after his day's labour, he finds himself in the dark, and in the power of an enemy it is impossible to subdue whilst he is awake, and to whose insatiable blood-sucking propensities he knows he must serve as a grand banquet if he happens to fall asleep. But happily experience had taught me a remedy for which these tormentors were not prepared, and lighting a wax taper, I brought it in turns close enough behind each of them to make them feel its warmth, when springing back through the flame, they were either burnt up, or singed their wings off and fell to the ground, never more to rise. In about an hour and a half I cleared the tent, as I thought, of them, and being exceedingly fatigued with the operation, I lay down, and was just about falling to sleep, when, to my great surprise, an infant outside the tent set up a fearful squalling close to my head, and the Indian mother, to appease it, commenced a lullaby ten times worse than the noise which the child made. This lasted incessantly for two hours, during which, to complete my discomfort, I heard the war-cry of so many mosquitoes wheeling round my head, and tuning their tiny hostile pipes, that it seemed to me as if I had done little or nothing in the way of their extermination. Worn out with the excitement, and forming determinations never to encamp in tall grass again, I at length fell asleep, and became the unresisting prey of these little demons, who, I found in the morning, had amply revenged on my face the slaughter of their race.

In the morning I found that I had been indebted to our friends the Menominies, with whom we had run the race the preceding day, for the squalling of the mother and the child: they knew very well that where we bivouacked there would be something to eat, and coming quietly to my camp, established the squaws to the leeward of my tent, whilst the men joined my people. They had had nothing to eat the previous evening, and I gave them some pork and biscuits, for which they thanked us.

At half-past 5 A.M. we got everything stowed into the canoe again, and pursued our way in a strong fog along the low flat banks of the river, filled with the zizania. Further on the country began to rise, and groups of trees to become more plentiful. At 9 A.M., having made about twelve miles, we landed to breakfast, and whilst this was preparing I climbed a lofty tree, and, the fog having cleared away, got an extensive inland view of the country, which was a perfect wilderness and nearly a dead flat, without any vestige of man or his labours, for the few Indians who frequent the country are all fish or rice eaters, or both, and seldom stray from the streams. The soil on the surface was a black vegetable loam, and beneath it nothing whatever was to be seen, as far as my opportunities went, but an incoherent whitish sand. Oak, ash, and elm trees, with many shrubs, grew in every direction. All this country obviously forms part of the immense area covered in ancient times with fresh water; and although the waters of the Wisconsin river, which I was now approaching, flow into the Gulf of Mexico, yet the elevation of the land which separates them from the Atlantic streams I am now upon is so trifling, that the Mississippi must have been comprehended in that area.

Having breakfasted we pursued our way cheerfully, the morning having become sunny and pleasant. A great number of large black water-snakes were basking on the muddy earth where the zizania grew; and as they heard the noise of our paddles, dropped into the water; but the young ones, who were yet without experience, kept their ground. I heard the *rail* frequently crying, and sometimes flushed them up. They appeared to me to be the same birds which abound near Newport, in the state of Delaware, where the zizania abounds so much. At noon the river averaged about fifty yards in breadth, and the banks rose twenty-five feet out of the water with a gentle slope to it. Here we came up with a mound about twenty feet high, where a famous chief of the Winnebagoes, called *Yellow Thunder*, is interred.

At half-past one P. M. we stopped for the men to eat and smoke a pipe in a country not very well wooded, open oak lands with low sandy bottoms, containing sedge, wild cane, and zizania. We were now about 100 miles from Green Bay, and a more perfect wilderness could not be imagined; nothing alive to be seen but black snakes, red-winged blackbirds, and the plaintive quail. Proceeding on our way we came up about 4 P. M. with two Menominey lodges, the people of which let us have six fish for some biscuit: the Indians called them *pashetāu*, and my men called them *chigon*, which was their imitation of the word *kēēgon*, the general Ojibway term for fish. We passed several primary boulders in the course of the afternoon.

One of the greatest sources of satisfaction to a traveller who is attached to geological pursuits, is to be found in the circumstance of his meeting with rocks of any kind. In this uninteresting wilderness, accompanied by illiterate men, I should have felt as lonely as if I had been in the deserts of Arabia, but for the chord which these boulders struck in me; and the moment I perceived them, all that existed of my lonely feeling passed away. I went to them with the eagerness of an old acquaintance, and having found out who they were, and informing myself as well as I could from whence they last came, I left them in a minera-logico-social pleasant state of mind, that lasted me for some time. It is one of the great charms of geological knowledge, that every rock, every pebble, every object on the surface of the earth and beneath it, forms an interesting link in that undefinable and rather awful world of existences to which they belong, and where man's intellect delights in roaming.

About half-past five, passed the *Sheshequāth*, or Rattle-snake River, as an Indian we met informed me it was called. I do not find this word in my list of western words, but in one of the dialects of the Six Nations, or *Iroquois*, as the French called them, they formerly made fierce war against the Indians of these more western parts, and have probably left this word behind them.

At 6 P. M., having made by computation about thirty-five miles paddling against the stream, and perceiving the men, who had been harassed by the storm of the last evening, were watching for me to give the signal, I landed on a level sandy loam. The truth was, I was so much afraid of those Indians following us up, who had come to our camp last night, that I had pushed on rather too far, and the little daylight we had left was consumed in pitching the tent, so that all our grand preparations for frying the *chigon*, which had been the subject of much conversation, were to be made in the dark. I anticipated a great deal of satisfaction on my own part in this rare dish of fried fish that was to be produced, and being determined to make a good dinner upon it, had the largest, weighing about 4 lb., reserved for the *bourgeois,* and consequently gave out no ham. It was my bad luck, however, to make a second bad dinner, for the *chigon* turned out to be so tough, dry, and good for nothing, that I abandoned it almost immediately, and had to take to some of the men's pork as a *pis aller.* When I had concluded my repast, I had to grope my way to the river in the dark to wash my greasy fishy fingers a second time, for the men were so happy bolting their food, and gossiping at the same time, that I was loth to interrupt them to bring me water again. The mosquitoes made another fierce attack upon me this evening, but I punished them severely, and did not lie down as long as I could find one with any wings to him.

We had our paddles at work again as early as 5 A. M., and as we were passing over a shallow sandy part of the bed of the river, I saw a unio walking in the water, and stopped a moment to observe him; his motion was slow but steady, moving with the umbones or heaviest parts of his shell foremost, having, according to correct principles, the bulk of his burden nearest to the power of traction. The river became very winding again, which made our progress in a straight line rather tedious. In a little more than an hour we reached the lodge of a chief called "the Sturgeon," but he was gone south with his band. These savages, as they are sometimes called, have one good custom, unknown to civilized men. When they go upon distant excursions, they leave their houses, containing what furniture, implements, and property belonging to them they do not wish to carry with them, with the doors unfastened, and frequently do not return until after an absence of several months. But the others never rob them or destroy their property in time of peace.

METHOD OF COMPILING A VOCABULARY.

Having made about twelve miles, we stopped to breakfast, and were under way again before ten. Our course to Fort Winnebago was S. S. W., but the river twisted about so that we were often going N. N. E. At 11 A. M. there were no longer any banks to the channel, and we appeared to be going through an ancient lake grown up with reeds and zizania. About 2 P. M. we had struggled through all this tall grass, and got to a lake called *Apachquāy*, or "Lake of Rushes." Three Winnebagoes here came to us with a deer they had killed and a wild duck, but they refused to part with the whole deer; they would let us have a part of it when we got across the lake, they said; so we crossed it upon a south-west course, by compass, to an Indian trader's by the name of Gleeson. We never saw the hunters again, however. This Gleeson had a Winnebago wife, who had borne him several little urchins, that were running about like wild animals. Her husband was from home, and whilst the men were cooking their dinner I entered into conversation with his wife, who was very civil, and spoke English tolerably well. This was a good opportunity of enriching my vocabulary, and I availed myself of it. I also read over to her the words and phrases I had already collected, and she gave me the correct pronunciation, which I noted down with care, as I always did when I had good authority. Their national name, she said, was *Howchŭngera*, the middle syllable having a strong nasal accent and being long, and the *e* penultimate being very short. A great many of their words have this nasal *ng*, as *whŭngera*, a man; and the termination *era* is very common to their nouns. The distance from this house across the country to Fort Winnebago was only twenty-five miles, whilst by water I was informed it was about sixty, owing to the serpentine course of the channel.

I left Gleeson's at half-past three P. M., and took to the lake again. Here we were obliged to paddle through an immense long field of zizania growing in the water. At half-past five we landed for the evening, and were obliged to encamp in the long grass, there being nothing else near us. I had a glorious scene here at sunset, that luminary lighting up with his parting beams several thousand acres of zizania, extending at least five miles in one direction and two miles in the other; the heads of the plant all waving gently about, as we sometimes see those of an extensive wheat-field do. When the grain parts from the head easily, the Indians enter amongst the plants with their canoes, and bending down the culminating part into them, thrash it out into the bottom as well as they can, until they have got as much as they can carry away. This must be a remarkable locality for the purpose. The grain was now generally formed, though not mature; the wild ducks concealed amongst the plants were quacking loudly, the red-winged blackbirds were issuing from them in clouds, and the night hawks (*Caprimulus*) were wheeling about and screaming in every direction. Take it altogether, it was one of the most rare and pleasing scenes I ever witnessed.

We had a heavy rain in the night, but when I rose in the morning, at 5 A. M., my Canadians, who had been muffled up in their blankets and exposed to the weather for several hours, were laughing and jabbering as if nothing had happened. They were good-tempered fellows, always gay, and only required gentle management and to be kept from temptation. They were very much

A FIRE LIT WITHOUT LUCIFERS.

pleased that their *bourgeois* spoke their language and condescended to sing with them, having usually been in the service of traders, whose only object was to make the most they could out of their labour. Leaving the bivouac about 6 A.M., we soon got into the river again, which was about fifty yards wide; but the rain recommenced with so much force, that we were soon completely wet through; we therefore stopped at some sandy ground about eight feet above the river, and having with some difficulty got up a fire, boiled our kettle and set the frying-pan a-going, with the rain pouring down upon us.

In very long and heavy rains it is sometimes found difficult to make a fire at all, especially one sufficiently brisk to boil a pot; but these men proceeded with great address to accomplish their purpose, and I never knew them fail to succeed. If the rain came down ever so hard, they dispersed in the woods to find broken branches and logs of fallen trees hid beneath others, and which were sufficiently dry to burn. Of these they always were sure to find a sufficient quantity to set the fire a-going. Meanwhile one of them carefully examined the decayed trees, should none of the fallen stuff appear dry enough for the purpose, and from the side opposite to the storm generally extracted a sufficient quantity of dry woolly decayed fibre, and making a little nest of it under his hat, took out his flint and struck it until a spark was produced: this he permitted to spread awhile in the dry fibre, and then depositing it in a larger nest of the same material, gently blew it into a flame, feeding it with the driest branches until the fire became so strong as to dry all the other matter that was heaped upon it, and thus a roaring fire was made despite of the torrent of rain that fell. I have often admired their ingenuity and perseverance in accomplishing this in the midst of a heavy storm of wind and rain.

This was one of those occasions when they got up an exceedingly fine fire in the midst of a deluge of rain pouring down upon us, and around which we all ate our breakfasts standing. As soon as we felt refreshed we started again. At half-past ten we reached a small lake, called *Lac le Bœuf*, about 500 yards broad, with pretty sloping banks, adorned with graceful trees. I observed some more boulders on the east side. The heavy rain prevented my stopping to look at some Indian mounds on each side of the lake, at the head of which was an eminence, called by my men *Fort Ganville*, probably the post of some old French trader. On leaving this pretty little lake, we found the river barely forty yards wide; and the rain ceasing, we pushed on as hard as we could, all of us paddling, to reach some favourable situation to build a good fire to dry our clothes, when suddenly the weather cleared up, and the sun came out so hot as to dry us in a short time, so that we deferred stopping until the hour for the men's dinner should arrive.

About 2 P.M., finding a commodious place, we landed, and as soon as the smoke of our fire arose, some wild-looking Winnebagoes came to us, all naked except their breech-clouts, and offered us wild plums and service berries. The first they called *chāngera*, the *ch* being a strong guttural; the other (*Sorbus am.*) they called *chāshera*, using the same guttural. I could get no information from these Indians: they seemed to be very poor; and as soon as I gave them some biscuit, they went away. My Canadians seemed to pity my simplicity in asking so many questions; and finding that I was not a trader, were at a loss what to make of me. They literally cared for nothing but eating, and as to their knowledge of the Indian tongues, of which they boasted when I engaged them, it amounted to nothing at all. If I asked them the Indian name of the *night-hawk*, the answer was, "Ah, ce b—— là, c'est le mangeur de marengoins;" and a rail, "Ce n'est rien qu'un mangeur de folles," meaning the wild rice. In this they copy the aborigines, who attend to nothing but the operations of nature, and have no artificial knowledge whatever.

At 2 P.M. we started again, and the river became so winding, sometimes going N. W., sometimes E. S. E., and indeed upon every point of the compass, that we as often had the sun on our right as on our left. I was exceedingly amused with seeing the tringa skip nimbly from one leaf to another, floating near the shore, to pick up the insects; they seemed to have remarkably fine sport. Having made by computation thirty miles, and feeling a little incommoded from sitting so many hours in wet clothes, I landed at a very nice spot, had a good fire built close to my tent, made a complete change of everything, and shaved for the first time since I left Navarino, now the sixth day. It was a fine evening, and there being nothing to prevent it, the frying-pan did its duty in a most satisfactory manner, and having made a comfortable repast, I lay down to sleep on a bed made of the straw of the zizania.

CHAPTER XIX.

REACH FORT WINNEBAGO.—MEET WITH THE FIRST TETRAO.—SLIGHT ELEVATION OF THE LAND SEPARATING THE EASTERN AND WESTERN RIVERS.—EMBARK ON THE WISCONSIN.—HORIZONTAL SANDSTONES.—A SHOT TOWER EXCAVATED IN THE ROCK.—BEAUTY OF THE VALLEY OF THE WISCONSIN.—REACH THE MISSISSIPPI.

I ROUSED my men before 5 A. M., and striking the camp, proceeded onwards. In every direction the country was covered with long wild grass; the buffalo, that formerly used to keep it down, having been driven to the other side of the Mississippi. This state of things will not last long, for the American population will soon drive the Indians after the buffalo, and the cultivated grasses will take the place of the wild ones. The scythe of what is called "civilization" is in motion, and everything will fall before it. Ere long the poor Indian will have to bid a final adieu to those plains over which he has so long wandered, and to seek and obtain a better subsistence on the other side of the Mississippi, than the hips and haws he finds in his native but unproductive wilderness. How long the white man will leave him in peace there, is an affair of the future: at present the race is advancing with a giant's pace, eradicating everything in its progress, first the buffalo and next the Indians; substituting for the unpretending barbarity of nature, the artificial government of *meum* and *tuum*, with the improvements in fraud and vice that are attendant upon those reasoning powers which make him so superior to the naked savage. Alas! if men are to be held accountable for the use they sometimes make of their reason, the Indian, with his tomahawk and scalps, need not envy the final judgment to be passed on his invader, who, planting himself here as his friend, has ended by exterminating him.

At 6 A. M. we passed some high sand-hills, called by Carver " small mountains."* This traveller, who passed through this country in 1776 in this direction, gives but a very meagre description of it thus far; and being one of the earliest European travellers in these parts of North America after the peace of 1763, I provided myself with a copy of his work, and took it in the canoe with me. Slight as his notices are, they are sufficient to convince me that he has been here. About half-past seven we passed the west fork of Fox River, said to be ten miles from the American post of Fort Winnebago. The stream had now diminished to about twenty yards in breadth. From this point we had frequently to struggle through the wild rice, which had all but choaked up the channel in various places; often paddling through the straw as if we were going through an inundated wheat-field. About eight I landed at a sand-hill, about eighty feet high, along which some boulders of primary rocks and limestone were lying. Ascending it, I observed several others in various parts of the country; but whether they have been produced by blown sand, or are the remains of ancient beds of incoherent sandstone, I could not ascertain: there was, however, an occasional appearance of stratification, which favoured the last opinion,

Here we breakfasted, and starting again about 9 A. M., got so entangled in the rice stalks, and canes ten feet high, that we could see nothing around us whatever. The channel was altogether obliterated, and the water became very shallow. Paddling became out of the ques-

* Carver's Travels, p. 41. London, 1778.

tion, and we all took to warping the canoe through, by hauling upon the tall stalks, upon a course by compass for Fort Winnebago. My fear was that we should work the canoe into an immense rice field, like that of the Lake Apachquay, and be very much embarrassed to extricate ourselves. Certainly, if night had overtaken us in this situation, we should have had to pass it in the canoe: but after two hours' hard work we got into clear water, and soon after 11 A. M. had the great satisfaction of seeing the American flag waving in a strong northwest breeze from Fort Winnebago. We now paddled away for the post, and reaching it soon after noon, I landed and presented myself at the quarters of Major Grant, the commandant, a very gentlemanly person, who received me with the kind hospitality with which American officers always receive travellers. This gentleman had been a long time on duty in the north-west country. The dinner went off very pleasantly; and when it was over, Dr. Foote, the very intelligent surgeon of the garrison, was kind enough to walk with me to some of the sand-hills I had seen in the morning. It was so long since I had seen any rocks in place, that I was rather at a loss about the geology of the country, and was exceedingly anxious to find out whereabouts I was. We had a very agreeable walk, during which we sprung several very large grouse (*Tetrao cupido*). These birds seem to flourish on this high dry land, for Fort Winnebago is most conveniently situated upon the dividing summit that separates the Atlantic streams from those that flow into the Gulf of Mexico; one of the first flowing at the foot of the fort, and the Wisconsin being distant only half an hour's walk.

The sand-hill we first reached was about sixty feet

WILD-RICE MARSHES.

high, and was formed of sandstone in place, rather incoherent, with the strata horizontal, and pleasingly coloured with streaks of red oxide of iron. The inspection of this outlier at once explained a great deal of what I had been observing for some days, but which I could not understand for want of the key. It was evident that an immense area of country had been, in ancient times, covered with a stratified arenaceous deposit, slightly coherent, and that this had been broken up and carried for the greater part away, when the waters had retreated in a violent and tumultuous manner. I found afterwards, that, although the Wisconsin empties itself into the Mississippi, passing the fort at a distance short of two miles, yet that the elevation of the ground betwixt the Wisconsin and Fox River was so slight, that once in six or seven years, when the flood in the Wisconsin is high, its waters overcome the difference of level and flow back into Fox River, so that a barge can at such times pass from one stream into another. I do not therefore hesitate to believe, that all the country, including the great lakes and the Mississippi, have, at a remote period, formed one great area of fresh water. One of the consequences of the removal of the ancient strata is the present depression of the surface of the country, the prevalence of wild rice marshes, and the deposition of sand over a great portion of the general surface. This loose sandstone reminded me so much of that which exists in the lead region of the state of Missouri, which I visited in 1834, that it struck me, for the first time, that the same formation might extend to the lead region of the Wisconsin territory, a fact that I should soon have the best opportunity of examining into.

Fort Winnebago, which, like all the American frontier

posts, is an exceedingly neat place, is built upon an elevated piece of land, with Fox River and the rice-marshes connected with it in front. To the south-west there is a range of hills, called Bonibou, which form an agreeable object. The fort is inclosed with a square picket, and contains two block-houses. At the period when this part of the Indian country was first occupied by American troops, the post was no doubt no more than adequate for defence against the Indians; but now that they are reduced to a state of insignificance, it would seem unnecessary to maintain a garrison here much longer. There is a military road, not yet completed, which passes near to the post, leading from Green Bay to Prairie du Chien : it is a wide path cut out of the forest, with the stumps of the trees razed close to the ground; and the streams are traversed by good bridges, this branch of the military service of the United States being always well performed.

Having got a comfortable night's rest in the fort, I rose at 5 A. M., and taking my towels, &c., went down to the river to wash myself, and see what my men were doing. They were all comfortably asleep under the canoe, except one man, who slept in the tent to take care of the *butin*. At seven I was called to breakfast with Major Clarke, and afterwards went to Dr. Foote's quarters, who presented me with a very large conch-shell (*Cassis c.*), taken by him from a very ancient and lofty mound, resembling those at St. Louis and on the Muskingum. These last appear to be the oldest monuments of this kind in the country, and have been attributed by some persons to a race of Indians that preceded the present red men : this shell, therefore, which I believe is not found at any point nearer than the Mexican side of the

DESCEND THE WISCONSIN.

Gulf, would seem to indicate the country from whence the race came that constructed the mound.

At 8 A.M. I bade adieu to the officers of the garrison, and turning my back upon the waters that flow into the Atlantic, I crossed the *portage*, and advanced to those that empty themselves into the Gulf of Mexico. The *portage* was a dead flat of black mud and sand, measuring exactly 2650 paces: it took me exactly twenty-eight minutes to walk across it. The canoe and luggage were conveyed to the shore of the Wisconsin in an ox-cart, and launched upon the river as soon as we reached it. It was a powerful black-looking stream, resembling the Arkansa, with broad sand-beaches, the whole breadth not appearing at the point where we struck it, on account of some islands which masked it; but it soon exhibited a breadth of 250 yards. After struggling so many days as we had against the current of Fox River, an exertion requiring so much care and labour as to keep down a great deal of enjoyment, it was exceedingly gratifying to find ourselves, on one of the most lovely mornings imaginable, carried down stream by a strong current of about three miles an hour, independent of our paddles; and all very much exhilarated, we went joyously and noisily down the waters that are tributary to the Mississippi, roaring out our *chansons* as we shot rapidly past the picturesque islands and graceful banks of a noble river I had never been upon before,—a feeling of peculiar enjoyment to me. The banks at first were low and verdant, with overhanging foliage, as were the beautiful islands which frequently presented themselves; whilst often the river expanded into an uninterrupted sheet of water, of a reddish colour, marking the quality of the soil it had passed through. The river, however, was so shallow in many places, that our canoe frequently grazed the bottom, and, going with unusual velocity, we more than once got so fast in the sand, that we found it difficult to force it back into deeper water. Upon such occasions, or at any difficult passes, the men never hesitated to jump out, knowing what frail vessels birch-bark canoes are, and that no time is to be lost. I never had men in my service more to be depended upon in emergencies of this kind.

About 10 A. M. we came up with sandstone strata, of the same character with those which I had examined at Fort Winnebago. At 11, the country began to rise, and became hilly in the distance. We passed a sandstone bluff sixty feet high, the strata still preserving that horizontal character which distinguishes the coal measures and the other intervening silurian beds I had left behind me, all of which laid above these rocks. The loose sand-banks of the river contained seams of red oxide of iron, shewing that they were derived from the strata the river had broken down, they being everywhere banded with red and yellow oxides. Our course being south-west by south by compass, we came up at noon with some pine trees, and a sandstone bluff on the right bank, 150 feet high. As a storm appeared to be rising in the west, I stopped here a short time, not wishing the men to eat their meal in so much discomfort as they had done upon other occasions; but we were soon off again, and got into a fine expanse of the river, free from islands, with lofty sloping banks, pleasingly interspersed with oak trees. At half-past 2 P. M. we passed an isolated ridge, standing a little back from the left bank, with a singular crest, rudely resembling walls and batteries, near 200 feet high. Every now and then we

BEAUTIFUL UNIOS.

passed heaps of dead valves of the unios, many of which, from their freshness, appeared to have been very recently dragged there by the otters and musk rats. I occasionally stopped to examine them, and sometimes obtained very beautiful shells, especially a large *U. rectus*, with a deep salmon-coloured nacre. The species generally resembled those in the Tenessee, Cumberland, and other western rivers, and confirmed my previous experience of the separation of Atlantic and Gulf species.

The day at length becoming cold and rainy, our musical propensities became dormant, and we went silently on anticipating the evening encampment and its comfortable fires, when we discovered that we had not exclusive possession of the country, a small canoe heaving in sight from below. On coming up with it we found it contained an old-looking Indian, his squaw and two young children: the squaw had some clothes on, but the man and the children were quite naked. They looked uncomfortable enough to be sure, but Indians are so accustomed to suffer in this manner, that they never complain. They are only really unhappy when they cannot procure food. I gave this poor family a few biscuits, and the woman seemed grateful.

At 4 P.M. we passed a picturesque-looking mass of horizontal sandstone, extending with some interruptions for about a mile, distant probably about forty miles from the *portage*; and at half-past five, observing a comfortable place, near to an ancient abandoned Indian village, I made, to the great joy of the men, the signal for landing. Whilst they were pitching my tent, I attempted to walk to an elevated ridge that appeared not very far from us, to get a look at the country, but I found it excessively fatiguing; the distance was greater than I supposed; the wild grass was wet and often up to my chin; night was coming on; I was alone and unarmed, and when I reached the foot of the ridge, and looked at the ascent, I began to think the wisest thing I could do was to return without delay, and I did return, but be-draggled in a most extraordinary manner. After regaling myself with dry clothes, a comfortable repast, and a lounge at the cheerful fire, I shut myself in the tent for the night.

My rest was a good deal disturbed by the mosquitoes, who had taken possession of the tent; and although I was up early, we could not start for a dense fog that was upon the river. I therefore amused myself with looking at the deserted wigwams near us. They were formed with nine poles, about twelve feet high, fixed into the ground in a circle, about two feet apart from each other, and their tops bent to a point and fastened together. These poles were strengthened with others interwoven round them, and the whole covered with birch bark. An Indian house of this kind costs but very little labour, and with a small fire in the middle, is comfortable in the coldest weather, the smoke escaping through a hole where the poles meet. The fog began to clear away at 7 A. M., and we resumed our voyage. At 9 A.M. we reached a shot-tower belonging to Mr. Whitney, on the left bank of the river, and landed there to breakfast. Mr. Whitney had entrusted to my care a large bag of silver money, with some other funds he wished to remit to his nephew and agent here. I had been very reluctant to receive it, as it not only brought me under a responsibility I was desirous of avoiding, but was an object that might have roused the cupidity of my men, and got me into a serious scrape with them. Indeed, I positively declined

AN INGENIOUS SHOT TOWER. 197

the proposition at first, but he had shewn so much obliging zeal in my service, that, upon his pressing me with some urgency a short time before my departure, I consented; and the treasure being put into the middle of one of my carpet bags, which contained some heavy fossils, was embarked. The men were so accustomed to see me bagging fossils and minerals of one kind or another, that they had no suspicion of this "*sacré sac*," as they called it, containing money. I had put this carpet bag under L'Amirant's care; it was his business to put it in the tent, and to stow it away again in the canoe. Upon these occasions, whenever he was about to lift it up, he always used to apostrophise it with, " Sacrè vilain matin, que tu est lourd."

As soon as the canoe was fastened to the shore, I told L'Amirant to shoulder the sack, and away we trudged with it to the agent's house, to which the name of Helena had been given, where I delivered my charge and took a receipt. Mr. Whitney's nephew and his wife received me civilly, and insisted upon entertaining me with breakfast, which when I had despatched, I went to see what they called the shot-tower, where lead brought from the lead district of Wisconsin, not many miles off, is cast into shot of various sizes. This shot-tower was not one of the ordinary columns, that rise to a great height from the surface, but was a cylindrical excavation, ingeniously made in an escarpment of the incoherent sandstone, 200 feet in height. The lead was melted at the top, and afterwards poured down to a chamber below. The whole contrivance did great credit to the projector. From the top of the escarpment I had an extensive view of the Wisconsin, with the broad bottoms of fertile soil on each side of it, forming altogether a rich valley, about two miles in breadth, once entirely occupied by this flood, in the ancient state of the river, and which had contracted itself into its present channel, either upon that last retreat of the waters of the country which I have before alluded to, or from its diminution by the gradual drainage of the country.

This phenomenon of rivers, with wide margins and terraces, is to be observed in every part of this continent; my attention was particularly drawn to it in 1807, on my first visit to Canada. In what is called the valley of the St. Lawrence, on the south side of that river, opposite to Quebec, there are abundant evidences of the water having retired from higher levels. This valley, which in many places is twenty miles broad, is bounded on the south-east by a more elevated country, once the right bank of the river. The strata, too, on each side of the valley appear, from mineralogical considerations, to have been once united; and the break in the continuity of the strata may have been produced by the retrocession of the river during long periods of time; though the difference of level does not appear in an abrupt form in the St. Lawrence, as it does in its tributary the Chaudiére, at its beautiful cataract, the bed of the river describing an inclined plane to the first great rapids west of Montreal. In many parts of the Potomac and James River, in Virginia, there is also abundant evidence of the same state of things. Indeed, it requires very little reflection to perceive that the retreat of an immense body of water, spread over a great portion of a continent, must be followed by the formation of such valleys and rivers, and that these valleys and their rivers must be the effects

INDUSTRIOUS INDIANS. 199

of such a cause. In treating, however, of these physical phenomena analytically, a distinction is to be observed. Some of the valleys may have been formed on the general retreat of the ocean from a continent on its first appearance, and some on the retreat of an inland sea of fresh water, such as that which has produced the valley of the Wisconsin, with its coves and dells coming into it at right angles, all abounding in natural and beautiful plantations of trees and shrubs. But whether these fine vales are owing to one cause or the other, it is evident that they have both been instruments in the hand of Providence to embellish that surface of the earth which was to be inhabited by the human family.

Mr. Whitney's agent informed me that galena was found within twenty miles of the shot-tower, and in examining some of the highest parts of the escarpment, I found a sparry calcareous rock, resembling that in which the galena is found in the state of Missouri, a fact which led to the inference that the galena of this district might also be inclosed in equivalent strata. I left Helena at 11 A.M. The morning was beautiful, and having made a good breakfast, I went gliding on and enjoying the scenery. Near 1 P.M. we came up with a mass of sandstone which had fallen off from an escarpment, about thirty feet in height, for about 200 feet in length; the water had underworn it, and being loose and incoherent, it had peeled off, leaving a smooth face. About 2 P.M. we stopped at a little cove to let the men dine, at a place where I found what I had not met with before, an industrious family, in a clean wigwam. There were two male Indians, and two women, with three male children, the males being all naked except their breech-clouts. The men were at work weaving matting, and the women were making mocassins. Some corn was boiling in a pot, and some venison was roasting on a stick. They offered us money for some biscuit, and were evidently familiar with the ways of white people, being in the habit of frequenting Prairie du Chien, on the Mississippi. As we were approaching this place, where we could replenish our stores, I gave them a liberal supply of biscuit, and in return they presented my people with a very dirty thin piece of venison.

About half-past 2 P. M. we were afloat again, and soon passed a fine stream coming in from the right bank. The country here was remarkably beautiful, the slopes of the banks gracefully wooded, and occasionally interrupted by coves. For a distance of about three miles the escarpments were about 250 feet high, the rock every now and then jutting out and taking a castellated appearance. It was evident, from the manner in which the sections presented themselves on the banks, that the surface of the country in the interior must be very undulating. I observed, too, that the incoherent structure of the sandstone had been favourable to Indian talent, the figures of deer, men, and horses —sometimes well executed—being cut in it, and sometimes painted with a red bole. The swallows had availed themselves of the softness of the rock by picking holes in it, and building their nests there in innumerable quantities. This loose texture of the rock is to be detected also in the tops of the hills, which are gracefully rounded off, the incoherent rock having yielded to the action of the atmosphere. In these parts of North America the arenaceous beds are of immense extent, and it goes beyond the power of man's imagination to form even a proximate idea of the ancient state of things which existed before the particles of sand, now so loosely combined, formed an integral portion of the hard quartzose rock, from which they seem to have been derived. How remote that period must have been from the present! About 6 P. M. we stopped for the night at a bold bank, up which the men had to carry the *butin* to a commodious encampment.

August 31.—On peeping out from my tent at 5 A. M., I perceived we were in the midst of a dense fog, and that the high grass was bent with the heavy dew; we, however, launched the canoe, and crept slowly along by compass until near seven, when the fog gradually rose, and again disclosed the beautiful shores of the Wisconsin. Soon after we reached Prairie de la Baie, where the scene was very pleasing, there being a fine level prairie to the south, terminating about a mile and a half from the river in gracefully rounded hills; whilst close to the edge of the shore were several Indian lodges, with the smoke rising from them; the departing fog, in the distance, creeping in a gauze-like substance along the flanks of the hills. The river here was studded with charming little islands; on our right the hills came down close to the water, and we had a beautiful cloudless morning, smiling on the most placid of streams. The picture presented one of the finest subjects for a landscape-painter, and I was tempted to stop a moment to enter a slight sketch of it in my portfolio. About half-past nine we stopped at the Rivière Bleu to breakfast. Here were some curious round hills, without any trees, with the sandstone strata cropping out from them, and fine slopes coming down to the river, covered with high grass. I ascended to the top of the loftiest of these, about 350 feet from the water, whilst my breakfast was preparing, and found a regular bed of cherty calcareous rock, containing mamillary quartz resting upon the sandstone. I was perfectly satisfied now, that this calcareous rock was the equivalent of that in the lead region of Missouri. Here I gave chase to a snake of a large size, resembling the rattle-snake, but without any rattles: these are usually called moccassin snakes, and I believe this was one of the trigonocephali, or serpents that flatten their heads into a triangular shape when angry. He escaped me, however, into some fallen rocks.

Having made a hearty breakfast we got afloat again, and about 1 P.M. observed a small prairie on the right bank with some Indian mounds: they reminded me of the lesson I got in Lake Huron, when violating the deserted tombs upon the small island, and I was far from offering any disrespect to these. About 2 P.M. the river began to widen, and we were rapidly approaching the point of its confluence with the Mississippi. I could already perceive the lofty right bank of that famous stream at the end of the vista; and being desirous of letting the men dine, and of taking a sketch of the confluence of these two noble rivers, I landed for an hour. At half-past 3 P.M. we bade adieu to the charming Wisconsin, and to the enjoyment of floating upon a favourable current, having entered upon the broad surface of the Mississippi, where our course was changed to north-north-west, and all our force was wanted to contend against the force of the descending stream. The river appeared at this point to be about 900 yards across; its waters were clearer than those of the Wisconsin, having deposited much of their sedimentary matter during their long course, a great part of which is through primary rocks. We soon came in sight of Prairie du Chien, an extensive level bottom or prairie, closed in to the east by a strong rocky bluff, which was no doubt once the bank of the river. A new scene now presented itself; there was a respectable-looking military post, cattle grazing, a village, and evidences of a settled population, to which I had been for some time a stranger.

CHAPTER XX.

REFLECTIONS ON THE POLICY TO BE OBSERVED FOR THE DEVELOPMENT OF BRITISH NORTH AMERICAN COMMERCE, AND FOR THE PROTECTION OF OUR COLONIES.

Having now fairly turned my back upon the lake country, I again suspend for a while the narrative of my tour, to introduce a few remarks which suggest themselves on reviewing the appearances presented by the territory left behind. And, first, as to those of a geological character.

Every observant traveller who passes along this line of country cannot fail to perceive evidences throughout its extent of the great modification of its surface from Michilimackinac to the Mississippi. At Michilimackinac the calcareous strata are broken up into brecciated masses. Further on, in the vicinity of Green Bay, are enormous outliers of those beds of sandstone superincumbent to the lower limestone near Navarino and at Kaw Kawning, and which were probably once continuous through an immense area of country. Again, near the Apachquay Lake the same incoherent sandstone appears to have been broken down to form the present loose sandy soil of the adjacent country. There is, therefore, upon the whole, reason to believe that the denuding force which acted when the general water level was lowered, and which perhaps brought the primary boulders from the north-west, have carried away a vast extent of mineral surface; and that all the great deposits of loose sand in the country about Lake Winnebago, as well as those in the valley of the Wisconsin, the coves and dells and *coulées* between the sand-hills, which now so much diversify the face of the country, are results of the same denuding force. These arenaceous deposits are of a character so totally different from those which form the surface of the district lying between the south end of Lake Huron and Lake Erie, that we must consider them as the results of the breaking up of the general ancient strata of incoherent sandstone.

But other reflections, of a perspective character, forced themselves upon me during my passage through the country, which perhaps will be thought to deserve more consideration by the British reader, since the existing political relations between Great Britain and the United States invest them with an immense importance.

The fertility and productiveness of the country I had passed through gave me the highest idea of its capacity for maintaining a great agricultural population. It seemed to me as if I had never been in a country where agriculture could be practised with less expense, or with greater success. The land was of an easily drained surface, exceedingly fertile, and without rock sandstones to impede the plough and other agricultural implements. The climate, too, tempered by such vast bodies of fresh water, is universally mild in the vicinity of the lake country, whilst the winters are severe enough to keep the insects within bounds. The population, already enumerated by millions, will soon be more dense than any other equal portion of the United States, and in less than fifty years may be estimated at twenty millions of people. Such is the future granary of America, capable of producing wheat, maize, and pork to any extent, for the occasional wants of Europe, and of absorbing its surplus manufactured articles, such as will be required for the consumption of an immense population in easy circumstances.*

The question, therefore, as to the direction in which the commercial exchanges of so great a population are hereafter to be made must ever be an important one, and especially to British statesmen; for if the commerce of the lakes reached a value as high as one hundred millions of dollars, or twenty millions sterling, for the year 1844, which has been shewn by a statistical report laid before the Congress of the United States, it must within the next half century quintuple that figure.

The Americans have long been aware of the immense resources of that fertile western country, and have already executed very costly internal improvements for the purpose of uniting it with their Atlantic ports by canals and railways, and securing to themselves the whole of the vast internal commerce of that region. Independent of the communications that have been successfully opened through the states of New York and Pennsylvania to connect the waters of Lake Erie with the Atlantic, they have constructed the important canal which connects Lake Erie with the Ohio river; besides the canals and railways, more or less finished, of the states of Illinois, Indiana, and Michigan, through which a large portion of their products are contemplated to be forwarded. And now, as if to monopolise the universal transportation to the Atlantic, they are projecting railway communications to connect the states of Massachussets, of New Hampshire, and of Maine, *via* Portland, with the waters of the St. Lawrence, *through the province of Quebec!*

Greatly as this characteristic enterprise and commer-

* The immense fertile district here alluded to comprehends a great portion of the States of Kentucky, Pennsylvania, Ohio, Indiana, Illinois, Michigan, and Wisconsin. *Vide* map.

A PROPOSED BRITISH IMPROVEMENT. 207

cial sagacity is to be admired, we cannot look to such a state of things, and to the facts also that the flour and provisions that reach the American Atlantic ports are charged with all the expenses of American labour, American transportation, and American navigation; and that the manufactures exported from England for the consumption of the western states are almost entirely conveyed in American trading vessels; without inquiring whether the commanding position of Great Britain, holding as she does a more extensive territorial empire in North America than even that of the United States, does not call upon her to secure a large share of these commercial advantages.

It is demonstrable that it is in her power to do so by adopting such internal improvements of her own as would not only secure the desired commercial advantages, but greatly contribute to the security of her colonies. We have in British North America Atlantic ports, and can connect them—as the Americans have already done theirs, —with our fine rivers, the St. John's, the St. Lawrence, and with the great western lakes, into the very heart of that fertile country which I have spoken of as the future granary of America.

A railway could be constructed from Halifax in Nova Scotia, or from the flourishing city of St. John's, on the Bay of Fundy, to the river St. Lawrence, at less than one-quarter of the expense that such a line would cost in Great Britain. From thence it might be continued to Montreal, to Kingston, and round by the north shore of Lake Ontario, *via* Toronto, to the Welland Canal, which is altogether in British territory, and connects the waters of Lake Ontario with those of Lake Erie. Or a railway communication could be carried

ried over land from point to point to the water communications, as, for instance, stopping at Kingston, and steaming across Lake Ontario to the Welland Canal.

Whichever of these modes of communication were adopted, it is evident, that, having advanced from the Atlantic by such a line to the western termination of the Welland Canal, an internal improvement would have been constructed all the way through British territory to the very central part of the United States; and at a point where we have a perfect right to be, since the frontier between British North America and the United States divides the great western lakes, giving to each country an equal right to their navigation.

I shall proceed to make a few remarks on the commercial advantages to be derived from such an enterprise, and then allude to those which are more immediately political, which I regard as important and certain.

And, first, as to the inestimable advantage of opening a practicable and secure communication through the British colonies to the great western lakes, with the view of *commanding the wheat and provision market* in the adjacent American states.

In peace or in war, it may be relied upon that the western Americans will be always ready to sell their products to whoever will take the trouble to go amongst them, and pay a good price; and that nothing is more certain than that the supplies from the western states necessary for the consumption of Great Britain, which under the present state of things reach us by the American communications, can even in war be securely diverted into those which it is now proposed to construct in our own colonies. This, which ought always to be a consideration of great importance, becomes intensely so at the present time, when all the contingencies appertaining to an invariable supply of food for the British population have received so much attention both in and out of Parliament; and when a general conviction has been produced, that emergencies requiring a certainty of supply may be of such frequent occurrence, as to make measures of this character the first duty of the Government.

The political advantages which may be expected from immediately carrying out the communication now proposed are various and striking; and I shall first mention one which deserves great attention. It is obvious, that, in proportion to the establishment of a constant and profitable commercial intercourse with the people inhabiting those central western parts of the United States, would be their inclination to the maintenance of friendly relations with us. And this may be illustrated by what has been passing before our eyes.

In a republic founded upon universal suffrage, demagogues will always be found contending for power and emolument, seeking to become the leaders of the masses by flattering their cupidity and their prejudices. Without the support of the western people of the United States, Mr. Polk could not have been carried into the Presidency, nor without it will he be able to secure his re-election. It was to gratify them, therefore, that he held out such magniloquent declarations about the Oregon territory, which, lying towards the setting sun, has greater temptations for them than for the citizens of any other part of the Republic. This, of course, produced corresponding heroic declamations from western members of the Congress, to propitiate their constituents for their own re-election. But if the negotiations respecting that question had brought into jeopardy any direct profitable intercourse that those constituents were accustomed to have with British capital, those orators, who, during the late congressional session, indulged so largely in the " Ercles vein," might have been counted upon as the most pacific and reasonable men in the national legislature. Happily, all men begin at length to perceive that commercial prosperity is the true basis of human contentment, and the effectual guarantee of peace to mankind.

Next in importance, perhaps, is the certain increase of prosperity which the execution of this measure would bring to Canada and the other British provinces. The Canadians, seeing their resources cherished by the foresight and power of the mother country, would have the strongest motives to entertain a loyal and good spirit towards her; and, becoming a prosperous people, would in time be in their feelings, as in their interests, a willing integral part of the empire of Great Britain.

Lastly, comes the great consideration of the security of our provinces.

It requires no argument to prove that a republican people, so notoriously unquiet as their geographical position and their democratical form of government have made the Americans, must always remain doubtful and dangerous neighbours, against whose future power every wise precaution should be seasonably taken. The prudent and the good of that country are without political power, and are becoming worn out with futile attempts to acquire it. Every generation being still further removed from the salutary examples of the founders of their Republic, it may fairly be assumed that power will hereafter, upon too many occasions, be placed in the hands of men, who, to promote their own ends, will indulge the

DEFENCE OF BRITISH AMERICAN PROVINCES. 211

masses in any extravagance, however wild. The threat, openly made in some of the American newspapers, that hereafter no European power shall have authority in North America, and which has been in a qualified manner insinuated by their highest authority, is to me, who have watched so nearly the progress of popular power in that government, ominous of a general political cry of that character within the next ten years.

In this point of view, therefore, a combination of such internal improvements along our North American southern frontier, as would secure to our provinces the greatest amount of commercial advantages, and which would furnish at the same time an efficient and rapid communication through them for the purposes of their military defence, is much to be desired; for the establishment of an exclusive British line of communication from our North American Atlantic ports to the western lakes, *extending along our whole Canadian frontier*, would enable her Majesty's Government, upon great emergencies, to convey in less than twenty days reinforcements to those great inland seas, where future conflicts will find their field if, in time to come, our country is brought to so melancholy an alternative. It deserves attention, also, that the notoriety of the fact of our being perfectly prepared would greatly tend to preserve the blessings of peace.

In making these remarks, I have not thought it expedient to allude to any physical or statistical details appertaining to the operations contemplated by the execution of the measure: they are far from being discouraging, and all fall into the class of ordinary enterprises of this character. Having had opportunities of becoming familiar with the construction of railways, I can speak with confidence on this point, of which I have thoroughly satisfied myself on traversing more than once the whole line which has been described from St. John's to Lake Erie, when all the physical difficulties which presented themselves to me were considered upon the ground.

These views were many years ago communicated to a few friends; but at that time no prudent man would have publicly proposed the investment of capital for such an object, lest he should incur the charge of being thought visionary. Until of late even New Brunswick has generally been considered a wilderness, possessing few or no resources that could aliment the capital necessary for the construction of a railway across the province. But in 1839, when it was the scene of my labours, as her Majesty's Commissioner in the dispute with the United States on the north-east boundary, I became satisfied that the project could be successfully carried out, and that it would soon be called for by a sound policy.

Whether such a line of communication betwixt our Atlantic frontier and the St. Lawrence should have its eastern termination at St. John's in New Brunswick, or at Halifax in Nova Scotia, it is of the first public importance that the line should be as *direct* as possible. The measure is of too national a character to be trusted altogether to private enterprise, which would be very likely to carry it by unnecessarily circuitous routes to serve private interests. But although charters from colonial legislatures are always exposed to such influences, the inconveniences attending them can be corrected by the Crown, which alone is competent to decide upon the true *direction* of the line.

CHAPTER XXI.

KINDLY RECEIVED BY THE OFFICERS OF THE AMERICAN GARRISON OF PRAIRIE DU CHIEN.—AN ASSINIBOIN IRISHMAN.—TALENT OF THE INDIANS FOR IMITATING THE CRIES OF NIGHT BIRDS.

I HAD become so accustomed to the independent feeling of a traveller in Indian lands, carrying my own comforts and my own little world along with me, and sure of my own rude, but clean, bed at night, that I felt shy at communicating with this post at Prairie du Chien, where I was more certain to meet with some of the restraints of society, than to find greater pleasures than I knew how to procure for myself. The scene, however, before me was a pleasing one, and some of the officers of the garrison coming down to the beach to learn who we were, I landed, and was conducted by them to their quarters in an extensive quadrangle in the fort. Here I had a commodious room assigned to me; and almost immediately afterwards, that most respectable and gentlemanly officer, Colonel Taylor,* the commandant, called upon me and offered all the services in his power. It is impossible to express by words how much a traveller in these rude countries is touched by such attentions; and certainly it is due to the officers of the American army to say, that upon all similar occasions I have found them as hearty and as hospitable as men know how to be.

* Afterwards appointed to the command of the American troops destined to invade the neighbouring Republic of Mexico.

Having seen my Canadians encamped in a proper place, had my effects brought to the garrison, cautioned them against getting drunk, made my *toilette*, and supped with the officers at the mess, I paid a visit to the commanding officer, from whose quarters we adjourned to a small theatre, which had been fitted up to amuse the men and keep them from dissipation, where some of the histrionically disposed soldiers were that evening to represent the comedy of "The Poor Gentleman." Miss Emily was personated in a most astounding manner; such a monster in petticoats, and stick in feeling, probably never was exhibited before. The only three decent performers were an Englishman, an Irishman, and a Scotsman; the rest seemed to have neither sense nor feeling. It was a crowded house, and, from the applauses that were occasionally given, and the criticisms that I heard, I perceived at once the importance of turning the attention of common soldiers to intellectual exhibitions of this kind, which, besides affording much gratification, cannot fail to divert many of them from sinking into low debauchery. At this post I was fortunate enough to find letters from my friends.

September 1.—After breakfast, whilst I was occupied in answering my letters, Colonel T. called and sat an hour with me, conversing about the state of this part of the country, and the condition of the Indians. Being a Virginian of independent fortune, who chooses to remain in the army only because he is attached to the profession, his manners, like those of many of the superior officers of the American army, who are men of education, inspire great respect. Having accompanied the Colonel to his own house, I proceeded to the old French village to call upon Mr. Douceman, one of the most respectable inhabitants there, who is one of the managers of the fur trading company; and having communicated to him my intention of proceeding to the sources of that important tributary of the Mississippi, the St. Peter's, he was kind enough to promise me introductions to his agents in the upper country. This important step being happily concluded upon, I determined to take a rapid look at the rocks in the neighbourhood, and lose no time in preparing for my departure.

Directing fresh supplies of provisions to be prepared for our voyage up the Mississippi, I walked across the prairie to the limestone quarries at the bluffs east of the garrison. The escarpment, which is near 400 feet in height, consisted of horizontal beds of non-fossiliferous limestone of a grayish-buff colour, laying beneath the incoherent sandstone we had just left behind, and abounding in cavities containing crystals of carbonate of lime and whiteish chert. Towards the top the slabs of limestone were occasionally made up of concentric circles of various sizes, some of which were two feet in diameter.

From this bluff I had a fine view of the Mississippi, upon which, as the season was passing rapidly away, I was greatly desirous of being once more. The whole valley, from the rocks where I stood to those on the other side, appeared to be about two miles and a half wide; the little prairie being near two miles of the whole, and the Mississippi contributing the rest. This, then, is the breadth of the ancient flood that rolled through these regions.

Having dined in a very agreeable manner with Colonel and Mrs. T., I walked in the afternoon to the French village, and amused myself with talking to the *habitans*, who seem to lead the same sort of idle and adventurous life that all the Canadians do,—perfectly happy when they have enough to eat, and superlatively so when they are drinking and dancing. I had made the acquaintance at Navarino of a Mons. Rolette, an "*ancien habitant*" of this place, who had been long engaged in the fur trade, and he arrived here this day. I found him a jolly, intelligent person, and a *bon vivant*. He gave me a good deal of information of the upper country, and insisted upon my taking up my quarters with him on my return.

The hard task now remained before me of collecting my men for our departure in the morning. I heard but indifferent accounts of them : they were acting more like wild men than tame ones, most of them being in a continual state of intoxication. Even Beau Pré had not been able to resist the fascinating temptations of the place; but he was not as bad as the rest ; and upon my reminding him of his promise to be prudent, replied, "Monsieur, ce n'est rien du tout; vous trouverez votre monde ramassé demain à l'heure convenu."

September 2.—This morning, as I expected, the men were, most of them, very drunk, especially L'Amirant, and two of them were missing, which obliged us to run in every direction to ferret them out. Seeing some newly-erected Indian lodges at the northern end of the prairie, about a mile from the settlement, I went there to look for the delinquents; and upon reaching them, found that the people who inhabited the lodges had only just arrived from Pembināw, on Red River of Lake Winnipeg. Amongst them was a wild dirty-looking fellow, who appeared from his countenance to have a little white blood in him ; and taking him for a half-bred Canadian, I went up to him whilst he was conversing, in what I afterwards found was a dialect of the Assiniboins, with a short Indian woman with a papoose at her back, and addressed him. He answered me fluently enough, but in a strange sort of French, that the squaw was his wife, that he had taken her to live with him three years before on the Shayanne, a tributary of Red River. They had left Pembināw, as many others were preparing to do, because there was nobody there to purchase their produce, which had accumulated upon their hands. He said the soil was exceedingly rich, and that the settlers had grown a great deal of barley upon it, which had been wasted because there was nobody to use it. He now inquired of me if he could descend the river in his canoe all the way to "une belle ville dont il avait entendu parler, qui s'appelait Orleans, et où il y avait beaucoup de gens?" Having satisfied him of this, he informed me that he was going there "pour avoir des nouvelles de sa patrie." But the French he uttered was such a *baragouin* as would not be comprehended if it were put down on paper; and supposing he had lived so long amongst the Indians as to have almost forgotten his native tongue, I asked him what language he preferred, and he answered, "J'aime mieux parler avec ma femme."—"Well," said I, "were you born in the Pembināw country, or in Canada?" To my utter astonishment, he answered, "Je suis né en Irlande." "What!" I exclaimed, "am I talking to an Irishman?" His English, in which he now began to speak to me, was about as bad as the French he had acquired by associating with the *voyageurs;* but I extracted from it that he had been an Irish sailor on a voyage to Hudson's Bay, and that about twelve years ago he had, after a great many incidents, reached Lord Selkirk's settlements on Red River.

This poor fellow had managed to run down almost to the zero of civilization; and beginning to feel an interest in him, I gave him some good advice. I told him he could encamp on the banks of the Mississippi all the way down to New Orleans, without being interrupted or without paying anything; but that when he reached the city he would have to give money even for the privilege of setting up his lodge; that he would have to work hard every day to maintain his family, and that in my opinion he had better return to Pembināw, where he would be always sure of plenty to eat. He said he thought he would go to New Orleans first, for he had some skins to sell, and could always return if he chose. Finding him bent on proceeding, I told him he would find plenty of Irishmen at New Orleans; a piece of information which seemed to encourage him, for he spoke cheerfully to the squaw, who smiled and said something in return, so giving him a dollar, and advising him not to get drunk, I bade him "Good bye."

What with this Assiniboinized Paddy and my drunken fellows, it was noon before we got away from Prairie du Chien. These Canadians become very sulky when they are forced away from a debauch, as they love to keep it up for several days, and to be dead drunk at least once a day. I was obliged to be very rough with two of them to get them into the canoe; but a serjeant of one of the American regiments, a very respectable man, had, with the permission of his officers, obtained of me a passage to Fort Snelling, at the mouth of the St. Peter's, and I was glad of his presence upon this occasion, for after we had got matters sufficiently arranged to push out into the river, the serjeant and myself were obliged to hold L'Amirant by bodily force until we were in the stream; but the moment we let go, the fellow attempted to jump overboard, and it was more than an hour before the fumes of the liquor had sufficiently evaporated to make him available again.

We passed Ferribaw's Prairie, an exceedingly pretty scene, terminated to the east with graceful green slopes, crowned with mural precipices resembling the castellated rocks on the Wisconsin, but more developed and imposing. The Mississippi here is more than a mile in width, including some very fine islands. The bluffs on the west side corresponded with the strata on the east, and consisted of limestone, alternating with sandstone and cherty beds.

Paddling against the current of the Mississippi we found a very different thing from descending the Wisconsin in the easy way we had done; and, as I thought the men would be all the better after their debauch for a long night's rest, I gave the signal, after making about twelve miles, to pull to a very charming-looking island, which offered a good encampment. I thought that at this distance from Prairie du Chien the men would hardly attempt to run back to their Cytherea, but determined to watch them closely. Just where we landed the islands were so numerous that it was impossible to see both the banks of the river: the grass was very high, and the mosquitoes very thick, but the same disadvantages presented themselves every where, and we made the best of our situation.

All the islands being upon the same level with each other, and with the prairies and rich bottoms on the river's bank, and the soil in all these situations being the same deposited vegetable sandy loam, it was at once evident that they were all portions of the general deposit which constituted the ancient bottom of the river, when it flowed close to the bluffs on each side, and which had been cut through by the existing stream since the last great retreat of the waters of this continent, which has been before alluded to. The number of these islands is so great in this part of the country, that it is sometimes difficult to preserve the channel. Once or twice we got into a *cul de sac* during the afternoon, and only found out our error by discovering, as we advanced, that there was no current. Below the mouth of the Wisconsin the islands are much fewer in number, the increased volume of the Mississippi having worn a great many of them away after receiving that powerful stream; and south of the Missouri to New Orleans, its waters being greatly augmented by that river, the Ohio, the Arkansa, and other streams, almost all the islands which formed part of the bottom of the ancient river are washed away: below the Arkansa not one is left, all the vegetable loam being carried down to enlarge the delta, which extends into the Gulf of Mexico.

September 3.—The fatigue of the preceding day sent me to my leafy couch with a headache; and not having succeeded in destroying all the mosquitoes in my tent, I passed a disagreeable night, and was glad to get up at break of day. A fine, fresh, and fair breeze was stirring; so rigging a small sail, and getting my somewhat sulky men aboard, we started at 6 A.M., and made fine way against the current. We passed numerous transverse valleys coming into the Mississippi at right angles, about 1200 yards wide, all of them presenting mural escarpments like those on the banks of the Mississippi. The Canadians call these transverse valleys "*coulées:*" none of them appeared to run very far into the interior, though some of them may be found to do so on inspection. As we advanced, I could perceive a long line of rocks jutting out from the escarpments, exactly upon the same level; the appearance was so unusual, that I landed to examine it, and found it was the siliceous and cherty beds I had seen at Prairie du Chien, which having resisted the degradation to which the lower and softer beds had been exposed, had become a sort of cornice to the whole line of the escarpments. This exceedingly curious state of the rocky beds is peculiar to this part of the Mississippi, and gives an idea of architectural design to the cliffs on each side of the river, as if some lofty wall had been constructed at the summit of the fine slopes which run down to the river.

About nine we stopped on the right bank to breakfast, at the foot of an elevated bluff, about 500 feet high, which I ascended. The top of this bluff was the natural summit level of the country; and although the traveller, when in his canoe, may think himself travelling between lofty mountains, as Carver and other early writers have expressed themselves, yet when he looks down upon the river from the summit level, he sees that the channel of the Mississippi, between bluff and bluff, is a trough which the stream has cut out of the main land, and that the two banks were once united upon the same level with that where he stands. The trough from the point where I stood was about two miles wide, of which the water occupied but a limited portion, the existing main channel of the river having a serpentine course from the east to the west side, sometimes keeping one side for several miles, whilst the rest of the width was occupied by low flat islands, divided by inferior channels, the whole width being about two miles. I could perceive that the bluffs on the east side were occasionally intersected by lateral valleys a mile in width, all of them well wooded; these last being again intersected by minor valleys running parallel to the line of the river. Everywhere mural escarpments were to be seen, and the same siliceous cornice peeping out. It would be difficult for a geologist to look upon a rarer or more instructive scene.

We left our breakfast fire at half-past ten, and near twelve passed a fine cape, on the west bank, rounded at the termination with a mural escarpment, fronting the river, that seemed a work of art. The main channel was about 350 yards wide; and the wind veering round, we were obliged to take down our sail, and apply to the paddles again. We now passed a deep cove, between two remarkable capes, with truncated escarpments: one of these capes had been called Cap à l'Ail, from the circumstance of wild onions growing on the banks of a rivulet in the cove. At half-past two P. M. my men pointed out to me the mouth of Bad-axe River, on the east bank, a stream where the Sacs and Foxes, who under the Indian chief Black Hawk had taken up arms against the Americans in 1832, received the fatal blow which crippled them as a nation. Colonel Taylor and other officers engaged in this affair, had given me an account of it, which appears to have been badly managed both by the Indians and Americans, the latter of whom had nearly lost all their advantages from the want of a commissariat.

About 4 P. M. we got into a calm channel, about 100 yards wide, which wound about very tediously. Immense quantities of scarlet lychnis, in full blossom, were growing upon the banks of the small islands. This breadth of 100 yards continued for about ten miles, when we

PROPENSITY OF THE INDIANS TO MURDER. 223

again got into the main channel, about 250 yards wide. A heavy rain now fell upon us, and we soon became thoroughly wet through, and so uncomfortable, that we landed on the west bank; and having got our fires built, and the tent pitched, I changed my clothes, and had stakes put round my fire to dry my wet garments upon. Leaving them to take their chance between the rain and the fire, I supped and lay down, whilst torrents of rain were pouring down in one of the darkest nights I ever saw.

September 4.—The rain did not abate until seven in the morning, and we waited awhile to get our clothes dry. As we were breakfasting, a Canadian reached our encampment in a canoe from the north. He informed us that he had spoken with some Ojibway Indians at the mouth of Chippeway River, consisting of a party of forty warriors, who were watching the Sioux (Nahcotahs), to strike them. This was not pleasing intelligence to us, for we knew that some time ago a party of young Indians, being disappointed in meeting with those they intended to attack, fell in with a white trader and his companions, near to where we now were, and being determined to have some scalps, contrived to put the white men off their guard, and murdered them all. We were not without our suspicions that this Canadian had invented his story, for the *voyageurs* are fond of exaggerating trifles; but as the safe rule is never to run any risk by giving these treacherous marauding Indians opportunities, his account served to put me more than ever on my guard. According to him we had not yet reached Bad-axe River; so that either he, my men, my map, or altogether were in error.

Leaving our encampment at 8 A. M., we pursued our way; but the rain returning in very copious quantities, we went muddling on in it until half-past ten, when we stopped to breakfast in a very uncomfortable manner; and getting into the canoe again at twelve, continued on amidst a perfect deluge of rain, until all of us being done up with *ennui* and discomfort, I turned into a pretty cove, about half-past four, under the bluffs of the east bank, and we set to work at the old business of building up good fires. Whilst these were burning up, having plenty of daylight before me, I commenced the ascent of the bluff, which was here about 500 feet high. I had dressed myself this day in a new suit of patent waterproof clothes and leggings, for which I had paid a corresponding price: according to the theory of the thing, therefore, I had some right to suppose myself dry and tolerably comfortable. Of this I had some misgivings when I landed, and had not proceeded far through the tall grass, which was loaded with rain, when I arrived at a perfect conviction that I had never been more thoroughly wet through in my life. Soon after I reached the top the rain ceased, and the weather became clear. I enjoyed here another of those magnificent views which abound on the heights of the Mississippi. The valley betwixt the opposite bluffs was here near three miles wide, and I seemed to look down upon an immense forest, growing upon innumerable islands, among which various streams were gliding. Some of the islands were so extensive as to contain ponds of considerable extent, and large areas of the zizania, already frequented by the wild fowl, which had begun to arrive from the north in immense quantities. In every direction the same features were exhibited; the bluffs of the opposite banks were always of nearly the same height; shewing in the clearest manner that the valley before me was an immense furrow, which had been worn out in the country by the long action of water. These scenes never satiate the eye and the mind; and I availed myself of every opportunity, when we landed, to renew the enjoyment of them. Whilst wandering about here, I sprung two beautiful broods of *Tetrao*, which immediately took to the trees. I could have shot several of them, but had not my gun with me.

Descending by a different direction, to examine a naked escarpment, I found the siliceo-calcareous rocks alternated often with sandstone, with strong beds of sandstone of a rather compact kind at the base; but I could find no fossils in any of the beds. Having reached the camp a little after sunset, I hastened to relieve myself of my bedrabbed patent water-tight garments; and after a hearty supper, commenced the fatiguing business of drying everything by the fire, which occupied me until a late hour. Meantime, my people, who cared nothing about being in wet clothes, as soon as they had made their accustomed carnivorous meal, and enjoyed their noisy conversation and their pipes, wrapped themselves up in their blankets, and were soon all asleep. Left, whilst standing by my fire, to the uninterrupted action of a busy imagination, I was struck by the apparently intelligent manner in which the owls and other night-birds answered each other. Every now and then an owl to the north, not more perhaps than 200 yards from the camp, would put his questions in a rather startling and distinct manner, and after a measured interval of time, the response, equally distinct, would be heard from the south, very near to me; there being to me, who have a very nice musical ear, a sensible difference in the intonation and modulation of the two voices. I was very much interested in this; everything connected with natural history is pleasing to me; and the effect was exceedingly increased by the locality, the adventurous life I was leading, and the hour of the night. But what, more than anything else, excited my imagination, was the knowledge I possessed that the Indians are such exquisite mimics of natural sounds ; and that one of their tricks, when hovering about a camp, is to imitate the cries of night-birds, to lull their intended victims into confidence, and to communicate to each other their observations and intentions. My men, too, before they went to sleep, had been loudly disputing about some murders that the Indians had lately committed in the upper country to which we were now going, upon white men. Several of these Canadians had passed successive winters in the service of traders amongst the Sioux and Ojibway, two nations always at war, were acquainted with their principal chiefs, and, espousing different sides, openly justified some of these atrocities. Even the serjeant who was with us had been a long time on service on the frontier, knew a good deal about the Indians, and spoke a few phrases, and could therefore take his share in these conversations. The noise therefore that these fellows had made, if any marauding Indians had been near our bivouac, would have completely revealed our situation. We were exactly in a position to be overpowered by half-a-dozen savages, intent upon plunder and scalps, for all my men were fast asleep, and upon a surprise would have been scalped before they could have stood upon their feet.

In this situation, whilst engaged in drying my clothes, with the notion in my mind that the owls might be wolves in sheep's clothing, sometimes the dull crackling of the fire at the men's bivouac, and sometimes an equivocal sound in the forest, made me more than once retire

MUSQUITOE MURDER.

to my tent, lest standing by the fire I should be too certain a mark for an Indian rifle. Having remained on the alert a sufficient time, as it appeared to me, to disclose any plan or stratagem, and having settled in my own mind what it was best to do upon every contingency, I retired to my tent, to rival the worst murders of the Indians, in an uncompromising destruction of myriads of mosquitoes; my satisfaction at seeing them jump back into the candle being equal to that of an Indian, perhaps, when he has torn the scalp from his enemy's head.

CHAPTER XXII.

AN INTELLIGENT INDIAN AND HIS FAMILY.—REACH WABESHAW'S BAND.—SCAFFOLDS FOR DEAD BODIES.—CARVER'S SUPPOSED FORTIFICATIONS.

September 5.—On putting my head out of the tent in the morning, I had the satisfaction of seeing that all my people were alive, with a tremendous deluge of rain pouring upon them. Almost nothing short of a tomahawk will awaken a Canadian *voyageur* who lies down after his day's work, with six or eight pounds of fat pork and biscuits within him. The torrent came down so incessantly, that we kept snug until about 10 A. M., when it began to abate, and striking the camp, we took to the river again. At 2 P. M. we met a party of soldiers in a canoe, going from Fort Snelling to Prairie du Chien with the mail. I stopped for the men to dine at a place where, upon some trees which the Indians had blazed or cut smooth on one side, figures had been painted in black, and were very tolerably executed. Two Indians were represented, each with a scalped prisoner, and two animals representing their *totem*, or the tribe they belonged to. A horse was extremely well done, and an Indian dog still better.

At 3 P. M. we came up with Prairie la Crosse, an extensive slip of low land, so named by the French from the Indians formerly resorting to it to play a game with racket-sticks, resembling very much the Scotch game of golf. About 4 P.M. the sun came out, and we had a beautiful evening : this encouraged the men to get up a *chanson*, and having all got into good spirits after the constant discomfort we had experienced from the wet weather, I made the signal for landing a little past 5 P.M. at a beautiful slope, with a magnificent escarpment overhanging it. Just as we landed, one of the men knocked a large *Tetrao* down from a tree, which was cooked for my supper. This bird was not particularly good, and, indeed, was only made tolerable by the slices of ham that were fried along with it ; however, I made a hearty supper, and reclining by my cheerful fire, was exceedingly amused in observing the gesticulation of my Canadians, their extreme eagerness about the veriest trifles ; incessantly did the *sacrés* and other profane expressions roll out of their mouths during the conversation which was carrying on betwixt those who were laid down and those who were standing up with their wet blankets spread over their backs to dry at the fire. Certainly a more careless, happy people can hardly be imagined.

September 6.—The rain began to come down in torrents again about 4 A.M., and peeping out of the tent, I saw all the people with their heads and bodies wrapped up in their blankets, profoundly asleep, and snoring as if nothing could awaken them. About 7 A.M. it cleared off again, and whilst they were striking the camp, the serjeant and Beau Pré killed five large birds like the one of the preceding evening. These birds are as yet so unaccustomed to man, that they sometimes permit themselves to be knocked from their roost. About half-past eight we passed a good-looking encampment of twenty Sioux lodges ; but the band was gone for the autumnal hunt,

At 10 A.M. we stopped to breakfast within sight of what my people called "La Montagne de Trombalo," of which I had heard a good deal said. At half-past eleven we were in the canoe again. Before we reached Trombalo, we observed many Indian marks upon the white sandstone rocks, which were again becoming the predominant beds, and further on the name of *Catlin*, the artist, painted in large letters. I wish this enterprising and very clever person had left his portrait on the rock, which he might very conveniently have done, for at this place it comes perpendicularly down to the river. A fine mocassin snake was swimming about here, having perhaps fallen from the rocks; after several attempts I got him alive into the canoe, to the great horror of the Canadians, who have an unconquerable aversion to snakes. With the aid of the serjeant I got the snake skinned very neatly, and afterwards made an excellent specimen of it.

At 2 P.M. we reached Trombalo, and as this rock had attracted a good deal of notice, I determined to examine it carefully. It is not an island, as it has been supposed to be, but is an outlier of the sandstone and limestone bluffs, running nearly a mile and a half east and west, being separated from the west bank of the Mississippi, and not from the east bank, as some travellers have supposed; for the west bank of the Mississippi is distant from it only about 1200 yards, whilst the east bank is separated from it by a distance of five miles, the intervening space being occupied by an extensive prairie with few or no trees, and extending east and west about twenty-five miles, and north and south about five miles. In ancient times the Mississippi has covered this prairie, which has then been a lake or enlargement of the river. The loftiest part of this outlier is about 500 feet high, and is separated from the bluffs by a shallow swamp, here covered with trees, through which, in a swollen state of the river, perhaps a boat might pass. From this outlier, or part of the bluff, thus standing as it were in the water, the early French travellers called it "La Montagne qui trempe à l'Eau," which is now corrupted to Trombalo.

Having ascended to the crest of this Trempe à l'Eau, I found it to be a non-fossiliferous limestone, only three or four yards wide, running from north to south about 200 yards, and falling off in a steep precipice to the west, with compact sandstone at its base. Whilst I was contemplating the magnificent view around me, I saw three Sioux Indians in a canoe approach our fire, and descending, I found the serjeant talking with them, and getting such information from them about the state of the upper country as the few words he possessed enabled him to do. Taking out my list of Sioux words, and pointing to the water, the fire, the trees, &c., they gave me the true pronunciation of the Indian names of these natural objects. I then asked them the name of the mountain at the base of which we were, and they answered "Minnay Chon ka hah,"—literally, as I afterwards found, "Bluff in the Water,"—than which nothing could be more descriptive.

We left this place about 4 P.M., and landed for the night at six, at a blacksmith's shop built by the United States Government, for the use of a band of Indians in this neighbourhood, but now abandoned. There was, however, a log hut, a blacksmith's shop, an anvil, some iron and steel, but nobody to take care of them. As soon as the tent was pitched, and our fires lighted, a very respectable old-looking Sioux Indian, who had espied us from an island in the river, crossed over to our camp in his canoe with two children, a boy and a girl about nine and ten years old. He walked up to me as I was entering some memoranda in my note-book, and extending his hand, said "Capitaine! Capitaine!"—the only word he knew out of his own language. I now took out my vocabulary, and sending for the serjeant, we soon got into a way of understanding each other. About the names of things we had little or no difficulty, for he soon saw that I wanted him to give me the pronunciation, and when I pointed to anything, he would name it two or three times, and when I had caught the sound, and pronounced it to him from my book, he would give an approving grunt and smile. But when I wanted to ask him questions about their enemies, the Ojibways, whether any marauding bands of either nation were out, and whether I was likely to meet with any of them before I reached Fort Snelling, we got into a perfect colloquial bog. I knew nothing but the names of substantial things. The serjeant had pretended he could converse; but when he was brought to the trial, he stuck fast so repeatedly, first trying a French word, then an English word, and then introducing an Indian word, in such a preposterous manner, that we made very little progress, and it soon became so ridiculous as to make me laugh heartily. The *cheval de bataille* of the serjeant was the word "washtay," which signifies "good, pleasing, satisfactory," and according to the serjeant, must have had a great variety of meanings; for when he was in a difficulty, he often began with it, always ended with it, and generally when he was at a loss for a word introduced it, meaning always an appeal to the Indian, whether what he was saying to him was satisfactory, or, in fact, whether he understood him.

Having been some time on the frontier, the worthy

serjeant had had various little dealings with the Indians, had picked up a few of their words, and not a few of their ways, and, except in the particular matter of understanding their language, was, in fact, a very accomplished dragoman.

One question which I told the serjeant to ask him was, " Who was the maker of the moon ?" which happened to be shining at that time. Pointing, therefore, to the moon, he began with "Washtay?" the Indian grunting assent, for it was exceedingly beautiful. Then he pointed to the little boy, and said " Washtay ?" Next he took hold of the Indian's arm, and said " Papa washtay ?" and there he left the question, to the great astonishment of the good Indian, who must have been exceedingly puzzled to find the moon, his son, and himself all put into the same pleasing category. As we obtained no results by this manner of putting the question, the serjeant suggested that I should send for one of the men who had passed two winters in the Indian country, and who boasted he could "parler sauvage tout comme le Français." Finding this Indian a very patient and good-tempered man, I really was desirous of coming to some understanding with him as to his notions of natural theology, and at any rate of ascertaining whether he had thought at all upon the subject. I therefore sent the serjeant for the man, who came scratching his head and grinning on finding he was going to be employed as an interpreter. Having received my directions, he propounded something or other to the Indian in a few barbarous words, which were perhaps some slang of the *voyageurs*, to which the Indian gave no answer, but by some low grunts. This fellow having had no better success than the serjeant, said to me, "Monsieur, c'est inutile; ce vieux b—— n'entend rien du tout;"

and believing that very likely to be the fact, I told the interpreter he might go back.

The old man remained very contentedly about two hours; I gave him a part of my supper, and biscuits and sugar for his children, which they were quite delighted with, the word "washtay" escaping them several times when they licked the fair white loaf sugar, which they put by after tasting it. When my supper was over, he rose, took his children to the canoe, and I saw him by the moonlight paddling over to the island. I now entered the tent and began my evening's work of bringing up my notes, at the close of which, hearing some unknown voices at my fire, I looked out, and lo! my Indian acquaintance, his two children, and two of his wives, each of them carrying a male papoose. I now understood why he had taken his departure so abruptly, without bidding me "Good bye;" the truth being, that, pleased with my kind treatment of him, he had determined to bring his ladies to my camp, and introduce them to the *Capitaine*. I received them of course very kindly, shewed them the tent, of which they expressed great admiration, and presented them with various delicacies, one of which had such an insinuating effect upon them, that they lost all their Indian reserve, ate everything that I placed before them, laughed as heartily as ever I saw women do, and seemed to be perfectly happy.

The irresistible elixir which unstarched these Indian belles was kept by me more as a medicine than as a cordial, for use upon extraordinary occasions, in various bottles inclosed in wicker-work to prevent breakage, for I never taste anything of the kind myself; and the form in which I administered it to these ladies may be best described, perhaps, as a "glass of pretty stiff hot brandy and water, with plenty of sugar in it." Seated amidst them near the cheerful fire, under the brilliant moon, I could not but contemplate with interest the condition of these poor people. It was evident they were good-tempered, confiding, cheerful, and grateful, and might in time, by kind and judicious treatment, be raised from their degraded position. Beau Pré now came up and said that L'Amirant had passed several winters amongst the upper Sioux, and spoke the Yankton dialect pretty well. I was delighted to hear this, and sending for him, asked him if he really could converse with these people. Upon which he immediately addressed the man, and in a few minutes I found, to my perfect satisfaction, that he could interpret betwixt us.

The Indian now informed me that his name was *Ompaytoo Wakee*, or Daylight; that he was brother to *Wabeshāw*, a celebrated chief, who with his band resided at their village built on a prairie on the right bank of the Mississippi, which we should see as we passed up the river. *Minnay Chon ka hah*, the outlier we had visited in the afternoon, was in fact, he said, a sort of island, as there was an obscure passage round it. Finding I could now keep up a conversation with him, I asked him "where the moon went to when it set?" and he answered that "it went travelling on until it came up on the east again." I then asked him "who was the father of the two little papooses?" when he answered that he was. We now came back to the old question which the serjeant had so bungled, and I asked him "who was the maker of the moon?" when he immediately replied "*Wakōn.*" I asked him "who Wakōn was?" and he said that every Indian knew that the moon (*wee*), the sun (*wee ompay-*

too, "sun day"), the lakes (*minday*), the river (*wāhpadah*), the trees (*chagn*), the sky (*māhpayah*), the stars (*weechāhpee*), were all made by *Wakōn;* and here he pointed to the heaven, and said that the Indians after death went to the hunting-ground where the sun rises, and afterwards to *Wakōn*. I asked him if they ever offered anything to *Wakōn,* and he replied that good Indians never forgot to offer to him ; and said that it was the custom of his band to go to the top of *Minnay Chon ka hah* at the season for hunting wild geese, and that they made offerings to Mangwah* Wakōn ("wild goose god"), that he might be favourable to them in their hunting.

Ompāytoo seemed pleased to be talked to about such matters; he expressed himself like a sensible and rational man, and convinced me that the Indians entertained juster opinions of natural theology than they had credit for. When we parted I gave the women pork and biscuit, and they presented me with some teal in return. At the last moment I desired L'Amirant to tell *Ompāytoo* that all good white men believed Wakōn made everything as well as he did, and that they prayed to him to be good to them. That there was only one *Wakōn;* and, as he made both the Indians and the white men, they were

---

* The Indians are not polytheists : they believe in one Creator of all things, and when they speak of the *wild goose god*, it is only on the particular occasion when they pray to Wakōn to give them a good hunting season of wild geese. An experienced western trader told me that he was once with a tribe of the south-western Indians on a wild horse hunt ; and that the chief, on the morning they went out, put a piece of bear's meat on a stake, and holding it up, said "I have always given you a share of everything I have killed since I was a man ; but I am growing old like yourself now, and cannot hunt as well as I used to do. I hope you will remember that, and help me to catch a good lot of horses, and I shall always think well of you as a *"wild horse god."*

brothers, and *Wakōn* was their father. That, therefore, we ought all to love one another, and that I hoped he would tell the Indians a white man had said so. He shook hands very kindly with me, and it was late in the night when they left my camp to go to their *weetah*, or island.

September 7.—A foggy morning delayed our departure until 7 A. M., when we got under way for *Wabeshāw's* Prairie. *Ompāytoo* had informed me last night that his brother was not at home, being gone on a visit to Roques, a Frenchman who traded higher up the river at the foot of Lake Pepin, and who had been many years married to a Sioux woman. The Indians had named this Roque, who had a red blemish on his face, *Wāhjustachāy*, or "Raspberry." I remember well *Ompāytoo's* words, when I inquired if his brother was at home: "Wabeshāw Wāhjustachāy teebee" "Wabeshew is at Wāhjustachāy's house;" so I determined, on our arrival at the prairie, to make my *dèbût* in the Sioux tongue in these very words, adding an interrogative tone to them. We soon reached it: it was one of those beautiful bottoms, or natural meadows, on the Mississippi, which are occasionally to be seen, about seven miles long in one direction, a mile and a half wide, and was bounded on the south by a bold high bluff. The village consisted of twelve large oblong wigwams, or teebees, covered in with bark, and two round lodges, made with poles and covered with skins. As we approached the prairie, a great number of men came to the landing-place, painted in the most hideous manner, one-half of their faces being rubbed over with a whiteish clay, and the other side all begrimed with charcoal; not that they were going to war, but because they were in mourning for the wife of a chief of the second class, who had recently died.

Near the village several death-scaffolds were erected, formed of four poles each, about eight feet high, with a floor made by fastening shorter poles to them about seven feet from the ground, and the frail structure shored up by another pole extending to the ground. Upon this floor a rude coffin was placed, containing the body, and from one end of the scaffold a sort of bunting was flying, to denote the rank of the individual. Across the end of the coffin a part of the top of an American flour barrel was awkwardly nailed, with the words "steam mill" branded upon it, now covering food for the worms as it once did for men. An old squaw was standing near the scaffold of the defunct lady, howling in a most extraordinary manner. Around these scaffolds were numerous inferior graves, some of them containing full-length corpses, and others only the bones of the dead after they have remained too long on the scaffolds to hold together. This custom of only interring the bones in the ground has been very general amongst the Indians of North America, and, as has been shewn in another work,* gave rise to an opinion, from the shortness of the coffins, that a nation of dwarfs had once existed.

Great numbers of children were running about in every direction, almost all of them with their faces begrimed; and near one of the teebees a little boy, about four years old, was sitting down with a tuft of eagles' feathers stuck in his hair, and his face entirely rubbed over with vermilion. Finery is the besetting sin of these savages; any glaring colour, any feather that has adorned a bird, they think must adorn them. Poor creatures! they have not the means of procuring the gaudy contrivances that administer to the vanity of

* Excursions through the Slave States, &c., vol. I. p. 180.

civilization, and they but avail themselves of what is within their reach to gratify the same passion. A great many of the bigger boys were amusing themselves with bows and arrows.

Whilst my people were engaged in preparations for our breakfast, I made the most of my time in strolling about the village. What most surprised me was the interminable number of narrow foot-paths that led from the village into the long grass, and supposing that all led to something or other, I entered several of them, treading however very cautiously, as I saw it was necessary to do, without at first suspecting what their immediate purpose was. I had with some difficulty got to the end of one, and seeing it terminate, and myself no wiser, I turned round, and the whole mystery became at length explained. A squaw came from the village, and entering the path where I was, squatted down, and having gone through some ceremony or other, arose and returned. Now it was just possible, since these paths were in the immediate vicinity of the graves, that this popping down of the ladies might have some smack of piety in it; but various *faits accomplis* I had cautiously avoided made me think otherwise; and remembering the state of our encampment when we first bivouacked at Lake Winnebago, I returned to the place where I was to eat my breakfast, to see that the men had not made their fire amidst some ancient Coprolites, and not liking the appearance of things, I had my breakfast taken to the canoe.

As soon as I had finished, being curious to see the interior of some of the *teebees*, I entered some of them, commencing with "Wabesháw Wāhjustacháy teebee?" which the women always answered in the affirmative, and in a tone of great kindness; so that I began to feel great confidence in the acquirements I had made in the Sioux language. All the women I saw were intolerably ugly, and appeared to be old without exception. What with hard work and bearing children, those who are only thirty years old appear to be sixty: their shrivelled faces bore strong marks of suffering, and were as utterly without attraction as those of female baboons: even the youngest were so dirty, that they were not pleasing objects. Nothing could exceed the disgusting filth of this village, with the lazy brutal appearance of its begrimed inhabitants; and I could not but wish that my friend Mr. Cooper, the author of the "Last of the Mohicans," whose fine imaginative pen has delighted so many readers, but who, I believe, has never been amongst the Indians, had been with me to see how impossible it was for such a forty-horse power of sentimentality as he ascribes to Uncas and his Indians to grow up amidst such piggish filth as belongs to a wild people like these.

We left Wabeshāw's village about noon, just as a flock of pelicans were crossing the river. The valley of the Mississippi is here near three miles in breadth, and the main channel about a mile and a quarter, bluffs and coves presenting themselves in every direction, and everywhere beautiful. We stopped for the night, at 6 p.m., at a pretty wooded slope on the left bank; and I was not much surprised to find myself attacked with an incipient sore throat, accompanied by a little fever, from having so often been wet of late, and from sleeping in a wet tent. The weather, however, had become more promising, and confiding in it and the temperate life I led, I merely put a piece of flannel round my throat, and lay down.

September 8.—I rose at sun-rise, and felt much better. It was a beautifully clear morning, and about six we got under way. The wind had been so high in the night, that I sometimes felt apprehensive for the tent, which had been incautiously pitched near some trees that were to windward; and trees on these slopes having but very little hold of the soil, frequently blow over. A tent should never be pitched without well considering the state of the ground, the wind, and the weather. As we proceeded, we met a canoe containing a naked brawny Sioux, two women, and several children. The serjeant asked him if they were his wives, when he replied that one was, but that the other was his mother. Upon which L'Amirant, who had a good stock of impudence, said "How do you know she is your mother?" Putting his hand on his breast, the Indian answered, " Mamma utah" ("I fed at her breasts;" *utah* means "to eat"), and certainly no answer could have been more simple or expressive.

We stopped to breakfast about 9 A.M., and enjoying this meal much more than I did my dinner yesterday evening, I considered myself out of danger of an attack of sore throat, an enemy I have suffered severely from. Here we shot a great many wild pigeons, which being fat were a very acceptable addition to our larder. I observed also a great many grey squirrels about, but no black ones, which I have seen abound so much in Upper Canada.

I had read with some interest, in Carver's travels, an account* of some curious remains of fortifications, which

---

* One day, having landed on the shore of the Mississippi, some miles below Lake Pepin, whilst my attendants were preparing my dinner, I walked out to take a view of the adjacent country. I had not proceeded far before I came to a fine, level, open plain, on which I perceived, at a little distance, he had seen "some miles below Lake Pepin," but I had not been able to find any one who could corroborate his account. We were now, by computation, very near the locality, and judging him to refer to the right bank of the river, although he does not say so, I frequently stopped, and either went or sent some one to take a look at the country from the top of the bank. L'Amirant having told me there was an extensive prairie not far

> a partial elevation, that had the appearance of an entrenchment. On a nearer inspection, I had greater reason to suppose that it had really been intended for this many centuries ago. Notwithstanding it was now covered with grass, I could plainly discern that it had once been a breastwork of about four feet in height, extending the best part of a mile, and sufficiently capacious to cover 5000 men. Its form was somewhat circular, and its flanks reached to the river. Though much defaced by time, every angle was distinguishable, and appeared as regular, and fashioned with as much military skill, as if planned by Vauban himself. The ditch was not visible, but I thought, on examining more curiously, that I could perceive there certainly had been one. From its situation, also, I am convinced that it must have been designed for this purpose. It fronted the country, and the rear was covered by the river; nor was there any rising ground for a considerable way that commanded it—a few straggling oaks were alone to be seen near it. In many places small tracks were worn across it by the feet of elks and deer; and from the depth of the bed of earth by which it was covered, I was able to draw certain conclusions of its great antiquity. I examined all the angles and every part with great attention, and have often blamed myself for not encamping on the spot, and drawing an exact plan of it. To show that this description is not the offspring of a diseased imagination, or the chimerical tale of a mistaken traveller, I find, on inquiry, since my return, that Mons. St. Pierre and several travellers have, at different times, taken notice of similar appearances, on which they have formed the same conjectures, but without examining them so minutely as I did. How a work of this kind could exist in a country that has hitherto (according to the generally received opinion) been the seat of war to untutored Indians alone, whose whole stock of military knowledge has only, till within two centuries, amounted to drawing the bow, and whose only breastwork even at present is the thicket, I know not. I have given as exact an account as possible of this singular appearance, and leave to future explorers of these distant regions to discover whether it is a production of nature or art."—Travels through the Interior Parts of North America, in the Years 1766, 1767, 1768. By J. Carver, Esq. Pp. 57, 58. London, 1778.

from Roque's, on reaching it about noon I landed there, and ascending the bank, perceived, through some evergreen trees, unusual elevations about a mile and three-quarters off. Directing the boat to wait for me, I immediately walked across the prairie, a distance of about two miles, and on reaching them entertained no doubt that this was the remarkable locality seen by Carver. It certainly was a very curious place: the prairie was entirely level as far as these elevations, and the surface was completely composed of dusty sand, covering a black alluvial mould.

The first of these certainly had the appearance of an ancient military work in ruins: it had a steep sandy slope to the top, and resembled a very irregular work, entirely covered with drifted sand, consisting of something like three bastions and various salient angles. Inside of the work was a large cavity, and a slope of twenty yards to the bottom. There seemed also to be the remains of terraces. Outside was what might, perhaps, without exaggeration, be called a ditch, whether made by men or the wind, with a terrace of eight paces broad to the north-east. The inside of the cavity was about seventy paces in diameter, and the whole elevation was 424 paces in circumference. Distant from this about 700 paces south-south-east was a second, resembling it in form and size; and 700 paces east-south-east from this last was a third, the largest of the three, being 1100 paces in circumference, having, like the others, what represented bastions and salient angles, and being capable of containing 1000 people. Its walls appeared lofty when standing on the outside, and there was a deep ditch on the south side. Further to the south I counted six more. Nor was there wanting what an observer might fairly call a communication from one to the other and to the river, for the ground was thrown up all the way to it. From the highest point at which I stood I could distinguish a line of similar elevations extending at least four miles.

At the northern end of this singular assemblage of elevations they most appeared to have been the work of art, whilst at the southern termination they gradually passed into an irregular surface, and became a confused intermixture of cavities and knolls, that I think might be satisfactorily accounted for by the blowing of sand. In this part, as Carver observes, were still a great number of straggling oaks.

It is possible that all this may have been done by the wind blowing a decomposed sandstone into these forms; but from the limited opportunity which I had of examining these appearances, I was far from being convinced of this. The substance of the prairie was a vegeto-alluvial deposit, having a light covering of sand upon it; and if it was the wind which had thus distributed the sand so evenly upon the surface, how are the raised lines which are continued down to the river, and the elevations which so much resemble fortifications, to be accounted for? The same wind could hardly at one time lay the sand equally upon the prairie, and at another build up structures so much resembling works of art. Those, however, who think so after personal inspection, are bound to satisfy themselves why the wind has not produced similar effects upon the surface in other parts of this extensive prairie? It is difficult to suppose a force of that kind proceeding uniformly to produce effects that so extremely resemble a line of defence constructed by a barbarous people. But after all comes the question,—what were these fortifications intended to defend? Carver certainly talks somewhat extravagantly when he speaks of their being fashioned with the skill of a Vauban. I regretted not having leisure to dig about them; but the sand was so blown over the whole, that it would have required a great deal of time to clear only a very small space away. Hereafter, when this curious place becomes more known and investigated, if Indian antiquities should be discovered commensurate with the extent of the work, such as the stone instruments and weapons of offence usually found about Indian encampments, it would decide the question.

At 6 P.M. we arrived at what is called the Grand Encampment, being an alluvial bottom with some scattered trees. Perhaps it may have received its name from the contiguous elevations I have spoken of. A great number of Indians had temporarily assembled here; and as soon as our canoe appeared in sight, they came to the bank and followed us along shore until we had selected our bivouac, which I was very careful to do in a place where these gentry had not been before. They were rather troublesome to us, were too numerous for me to gratify them all with presents, and I could find no chief amongst them.

It was evident that I was getting into a part of the country very much overrun with the *Sioux*, and that I could not advance comfortably without a regular interpreter, through whom I could maintain a good understanding with them. As far as I could make it out, all the Indians we should now meet on the right bank of the Mississippi were bands of the widely-spread people who had received the name of *Sioux* from the French, a term now recognized by the Indians. On the other side of the Mississippi the country was possessed by the *Ojibways*, a still powerful people; and betwixt these two races, only divided by the Mississippi, as fierce an antipathy existed as ever prevailed betwixt the two nations who inhabit the opposite sides of the British Channel.

Hastening to get my fire built, I retired to my tent to eat my supper, leaving the men to squabble with the Indians. The usual quantity of pork and biscuit—a pound of the first and two pounds of the other—for each man had been already served out, and the provision-bags replaced in the tent. I knew the Canadians would surrender no portion of their allowance to the importunities of the natives, and hoped that, finding they could obtain nothing, they would go away to their own fires, which at length they did, and we were left in peace. During the night I looked out to see if anything was going on, but the Indian bivouac was as quiet as our own. If they had had any whisky we should have had a mad uproar all the night; but the wise regulations of the United States Government preventing the introduction of ardent spirits amongst the Sioux, and which seem to be faithfully carried out, were made evident by the silence of the night.

CHAPTER XXIII.

REACH LAKE PEPIN.—HEAR THE CATARACT OF ST. ANTHONY.—REACH FORT SNELLING.—ENGAGE MILOR AS A GUIDE, AND GET INTO VERY BAD LODGINGS.

September 9.—We got the canoe under way at the dawn, and plying our paddles, reached *Wajhustachay's*, or Roque's, at 7 A. M. The house of this trader was well situated at the south-eastern end of *Lake Pepin*, upon the edge of a high prairie fifty feet from the water, on the right bank of the Mississippi. It will make an excellent site for a town, there being a little stream emptying into the Mississippi, wide enough for boats to go up into the prairie some distance. On the opposite side of the Mississippi is Chippeway River, one of its most important tributaries in this part of the country, the sources of which are at a great distance to the north-east, not far from Lake Superior.

At this place I found Wabeshaw, the chief of the band I had visited the preceding day, with some other chiefs. He was dressed in a red-coloured garment, and acted and spoke like a person still conscious of possessing some authority. Roque was from home, but we found his wife, an active bustling Indian woman, who seemed to be a very good housekeeper, and from her I procured a supply of potatos and a bottle of fresh milk. She had two daughters by this Frenchman, one of whom I saw, a rather pretty half-breed girl, about eighteen; the other was married to a Frenchman, and lived with him in a small hut close by. I suppose M. Roque, like many others of his countrymen, had shaken hands with civilized society, for everything about his house was perfectly Indian.

Wabeshaw was grave, and not communicative. I understood afterwards that he was dissatisfied with the proceedings of the agents of the United States, and looked with great anxiety to that much-feared moment, when he, too, would be called to a treaty of cession of his lands, and be compelled to move to some distant country. He therefore dreaded the appearance of white men. I had, however, some conversation with him of a general nature. He told me that they had no name for the Mississippi, but *Wāhpadah Tanka*, or "Great River;" and none for Lake Pepin, but *Minday Tanka*, or "Great Lake." Indeed, when we consider that this immense continent was occupied by various races of savage people, speaking different languages, and each of them before the arrival of Europeans in America inhabiting and hunting in particular districts, without issuing from them except when upon warlike excursions, we see the impossibility of the word "Mississippi," or any other word, having at any time been a general name for this stream amongst the Indians of North America. In many of the dialects of the Lenape, and of the aborigines settled upon the Atlantic coast, the word *seepee* meant river; and in the Ojibway, and even Knistenaux, which are northern branches of the same family, it means the same thing. The early French adventurers, as they advanced westward, appear to have carried this word with them, and adding the word "Missi" —not in any Indian tongue that I have any knowledge of—to it, we have thus obtained the word "Mississippi," which some writers, without authority, have stated to mean the "Father of Rivers,"—a rather nonsensical interpretation, since, being a flood resulting from the confluence of many streams, it might with greater propriety have been called the "Son of Rivers."

Taking leave of Madame Roque and her guests, we pushed off into the lake, accompanied by two canoes, in one of which was a young buck of an Indian, with an eagle's feather stuck in his hair, and long strings of beads depending from a slit in his ears: in the other were two squaws, with long flowing black hair, and a little boy; the oldest woman sat in the stern of the canoe, and guided it with her paddle, whilst her companion and the boy worked away vigorously at their paddles. Each of the women had a petticoat on, and a jacket slightly fastened with a silver brooch.

About half-past eight we landed on a sandy beach, on the east side of the lake, to prepare our breakfast. I had purchased a fine cat-fish of the Indian in the canoe, and they were frying part of it for me when one of those north-west winds, which at times agitate this lake so fearfully, and which had been rising for some time, came down upon us with such force that we were in an instant covered with flying sand, and our breakfast preparations utterly ruined. This lake trends north-west and south-east, and being completely raked by these occasional high winds, is at such times very dangerous for canoes. On re-embarking we found our situation far from being an agreeable one; the waves of the lake were very high, and, as we advanced upon the broad lake, became tumultuous. It required the greatest dexterity on the part of Beau Pré to keep the head of the canoe in a proper position. It was evident that a slight mistake would immediately be fatal to our frail machine. More than once I had my apprehensions about the result, for it being necessary for us to cross the lake to the right bank, we found an unexpected high sea in the middle, and not daring to steer in the trough of the waves, were obliged to keep the canoe's head to the wind. All our men were grave, none of them spoke, and all I said once or twice was, "Prudence toujours, Beau Pré." He was very prudent, and by taking every advantage of an occasional lull, we at length got into smoother water, under the lee of the right bank. Here my apprehensions being over, I became sea-sick, and upon reaching a point of land called by the French Pointe aux Sable, was glad to get ashore near the remains of an old French trading post. Nearly opposite to this place there is a bluff on the other side of the lake, distant about three miles and a half, of rather a remarkable character. It is an escarpment fronting the south-west, about 1400 yards long, lying between two well-wooded coves, with a vertical depth of horizontal beds of about 150 feet, and a wooded slope from it to the river. It is now called "The Lover's Leap," a story being attached to it of some Indian Sappho, which is probably an invention suggested by the perpendicularity of the precipice.

The wind having lulled a little, we re-embarked and got to the head of the lake about 5 P. M., which by computation appeared to be about twenty-one miles distant from the south end. There are two large channels at the head of the lake, and we took the one dividing the right bank from an island about twelve miles long, edged all the way by lofty and beautiful trees. We stopped at a very commodious camping place, upon the island, a little before six; and having got my tent pitched, I sat down to a hearty supper of fried cat-fish, decidedly the best fish I have tasted in the western country.

September 10.—We struck our camp at the dawn, leaving our excellent bivouac, with its smooth, clean ground, and abundance of the best dry fire-wood. All were delighted at having exchanged the turbulent and dangerous surface of the lake for the secure amenity of the river. About 7 A.M. we stopped at an Indian village, consisting of eight large teebees erected near the bank of the Mississippi. On our arrival a number of Indians of both sexes, children, and dogs, issued from them. We had taken them by surprise, for they appeared all to have been sleeping when we came up, and were roused by the sound of our paddles. The principal chief was *Māhpayah Māzah*, or "Iron Cloud"; there was also another chief, called *Māhpayah Mōnee*, or the "Cloud that Walks." Some of the Indians at this place had come from a great distance, and being unaccustomed to see white people, were very curious. I wore a large Mackinau blanket coat of a bright green colour, which attracted their attention; and being told I was the chief of the party, they followed me wherever I went. We were surprised to find the two canoes here which had left Roque's with us: they must have worked very hard to have outstripped us, one of them only having a pair of paddles; but the Indians are more skilful than the whites in the management of canoes, and we probably lost a great deal of time upon the lake. The maize they raised here appeared to be of a very good quality.

At half-past 8 A.M. we reached six lodges full of Indians, all busy drying their maize. The men were fine brawny-looking fellows, all, as usual, in excellent condition at the end of the summer months, and what rather surprised me was to see them working as hard as the women. We stopped and had a few moments' conversation with them, during which they informed me we should soon reach a tributary of the Mississippi, called Hōhāng, or "Fish River," giving a nasal termination to the word, which reminded me of the Winnebagoes. All these Indians had very fine teeth. From hence we crossed to the left bank, which is low and rolling, and without those fine escarpments we had found below. At nine we stopped to breakfast, and were overtaken in a short time after by our Indian fellow-travellers of Lake Pepin, with some other individuals they had taken on board. There was a frightful-looking old squaw, with a little boy, a youth about twenty, with strings of wampum hanging from his forelocks, and his face all be-grimed with charcoal, whilst his sister, a tolerable-looking young squaw, about nineteen, had only a black grimy spot on each cheek. The journey they were upon was connected with the death of a relative, and the party had gone into cheap mourning, which, nevertheless, amongst these simple and rude people, is the symbol of wounded affections. The old crone, as soon as she arrived, came to me and begged some gun-flints, and I gave her a couple, as well as some biscuits. They had got a quantity of half ripe sour wild grapes in their canoe, and were eating them with apparent satisfaction. I had repeatedly observed that they permitted their children to eat as much as they pleased of these harsh fruits, the consequence of which was, that they all had violent bowel complaints, of which many died.

About eleven, the wind coming aft, we rigged a sail and glided along very pleasingly. At 1 P.M. the banks became again about 300 feet high, the escarpments coming down to the water's edge; and at half-past four we had nothing but round knolls on the left bank about 100 feet high, all well covered with grass. Here we came in sight of the *Hōhāng*, or as the French call it, the St. Croix river, which I suppose to be about thirty-eight miles from Lake Pepin. I left the canoe for a moment, and ascended the bank, from which I saw that this stream, about two miles from its mouth, becomes a lake, and that its left bank was low, and exhibited some beds of horizontal limestone. From this point the Mississippi became gradually narrower, diminishing to 250 yards, where there is a prairie on the right bank, and at length, after winding very much, becoming only 100 yards wide. Here I stopped at half-past 5 P. M. for the night, on the right bank, at a fertile bottom, where there was a small deserted house not far from our bivouac, once occupied by a trader of the name of Brown, formerly a discharged soldier. This Mr. Brown, the serjeant informed me, was a gay deceiver amongst the Indian fair. First, he married, after the Indian fashion, a half-breed young beauty, the daughter of a person named Dixon; then, becoming tired of her, he took another wife of the same degree, a daughter of a Mr. M‘Kay. They had both of them lived with him at this place. But casting off the second, he had acquired such an exceedingly bad character for abandoning his women and children, having played the same trick with two or three white wives in the States before, that he had found it convenient to move away to a very remote part of the Indian country, where he was unknown.

Whilst the men were pitching the tent I heard a deep throbbing sound coming at intervals from a great distance, which the men told me proceeded from the cataract of St. Anthony. The evening being fine for fishing, I took the serjeant with me, after I had supped, to an Indian lodge I saw at a distance, hoping to be able to borrow one of their canoes, our own having been landed for the men's bivouac. We found an old squaw, her son, and some young children at the lodge, but no canoe. I therefore promised the youth a piece of pork if he would go with the serjeant and bring a canoe, for we were very sure they had hid the one which belonged to them; but the little fellow refused to go unless he was paid first, so I told the serjeant to return to the camp and procure a piece. But now another difficulty arose; the old squaw would not let me stay by her fire until they came back, because she said her children would be frightened and would cry. All this distrust, as I found afterwards, was owing to the ill-conduct of the soldiers and other white men at Fort Snelling, who often took the canoes of the poor Indians without their consent, and did not return them. Indeed, I was sorry to learn from the serjeant that they were not famous for keeping their word with the natives at all. We procured a canoe at length, but had no success; and I retired to my tent rather late, listening to the throbbing sound of the cataract until I fell asleep.

September 11.—This being a place where we were very much annoyed with the mosquitoes, we were glad to pursue our course early in the morning. We found the river free of islands, and not more than 150 yards wide. On our way we met a canoe with Mr. Johnston, a half-breed brother to Mr. Schoolcraft, who had been serving as interpreter to a party of surveyors that had

A NOBLE-LOOKING INDIAN.

been running a divisional line betwixt the Sioux and the Ojibways. He was an intelligent person, and gave me a great deal of information about the Indian country as high up as Otter Tail Lake, which I returned in news about his friends at Michilimackinac. Immense quantities of wild grapes, but of a very inferior quality, were growing in this part of the Mississippi. At 9 A. M. we stopped to breakfast, and were soon joined by five canoes with Indians, including the old mourning party of Lake Pepin. All of them were hideously daubed with black and white. In one of the canoes was a youth of a remarkably noble figure, most woefully begrimed and covered with dirt, with a ragged blanket spread over his shoulders; but notwithstanding these disadvantages, there was an air of superiority so strongly implanted in him by nature, that no filth could obscure it. I never before saw a human being that had such an imperial air, and so fine a carriage of his person. If it had pleased God to fashion all kings and princes after the model of this savage, men would never have doubted of royalty being of divine origin, not even in Portugal.

Having breakfasted and regaled our begrimed companions with a little pork, we all started again, and soon came up with another village, consisting of six teebees, where our Indians stopped. Beyond this place I landed to examine some rocks in place, consisting of a tough and contorted limestone; and a little higher up the beds became very cavernous, and contained concentric masses like those at Prairie du Chien: in some of them the laminæ undulated and often affected the concentric form, as if the mineral had a tendency to resolve itself into a globular state. The Mississippi was singularly beautiful here, flowing in a stream of about 300 yards wide through its banks, lined with fine forest trees, vines, and shrubs, the limestone frequently showing itself near to the water.

At 4 P.M. we stopped a short time at the village of *Tcháypehámonee*, or the "Little Crow" (all the villages go by the name of the chief). The Indian men were principally gone to hunt the buffaloe, but the women and children, a sad squalid-looking set, came running down to us to obtain pork, which, after I had distributed some amongst them, brought out an elderly man with four fine wild ducks, which he bartered with us as we were leaving the place. Two years ago this Little Crow band was almost destroyed by their mortal enemies the Ojibways, who, whilst they were hunting at the upper end of Lake St. Croix, surprised them in the night and massacred forty of them. About 5 P.M. we came up with a bluff of incoherent sandstone about 180 feet high, like that on the Wisconsin. The Indians say there was formerly a large cave here, but that the rock fell in and covered it up. I landed, and endeavoured to trace some vestige of the cave, but in vain, a talus of hundreds of tons of fallen rock covering the entire slope. We now crossed over to the opposite side and encamped.

September 12.—In the morning we were embargoed by a dense fog until near 8 A.M., but at length got away, and found the banks of the river for some distance flat and woody, the soft sandstone having evidently been removed. In the course of an hour we came abreast of another bluff, receding a little from the river, with a short ravine leading to it, from which issued a spring of good water. I landed, and following it about

200 paces to a cave, found it was a famous locality which some of the chiefs had described to me as *Wakōn Teebee*, or "House of the Spirit." The ravine ended in a circular wall of soft sandstone, about forty feet high, to the right of which is the entrance to a very fine cave, about eighteen feet in height and thirty feet wide. After advancing a few steps the cave lost its dimensions, became six feet and a half high and ten feet wide. I entered it forty paces, when the stream which ran down the centre of it, and which was the one we saw on landing, overflowed the ground, and became too deep to walk. From hence I heard a rumbling sound of falling water within the cave, and throwing stones as far as I could, I could distinguish by the sound that they fell into deep water. Like many other caves, this appears to have a reservoir of water in it arising from springs, that in long periods of time have effected the excavations in the rock, which is so soft and incoherent as to be easily cut by a knife. I found many pebbles of primary rock in the cave, which must have been brought there by floods subsequent to its formation.* This cave is very well described by Carver, who mentions the figures which the Indians had cut in the rock, and which I also observed there.

Leaving this very curious cave, which I regretted not being prepared to explore, we recommenced our voyage, and passing the mouth of the *Minnay Sotor*, or St.

* In a communication made by me to the Geological Society of London, in 1828, a cave is described in the Helderberg mountain, in the state of New York, containing a thick bed of detritus, consisting of slate, limestone, and primary rocks, through which a stream flowing from a reservoir of water has worn a passage. This cave is many hundred feet above the level of the existing waters.

Peter's river, soon after 10 A. M. came in sight of Fort Snelling, the last American garrison in the Indian country. This imposing-looking post is situated on the top of a bluff on the right bank of the Mississippi, which fronts a water communication betwixt this river and the *Minnay Sotor*, the mouth of which being somewhat hid by a low flat island, was not observed by Father Hennepin when he ascended the Mississippi in 1680. This communication is, in fact, a *cut-off* or channel which the waters of the river have made into the St. Peter's, the current running in that direction. The bluff presents a fine section of the horizontal rocks, and I was very much struck with the noble appearance of the fort. Here we landed, and giving directions to the men to pitch the tent on the plain below, I commenced the ascent of the hill to pay my respects to the commandant, examining cursorily the limestone beds superincumbent upon the soft sandstone, in which were a great variety of fossils, such as *orthocera, bellerophon, fucoides, orthis,* and other fossils characteristic of some upper beds of silurian limestones. Upon entering the quadrangle of the fort, Major Bliss, the commandant, advanced to meet me: he appeared a straightforward soldierly sort of person, and very civilly said he would order my luggage to be taken to a room, adding that he would be happy if I would drink tea with himself and his lady in the evening.

I was now presented to some of the officers, and then permitted to stroll about and look around me; after which I returned to the fort at the dinner-hour, thinking it possible some charitable Samaritan might ask me to dine; but that interesting moment slipping away, I found Duke Humphrey was likely to be my only patron. I determined, therefore, to lose no time in making arrangements for my departure, and, descending to the bivouac of my men, got into the canoe, and was paddled over the St. Peter's to Mr. Sibley's, the agent of the fur company, to whom I had letters of introduction, and upon whom I relied to procure me a good guide and interpreter to accompany me in my projected adventure to the sources of this fine stream, which rise at the Côteau de Prairie, a dividing ridge that separates them from the waters of the Missouri. The Indians in that part of the country had not hitherto mixed with any white men who were not traders; and it was essential to my safety and successful progress to take every proper precaution, and especially to be provided with a respectable guide and interpreter known to the Indians.

Mr. Sibley received me very kindly, and immediately offered me quarters at his house, which I certainly should have accepted, if I had not thought it might give umbrage at the fort. Having explained to Mr. Sibley my intentions and wishes, he confirmed me in the opinion I entertained of the expediency of engaging a guide, and was kind enough to say that he had a half-breed in his service who was exactly the sort of person I wanted, and that, if I approved of him after conversing with him, an arrangement should be made for him to accompany me. The man was immediately sent for, and soon after arrived. He was a fine Frenchman-looking Indian, about fifty-five years old, tall and active, and was, as he told me, the son of a French officer by a Saukie woman; "et c'est pour quoi, Monsieur," said he, "la compagnie" (the fur company) "m'a donné le nom de *Milor*." The *sequitur* was not very clear, but the name was a very good one, and betokened some good qualities, of which Mr. Sibley said he possessed a great many, besides speaking the Sioux and other Indian tongues perfectly well, and having been familiar from his youth with every inch of the country. Being prepossessed with his appearance and pleased with his conversation, I immediately engaged him, considering myself very fortunate in obtaining the services of such a person.

Mr. Sibley's agency was well situated on the right bank of the St. Peter's, about three-quarters of a mile from its mouth, opposite the small island of alluvial soil called Terribaux, from a French trader, which lies betwixt the river and the channel at the foot of the fort. The St. Peter's from hence can be seen coming in from the south-west, winding through the country in a pleasant fertile vale of about a mile and a half in breadth, its banks having a general elevation of about 120 feet.

Having given Milor my instructions, and directed him to be constantly in attendance at the fort, that I might devote every leisure moment to the acquisition of information from him about the state of the upper country, where I now proposed to proceed, I returned to Fort Snelling in time to drink tea with Major Bliss and his lady, who entertained me hospitably and agreeably; but what with bustling about in the cave in the morning, the fatigues of the day, and the horrible atmosphere of tobacco smoke I had been obliged to breathe at the agency of the fur company, where all hands appeared to be constantly smoking, a nervous sick head-ache which had seized me became so violent, that I asked to retire. In such a state of distressful feeling as I experienced, I longed for retirement in the comfortable room and nice sweet bed that I was sure were destined for me. The Major was kind enough to direct an orderly to show me to my apartment; so bidding them "Good night," I followed him, not up stairs, but across the quadrangle a considerable distance, to a door which was fastened by a padlock; having unlocked which, the orderly told me to enter, and shutting the door upon me, left me in the dark. From the confined air, and the villainous musty smell which prevailed, I thought the fellow had left me to obtain a light, and after waiting a short time and not hearing his footsteps, I opened the door and called out to him, but no one answered, and he never returned.

Fortunately there was some moonlight which enabled me to see my luggage not far from the door, and it appearing to me that this was likely to turn out to be the nice comfortable room my imagination had been indulging in the contemplation of, I determined to turn my ill luck to as much advantage as I could; and taking out the materials for procuring a light, and the lantern belonging to my tent, I soon was enabled to take a partial survey of my lodgings. It was an old dirty, ill-smelling, comfortless store-room, which had been assigned to me to sleep in: it appeared never to have been swept out, and the floor was covered with casks and boxes, and all sorts of unseemly things. No bed, no mattress, nothing, not even a light, had been provided for me. Not a rancho in South America ever offered less comfort to the weary traveller, for there the nights are warm at least, but here, to increase the discomfort, it was very cold. There was, however, an old ricketty table in the store-house, so, placing my mattress upon it, I lay down, and drawing one of my buffalo skins over me, I entered upon the tedious occupation of hoping rather than expecting that I might get a sleep in such a place. I saw that I had committed a great error in not keeping my comfortable tent pitched for my own use, and was determined not to surrender it to my men upon another occasion, unless I had first made sure of something better. In the meantime I could not but reflect upon the contrast betwixt the very kind attentions I had received at the other American posts, and the want of them I experienced here. The reason was not very obvious. The commandant and his lady had entertained me with a very cheerful kindness, and knowing I was indisposed, could not have intended this sort of treatment for me. I therefore came to the conclusion that there was some misunderstanding; that the commandant might have thought the officers would take care of me, and the officers might have thought the same thing of the commandant. It was possible, too, that none of them might have a second bed, or indeed a room to spare. I had hitherto found all the officers at the different posts quite friendly and obliging, and I determined to shut out every thought from my heart that these gentlemen intended to be otherwise. Having got into this comfortable state of mind, I at length fell asleep.

CHAPTER XXIV.

AN EVANGELICAL PRETENDER TO SANCTITY.—THE FALLS OF ST. ANTHONY.

September 13.—In the morning I awoke rather feverish with a severe head-ache, and having managed with some care to get off my table without breaking it, I hastened to open the door in order to let in as much air as I could, and going into a narrow corridor, found I was not far from the quarters of the next senior officer, who appeared to be entertaining his family with some very bad psalm-singing. Having found a person to procure me water, I made my *toilette* as quick as possible, with the agreeable prospect before me of having to trudge to the bivouac of the men to obtain some breakfast, or to cross the St. Peter's again to Mr. Sibley's, where I was as sure of getting a hearty meal, as of getting plenty of tobacco smoke along with it. Just as I was on my way, the orderly made his appearance with an invitation to breakfast with the commandant; and as violent head-aches and long walks do not harmonise well together, and I was anxious to be on good terms with the worthy Major, I followed the orderly across the quadrangle again with more satisfaction than on the preceding evening. I was glad I did so, for I got an excellent cup of tea and some pleasant conversation out of the Major; and feeling better, walked into the country to see a very pretty waterfall of about fifty feet, made by a rivulet twenty feet broad, on the right bank of the Mississippi, which by recession has cut out a small gorge for itself through the incoherent sandstone. I obtained a great many fossils from the calcareous strata overlying this sandstone during my walk, of the same kind with those found in the beds at the fort. On my return Dr. —— invited me to partake of his dinner, which, from the unaffected kindness of his manner, I am sure he wished had been better.

In the afternoon, Milor having called, I took a walk with him into the country, and found that he was a person in every respect suited to my purpose; he spoke French very fluently, was remarkably intelligent and active, and entered with zeal into my plans, which not only embraced a geological *réconnaissance* of the country, across the Côteau de Prairie, from the sources of the St. Peter, as far, if possible, as the village of the Mandans, on the Missouri, but as accurate a knowledge as could be acquired whilst he was with me of the Sioux tongue. He had been brought up amongst them, and told me he considered it as his native language: he knew almost all the distinguished chiefs personally; and from the many expeditions he had made amongst them in the service of various traders, was known to every band throughout their extensive country. He had all the prejudices of a Sioux against the Ojibways, had been engaged in many hostile affairs with them, and told me that being once pursued hotly by a party of them, he was compelled to fly on foot the distance of 100 miles within the twenty-four hours, to escape being tomahawked. I had therefore some guarantee for his vigilance and care of our party whilst conducting us through the upper country. Before we parted, I told him that I should prepare lists of the names of everything in nature, as well as phrases, in the French language, and that when we were in the canoe he should act as my schoolmaster, and translate them into the Sioux, giving me at the same time the exact pronunciation, which I had the means of committing to writing. I also asked the great favour of him, as he would sit next to me in the canoe, to smoke as little as possible, as it always made me sick, and gave me a head-ache, to which he replied that he only smoked the *kinnekinnic*, which is a mild preparation of the inner bark of the willow, mixed with a little tobacco; "Mais pour vous servir, Monsieur, je ne manquerai pas de faire ma petite fumée seulement lorsque la journeé est faite."

With this capital understanding with Milor I dismissed him for the night, and returned to the fort, having engaged to drink tea with the Major and his lady. Before I went to their quarters, some of the officers came to see me in my store-room, and expressed their great dissatisfaction at the shabby lodgings which had been assigned to me. I now learnt the secret history of my ill luck. The commandant's lady had been for some time without a servant of any kind,—a state of things which must often occur at so distant a frontier,—and this was the reason why I could not sleep at their house; but the Major was ignorant that I had been put so unceremoniously into a cold store-room. He had told the second in command, Major L——, a long-legged, self-sanctified, unearthly-looking mortal, who was always singing psalms, and boreing the garrisons where he lived with temperance societies, pious exhortations, and puritanical factions, to assign me quarters. Now, unfortunately, I had brought no letter of introduction to him from any of his brother saints, and being without their *shibboleth*, he took it for granted that I was in a reprobate state. Considering himself, therefore, as a living rod in soak to tickle up sluggish Christians, he condemned me to all the privations it was in his power to inflict before he had even seen me, and before I had even heard that such a "burning light" as himself existed. It was at his quarters I heard the psalm-singing in the morning. I soon learnt that he was universally despised, and besides being a shabby sordid person, was considered but as being a pretender in the sanctified line he had selected for himself. I perceived, however, that notwithstanding he had lost every trace of respectability by his absurd affectation of piety and purity, that it would not be prudent for me to express any dissatisfaction with his uncharitable and inhospitable conduct, since Major Bliss, being a manly soldier-like person, the very reverse of this mundungus, might have resented his conduct, and an unpleasant disagreement might have been introduced into the garrison in consequence of my arrival. I therefore determined to keep my quarters, and make the best I could of them.

The evening passed very pleasantly at the commandant's: himself and his lady were full of kind attentions to me. They had a fine young boy, an only child, greatly in want of education. I could not but admire his mother, her strong affection for him, and her self-devotion to the comfort of the only two beings in the world she seemed to love: and when I told her that so fine a youth must not be permitted to vegetate at a military post on so remote a frontier, where there was nothing good or useful for him to learn, I found that I had touched a string which made them both very grave. We afterwards resumed the subject; and so much was said about the great duty of parents giving their children a good education, that she admitted she must part with him some day, but said she felt so unhappy when she thought of it, that she had not the courage to dwell long upon the subject at a time. I left them a little after nine, and crossing the quadrangle alone, regained my musty and melancholy store-room, and having obtained a light, mounted my table once more.

September 14.—I arose at break of day, and feeling much better, went down to the bivouac. The men were all snoring in the comfortable tent, which was redolent of tobacco. I roused them and ordered the canoe to be ready in an hour to take me to the Falls of St. Anthony, and returning to the fort breakfasted with the commandant and his lady, and receiving their willing consent to take their son with me, sent an invitation to the doctor and a young officer of the name of D—— to accompany us. They soon joined us, and we walked down to the canoe and embarked. We had between eight and nine miles to go against the current, which made our progress very slow. The bluffs had the same character with those opposite to Fort Snelling, but diminished in height as we proceeded, being about eighty feet high, coming down to the river with occasional slopes and bottoms of low land, the river averaging about 100 yards in breadth. As we advanced but slowly, we landed on the left bank, and ascending to the top of the bluff, got upon an extensive and beautiful prairie. We had not gone far before we started a prairie wolf, a small fox-looking animal of a reddish gray colour. This little vulpine burrows in the ground, and is become, as it is said, so sagacious, that when it hears the sound of a gun it peeps out of its hole, anticipating a feast from the offals of the buffalo. I also killed a large snake of the mocassin kind, like that we had found in the water when ascending the Mississippi.

After a short walk we came in sight of the Falls of St. Anthony, which perhaps look best at a distance; for although upon drawing near to them they present a very pleasing object, still, from their average height not exceeding perhaps sixteen feet, they appeared less interesting than any of the great cascades I had seen in North America. Father Hennepin, the first European who visited them, assigns them a height of from fifty to sixty feet, exaggerating them as he had done the Falls of Niagara, which he stated to be 600 feet high. Carver, who visited them in 1766, says, "they fall perpendicularly about thirty feet;" but Colonel Long, of the United States Service, a person remarkable for his scientific accuracy, made an actual admeasurement of them, which gave about sixteen feet.

The line of the cascade, like that of Niagara, is interrupted by a small island, and, including it, has an irregular curvature of about 650 yards from bank to bank, the river contracting below the falls to about 180 yards. The current above the cascade is very strong, and comes dashing over the fractured limestone of this irregular curvature, where it recedes and advances with great variety of plays, so that in its details this is a cascade of very great beauty, its incessant liveliness contrasting pleasingly with the sombre appearance of the densely wooded island, and presenting to the observer that element in motion which has so much modified the whole channel of the Mississippi. But as, under this view, the Falls of St. Anthony furnish a remarkable illustration of the natural method by which interior lakes of great dimensions, and marecageous districts of great extent, are drained, and their surfaces rendered fit habitations for man, this subject will be reserved for the next chapter.

CHAPTER XXV.

ON THE ANCIENT STATE OF THE MISSISSIPPI AND OTHER AMERICAN RIVERS, AND THE MANNER IN WHICH THEIR PRESENT CHANNELS HAVE BEEN MODIFIED.

THIS cataract, like the more celebrated one of Niagara, belongs to that class of waterfalls, where the rivers being projected over compact mineral beds supported by soft shales or incoherent sandstones, these last are loosened and washed out, and the superincumbent strata losing their support, fall down from time to time, whereby cataracts in long periods of time shift their places, and finally, by this kind of recession, cut gorges of great length towards their sources, and thus effect the drainage of immense continents. In mountainous countries composed of primary rocks the process is more slow, the excavation of the channels of their rivers not being accomplished by this subtracting or undermining operation, but by a molar or grinding process, whereby pot-holes or cylindrical cavities, in great numbers and of large dimensions, are drilled or ground in the face of the rock, until its cohesion affording insufficient resistance to the increased volume of water during the periodical floods, immense masses are precipitated below one after the other. Of this method a beautiful illustration will be exhibited in the second volume.

The spectacle which the channel of the Mississippi presents illustrates in a remarkable manner the ancient state of the country before this drainage took place, and the manner in which it has been effected. From the Falls of St. Anthony to the mouth of the river in the Gulf of Mexico, the distance may be estimated at 2300 miles; for the first 1200 miles of which southward, the broad valley, as has partly been shewn in the preceding pages, in which the river flows, is generally from two to three miles in width, and is bounded by escarpments of calcareous beds resting upon loose sandstone, from 200 to 400 feet in height, with slopes coming down to the river; being, in fact, a talus formed of the ruins of the strata, now covered with a sod, and in many places wooded down to the water. From the summit of these escarpments the spectator sees beneath him an immense trough, which has been excavated out of the general level of the country, and which from some distance north of Lake Pepin to Prairie du Chien is almost filled by well-wooded islands, some of them ten or twelve miles long, amongst which the waters of the Misssisippi meander in various streams, the main channel shifting its course occasionally from one bank to the other. Here and there lateral valleys are seen coming in through the escarpments at right angles to the river, and connected occasionally with extensive alluvial plains running into the country for several miles. Descending into the trough he finds all the islands upon the same level with each other, and with the alluvial bottoms he had before noticed. A further investigation shows him that the soil of all these alluvial plains and islands is identically the same, being a light vegetable sandy loam, containing many remains of decayed freshwater shells; so that at length his judgment becomes satisfied that all these islands and bottoms are portions of a general deposit effected at the period when the voluminous river occupied the whole breadth of the valley from escarpment to escarpment, and when the alluvial plains, as well as a great portion of the upper country, were under water.

The solution of the whole physical topography of the river now presents itself; the observer perceives that there has been a great reduction of the volume of the ancient river, and that the present stream, when compared with it, is but an insignificant rivulet, that has worn for itself a channel in the old muddy bottom that was deposited in very remote periods, but which, since its desiccation, has been converted into fertile islands covered with luxuriant forests, and plains or prairies bearing a rank herbage.

Nor does the fact of the total absence of alluvial islands in the last 500 miles of its course south of the Arkansa, and the comparative scarcity of them from that point to Prairie du Chien, militate against this opinion. We have seen that for some distance north of Lake Pepin, as far as where the Wisconsin joins the Mississippi, islands are very numerous; but from the moment this last is increased by the ample volume of that stream, they become comparatively rare, because the increased aqueous force acting upon the loose texture of the old muddy bottom, especially during the periodical floods, has greatly diminished them both in number and size. Further to the south, after the river has received that mighty flood the Missouri, scarce an island is to be seen; and when it has been joined by the Ohio, the Cumberland, the Tenesse, the Arkansa, and Red River, nothing exists in the form of one,—everything has been swept away; the waters spread over the whole surface of the valley, and hasten to the Gulf of Mexico, to enlarge that delta which is the offspring of the ancient deposits of the Mississippi and its tributaries.

There is, however, an exception to this state of things on the line of the Mississippi, which deserves to be noticed. In the midst of that part of the channel where the islands are most numerous, Lake Pepin, which is only an enlargement of the river for twenty-one miles in length, is without islands, being a sheet of water covering the whole space from escarpment to escarpment for three miles in breadth, representing as far as it goes the ancient state of the river. That there should be no islands for twenty-one miles is an anomaly, the solution of which upon first consideration is not very obvious. Is it that the violent north-west winds which prevail have kept the waters in a turbid state, and thus prevented the deposit of that alluvial matter of which the islands in other parts are formed? and has not the great volume of the Chippeway river, which joins the Mississippi at the south end of the lake, so dammed up the water as to cover the partial deposit which has been made, and thus prevented the growth of trees and shrubs? Some cause —if indeed the lake is not much deeper than any other part of the channel—has certainly prevented sedimentary matter from forming here as it has done in other parts, and winds and high waves suggest themselves with some plausibility.

But the evidences of the state of things which has been described are not confined to the channel of the Mississippi. There is not one of the large Atlantic rivers which does not furnish proofs that at some previous period its volume was several times larger than it is at this day, and that there has been a great diminution of the fluviatile waters of the continent of North America.

As we ascend the St. Lawrence and approach the city of Quebec, we perceive on its right bank an alluvial plain from fifteen to twenty miles in breadth, bounded by cliffs that were once the ancient limits of the river. In the villages and solitary cabins of the Canadian peasantry, now erected upon that plain, not a well has been dug which has not furnished conchological proofs of that fact. Proceeding onwards, instances of a like kind, but more limited in their extent, are to be observed in various localities before the traveller reaches Lake Ontario, especially on the course of the tributary streams. At Lake Ontario the ancient banks of the water are found at great distances from its present shores, both on the north and south side. Reaching the neighbourhood of the Falls of Niagara, we find fresh-water shells of the kinds which inhabit the modern streams, on conspicuous heights of land in the vicinity of Lewiston, as well as upon Goat Island, above the level of the existing river. The same proofs are repeated in the vicinity of Lake Erie, on the south shore of which a flat alluvial plain presents itself, extending several miles inland from the banks of the lake, which are themselves from 50 to 100 feet high. From the wells, also, dug in this plain unios, anadontas, melanias, and other fresh-water shells are frequently thrown out; whilst to the north, on the isthmus separating Lake Erie and Lake Huron from Malden to the shore of this last lake, a distance of seventy miles, we have, as has been before stated, a level alluvial country, containing quantities of decayed fresh-water shells, proving that the whole region once formed a large lake, and that the land there is an ancient lacustrine deposit.

Continuing westwards from the waters of Lake Huron to the sources of Fox River, which empty into that arm of it called Green Bay, we find that these last are only divided from the waters of the Wisconsin, which flow into the Mississippi, by a narrow slip of level land not two miles broad, across which, so slight is the difference of level, boats even now pass when the waters of the Wisconsin are high. Thus we trace a freshwater communication of ancient times from the St. Lawrence to the Missisippi, embracing an immense portion of the present dry land of the continent, and have the evidences before us of an extraordinary diminution of the fluviatile waters in those monuments it has left behind, the margins of the lakes and rivers, the terraces they have abandoned, and the rich alluvial deposits which now form part of the most valuable lands of Upper Canada, and of adjacent parts of the United States.

It seems impossible to admit the facts which I have noticed, without subscribing to the opinion, that in ancient times the lakes and rivers of North America were of much greater magnitude than they are at present: indeed, the proofs which have been adduced of that fact are in an equal degree repeated upon the course of the other great American rivers; for whether examining the St. John's, in New Brunswick, the Hudson, the Delaware, the Susquehannah, the James River, the Ohio, the Tenessee, the Arkansa, or Red River, I have invariably noted corresponding modifications of their channels.

We can gather from this truth, that, in the computation of any period, which, according to some writers, may be reasonably assigned for the change of place of any cataract, the existing state of rivers ought not to furnish the only data, since the progress of degradation would necessarily be greatly accelerated during a state of things when the dynamic force of the acting agent was perhaps ten times as great as in modern times. The Falls of St. Anthony well illustrate this. The observant traveller who ascends the Mississippi from the point where the escarpments first appear, sees in them the results of an operation of one and the same kind ; and when at length he overtakes the cataract, he sees in it the powerful natural agent which has excavated the valley he has followed so great a distance. But if, desirous of computing a period within our own chronology for the accomplishment of so stupendous a work, he were to assume nothing beyond the force now in action, he would find himself baffled beyond all hope of extrication. Father Hennepin found these falls 164 years ago at the same place, as far as we can understand him, where they are now. Carver, who visited them in 1766, now seventy-eight years ago, speaks of the small island near the centre of the cataract, though rating its dimensions, as he did the height of the fall, very inaccurately. So that we are, perhaps, within bounds, when we suppose that the cataract has not receded more than twenty yards in the last 100 years, and probably not more than 400 yards in the last 2000 years. If the waters of the Mississippi then had never been more powerful than they are at present, how many millions of years must have elapsed during the accomplishment of this long excavation, especially if we make allowances for the height and breadth of the valley south of the Falls of St. Anthony, which exceed fourfold those at the point which the cataract has now reached !

It would seem, therefore, to be a vain attempt to assign any portion of the mysterious past for such a work as the excavation of the channel of the Mississippi. Neither is it necessary to the progress of science that we should engage in such an unsatisfactory under-

PERIODS OF EXCAVATION.

taking. The observer of nature finds ample scope for the fruition of his intellectual powers, in considering the details of these operations, and referring their results to the great class of providential arrangements for the benefit of the human family; since, without them, the lakes and marecageous surfaces of continents would be unfitted for the habitations of men. In our own island those portions of gorges which are to be observed of a character similar to those of the Mississippi, are not to be traced to their sources, as we can do those of an extensive continent like North America, since our island is but a fragment detached from the European continent, of the ancient extent of which we can now allege nothing, and the sources and courses of whose ancient rivers, of which these insular gorges are but an insignificant part, are for ever obliterated.

CHAPTER XXVI.

EMBARK ON THE MINNAY SOTOR.—REFLECTIONS ON THE RUIN IMPENDING OVER THE INDIANS.—THE PROPER NAME OF THE SIOUX, "NAHCOTAH."—THE GEOMYS, OR MUS BURSARIUS.

WITH the aid of the current we returned to the fort in an hour, accomplishing in that brief period what it had taken three hours to do when ascending the river; and after making a hearty supper with my kind friends the Major and his lady, I retired to my quarters. In the morning we had cold stormy weather, but Milor was punctual, and came to my den soon after daylight, with a report that the provisions and other things in preparation for our expedition would be ready in the course of the day, advising me, however, not to start until the storm had abated, which he thought was likely to last a day or two. As soon, therefore, as breakfast was over at the commandant's, I took a walk of half a mile to see the agent for the Indians on the part of the United States, a gentleman from Virginia of the name of Tagliaferro, which the Americans pronounce Tollaver. He was living in a tolerably comfortable house with his lady, who had a very fair share of personal beauty. The Sioux have translated his name literally into *Mahzah Baksah*, or "Iron-cutter." I remained here an hour, trying to pick up information, but Major T. appeared to have less information at the service of a traveller going amongst the Indians than any person I had yet met with occupying his official situation. He told me, that if at any time during my journey I wanted assistance, it would only be necessary for me to mention his name. Others, however, who knew him, told me afterwards that it would be of no use to me, so it was to be hoped I should never stand in great need of those talismanic words. From the agency I crossed the St. Peter's, to consult Mr. Sibley about some matters, and to see some Indians who had just arrived from the upper country.

I have before observed, that one of my motives for ascending the St. Peter's was to examine a locality of some celebrity amongst the first French travellers who penetrated into this part of the country, and of which the Indian tribes there might be supposed to have some knowledge. From Charlevoix's "Histoire de la Nouvelle France," and from some old inedited French authorities, it appears that Monsieur le Sueur had discovered a mine of green cupreous earth near the mouth of the largest tributary stream of the St. Peter's river, distant from the mouth of this last about forty-five leagues; and asking, through the Count de Frontenar, the Governor-General of Canada, permission of the French court to open the mines, he went to France in 1697. Having received a commission to that effect, he returned to America with thirty workmen, and reaching the mouth of the Mississippi in December, 1699, ascended that stream to the mouth of the St. Peter's, which he entered the 19th of September, 1700. Advancing up it about forty-five leagues, he came to the Rivière de Terre Bleu, its principal tributary, near the mouth of which, in north lat. 44° 13', he built a stockaded fort, and named it Fort l'Huillier, after an enterprising patron of his, who was a *fermier-général* under the government. Charlevoix states the copper-mine to have been only three-quarters of a league above this fort, and that in twenty-two days they obtained 30,000 lb. weight of the ore, with the greater part of which having reached the mouth of the Mississippi again on the 10th of February, 1702, about 4000 lb. weight of the best ore were selected and sent to France. The mine was stated to be at the foot of a mountain ten leagues long, that seemed to be composed of the same substance.

From the subsequent silence of French and other writers on this subject, a fair inference was to be drawn that there had been a great exaggeration in the account of this affair, and that either M. le Sueur's green cupreous earth had not corresponded to the expectations he had raised, or that the whole account of it was to be classed with Baron Lahontan's " remarkable voyage upon the Long River, to the country of those imaginary nations, the *Gnacsitares* and the *Mozamleeks*, which last were clothed like Spaniards, and had thick bushy beards." *

It was improbable, however, that the whole story was an invention. I had seen many indications of cupreous veins since I left Michilimackinac; the river Terre Bleu was well known to exist, and its name might be derived from the admixture of its waters with some mineral colouring matter. I had determined, therefore, to investigate the point, and settle it once for all. Milor

---

* Lahontan had really descended the Wisconsin to the Mississippi, in 1689, and having there got an imperfect account of St. Peter's river, the sources of which rise very near to those of some of the tributaries of the Missouri, he founded a fable upon it, which to every one who has explored that country bears intrinsic evidence that he never ascended the Mississippi as high as St. Peter's, which is his " Rivière Longue." Of his talent for exaggeration it is sufficient to say, that, after seeing Niagara, he describes the cascade to be 700 or 800 feet high, and half a league broad.

had never heard of a copper-mine up the Terre Bleu, but one of the Indians, an elderly chief, who had just reached Mr. Sibley's from the upper country, stated that there was a place near the mouth of the Terre Bleu to which the Indians resorted to collect a green earth which they used as a pigment to paint themselves, and that he had seen it himself in place. I therefore desired Milor to obtain from him the most exact details of the locality, as it was probably the one alluded to by Charlevoix. The weather continued exceedingly wet and stormy, as it frequently is on the eve of the equinox; and re-crossing the river in the evening, I went to my disagreeable den, hoping it would be for the last time.

September 16.—In the morning the cold rain continued to fall heavily, and left little or no prospect of my being able to get away during the day. Milor came over and advised our remaining, as he said it would be impossible for us to get everything stowed away conveniently, and the country would be so deluged with water as to make the camping places uncomfortable. Having breakfasted as usual with the commandant, I retired to my quarters to get a lesson in the Sioux from Milor, who gave me an addition to my vocabulary of 200 words, with their pronunciation. The weather clearing up at noon, I walked to Major Tagliaferro's to bid him adieu; and being pressed in a kind manner to pass the evening with them, I remained. We had a cheerful fire, and a comfortable cup of tea; and when night came, and I had to walk over the wet cold prairie to my dirty store-room, I felt rather loth to exchange so much comfort for the dingy receptacle that was to harbour me for the night. This, after a comfortless walk, I reached once more, and upon opening the door, the damp confined air occasioned by the wet weather was so oppressive, and smelt so horridly, that I was almost upon the point of returning to Mrs. Tagliaferro's to ask permission to sleep by her fire-side; and I verily believe I should have done it, but for an apprehension of hurting the feelings of the commandant. I therefore reluctantly mounted my table, and drawing my bear-skins over me, fell asleep whilst forming determinations, that, under any circumstances, this should be the last time this old filthy warehouse should number me amongst its articles.

September 17.—Milor entered my den soon after daybreak and announced a fine morning; upon which cheerful intelligence I told him to go to the commandant's, and ask for assistance to take my luggage to the canoe, and then to make everything ready for our immediate departure. The orderly soon made his appearance, bringing me water, with a message from the commandant that breakfast was waiting for me as soon as I was ready; but before I had left the store-room the worthy Major himself came, and seeing for the first time what abominable quarters had been assigned to me, expressed his regret in very strong terms, saying that it was altogether contrary to his directions. I felt well assured of this, as it had been told me in confidence the day before that the proceeding was entirely owing to his second in command, who, if I would have attended his insane ravings and psalm-singings, and made him a handsome present into the bargain, would have given me a bed at his house. And this was the punishment he had inflicted upon me for not doing so; such pitiful and spiteful devils men sometimes become, whilst they are fancying themselves so very good.

Having breakfasted and taken my leave of Mrs. Bliss, with many sincere thanks for her attentions, I walked to the river, accompanied by the commandant and several officers of the garrison. He here repeated his regrets, and desired me on my return, if I did not cross the country to the Missouri, to send my luggage to his house on my arrival, and establish my quarters there. I now bade them all adieu, and stepping into my canoe, the men set up a barcarole and chorus, and paddled over to Mr. Sibley's to take in Milor, whom I found waiting for me. Here we had another set of adieus to make, and having established Milor near to me in the canoe, we started our paddles upon the St. Peter's about 9 A.M., with a fine sweet fresh breeze, and a world of adventure before us, in a region unvisited by civilization, and in advance of all the frontier posts of the United States.

The morning was bright, and our spirits were buoyant. The very thought that you are in a region where you depend entirely upon your own exertions and prudence, where the laws and regulations of society have no control over you, where everything is new, and where every hour may be pregnant with adventure, makes you at once bold and cautious, thoughtful and gay. I know not when I have felt more happy than upon this occasion; and it increased my satisfaction to see my men so sober and in such fine spirits, and so much delighted as they evidently were to have Milor with them.

The course of the St. Peter's was very serpentine: as we advanced, we found it about 125 yards wide, with low fertile bottoms on each side, and gracefully wooded slopes leading from them to the uplands. We went nearly south by compass; the great bend of the St. Peter's, where the turn is made to the north-east, being in about 44° 12′, whilst the source is in about 46°, and the mouth in 45°. About half-past 10 A.M. we reached the Indian village of *Wāhmundēe Tanka,* or "Great Eagle," consisting of six teebees on the right bank, and some lodges on the opposite side. The band was from home, on the prairies hunting buffaloes.

The reflections which I had before made on the condition of the Indians again occurred to me. Indeed, at every step a traveller makes in this country, he sees more distinctly the ruin that is impending over them. Before the white man invaded them they possessed all the country, could command all the game in it for their subsistence, and use their skins to clothe themselves with. The Indian could conceive of no wealth beyond this, for there was the certainty of animals being always plentiful, the population, from causes inherent to the condition of the aborigines, not increasing after the rate of that of an agricultural people; but white men have taught them to abandon the use of furs, and to substitute blankets for them; they have now acquired wants formerly unknown, such as whisky, tobacco, arms, and powder. To acquire these, the Indian must make long journeys, must kill all the animals he meets with, not to subsist upon, for the flesh for the greater part is left to rot on the ground, but to carry the skins to the trader to discharge his debts, knowing well at this time that an unpunctual Indian gets no more credit. Already game is becoming scarce; by and by there will be no skins to be obtained in these regions; the trader will abandon them; and thus the Indians will discover that there is no one to supply their wants, and that their dependance upon the traders has led to their ruin. This state of things would cause their immediate extinction, but for the policy of the American government, which, before the extreme point of want overtakes the Indian, seizes, under the form of treaty-bargain, all his land, and drives him to a more distant region.

At half-past eleven we reached another small village, about three leagues from the fort, the residence of a chief who is known to the French traders by the name of Penichon: this also was deserted by the band. The river a little beyond this contracted to about eighty yards in width, the banks being very low. We stopped for the men to dine at a stream, very narrow at its mouth, which comes in on the right bank, called *Kāhkahīnhahāh*, or "Where the Elk was put," from some tradition of the Indians, and pursued our course afterwards along the beautiful sloping banks, covered with wild grass, and crowned at their summits with fine trees.

I found Milor intelligent and anxious to oblige: he had the physiognomy of a French gentleman of the *ancien régime*, and a good deal of the polite manner of one. He told me that he did not know exactly how he had obtained the name of Milor; that he had always been told that his father was a French officer; but added, "Il se peut, Monsieur, que ce fut un Milor Anglais." No doubt he got the *soubriquet* from some circumstance or other when he was very young. The national name of the numerous Sioux tribes, he informed me, was *Nāhcotah*, and not *Dahcotah*, as it has been hitherto supposed to be. Nāhcotah, he said, meant "the connected people," just as Lenni Lenape means "the original people" with the Delaware Indians. Dahcotah is a name given to them by other Indians, who claim kindred with them, and means "mes parens," or "my relations." But the confusion which prevails respecting the proper names of the Indian tribes, the frequency with which names given to them by their neighbours are substituted for the national names they recognise themselves by, and the consequent adoption of them by the white people, is a subject which ought to be discussed apart; and for the present I shall continue to call these tribes by their universally received appellation of "Sioux," which is an abbreviation of the name given to them by the old French writers, of "Nadowessioux."

The Indian name of the St. Peter's is "*Minnay Sotor,*" or "Turbid Water;" the water, in fact, looking as if whiteish clay had been dissolved in it. At half-past 3 P. M. it widened to about 100 yards, with beautiful high grassy slopes. I landed at one of these gentle lawn-like slopes, and, ascending to the summit, had an immense extent of prairie-land before me, covered with wild grass; and advancing a short distance, sprung a large brood of heavy grouse (*Tetrao cupido*), which flew but a very short distance. This incident brought the moors of Yorkshire and the days of my youth vividly to my memory; indeed, the resemblance was perfect.

At a quarter past four we passed a village called *Shākpay*, or "Six," the name of the chief of the band: it consisted of seventeen large teebees, all of them closed, the band being gone to the Shayanne to hunt buffaloes. This is called nine leagues from the fort. The teebees were on the left bank, and the burying-ground, with some scaffolds, were on the opposite side of the river. About 5 P. M. two young Indian girls rushed from the left bank from amidst some bushes, and, jumping into a canoe, paddled with desperate energy to get away from us. They were evidently terrified at our appearance, thinking perhaps we were those Ojibways they had been taught to dread so much, or perhaps entertaining an equal dread of white men, for the soldiers of these frontier posts are not scrupulous. Our men frightened them still more by shouting after them, and striking their paddles in the same direction; but I immediately ordered them to turn the canoe in an opposite direction, to convince them we intended no harm, for the young things paddled so desperately, I was afraid they would overset their canoe and be drowned. For more than a mile, however, they continued their exertions, nor relaxed until they felt sure they were out of our reach. A little further up we came to the village to which they belonged, consisting of half a dozen lodges on the right bank, with a great many children playing about them. We stopped there a moment, and when the women saw Milor, whom all seemed to know, they came to the canoe, and greeted him with salutations and smiles. I desired him to explain to them that the little girls had nothing to apprehend from us; and when he had told them who we were, and how friendly our intentions were to them all, they seemed very much diverted with the fears of the children; so, leaving them some pork and biscuit, we parted very good friends with them. Milor, by his own account, had had several wives; and when I asked him how many children he was the father of, he answered, "C'est difficile à dire, Monsieur; les femmes savent mieux que les hommes qui sont les pères des enfants."

At half-past 5 P. M. we landed on the left bank to encamp for the night, establishing our bivouac on a high bank, amidst a profusion of wild grass, six feet high, which the men had to cut out with their bush-hooks; so that when the *emplacement* was in order, and our fires briskly burning, we occupied an area surrounded with lofty grass; amidst which the dense smoke and the crackling flames, that made a singularly loud noise in the wild inclosure, assisted to make the scene quite melo-dramatic. I made an excellent supper of my good tea, bread and butter, fried ham and eggs, taking especial good care to eat these last out of the frying-pan. On leaving Navarino, it was thought one frying-pan would suffice for the party—an economy which had produced great inconvenience to myself, as I was obliged generally to surrender it too soon for the use of the men. Having now one for the parlour, and another for the kitchen, I was quite independent of the rest of the party, and I am not acquainted with a more desirable dish for a hungry traveller in the Indian countries than ham and eggs, soaked biscuit and sliced potatos, all nicely fried together, and eaten hot out of the pan. Of these I made a stupendously satisfactory meal; and, rejoicing that I should no more have to retire to the musty and detestable store-room of the evangelical major, I lay down on my clean pallet in my neat tent, and soon composed myself to sleep.

September 18.—I was up with the earliest dawn, and rousing my men, we got under way amidst a most magnificent sunrise. The additional provisions I had laid in for my voracious party at Fort Snelling, and the enormous quantity of potatos, cabbages, and onions which Major Bliss had permitted my Canadians to take from his garden, had, on our departure from the fort, brought the gunwale of the canoe to within four inches of the water; but our maxillary powers had received an important reinforcement in Milor, and I thought I could perceive that we already floated a little higher in the water. To be sure, we were too deep for rough water, and, loaded as we were, never could have crossed Lake Pepin safely in fresh weather. Milor, to whom I mentioned my appre-

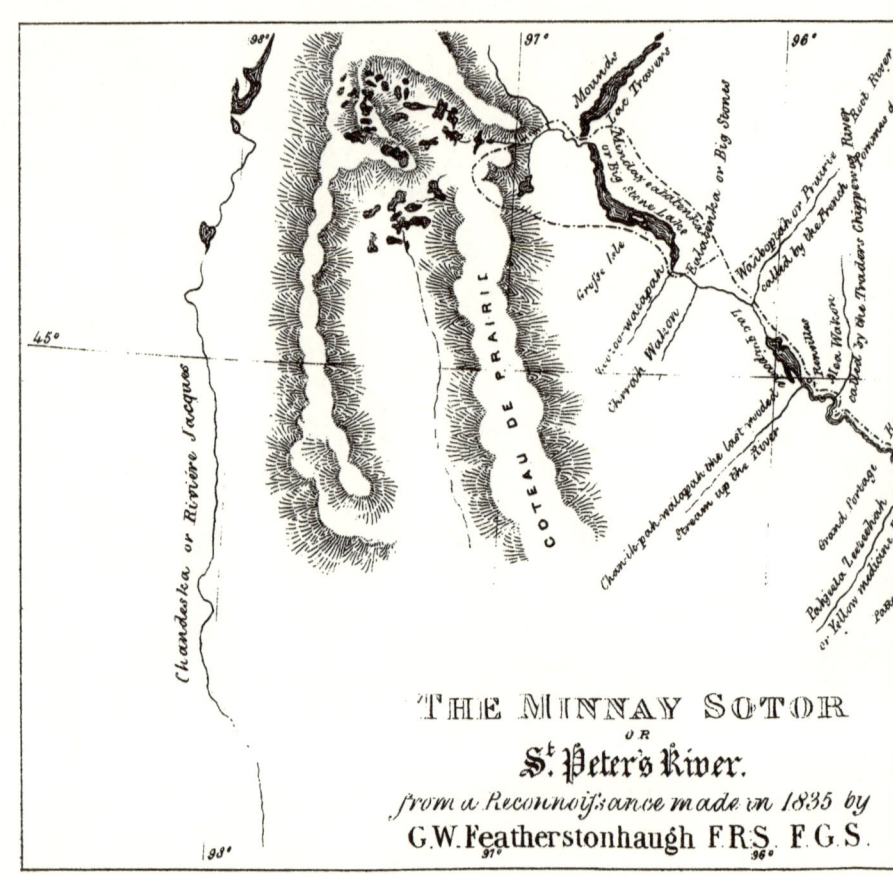

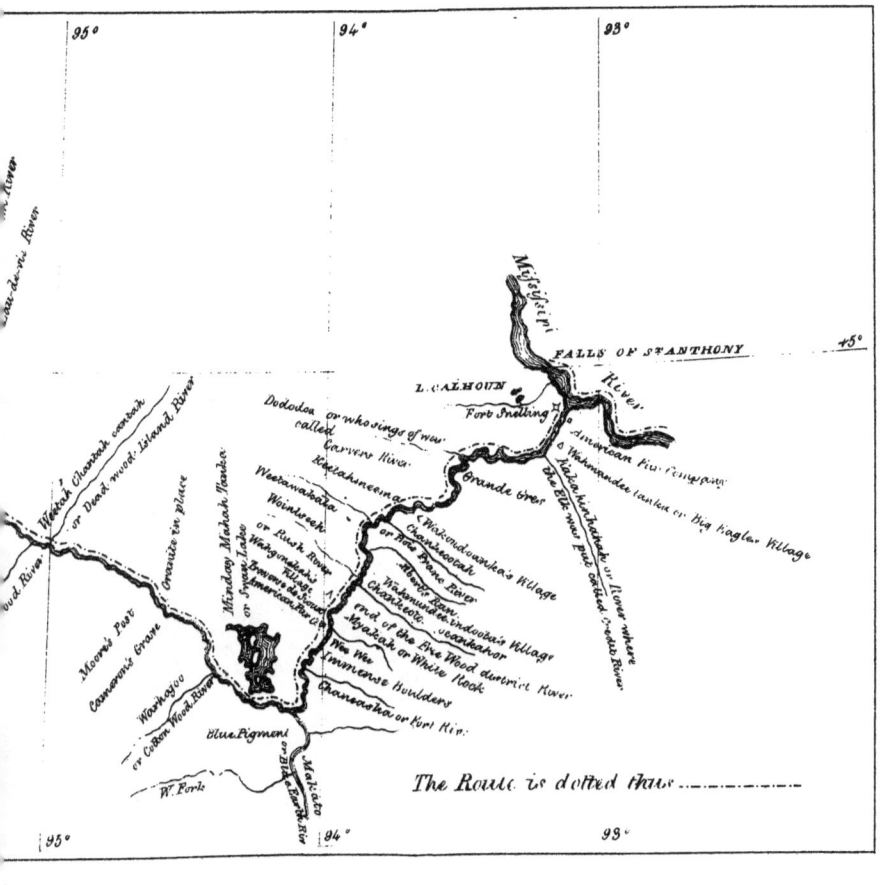

INJUSTICE DONE TO CARVER. 289

hensions on this account, told me we had no lakes to encounter on our way to the sources of the river, and that the water would be always smooth, except where the rapids were, which were several days distant. "Ne craignez rien, ne craignez rien, Monsieur," he said; "je vous reponds pour ce danger-là. Un canot léger fait peur plus qu'un canot pésant."

The river now wound through a rich bottom, and was about 100 yards wide. We passed a small prairie on the left bank, estimated to be twelve leagues from the fort, the edge of which is only twelve feet above the river. At nine we stopped to examine a stream on the left bank, with a strong current not more than twenty feet broad. Its waters were low, but, from the height of the banks, it was evident that the volume of water is large in the season of floods. Milor said the Indians called it *Dododòah*, or the "Singing of War," from the Nahcotahs once assembling to sing the war-song there. It is the same distance that Carver assigns to the river which he has given his own name to,[*] and I suppose it to be the same.

In the narrative of Major Long's interesting expedition to Lake Winnepeg, &c., Carver is slightingly spoken of, and I think great injustice done to him. It is true, that, like many travellers, he has fallen into mistakes when venturing to give a detailed account of wild, unexplored countries, which had not fallen under his immediate notice; but he certainly visited the countries he has described, and must have been a person of great energy and courage, to attempt the journeys he performed at that particular period. I have great pleasure in saying, that, having followed him to the extent of his journey, with his book in my hand, I can express my confidence in him.

[*] Carver's Travels, 1778, p. 74.

A NATURAL OBELISK.

A short distance from *Dododōah* another stream came in, about thirty feet wide, from the right bank, which Milor had no Indian name for, but called it Le Grand Grès, and here we stopped to breakfast. I afterwards learnt that it had its source near a very remarkable outlier or pillar of sandstone, about thirty miles from its mouth. This pillar is situated on what is called the Big Prairie, and can be seen for a distance of twenty miles, somewhat resembling a church with a cupola; the lower part being a huge column, sixty feet high, and

twenty-five in diameter; and the upper part being thirty feet in height, and varying from two and a half to fifteen feet in diameter. This curious obelisk of sandstone is one of the proofs of the ancient continuity of strata, and of the general reduction which has taken place of the mineral structure of the country. For these particulars, as well as for the accompanying outline of Le Grand Grès, I am indebted to a traveller who had visited the locality and made a sketch of the pillar.

Pursuing our course, we came to some rapids, about

half-past eleven, which were exceedingly strong; but keeping close to the right bank, and holding on to the bushes, we warped ourselves through in a very short time. About 700 yards further up we met with other rapids, and then sandstone in place. About 1 P. M. we came to *Weeahkōtee*, or the "Sand Hills," where there is a village, the inhabitants of which, Milor said, were gone to some lakes to collect wild rice. The sand-hills now began to rise very high. At 3 P. M. we stopped for the men to dine at a slope on the right bank, up which I ascended; and after struggling for 100 yards through the matted bushes, entangled with wild peas and vines, I reached the top, and found a very spacious prairie, thrown up into myriads of hills, made by what have been called prairie dogs. These interesting little animals have been called so probably from the indistinct sort of barking they make, for they have no resemblance to dogs, either in their appearance or habits. In size they are like a large rat, about ten inches long, with a reddish-green fur, and sit upon their hind legs like a squirrel on the top of the hillocks they have thrown up; from whence, on the approach of danger, they quickly retreat into their burrows. They are short-legged, and have sharp crooked nails to their anterior feet, for the purpose of burrowing. Nature has curiously provided them with deep pouches, opening externally from their cheeks, and enlarging the sides of the head and neck. The first specimen which was produced had these pouches turned inside out, as though the animal had a bag on each side of the head, and in this odd manner it is figured in the Linnæan Transactions, and in Shaw, vol. 2. Raffinesque gave it the elegant name of *Geomys*, and Shaw, of *Mus bursarius*.

CHAPTER XXVII.

PASS CHAGNKEEOOTA.—TREES TAKING THE AUTUMNAL TINT.—TRAVERSE DES SIOUX.—IMMENSE ABUNDANCE OF BOULDERS.—REACH THE MAHKATOH. —LE SUEUR'S COPPER MINE, A FABLE.

From the brink of this prairie I had a fine view of the line of the river and the country around. The stream had a graceful serpentine course, and the trees on its left bank were beautifully distributed in natural clumps and lines, and everything assisted in the perfect and general embellishment of the scene; even the uninterrupted solitude of the prairie was full of enjoyment. The wild man, who is killing the goose for the golden egg, has abandoned it, after frightening the buffaloe away, and a country containing every requisite for human welfare is vacant of industry. Perhaps this state of things is to be as much attributed to the folly of the Indian as to the cupidity of the white man: the simple and ignorant savage, if he had not surrendered himself so easily to the artificial habits he was lured into, might have maintained his empire here a long time. It is impossible to look around one of these desolate and deserted prairies, without thinking of the quick ruin that has overtaken this unfortunate race; and the traveller re-peoples them in imagination, with the same ardour as when, contemplating the graceful solitude of Rivaulx Abbey, he would wish to see the venerable monks re-appear in their mouldering cloisters. To me these walks from the canoe to the upper prairie were always sources of pure enjoyment.

We got under way again at 3 P. M., and soon after killed three grouse from the canoe. The banks of the left side here were very beautiful; the hills were conical, and about 100 feet high; whilst the coves, or *coulées*, that separated them, resembled amphitheatres covered with verdure, and crowned at the top with graceful trees. At 4 P. M. we came to *Kāhtameīmah*, or "Round Prairie," a lofty level about 100 feet high, with a fine slope covered with grass. The Indians have given it this name because it is nearly encircled by woods. A storm threatening from the north-west, I stopped a little before 5 P. M. at a clean and commodious place for the night, and as soon as the tent was pinned down, and the fires were crackling, had the grouse transferred into a pot, and covering them up with rice, a pillau was brought to my tent in about an hour, that placed me for the moment on a par with the most distinguished living gastronomer. Milor, to whom I gave one of the birds, weighing upwards of two pounds, and a dish of the rice, said, when he came to assist me with my vocabulary after supper, "Que ce potage magnifique lui avoit fait du bien, et lui avoit disposé a manger son souper de tout son cœur;" so that the pillau did not seem at all to have prejudiced his performances with the men at the boiled pork and potatos, for this is a dish which the *voyageurs* stick to until their mouths, what with eating and talking, can do no more duty.

September 19.—I rose at 5 A. M., and everything being carried on board, we resumed our journey, and, paddling along, came about seven to a village on the right bank, belonging to a chief called Wakondoānka, or "Lively

Spirit," but better known to the *voyageurs* by the name of Le Bras Cassé, on account of his having had an arm broken. About 7 A. M. the river was only about sixty yards wide, and the banks very low and woody. We passed some poles belonging to Indian lodges, standing a foot deep in the water. Some Indians had encamped on a sand-bar, near upon a level with the stream, and, the river suddenly rising, they had escaped and left their poles: this was a lesson to us. About eight we reached the *Chagnkeeōota*, or " Free-wood River," coming in on the right bank, and soon entered an extensive forest from which that stream takes its name, through which the St. Peter's wound and turned for several miles. The forest is said to extend from twenty-five to thirty miles on each side of the river, and the district consisting of low, swampy land, in which deciduous trees grow, the Indians have called it " free wood," in contradistinction to the wood that is evergreen and tough.

About nine we stopped to breakfast at a place where immense quantities of small wild beans were growing; and here I perceived with regret that the trees were beginning to assume the autumnal tint—Nature's universal signal to the wanderer in these regions to be diligent before the winter surprises him. A little further on a new feature appeared in the banks of the river,—a tenacious blackish clay, with primary gravel. At 1 P. M. we passed a small stream on the left bank, which Milor said extended far into the country. It is called *Wēetah Wakātah*, or " Tall Island," from having its source in a lake containing an island standing high above the water. Upon all occasions the Indians appear to name localities from natural circumstances or incidents, and never to adopt arbitrary or fancy names. About 2 P. M.

SOCIAL DISPOSITION OF THE OWL.

we got out of the forest, and came upon a very handsome bend of the river, changing the scene from the sunken forest to high bluffs of land and clay, beyond which a charming prairie appeared on the left bank. Passing this, we came up with a stream on the right bank, with a great deal of primary gravel in its bed, which, in addition to other observations I had made, led me to anticipate a change in the stratification of the country. A short distance beyond this stream some calcareous rocks were in place, containing thin beds of fawn-coloured limestone, partially vesicular. The mineral structure of these beds resembled that of the galeniferous rocks of Missouri so much, that I think it not at all improbable galena may hereafter be found in this part of the country. In the course of this morning I met with some new varieties of helices and other land shells.

At 4 P. M. we reached the village of Wāhmundee Indōotah, or "Red Eagle," situated on a prairie on the right bank, but the band was out on their autumnal hunt; we, however, got some grouse here, and pursuing our journey, stopped at half-past five for the night at a clean dry place on the right bank, and the bivouac being in order, concluded the evening by a capital dish of grouse pillau.

To-day, the weather being fine, with a cool elastic north-west wind, the men paddled with spirit, and we made by calculation about thirty miles against the current. The owl of this part of America is a very gossipping bird: every night numbers of them commence a general hooting, which they continue to a late hour. Milor had told me the first evening that this was a sign of rainy weather; but I imagine it is merely a social noise they make, for I have often observed, that when a single owl hoots in the night, if you mock him tolerably well, he is sure to enter into conversation with you. I have also heard them hoot by day when the sky is much overclouded, the light being then much more agreeable to them than that of a bright sun.

September 20.—After a comfortable night I rose before day, and got under way before sun-rise, leaving our blazing fires behind us as though they were standing guard over our abandoned bivouac. About 7 A. M. we passed *Wōintseah Wahpahdah*, or "Rush River," a stream about forty feet wide, which comes in from the left bank through prairie land. At eight we passed another small river on the right bank, called *Chagn Keeōotah Oeānkah*, or "End of the Free Wood." This is computed to be ten good leagues from the beginning of the free wood district. At half-past eight we stopped to breakfast at the foot of an extensive ridge about 150 feet high, running N.N.E. and S.S.W.; and whilst the men were preparing our meal I went to the top, where I found a very extensive dry prairie resembling an English moor, occasionally diversified with clumps of trees : the grass was low, being destroyed by the geomys, which had thrown up countless myriads of their little hills. The view from hence across the river was very beautiful; the St. Peter's wound through the country, shining like burnished metal, and I observed a stream enter it from the north-east, traversing the prairie, and occasionally enlarging itself into considerable lakes.

It had often struck me that in magnificent solitudes like this, a man, but for his affections, might come near to realizing the thought that he was alone in the world; yet, when turning his thoughts to those he loves, how soon he peoples the world again with beings present to the fancy, though separated by thousands of miles. How readily and rapidly the thoughts fly to the most remote points! The velocities the body is capable of, cease to astonish us when we compare them with the telegraphic operations of the mind. Every where around the soil appeared to be fertile, indeed nothing seemed wanting to make it a farmer's paradise at some future day. Grouse were abundant, and rose booming and screaming in every direction. I picked up a fine elk's jaw here, and having taken the teeth out, finished my agreeable ramble and returned to our fires.

Arriving there wet through in my lower garments from the heavy dew, I learnt, to my profound vexation, that my private tea-kettle, and some other things belonging to my *batterie de cuisine*, had been left at our last night's bivouac, owing to our coming away before daylight. Upon this occasion I gave my Canadians to understand that I could " Peste!" and scold as glibly as any of them; and not knowing what excuse to make, they at last proposed that L'Amirant should be crossed over in the canoe to find his way to the bivouac on foot and bring them back. But it was becoming rainy and cold, time was precious, and I was afraid something might happen to the fellow, so, after some reflection, I determined to go on without them. The water could be boiled in an open tin vessel we had, and, at any rate, that important instrument the frying-pan was safe. If that had been amongst the delinquents, L'Amirant would certainly have had to trudge.

At half-past one P. M. we came again to rocks in place on the right bank, at a locality called by the Indians *Mȳa Skah*, or "White Rock," where there is an escarpment of fifty feet, consisting of forty feet of clear granulated sandstone, with occasional flinty concretions, capped by ten feet of fawn-coloured limestone, being a sort of repetition of the beds on the Wisconsin river. At the junction of these two beds there is a narrow seam of greenish-blue silicate of iron, which Milor said was a kind of pigment the Indians valued much to paint themselves with. Here I observed several nests of the cliff swallow, built against the face of the rock. This species is said to be gradually advancing from the distant parts of the western country. At half-past two we passed the village of *Wahgonakah,* or "Big Leg," the band inhabiting which were gone to gather wild rice. About 4 P. M. we reached a place called Traverse des Sioux, and passed a trader's on the right bank called Preston. The Sioux, who in old times came from the south to trade with the French, used to cross the river here. A little further on I landed at a prairie, and walked to an agent of Mr. Sibley's, of the name of Le Blanc. I found him at home with his Sioux wife, and some very nice little children. Having made him acquainted with my misfortune, he very obligingly offered to repair it by lending me an iron tea-kettle; and finding it would not deprive them of any comfort, his wife having another, I returned to the canoe with it in my hand. As I approached the men, I heard one of them say "Voilà le bourgeois, qui est content."

We left this place at 5 P. M., and soon after passed a stream on the right bank, called *Wee Wee,* or "Moon Creek." Its serpentine course is divided so equally into curves, that the Indians, who always name things from nature, have called the curves moons. With the Nahcotahs the word *wee* is used for both sun and moon; in fact, it means luminary, for they say *ompáytoo wee*, "day luminary," and *heeyáytoo wee*, "night luminary." At 6 P. M. we stopped for the night.

September 21.—The morning was fine, but very cold; we, however, started as the sun was rising, and soon came up with a long bluff of sandstone, capped with a thin bed of limestone, on the right bank. We computed our bivouac of last night from Fort Snelling to be about 125 miles. The river was now about 100 yards wide. At 9 A. M. we landed to breakfast at a high bluff called by Milor *Makássa Oasa*, or "White Earth." Having contrived to reach the top, I found an extensive prairie, presenting an odd and picturesque appearance. From the bank it stretched several miles back into the country, without a tree, and then rose into an elevated terrace bounded by woods. But that which gave it a very peculiar character was the tens of thousands of huge boulders scattered about in every direction, looking like petrified buffaloes. Upon walking to examine them, I found that a great many of them were granite, but that the greater portion were blocks of limestone, that had been torn up from the strata with great violence. These were the first granitic boulders I had met with on the St. Peter's,—many of them would weigh from 50 to 100 tons,—a circumstance which indicated the vicinity of granitic beds. To the south was a low prairie with a lake, and to the west was another beautiful prairie, bounded by elegant wooded slopes on the left bank of the river. From the top of one of the boulders I made a hasty sketch of this pleasing scene. Milor had warned me against extending my walks too far; observing, that wandering bands of Sissitons were sometimes prowling about, who did not hesitate to scalp any one they met, who was unarmed and without assistance. I was, therefore, habitually cautious, and, as I could command the whole country around from my position, felt very secure. To be sure, it was barely possible that Indians might be hid behind some of the boulders; but I could always make a good run for it to the river, and, by shouting, could soon draw Milor and the men to my assistance. Reflections and precautions of this kind always gave an additional interest to my walks.

After a hearty breakfast, I left this interesting place, and about half-past eleven passed an island about 400 yards long, the largest we had yet met with: a little beyond it was a well-wooded bluff on the left bank, with the sandstone down to the water's edge. The river here was about ninety yards broad, and the current very strong, a sure indication of our not being very far from the Blue River. At half-past twelve we passed some bold grassy bluffs on the right bank, with numerous large boulders on their slopes. Immediately beyond them the *Chaneāska*, or "Fort River," came in, so named by the Nacotahs upon the occasion of a fight between them and the Hāhatōna, or "People of the Falls," a name they give to a band of the Ojibways who reside principally near the falls on Chippeway river.

At 2 P. M. we stopped for the men to dine, whilst I collected some fine unios in the river. From this point the bluff becomes very strong again, especially on the right bank. At five we stopped for the night, as we wanted an hour's daylight to repair the bottom of the canoe, the gum of which had peeled off, as it is apt to do in frosty weather, and caused several leaks. We had killed some fine fat plover in the course of the day, and I had them boiled for my supper, a method of cooking those birds not greatly to be recommended.

REACH THE MAKATOH.

September 22.—I found it very difficult to keep myself warm during the night, which was very cold, and was glad to leave the tent at 5 A. M., and go to the fire. The wind was sharp from the N.W., and Fahrenheit's thermometer stood at 34° in the tent; but on going to the river I found a still more unwelcome symptom, ice having formed at the edge of the stream. We had, however, a fine sun-rise, and soon got away. At 7 A. M. we passed a low bluff on the right bank, which Milor said was called Mȳhākee Sāba, or "Black Bluff." The maple trees had already got their bright autumnal tints, and the dogwood and sumac had become purple and scarlet. Milor observed that my excursion should have been commenced a month earlier, but that the autumns are usually very fine in this part of the country, and a great deal of ground might be got over yet in season. About eight we came to a fine reach of the river, with a rich wooded slope on the left, where the sandstone bluff was 150 feet high. Milor said that a very black-coloured rattlesnake abounded there. I had met with a great many mocassin snakes without rattles, but had not met with one snake that had rattles since we left the Wisconsin.

Soon after 8 A. M. we came to the mouth of the *Māhkatoh*, or "Blue Earth River," a word composed of *māhkah* ("earth") and *tŏh* ("blue"). This was a bold stream, about eighty yards wide, loaded with mud of a blueish colour, evidently the cause of the St. Peter's being so turbid. It was not far from the mouth of this river that M. le Sueur was asserted to have discovered in 1692 an immense deposit of copper ore. No traveller had ever entered the river to investigate his statements; I therefore directed the head of the canoe to be turned into the stream, the entrance into which lay S. 10° E.

The current was exceedingly strong, and my men had to struggle very hard with their paddles to overcome it. Having ascended it about a mile, we found a Sissiton family established with their skin lodge upon a sand-bar —a fortunate rencontre, as it gave us an opportunity of asking for information respecting the object we were in search of. The head of the family immediately told Milor that the locality where the Indians collected the blue pigment was up the right fork of the river, and that we should reach it in an hour and a half. He added that he had killed a deer the preceding evening, and if we would give him some pork he would give us venison in exchange. All this was joyful news, so I landed upon the sand-bar and went to the lodge. The party consisted of three stout men, two women, and four children. The skin of a fine buck was spread out to dry behind the lodge, and some of the meat, in small pieces, was drying upon sticks near the fire.

It certainly looked very uninviting; and I told Milor to inform the women that I wanted a large joint, and not little smoked pieces, upon which one of them replied that there was one in the lodge. Accordingly, putting aside the skin curtain, we entered this Indian larder to look at it, when it turned out to be part of the breast lying on the ground all bloody and dirty, upon which a little naked boy was squatted down on his haunches. I looked at this delicacy more than once, and then told Milor I could not eat it, and therefore should not have anything to do with it. His answer was, "Mais, Monsieur, c'est bien bon lors'qu'il est cuit." Reflecting, however, that my scruples might not be quite so strong when I was hungry, we finally accepted it; and the Indians, who had not had any pork in a very long time, were highly delighted with their bargain. These people constantly asserted that they knew of no remains of any old fort or stone building in that part of the country; so that Le Sueur's fort, if he had ever built one, must have been constructed entirely of wood.

Whilst we were negotiating this exchange it began to snow for the first time this autumn, a not very pleasing incident to us, for snow upon these excursions is the precursor of many discomforts, interfering seriously with bivouacs, and offering many other impediments. Pushing on, we passed a singular conical grassy hill on the right bank, which commanded all the vicinity, and appeared to me to be a likely situation for the site of Le Sueur's fort. We stopped to breakfast about ten on the left bank, the men appearing to be very much worried with the snow, and unwilling to leave their comfortable fire when they had done. I got them away, however, about eleven, and we hastened on.

The Māhkatoh appears to form about half the volume of the St. Peter's, and is a very rapid stream. The Sissitons we had met told us it forked eleven times, and that the branches abounded in rapids and shallow places. About twelve we came to a fork or branch coming in on our right, about forty-five yards broad, and we turned into it, having a well-wooded bluff on the right bank about ninety feet high. The stream had very little current, owing to the main branch, which we had just left, rushing down with great velocity, and making backwater here. We had not proceeded three-quarters of a mile when we reached the place which the Sissitons had described to us as being that to which the Indians resorted for their pigment. This was a bluff about 150 feet high on the left bank, and from the slope being very much trodden and worn away, I saw at once that it was a locality which for some purpose or other had been frequented from a very remote period. We accordingly stopped there; and I told the men to make a fire and warm themselves whilst I examined the place.

As soon as I had reached that part of the bluff whence the pigment had been taken, Le Sueur's story lost all credit with me, for I instantly saw that it was nothing but a continuation of the seam which divided the sandstone from the limestone, and which I have before spoken of at the Mȳah Skāh, as containing a silicate of iron of a blueish-green colour. The concurrent account of all the Indians we had spoken with, that this was the place the aborigines had always resorted to to procure their pigment, and the total silence of every body since Le Sueur's visit respecting any deposit of copper ore in this or any other part of the country, convinced me that the story of his copper-mines was a fabulous one, most probably invented to raise himself in importance with the French government of that day. Charlevoix having stated that the mine was only a league and three-quarters from the mouth of the Terre Bleu, made it certain that I was now at that locality, and the seam of coloured earth gave the key to the rest. Le Sueur's account of the mine being at the foot of a mountain ten leagues long was as idle as the assertion that he had obtained 30,000 lb. of copper ore in twenty-two days, for there is nothing like a mountain in the neighbourhood. The bluff, to be sure, rises to the height of about 150 feet from the river; but when you have ascended it you find yourself at the top of a level prairie, so that what might to an inexperienced traveller appear to be a mountainous height, is nothing but the summit of the gorge which the river has cut out.

CHAPTER XXVIII.

ASCEND THE MAKATOH AGAIN.—THE VOYAGEURS UNWILLING TO PROCEED.—MILOR'S GOOD CONDUCT. — MINDAY MANGWAH, OR SWAN LAKES. — PAHKAH SKAH, A BEAUTIFUL HALF-BREED, ABANDONED BY HER FATHER.— CAMERON'S GRAVE.—MILOR'S ESCAPE FROM STARVATION.—GRANITE IN PLACE.

FINDING the copper-mine to be a fable, I turned my attention to the possibility of getting from hence across the country to the red pipe-stone quarry on the elevated district called the Côteau du Prairie, which divides the St. Peter's from the waters of the Missouri; and I walked into the interior about two miles, in the expectation of getting a glimpse of some spur of the Côteau; but nothing of the kind appearing, I returned to consult Milor. He dissuaded me strongly from attempting it, urging that we should have upwards of 150 miles to walk, carrying every thing with us; that little or no game would be found, water being very scarce in that direction. He said there was not a hill of any kind betwixt us and the Côteau, but that the country gradually rose to its summit; that, if there had been any copper-mine in the country, he must have heard of it, having frequently crossed betwixt the St. Peter's and the Missouri; and that, if he had heard of one, he certainly would have gone to see it. Objects of this kind, he assured me, were remarkably well known to the Indians, who wandered about in every direction, and who always attributed a mysterious importance to conspicuous natural objects. He added that the locality upon the Côteau, where the

Indians obtained the fine red clay of which they made their pipes, was very curious, but was not connected with any metal whatever.

Seeing there was nothing to be obtained by advancing further in this direction, and the low state of the river, and the impediments presented by the numerous rapids, rendering it almost impossible to ascend the Makatoh much farther, I turned my back upon this romance of Le Sueur's Rivière Verte, and passing swiftly down the current, got into the St. Peter's again. The moment we got into the water of this last river, where it is not mixed with that of the Makatoh, we found it exceedingly limpid, and altogether distinct from the turbid state of its tributary; a certain indication to me, that we should soon find the St. Peter's running through a primary country. There was no sensible current for some distance, owing to the backwater made by the Makatoh, the channel was about 100 yards wide, and the country extremely beautiful; the prairie occasionally coming down to the water's edge, whilst at other times bold bluffs arose with well-wooded slopes, interspersed with graceful clumps of trees.

About half-past five P. M. I landed for the night at one of the loveliest encampments I had yet met with; charming slopes, with pretty dells intersecting them, studded with trees as gracefully as if they had been planted with the most refined taste; everything indeed around was inviting. I could not but think what a splendid private estate could be contrived out of so beautiful a territory, A mansion, built on one of those gentle slopes, backed by thousands of well-formed trees, decked in their autumnal colours; thousands of acres of the most fertile level land, with the river in front, and a world of prairie in the rear, abounding with grouse. Yet with all this, how much nearer would a man be to happiness without society? This reflection, with other considerations, determined me to leave it to others to build houses here, and to content myself with making use of these pretty corners of the world, merely as amusing spectacles that gratify the taste for the moment; and to seek for happiness only where the welfare of those we love can be promoted, and which the most obscure corners are often better fitted for than the most enviable domains.

I was sorry to discover at night that my men were not proceeding as cheerfully as usual. I had apprized Milor, when I determined to leave the Makatoh, of my intention of pushing on to the sources of the St. Peter's. This he had communicated to them, but they were unwilling to go further to the west: they were well fed, yet the nights were beginning to be very cold, and they thought I ought to have provided a tent for them. These fellows, when on their Indian expeditions, had lived principally with the Ojibways, and had strong prejudices against the Sioux. To go to the sources of the St. Peter's, it would be necessary to pass Lac qui Parle, about ten days higher up. Some savage murders had been committed lately upon the Ojibways by other Indians, and the perpetrators had all rendezvoused at Lac qui Parle. Some of the reckless fellows called pillagers were said to be there, with other bad characters belonging to the Yanctons, Assiniboins, and other bands bordering on the Missouri. Having listened to all these stories, I asked Milor's opinion, who stated that we were perfectly safe if the men only acted prudently, and that their fears were very much exaggerated. I had no choice now but to turn back or face the savages, whose very wildness, so untamed by intercourse with white men, made me anxious to see them; but, as I did not wish to give

x 2

up the idea of crossing the country from the sources of the St. Peter's to the Mandans, on the Missouri, I told the men that I should act with the greatest prudence, but that nothing should change my purpose of advancing, until I got an opportunity of crossing to the Côteau du Prairie: that my life was as valuable to me as theirs could be to themselves; that Milor was known to all the Sioux; and that we should be quite safe amongst them, if they only acted discreetly; and that, if they continued to act as cheerfully as they had hitherto done, I would give them marks of my friendship when we parted. Finding that I was of good heart, and that Milor derided their fears, they assented to go on, and said, " Le bourgeois fera comme il voudra."

September 23.—We passed a cold night; the thermometer was as low as 32° in the tent, and ice had formed at the edge of the river; we had, however, a fine clear sun-rise soon after we got under way. Immense primary boulders appeared now in every part of the country. About 7 A.M. we passed a broad trail quite fresh—the trees and bushes being blazed and otherwise marked. The men did not like these appearances, and shewed as many apprehensions as if they were in an enemy's country; but Milor explained to me that this was the trail of a band of Sioux, that had crossed the river here on their way to the south. The St. Peter's was now only about fifty yards broad, and was becoming shallow. A great profusion of unios were lying in the sandy bottom, buried to their umbones; the species called *fasciatus*, with singularly beautiful nacres tinged with a brilliant carnation, being the most prevalent. I made a good collection of these shells, none of which were decorticated. About nine we stopped to breakfast, and built a rousing fire to warm ourselves; when, having got into good spirits, we resumed our paddles, and about half after ten passed a large mass of sandstone in the middle of the river. At noon we came abreast of *Minday Mangwāh*, "or Swan Lakes," about a league from the left bank. *Mangwāh* is an imitation of the cry of this bird.

Milor computed the distances to Lac qui Parle as follows:—From *Mȳa Skah*, or "White Rock," to the *Warhajōo*, or "Cotton-wood River," which we were approaching, thirty leagues: from thence to *Chagn Shȳahpay*, or "Red-wood River," forty leagues: thence to *Pahjēētah Zezēēhah*, or "Yellow Medicine River," fifteen leagues; and thence to Lac qui Parle, twenty-five leagues; so that we had at least eighty leagues to go amidst the windings of this stream, before we should reach the latter place.

At 3 P. M. I stopped to let the men eat, but took occasion to tell them that the days were getting very short, and that we should save a great deal of time, if they would make their principal meal at the close of the day, as I did. The proposition was not well received, and I thought it wise not to press it, as Jean Baptiste likes to make every meal a principal one, and they were evidently going on contrary to their inclinations. At this place the banks of the river consisted of about twenty feet of an ancient lacustrine deposit, containing great quantities of planorbis, anculotus, &c., of which I made a collection.

The men only remained half an hour eating, and when we were under way again, got into one of their cheerful lively humours, favouring me with some of their best barcaroles. They liked Milor, and I perceived that he had been talking to them. At a quarter-past four P. M. we passed some bluffs of red earth with numerous boulders on the slopes. From this colour of the earth, an approaching change in the rocks appeared probable; but the banks continued the same until past 5 P. M., when all of us being fatigued with vigorous paddling, and the canoe leaking again, I selected a tolerably good encampment, and we commenced the usual preparations for the night.

September 24.—We got under way very early, and before 8 A. M. came to some rocky bluffs on the left bank, of a peculiar appearance; and, on landing to examine them, I found they were a hard, compact red sandstone—the lowest beds being a fine-grained stone, of a brick-red colour: on the surface were numerous pot-holes, some of them a foot in diameter, and quite deep. The rocks appeared to have been very much water-worn, for they were as smooth as metal, and in some places rather difficult to stand upon. At some distance from the bank, immense masses were lying about close to each other, as if they had merely been loosened in their situs. We seemed now to have got beyond the calcareous strata. At 9 A. M. we reached the *Warhajŏo*, and I made an attempt to ascend it a short distance, but we found it too shallow to proceed far; and continuing our way up the St. Peter's, we soon passed another broad trail, and a Sissiton village, but without inhabitants. Our distance from the mouth of the St. Peter's to this place was computed by Milor to be, by the windings of the stream, about 210 miles.

Making a hasty breakfast in the neighbourhood of the village, we pushed on, the river becoming 100 yards broad again; and at 11 A. M. came to *Eepah Haska*, or "Long Point," a narrow isthmus, which runs three-quarters of a mile into the river, and is not more than fifteen feet wide. Here I observed a great many trees of the sugar maple (*Acer saccharinum*). After coasting this point, the river stretched near the distance of a mile N. 30° W., with a fine breadth of about 110 yards, the water being perfectly smooth, and a prairie on the right bank. About noon we came to another long point of a similar character, and found the Zizania abounding in the neighbourhood. This was a hot day; and having stopped to refresh the men at half-past one, we proceeded and passed a fertile bottom, with a beautiful open wood growing on it. Nothing can be more pleasing than this portion of the St. Peter's, which, sometimes holding a serpentine course to one bank, and then taking a graceful curve to the other, always when it approaches a bluff, leaves a pleasing prairie on the other side. Sometimes, for a considerable distance, the river and the bottoms occupied a space equal in breadth to a mile and a half. The general amenity of the country put us all into high spirits; and just before 5 P. M., whilst we were paddling away, and screaming a Canadian boat-song at the top of our voices, we suddenly came up with several canoes on the left bank, fastened to the bushes, with a lodge containing four stout men, several women and children, and a very beautiful young half-breed girl, about seventeen years old, with fine flaxen hair. They had heard our screaming before we came in sight, and were not a little flurried; but the appearance of Milor calmed them, and they came to the water-side to speak to him.

We stopped for a short time, and missing the flaxen-haired beauty, with whose unusual appearance, so much contrasted with the coarse, black, wiry hair of the others, I had been very much struck, I told Milor to ask where she was, when they pointed her out to me hiding herself behind one of the trees. Perceiving we were white men, and knowing she was the daughter of a white man, a modest feeling, which the others seemed to be strangers to, had taken possession of her, and she was evidently reluctant to show herself. Upon inquiring into her history, I learnt that she was the daughter of an American trader named Robinson, who had lived some time among the Nacotahs, by an Indian woman, who had lived with him as his wife. Having collected his debts in the Indian country, he left his family under pretence of business at Prairie du Chien, and had never returned to them. This beautiful creature, being thus abandoned by her father, had been brought up as a savage; but ignorant as she was of the ways of civilization, the modesty of her demeanour betrayed the consciousness that she was connected by blood with the white race. Upon being informed of these circumstances, I was exceedingly touched with the hopelessness of her condition, for independent of her beauty, there was a gentleness and shyness of manner about her which seemed to implore the protection of the race she had sprung from. Before we left the place, I sent her by Milor some pork and biscuit, and a new silk handkerchief, a somewhat extraordinary present, to be sure, to a young beauty of seventeen, but she received it very pleasingly; perhaps, after all, she may be less miserable here than if her father had taken her with him. The head man of this little band was called *Chas kās keeah*, or "First in Age." This being the season for musk-rats, as the traders call them, they had taken an immense number of them, which they had skinned, and the carcases, which they are very fond of, were drying on sticks over a slow fire. In twenty days they had taken 1200 of these animals. Some of the traders at Prairie du Chien told me that these creatures increase in number now that the foxes and other animals are diminishing.

The *sīnkepay*, as the Nacotahs call the muskquash* or musk-rat of the traders, is much larger than the common rat; it has a reddish-grey fur resembling that of the beaver, and in common with that animal constructs itself a conical mud house, where the situation admits of it, above the surface of any body of water where a root grows, which it subsists on during the winter, and to which it has access by a hole in the bottom. I have occasionally seen skins of this animal of a fawn colour. Besides this famous supply of musk-rats they had a large pile of wild ducks and teal which they had shot, together with a fine heron. All the Indians looked strong and hearty, in consequence of the abundance of animal food at this season of the year.

As I was stepping into the canoe to depart, some of the women came and told Milor that if I did not give them also some pork and biscuit, "it would not be me"—an oblique piece of flattery intended to provoke my generosity. I told them that I had given some to the young girl because she belonged to my race, but that I would give them also some, and begged they would always be kind to her, as the poor girl had lost her father. They answered that white men came amongst them and took wives, who thought of nothing but taking care of their children and their goods when they were travelling about the country; and that when they had collected all their skins they took everything away, and never came back again. That this was what Robinson had done: he had told his wife he was going a journey, that she must take care of the little boy and the little girl they had, and he would soon be back and bring them all new clothes; that

* This word is corrupted from some dialects of the Lenape, and means "red."

he never came the first winter, and when their old clothes were worn out he never came with any new ones; that he never came for fifteen winters, nor ever sent her a message; that *Pāhkah Skāh,* or "White Hair," was now seventeen years old, and her brother was a very good hunter. I desired Milor to tell them that perhaps Robinson was dead; but they said that Milor knew better, for he had seen him two years ago at Prairie du Chien. Upon which I answered, that there were bad men amongst the whites as well as amongst the Indians, and that good white men loved their wives and children, and took care of them as long as they lived. They laughed, and asked Milor if I was going to stay in the country, and intended to take a wife? I answered that I was afraid the white men had got such bad characters that I should not be able to get one; when they all laughed and exclaimed with one voice, that, if I wintered in their neighbourhood, I should have Pahkah Skah!

A great deal more has been written about the austerity and reserve of Indians than is true. If you are uniformly kind to them, and generous when it is convenient to be so, they are as open-hearted and merry a race as ever I travelled amongst. These were a remarkably good-tempered, pleasant set; and we had become so well acquainted, and it was drawing so late, that at one time I thought of pitching my tent here; but on looking round, I saw many reasons against it, so we bade them "Good bye;" and paddling on a couple of miles, made our bivouac in a charming, clean, open wood on the right bank.

September 25.—After a comfortable night's rest, we hastened to get everything on board, and were on the water at sunrise. At eight we passed a place on the right bank, where Milor buried his bourgeois, a Mr. Cameron, in 1811. He was an enterprising, sagacious Scotchman, who had amassed a good deal of property by trafficking with the Indians; but with him, as with many others, the word "enough" meant a little more than what he had got, and whilst upon one of his expeditions he was taken ill in his canoe, was landed, and died in the woods. Milor told me, upon this occasion, how nearly himself and three others in the service of Mr. Cameron had been starved to death; and as it illustrates well the privations which those who engage in these trading adventures are sometimes exposed to, I shall give a sketch of his narration.

The winter was advancing fast upon them, and they had delayed so long collecting their packs of skins, that the ice formed one night too strong to permit their descending the stream in the canoe. There was, however, some hopes of a thaw, and they kept waiting from day to day until their provision, of which they had but a slight supply, was exhausted. They had nothing left now but to leave their packs of skins under the canoe and take to the woods, in the hope that Cameron, who was at a distant trading post below, seeing the state of the weather, would send relief to them, and that they should meet it on the way. The snow was too deep to enable them to carry any burden, and with their last meal in their pockets they commenced their journey. They met with no game of any kind for the first two days; and on the night of the second, having nothing whatever to eat, they were reduced to the necessity of stripping some bark from a tree to masticate. In the morning the severity of the weather increased, and no alternative presented itself but stopping to die on the way, or making the most desperate effort to extricate themselves. On the evening of the third day two of the men became weak, and frequently urged the others to stop; but as it was always found a difficult task to persuade them to go on again, Milor always opposed these delays. These poor fellows were gradually losing their judgment; they knew that delay would be fatal to the whole party, yet the sense of present distress took away all reflection from them. Milor, who was ahead of them all, came before night to a place somewhat sheltered from the wind, which was very piercing, and seeing some signs of the bushes having been disturbed, he stepped aside to look, and found a dead Indian beside the remains of a small fire. He had no provisions with him, and had probably been crossing the prairies to join some band, and the whole country being covered with a deep snow, had lost his way.

Milor now shouted to the men to come on, and they, hoping for good news, hastened to the place. Pointing to the dead Indian, he told them that would be their fate before morning if they stopped. Being somewhat frightened at this, they kept up a pretty good pace until a late hour; and Milor being in a part of the country he was acquainted with, took one of the most active of the men with him, and, after great exertions, they had the good luck to catch two musk-rats. With these they returned to the men, who had built up a good fire, and having eaten one of the animals they lay down to sleep, and rested very well. In the morning they ate the other before starting, and, as they felt a little more cheerful, Milor told them, that, if they would walk like men, he would take them to a place where there were plenty of musk-rats, and that, as soon as they had laid in a supply of them, they would strike across the country to Traverse des Sioux, where they would be sure to hear of Cameron and get food. For two days, however, they caught nothing more, and all began to be sick and to despond. On the sixth day they caught one musk-rat, which raised their spirits a little. on the seventh they caught another, but that night all three of the men fell sick, and in the morning he could not persuade them to stir. Uncertain whether to abandon or stay by them, he went to the river and tried several places in vain for musk-rats. The weather, however, became more mild, and he returned to the fire to tell the men they were going to have fine weather, and that he was sure Cameron had sent somebody to meet them with provisions: this encouraged them a little, and they agreed to go on.

They had not been marching an hour, when Milor, looking attentively to the south-east, declared that he saw smoke in that direction, and that there must be a fire: this, as Milor said, had the effect of a glass of *eau de vie* upon them, and they went briskly on for two or three hours; but this cheering sign disappeared, and the men were beginning to despond again, when the thought struck Milor, that, if any party was coming to their relief, they would naturally be keeping a look-out also. He accordingly directed the men to build up a fire, and to put a quantity of wet bark upon it to make a heavy smoke, whilst he would go to the top of a bluff and observe if the signal was answered. In less than half an hour after he had gained the bluff, he saw a thick column of smoke arise to the south-east, and not more than three miles distant. He immediately waved his cap, shouted to his companions, and set off in the direction of the expected aid. It was indeed the relief they expected: two men, each with a pack containing pork and biscuit, had been despatched from Traverse des Sioux, and Cameron, with three others, were to leave it in a canoe if an expected thaw admitted of it, and at any rate were to start with an additional supply. Milor having refreshed himself, set out to meet his comrades with the reinforcement. "What did they do when they saw you?" I asked Milor. "Ces gaillards-là ont commencés à danser, Monsieur," was his answer.

This incident in the adventures of Milor is very much to the credit of Cameron, who made so resolute an attempt to relieve his poor *engagés*, when the chances were so much against his succeeding. It was during the same winter that a band of 164 Yanctons, seeing that all their families would be starved to death if they did not make a great effort to obtain some provisions, started with the snow three feet deep, in search of the buffaloe, which were said to be between the *Shayanne* river and *Minday Wakon*, or "Lake of the Spirit." The unfortunate savages never met with the buffaloe, and, with the exception of three or four of their number, were frozen to death—the deep snows making it impossible for them to extricate themselves.

A little after 10 A. M. we came to a mass of granite in place, which Milor estimated to be fifteen leagues from the Warhajōo. Hereabouts then was the junction of the sandstone I had so long kept company with, with the granite; for it appeared to me that the peculiar red colour of the sandstone of yesterday was derived from its contiguity with the granite which had altered it. Huge masses of this primary rock were scattered about on both sides of the river : here was, no doubt, the original situs of the boulders I had passed below. The river now contracted to about fifty feet. At half-past 11 A. M. we came to the trading post of a Mr. Moore, on the right bank of the river, then encamped in a tent, but who was building a small house, consisting of two rooms—one for himself and family to sleep in, the other to contain his goods. His wife, a middle-aged bustling Indian woman, seemed to be heartily engaged in the work. Their children were very Indian in their faces—small eyes and large cheek-bones; the half-breeds appearing always to show more of the Indian than the white man. Mr. Moore was a thin, good-looking man, about forty-five years old, but intelligent, and gave me some interesting information: he said that the Côteau du Prairie was about fifty miles west of his post; and not more than ten miles distant from Big Stone Lake: adding, but I thought erroneously, that it consisted principally of sandstone and limestone, the beds of which extended to the Shayanne River. He stated also that he had seen fragments of coal on Lake Traverse, and that I might proceed in full confidence that I should find the Indians peaceably disposed. The winter, he observed, rarely set in until the end of October; but that it gave very little notice in this part of the world—extremes of mild and severe weather taking place within twenty-four hours. Indian corn, he informed me, ripened very well where he lived; and that next year it was his intention to plant both corn and potatoes. The fact of maize ripening well is a sure guarantee for a great increase of the white population here. Where this valuable grain comes to maturity so far north (44° 30'), all other grains flourish; and the ground here is exceedingly fertile.

We now took leave of Mr. Moore, who, I learnt from Milor, had been a great many years in the Indian country, and had taken to wife the half-breed daughter of a Mr. Hart, another white trader. Moore had formerly been connected with an American fur company, but was now established as an independent trader—an annoyance which these companies are not slow to rid themselves of. Milor informed me that Mr. Sibley intended sending up a barge with goods very soon, and establishing a trading-house opposite to him. This competition, as long as it lasts, will be greatly in favour of the poor Indians, who at present are obliged to pay as much as sixty musk-rat skins for one blanket.

We shot three cormorants on the wing this morning from the canoe, to the great joy of the men, who make no scruple of putting every thing that falls in their way into their pot to boil with the pork. The navigation of the St. Peter's, as we approached its sources, had many embarrassments in the great number of sand-bars and snags, which the *voyageurs* call *chicots;* but they shew great skill and prudence in their canoe management, seeming to know, from the appearance of the water, whether they ought to go slow or quick: they had already brought our frail but well-constructed bark vessel about 900 miles, and it was as sound as when we first started. At half-past two we had granite in place on the right bank, and lofty upland in front. I landed here, and went to the summit, where I found a boundless extent of prairie, without a single tree, on each side of the river. The valley was about two miles in breadth, consisting of beautiful fertile bottoms, through which the narrow stream meandered, looking, at a distance, like a bright silvery riband. Upon the slope of the banks a great part of the wood was dead and black from the fires of the preceding year; and I observed that the men always preferred to encamp in similar situations, because the wood burnt briskly, and took them less time to collect. About 5 P. M. the masses of granite in place extended almost across the river, and finding a convenient situation near them, I made the signal and we encamped for the night.

CHAPTER XXIX.

HOW TO COOK A RACOON. — MAKE A CACHE OF OUR HEAVY ARTICLES. — A GRANITE COUNTRY.—PROWLERS ABOUT OUR CAMP.—THE GRAND PORTAGE.

September 26.—Having roused the men at 5 A. M., they proceeded to gum the bottom of the canoe, which had suffered a little amongst the shallows and snags of yesterday, during which time I collected some fine unios. We started soon after six, and passed a rapid with a fall of about twelve inches. Having got into still water, the men, who had gorged themselves to a late hour the preceding night with the cormorants and pork, seeing a racoon running on the shore, set up the cry of *"Chat sauvage!"* and, pulling away for the shore, all jumped out without "By your leave" or "With your leave"—Milor and myself, who had not seen the cause of this general animation, remaining on board. A small *coulée* came into the river close by, and, the animal taking that direction, the men followed, making as much noise as if they were contending with a stag. We now jumped out, and fastening the canoe, hastened to the *coulée*, where, after a long search, the poor animal was at last detected and immolated. He had been to the river-side looking for crawfish, which the racoon in this part of the country is very fond of; so that the avengers of the craw-fish came upon him at an unlucky moment.

The weather was beautiful to-day, warm, sunny, and serene, with a slight haze, resembling what is called in

North America the Indian summer. We made a hasty breakfast upon a *battue* or beach, and pushed on again, all anxious to make the most of this pleasant season. I had frequently heard this periodical serene part of the autumn attributed by persons living on the Atlantic to conflagrations of the dry grass on the immense western prairies of the Indian country; but I now found the same phenomenon in the prairie country without a fire of any kind. We must look otherwise therefore for the cause. The river now became so embarrassed and shallow, that we could no longer use the paddles, and were obliged to take to poles. About 1 P. M. we were obliged to stop and unload the canoe, the bottom having got torn a little. Whilst some of the men were attending to this important business, the others began to prepare their dinner, and being curious to see how they would cook the racoon, I remained by their fire. A more summary exercise of the culinary art I never saw. Having made a fine blazing fire, they tied his hind feet to a piece of stick, and his head to another; two of them then held him in the blaze until all the fur was singed off, and then slightly eviscerating him, consigned him in that state to the pot, covering him over with pieces of fat pork to keep him down. They seemed to enjoy their repast immensely, for their talking and laughing was incessant.

We got under way at half-past 2 P. M., and soon found the river diminish from two feet and a half to one foot, the water beautifully transparent, and the unios stuck in countless numbers in the pure white sand, so that I could, by baring my arm, select them as we went along. The stream began to be very narrow; in one place the trees had fallen across, and it took us a long time to get through. Our voyage now required unceasing exertion;

we were constantly stopping to drag the canoe over the sand-bars and remove snags; and all of us fatigued, were glad to encamp about half-past five P. M.

September 27.—We had another beautiful morning, and were afloat before 6 A. M. At seven we had not quite a foot of water, and I began to entertain apprehensions for our future progress; the stream was becoming more shallow every mile, and it was evident that this not being the rainy season, there was reason to apprehend we should have to put our lading in a *cache,* or hiding-place, and take to the prairie. The Canadians, instead of encouraging me, and suggesting prudent plans for pursuing our journey on foot to Lac qui Parle, rather tried to conjure up difficulties, saying we had enough provisions to take us back again, which we should not have in three or four days. Milor gave it as his opinion that we might get the canoe on as far as Lac qui Parle, but no farther. I therefore told them, that, whatever might be their opinions, I had determined to go on, and if the water should fail us, we would all take to the prairie; but that it was childish talking about it until we were compelled to stop; and that meantime every man must use his best exertions. Finding me resolute, they went on in a dogged sort of manner, to which I paid no attention, only giving my orders, as I always did upon these occasions, in a sterner manner.

At half-past seven we passed a small stream on the left bank, which Milor called *Weētah Chagntah Eahāntah,* meaning the river which flows from a "lake, with an island whose dead wood falls into it," or Dead Wood Island River, as I have called it in the map. The traders have given it the name of Beaver River, an absurd name, seeing that all the streams had these animals upon them. My feet becoming cold, I landed to walk in the prairie, and finding it warm and pleasant exercise, soon left the canoe far behind me. Having gained the upland, I had another of the magnificent views of this unpeopled wilderness. The line of the St. Peter's was well marked by the trees growing on each bank : and these, owing to the narrowness of the stream, effectually concealed both it and the canoe ; but from the screams of the flights of wild geese, that were hovering over it as they rose from the river, I could know exactly the point where it was. I had frequently observed, also, that these birds turned a little out of their line of flight when they perceived us, and flew over the canoe : upon one occasion we winged one of them, and as the bird kept falling and using the other wing, the whole flock lowered itself, as if with the intention of assisting their wounded companion.

Descending to the river to a convenient point for us to breakfast at, Milor, when the canoe came up, advised that we should make a *cache* of everything not necessary to us, in order to lighten the boat: selecting, therefore, all my best specimens, both of fossils, minerals, and shells, I had the rest, which weighed two or three hundred pounds, put into bags, and having dug a hole amidst the bushes, we put the bags with various other things into it, and, covering it carefully up, we breakfasted and left the place—it being understood that if the party separated and returned by the Missouri, those who re-descended the St. Peter's were to re-embark what we had placed in the *cache*, and deliver them at Fort Snelling or Prairie du Chien.

We left the *cache* at 11 A. M., much more buoyant than before, and got on without striking the bottom so often, passing soon afterwards a stream on the right bank called *Chagnshāhyapay*, or "Red-wood River." This red wood is a particular sort of willow, with an under bark of a reddish colour, which the Indians dry and smoke. When mixed with tobacco it makes what they call *Kinnee Kinnik*, and is much less offensive than common tobacco. The St. Peter's now became wider, but was shallow. Milor said we were now eight leagues from some strong rapids, named from a man called Patterson, who wintered there once, and who, from wearing a bear-skin cap, was called *Wakon Apāhhah*, or "Bear's head;" *Wakon Sēejah* which means a "bear" in Nacotah, is also the name they give to the devil; *Seejah* meaning "evil," hence *Wakon Sēejah*, "Evil Spirit." This name was probably first conferred on the grizzly bear, who is rather too strong for the Indian.

At two, at the place where we stopped for the men to eat, the grass had become so dry that the fire began to run in it. Milor stated that we must soon expect to see prairies on fire, for many of the Indians were so careless, that they left live embers at their stopping-places. I could not understand from him that they ever purposely set the prairies on fire. A huge perpendicular granite rock was standing alone here on the right bank, and further on we passed a fine escarpment of vertical granite, fifty feet high, and about 150 yards long, upon the face of which several swallows had built their nests. At 5 P.M. we encamped at a small cascade running across the channel, called *Hhāhhah* ("The Falls"), the *Hh* being pronounced as a suppressed guttural. I chose the place of our bivouac in a pretty wood on the right bank, with a prairie behind us, bounded by rugged granite hills to the south, resembling parts of Dartmoor. In our front we had the falls and a curious basin excavated by them. In approaching this basin the river flows through a passage it has worn in a ledge of granite stretching across the channel about S. E. and N. W. by compass. The passage through which the water flows is about thirty-five yards broad, and the ledge continues to the left about 100 yards, and twenty yards broad, with a slope of 20° N. E. by N. This slope is as slippery as metal, and has evidently been produced by the friction of water continued for a long period. But betwixt this slope and the cascade is an excavated basin about fifty yards by forty. It is evident that in ancient times, when the volume of the river was many times greater than it is now, the ledge of granite extended across the channel, that its greatest force was exerted upon that part of the ledge where the present narrow entrance to the basin is, and that the cascade by recession has shifted its place to where it now is, and commenced, by its eddy, the excavation of the basin. I consider this an instructive instance, as well of the greater amplitude of the rivers of this continent in former times, as of the power which water exercises upon the bed over which it passes, and excavates its channel by recession.

September 28. — We rose at 5 A. M., and having well gummed our canoe, and got every thing on board, proceeded to the cascade. Here we unloaded it again, and one of the men going into the river where the water projected over, contrived, with the assistance of the rest below, to hoist the canoe to the top. Nothing could exceed the care and judgment of the men upon this and similar occasions. They considered the canoe as the ark of their safety, and upon all difficult occasions were entirely to be depended upon. When in the midst of their jokes and merriment they would come to a difficult rapid, it was admirable to see how vigilant they would instantly become. At a word from the steersman one or more of them would jump breast-high in the water to steady the canoe and guide it amidst the sharp rocks through which the river came boiling down. This they would do several times a day without complaining; and upon this occasion, on a very cold morning, a few minutes after starting, four of the men stood breast-high in the water to steady the canoe, whilst the man above drew it up with a rope.

We soon reloaded, and at 7 A.M. were afloat again. From this place Milor said it was ten leagues by land to Lac qui Parle, a good day's journey to a stout walker, but a troublesome one when the grass is high. The banks of the river were generally low, but occasionally immense bluffs of granite came jutting in, maple, oak, poplar, and willow abounding. Milor informed me that the sugar-maple was a great blessing to the Indians; for that often in the spring, before the snow has melted, and they are almost reduced to starvation, they watch the maple-tree, and as soon as the sap begins to run in March, drink it and soon recover their strength. They also in great emergencies find much nutriment in a creeper which twists round the tree, and which they call *bois de tort*.

As we advanced the quantity of wild ducks and geese became enormous; but they were shy, and generally rose before we could get within shot, for it was impossible to make my men preserve silence; but the bends in the river being very short here, owing to the resistance of the granite, sometimes when we suddenly came round one of the points, we used to knock a good many of the birds down: all of them were fat, and many of them had the most beautiful plumage, especially the gaudy-crested wood-duck, which is a common bird here.

At 8 A. M. we reached Patterson's Rapids, which in fact do not deserve that name. It is true the bed of the river appears so much obstructed with rounded masses of granite, as to make it a difficult affair to get a canoe through at low water, but there was no boiling and foaming of the stream, so as to give it that character which distinguishes what are called rapids. All of us, however, except two, landed to lighten the canoe, and walked through a wood to a fine prairie bottom with the wild grass six feet high. Here, near to the river, we fell in with the track of the *charette* road of the Fur Company. Milor informed me that their goods were sent up the river to this point, and then put into carts or *charettes* with two wheels and one horse, and sent across the prairies to their different trading posts. It was a new and welcome sight to see ruts made by wheeled carriages, although they reminded us of civilization, rather than introduced us to it.

The rich prairie bottom I was now traversing was at least one mile broad, and extended far upwards along the course of the river. What a meadow for a farmer! Tired of walking in the high grass, I made for the upland prairie, the surface of which consisted of a light sandy soil; but the infinite number of small hills of rich black mould, thrown up by the geomys, shewed the fertility of the subsoil. Seeing some eminences at a distance on the prairie, which I thought might be lofty enough to give me a view of the Côteau du Prairie, I made for them, believing them not to be more than a mile and a half distant; but such is the deception in prairie distances produced by objects in situations where there is nothing to compare with them, that that which appears near is often distant, and that which appears large is often small.

Thus, these eminences, instead of one mile and a half, were at least four miles distant, for it took me more than an hour to reach them; and instead of being high, were so low that they appeared quite insignificant. I could now understand why a bear had been mistaken for a buffalo; for it seems that upon these immense prairies, where there is nothing to interrupt the general level, any object, however small, is, for want of something to compare it with, invested by the imagination with dimensions that do not belong to it.

I now turned back to seek the canoe, having got a sick-headache by walking too far before breakfast: it had got ahead of me, but I soon overtook it, and was glad to take a cup of tea and eat a cold wild duck which had been boiled the preceding day. Having got under way we set to work vigorously with our poles, but soon came to other rocks in the river, which obliged some of us to land and lighten the canoe. Whilst on the upland prairie I found some slabs of flat salmon-coloured limestone, that had been brought here apparently from the north-west, from whence I concluded the granite stretched to the north-east, and that the limestone we had travelled with so long was north-west of us at no great distance.

We found the wild fowl less shy now that we had left behind us the landing-place of the Fur Company, owing, no doubt, to the birds below being a good deal harassed by the people in the service of the traders. We got as many as we wanted, all of them exceedingly fat; and some of them were so like the canvass-back in every particular, that I could see no distinction. The unios were singularly beautiful in this part of the river, especially the *Unio fasciatus*, some specimens of which outstripped in elegance any I had yet seen.

About 2 P.M. the river became so shallow that there was no longer any channel. We were all, therefore, obliged to get out, and the men dragged the canoe through the sand as well as they could. This was a tedious and fatiguing day, and we were glad to encamp at 5 P.M. Our progress had not been great during it, but I told the men that we had overcome all the difficulties that presented themselves, and to-morrow, after a night's repose, we should be ready to do the same thing again. They appeared more reconciled to going on than they were, for they knew that every day made the water shallower below as well as above, and that they would have plenty of hard work if we were to return before it rained and swelled the river. But these Canadians did not think much beyond the moment: what principally occupied their minds were the facts that we got more wild ducks and grouse than sufficed to subsist our party daily, and that all this fine living would soon be at an end if we were to turn back; and as I was convinced that the Indian summer would last for some time, I was no more afraid of their opposing my wishes at present. Our constant dish now, both for parlour and kitchen, was a pot of grouse, wild ducks, and biscuit all boiled up together. The *potage* which this made was the delight of the men: the pork and ham we saved for our return.

September 29.—The night was a very cold one, and I was glad to rise with the dawn. Whilst I was washing at the river, Milor and the men came to inform me, that during the night they had heard men whistling, which was answered, and then the occasional crackling of dry branches, as if of men walking stealthily about: this was repeated an hour before day. They were all quite sure of the fact, and thought it was a party of young Ojibways, four in number, prowling round to take Sioux scalps. Attracted by our fires, they had cautiously examined our strength, and finding that we were white men had moved off; yet, if they had fallen in with one or two of us, and could have overpowered us, they would have done so, for the young Indians who are out in pursuit of scalps never return without them if possible. Milor said that the chiefs found it very difficult sometimes to keep the youths within bounds ; that, notwithstanding the restraints laid upon them, and their being watched, they often got away in the night, and rather than return without a trophy, would murder a lone woman or a child, or any one they could overpower, knowing that if they got safe back with a scalp everything would be overlooked. The women, it seems, always take the part of the delinquents, and, although they are no better than the menial slaves of the chiefs, still they have a great deal of influence over them. So true it is, that in all situations of life men cannot live without the society of women, and that they generally find out they cannot lead quiet lives without they permit their better halves to do just as they please.

In the morning we were so much occupied with gumming the canoe and thawing our frozen things, that we did not get away until 7 A. M. I continued on foot to the mouth of the *Chāhtāhn Boah*, or "Sparrow-hawk River," a stream about twenty-five yards wide, when the canoe coming up I embarked ; and not long afterwards we passed another stream on the opposite or right bank, called *Payjētah Zezēēhah*, or " Yellow Medicine," from a yellow root which the Indians procure here for medicinal purposes. The St. Peter's was about eighty yards wide here, the banks flat and abounding in zizania and wild ducks and teal, that flew up in clouds as we advanced. At

9 A. M. we stopped to breakfast : it was a fine autumnal morning, sunny yet cool. The leaves were falling from the trees very fast; they froze in the cold nights, and the hot sun succeeding hastened their fall.

At 1 P. M. we reached *Minnay Cháhháh*, or "Waterfalls," from whence it is about two miles to the *Grande Portage*. Here we all got out of the canoe, and the men entering the water as high as their waists, commenced dragging it through a rather turbulent rapid about 100 yards in length. Ascending the uplands on the left bank with Milor, I had a charming view of the country. The breadth of the valley was still about two miles : immense rugged masses of black-looking granite lifted up their heads throughout the whole line of it, which was very serpentine. On descending to the river, I found the men had taken all the lading out of the canoe, the gum having cracked owing to the frost, and given way generally whilst they were dragging it. This caused a detention of more than an hour; and learning from Milor that there were four more rapids in advance, I took to the uplands again on the left bank, having an immense prairie on my right. Walking along the crest of the uplands, and occasionally watching the progress of the canoe, I came to a ravine at least 800 yards wide, very profound and thickly wooded; and seeing two others of a similar kind ahead, I did not care to descend into them alone, as they were exactly such places as marauders would select to hide themselves in, and descended to the river again. This I did with reluctance, being in a good humour for a long walk; and certainly a fine stretch along the edge of a boundless prairie, with a river below you flowing through a beautiful valley, is a source of much enjoyment. During my walk I had again occasion to observe, that, in considering the causes which have led to such extensive plains being totally without trees, it is to be borne in mind, that wherever there is water and shelter there trees always grow.

The other rapids beyond the *Minnay Chahhah* all occurred within the distance of a mile, so that in fact the men were always in the water. About half-past three P. M. we reached the Grande Portage. Here we came upon an uninterrupted succession of violent rapids for three miles, so leaving two of the men to conduct the canoe through this long line of breakers, we landed the luggage and the greater portion of the provisions; and each of us taking something, commenced our march across the Grande Portage, which is about a mile and a half broad. Each of the three Canadians took about 100 lb. weight upon his shoulders, and looking at nothing but his feet, trudged away with it without a murmur. This they are accustomed to do from their youth upwards. I saw, however, that all the men were fatigued and would be much better for having dry clothes; therefore we drew near to the bank of the river where the canoe must pass, at a place about half-way across, and selected a place for our night's bivouac. The canoe having reached us we pitched the tent, and having built up our fires, lost no time in making ourselves as comfortable as we could.

September 30.—At day-break we put ourselves in motion again, and taking my portfolio and instruments, I proceeded to the west end of the *portage*, which was across a fertile bottom, with immense masses of granite all quasistratified, in lamina of about an inch broad, distributed about. In some places these masses were twenty feet high, and dipped to the south-east. Some of these laminated masses were in a vertical position. Most of them were a red quartzose granite, with a slight quantity of mica; but some were gneissoid, and from some of the masses I collected good specimens of both granite and gneiss. Having got everything across the *portage*, and being joined by the canoe, we re-embarked, and got with much pleasure upon a smooth stream about eighty yards wide, as great a luxury to us as leaving a bad road to enter upon a good turnpike is to travellers. I could not but admire this morning the address with which these *voyageurs* carried their loads on crossing the *portages*. A large bag full of something was first put on the back of the head and neck of one of the men, with a collar round it and the forehead to prevent its slipping off; upon that a heavy bag of biscuit was placed, and above that again one of my largest carpet bags containing minerals and shells. Thus loaded and bending down, the man, keeping his eyes fixed upon the trail and his feet, and never attempting to look up, went for near a mile without stopping. L'Amirant, who was a stout young fellow, always carried my luggage, as I wished to have the same man always accountable for it, and he never used to show anything like impatience, except when it came to the carpet bag, and then he would say, " A présent ce s—— sac avec les pierres."

CHAPTER XXX.

CAMP NEARLY BURNT. — REACH LAC QUI PARLE. — TURBULENT CONDUCT OF THE SAVAGES. — DANGER OF BEING PLUNDERED. — THE AUTHOR'S SPEECH TO THE CHIEFS.

This was a beautiful and a warm morning, with a perfectly serene sky, and we moved along very agreeably amidst extensive areas of wild rice and clouds of wild ducks until we came to more rapids—three of them coming in near to each other, and a fourth lying in wait for us a mile further on. We therefore lost a great deal of time in landing and re-embarking; but the men behaved very well, and their conduct was the only thing I was anxious about. Having passed these rapids, we had flat banks without trees, or only two or three here and there, the river spreading itself to the width of 110 yards, and winding about as it were in an immense meadow. The prairies now began to look brown, like the English moors, the water was still, and we paddled away at the rate of four or five miles an hour, the men singing Canadian boat-songs, and only interrupting them to halloo at the top of their voices, now and then, when the otters were seen swimming about amongst the zizania. Milor said that buffaloes were killed here about five years ago, but that he thinks the animals have been so persecuted that they will never return.

We stopped to breakfast about half-past nine A. M., and started again in forty-five minutes. The musk-rats were already at work building their conical houses on the marshy grounds, with mud and the straw of the wild rice, against the approach of winter. As we advanced through these low rice-grounds, clouds of wild ducks rose on the wing, and we killed them at our leisure from the canoe. Nothing tended to keep up the good-humour of my Jean Baptistes, so much as seeing piles of these beautiful birds, all as fat as they could be, laid in the canoe. I became now more than ever persuaded that the most scientific as well as the most humane way of the few governing the many is to do it *par le ventre*. At half-past twelve we passed a broad gap in a bank twenty feet high of clay and sand, which Milor said was made by an immense herd of buffaloes that crossed the river here eighteen years ago.

About 3 p.m. we came to a stream on the left bank about fifty feet wide, called *Mēa Wakon* ("Spirit Medicine"); and here we saw that the prairie was on fire at no great distance from us. The river now contracted to thirty-five yards, and became more narrow as we advanced. We pushed on, and about half-past five made our bivouac for the night amongst some very high grass and weeds, not being able to select a better place. From this place Milor said it was not more than two leagues to Lac qui Parle by land, but that it would be five by water. When night fell the prairies both north and south of us shewed themselves brilliantly on fire, though perhaps eight or ten miles off. Before we lay down I pointed out to Milor the danger of our situation, encamped in high thick grass; and as it was evident, that, if the wind should change, the fire might gain too rapidly upon us, I directed the men to have every thing ready to retreat to the river if such a danger should be imminent. Milor promised that he would keep a good look out during the night, and I found he was to be relied upon, for having turned out twice, to see how the fires were going on, I found him both times watching.

October 1.—But we were all too much fatigued to keep up a perpetual vigilance, and having fallen into a profound sleep, were not aware that a high wind had arisen about two in the morning, which, driving the flames with wonderful velocity, had set everything on fire down to the water's edge, except the low bottom upon which we were, and which was saved by the grass being rather green and wet. The men, who were awoke by the fire roaring within two or three hundred yards of us, rose in alarm and came to my tent. Upon examining our position, we came to the conclusion that the fire had passed the bottom on which we were on both sides, and that it was the juicy green grass which had saved us; the which, if it had been dry enough, would have got into immediate conflagration, and, in the confusion created by the flames and the volumes of smoke, we should most probably have not been able to save anything, and might some of us have perished. Looking back to the danger we had incurred, I felt very much ashamed of my own want of vigilance, and told Milor how much we were in want of a Providence to take care of us, since it was evident we all preferred sleeping to taking care of our lives. He admitted that we had not acted with prudence, and told me that three Nahcotahs were suffocated last year, having laid down where the grass was dry and thick, and that the fire having got into it, the smoke had first bewildered and then suffocated them, they being found each of them in a different place, where they had fallen after struggling in vain to escape. Buffaloes also perish, for when surrounded by raging volumes of flame, the smoke first blinds and then suffocates them. It requires to have seen the tremendous columns of smoke that sometimes rise, to understand how it is that wild ducks are said to be sometimes unable to escape.

We remained watching the fire until 3 A. M., when it having reached the river and expended itself, we lay down again. When morning dawned, we perceived, from the mantle of nature being changed from a russet-brown to a deep black, that the prairies had been all burnt close to the ground; and amongst the drollest contrasts I have ever seen, was, I think, that now presented to us, of a serene sky with a brilliant sun shining upon a black world.

At about half-past six we re-embarked; the stream having now become a rivulet not more than twenty-five yards wide, the borders of which were covered with interesting plants. At 9 A. M. we stopped in a clump of sugar-maple trees to breakfast, where we found a great number of little wooden troughs, which the Indians, after making an incision in the trees, place beneath them to collect the sap: here, also, were their spring teebees, which they inhabit at that season. Directing the men after breakfast to proceed up the river, I walked about a mile through the alluvial ground adjacent to the river, and got upon the upland, from whence I had a boundless view over the prairie to the south and south-west. The valley beneath me, the soil of which was entirely formed of fluviatile deposit, was still about two miles broad, and shewed how vast the volume of fresh water had formerly been. Here I had again occasion to observe how much the fertility of these prairies or uplands is injured by these annual conflagrations, the vegetable matter being burnt, and everything on the surface incinerated, so that the wild grass on these extensive plains becomes short and wiry. Granite boulders, occasionally mixed up with others of a soft pale-coloured limestone, were lying in great quantities upon the river slopes.

The regularity of the serpentine bends of the river was admirable : from the point where I stood I could see the stream at the termination of six different bends, at each of which the canoe appeared by turns. On descending, I measured the neck of one of these bends, and found it to be sixty yards broad.

At length the stream, constantly diminishing in width, became blocked up with fallen trees, and it was exceedingly tedious to stop so often to cut our way through them; but we took them patiently in succession, and having got through the worst part, came to a small cleared piece of ground on the left bank, where we found vestiges of white men, for a log-hut was building, and there were three Indians, two of them clad in old British uniforms. These men came running down to the bank, and one of them fired his gun over our heads as a salute. Milor now found out from them that the log-hut was erecting for a missionary, who was in the neighbourhood making some hay he had cut. As soon as they had given us this information, they set off scampering to Lac qui Parle, to announce the arrival of strangers. A little after 1 P. M. we passed a small stream coming in from the right bank, called Chagn Ikpah, or "the last stream with trees" before reaching the lake.

We paddled away as fast as we could, that we might reach the trading post before any persons had assembled at the landing. The stockaded fort of the agent of the post was about three-quarters of a mile from it, and I wished to land quietly, rather apprehending some trouble from the confusion of an Indian mob, and entertaining a worse opinion of the wild people we were about to meet, than perhaps they deserved. But we were too late. The party we had seen must have speeded as though they had borne the "fiery cross," for, on reaching the landing, we found at least 100 Indians, stout, brawny, athletic young fellows, most of them with buffalo robes on, the rest naked; some painted red, some black, some black and white, and indeed begrimed and bedaubed with all colours. Many of them had eagles' feathers in their heads, and the greater part of them was armed. There were also a great number of women and children, and others were flocking to the place.

On making our appearance an immense yell was set up by this strangely painted and savage-looking company, which, if I had been conscious of being under the guidance of Charon, instead of Milor, I should readily have supposed was a set of ministers of vengeance from the infernal regions, assembled to pay me off for past scores of the flesh. The conduct of the male savages especially was very tumultuous for some time, shouting, screaming, and brandishing their arms. We learnt afterwards that we had taken them all by surprise, and that the general idea was that we were not come on a friendly errand, the Indians supposing us to be a party sent from Fort Snelling to arrest the Sioux who had lately murdered the Ojibways, and being disposed in fact to treat us rather roughly; whilst Renville, the half-breed, who acted as agent for the Fur Company, supposing we were come on a rival trading expedition, shewed his unfriendly disposition by not coming down to the landing-place to meet us.

It was at once evident that some untoward accident

might happen if great prudence and steadiness were not observed. A quarrel of any kind would have led to the general plunder of our party, and perhaps to something worse, without any hope of a remedy or moderation, where there was no law and every desire to appropriate what we had. Revolving all these considerations rapidly in my mind, I called to Milor to come with me, and jumping instantly ashore without any arms, ordered the men to put back instantly into the stream, and not to approach the bank until I directed them. By this measure we secured the canoe from being plundered, and taking my stand by Milor, he immediately began to harangue them, and told them that we were not going to trouble any body, that we were neither officers nor traders, and were nothing but travellers come to see them and their country; that I was the head of the party, and intended to go at once to the fort to see Renville and the chiefs, and make a speech to them. Several Indians were present who were acquainted with Milor, and these declaring in our favour, a general yell of satisfaction was set up, and the whole party moved on to the fort, which was a building made of squared timber and well stockaded.

By this time a prodigious number of Indians had collected, and I was accompanied by a most extraordinary *cortège*, for, when the first runners had reached the village to announce our arrival, all the dandies of the place had hastened to make their *toilette*, and certainly they were so bedaubed and painted, and bedizened, that to me, who had been so many days quietly gliding through these extensive solitudes without any intercourse with mankind, it appeared as if the curtain of some great theatre had suddenly drawn up, and discovered a stage filled with all sorts of grotesque diabolical figures—tall, insolent-looking young fellows, six feet two or three inches high, with wiry, black, coarse hair, clotted with bear's grease, and profusely rubbed through with vermilion. Some of them had their faces entirely covered with it, whilst others had daubed their countenances with whiteish and blueish clay; and not a few of them were adorned with a broad ring of dirty white round each eye, the rest of their faces being completely blackened over with burnt wood. A few who were the most *recherchés* in their costume, had vermilion faces fantastically streaked with black and white lines. Dirty eagles' feathers were in great profusion in their heads, and in most instances this excess of *parure* was finished off by what generally sits gracefully on an Indian, a toga, consisting of a dirty blanket, the back part of which was also rubbed over with vermilion. This, the use of which is for cold weather, these youths constantly threw open, displaying their manly chests and well-turned limbs.

The ladies were not in such decided *habit habillé*. Most of them had a little vermilion rubbed through their wiry black hair,—modestly contenting themselves with this and an extremely filthy blanket thrown over their shoulders. Some of the young girls, of about fifteen years of age, had very pleasing countenances, and a good and feeling expression of the eye, but they were not otherwise very attractive; most of them had a circle of thickly-daubed vermilion of about two inches diameter on each cheek, intended, no doubt, as beauty-spots; and as to their persons, I am sorry to say nothing could be less inviting, for they appeared to be from top to bottom in as dirty a state as can be imagined. All the Indian women, except the old crones, seemed to be fat, this being the season of the year when musk-rats and maize abound, and in this they appropriately resembled the wild animals.

The hurly-burly made by the quasi-devils that surrounded me had now taken a rather merry, but still insolent character, and perhaps no living picture could come nearer to the scene than that extraordinary one in the "Inferno" of Dante,* where the imps are so admirably pourtrayed. To be sure, our advent was a memorable one in the eyes of this wild community: the circumstance of a number of white men suddenly appearing amongst them could not but create a sensation, and although their conduct was at times very uproarious, I must say that they were moderate enough to content themselves with shewing that I was completely in their power.

On reaching the fort, Renville advanced and saluted me, but not cordially. He was a dark, Indian-looking person, shewing no white blood, short in his stature, with strong features and coarse black hair; his physiognomy was wily, but he was not without a little touch of French manners. He told me that the Indians were very uneasy at my coming into their country, without first apprising them of my intention. I replied, that my principal object was to see so fine a people as the Sioux, of whom I had heard a great many pleasing accounts: that I was also desirous of seeing whether there was any coal or lead in their country, having been instructed how to find coals and metals that were in the earth, but that he might believe me when I told him that I was not a trader, and that, as soon as I had reached Lake Travers, my intention was to examine the Côteau du Prairie, and cross it to the country of the Mandans, if the season permitted me, and then return to the Mississippi by way of the Missouri

* "Inferno," canto 21.

river. This plain story made Renville my friend, who advised me instantly to make a speech to the chiefs, and offered to be my interpreter. I should certainly have preferred Milor, for I could have depended upon his rendering what I should say faithfully; but, as he would be present, and could detect any mistake or misrepresentation, I accepted Renville's offer with thanks.

We now entered a spacious room in the fort, and whilst the chiefs were arranging themselves in a circle on the floor, and Renville had disappeared to give some orders, I directed Milor to interrupt Renville if he did not fairly interpret what I should say to them. The chiefs being all squatted on the floor, each with his pipe in his hand, and Renville being returned, I took my station opposite to the principal chiefs, with Renville standing at some distance in a line on my left hand, and Milor two or three paces from him a little in advance, and inclined towards me.

I commenced my speech by saying, in French, that I was not a trader, that I had nothing to sell, and did not want to buy anything, except some very good tobacco, which I was told Renville had to sell. That I did not use tobacco myself, because it made me sick at my stomach, as it sometimes made their young children, but that I should buy it to give to the brave warriors I was now talking to, because they loved tobacco, and I wanted to begin at once by shewing them that I had a great friendship for them. This opening produced a general grunt of satisfaction, and I saw at once that we should soon be ready to swear eternal friendship; for upon Renville's adding that I had already communicated that intention to him, it was nothing but " *Ungh, ungh, ungh !*" ("Hear, hear, hear!") round the circle. Indeed, Milor, after the interview was over, said, as we were going to the river to call the canoe to the shore, "Monsieur, vous avez commencé votre discours de la manière la plus juste. Le tabac a mis tout le monde de votre côté."

Feeling encouraged by having my audience with me, I proceeded to say that I had been a great traveller, had seen a great many people, and having heard what a fine race of men the Nahcotahs were, I had come to see them and their fine country: that I had been told it was not good to come to Lac qui Parle, because there were wild young men, that had occasioned disturbances, and might hurt me and my party; but that I did not believe it and was not afraid, because I was not a coward, and because I knew that in all countries where there was one bad man there were one hundred good ones, and that for my part I came to see the good ones, and not the bad ones. (Here we had a lively grunt of a friendly character.) That I was very glad to have got amongst them to see such a fine race of brave men, and to be able to say to my friends when I returned, that I had seen so many bold warriors and so many happy people, all looking so well, and to find that they were at peace and not at war. That I had brought no arms with me, because I knew I was coming amongst friends and not amongst enemies, and that I knew I was safe in the Nahcotah country, because the Nahcotahs were wise men, and knew that if any bad Indians did me any harm, the Great Father of the whites would send people to learn what they had done with me. That they would see that I should act without any fear, and just as I should do in my own country; and that I hoped, if they were satisfied with what I had said, that their principal chief would rise and shake hands with me.

CHAPTER XXXI.

THE CHIEFS PRESENT THEIR PIPES IN TOKEN OF FRIENDSHIP.—HUGGINS, A YANKEE MISSIONARY. — THREE OJIBWAYS SCALPED. — A SCALP-DANCE. — PLEASING MUSIC OF THE SQUAWS.

As soon as Renville had rendered this into their language, Milor spoke to him in Nahcotah, when Renville told me he had taken the liberty to say that *I* had desired to shake hands with all the chiefs. It was no doubt well meant, but I told him it was wrong in him to do so, and bade him tell them that he had mistaken me, and that what I wished to say was, that, if they were satisfied with what I had said, I should be glad if their principal chief would rise and shake hands with me; which when he had done, their two senior chiefs arose and came and shook hands very cordially with me, offering me at the same time their pipes to smoke as a token of friendship. I told them that I valued their friendship very highly, and that I should always remember with great satisfaction that they had permitted me to carry their pipes to my mouth; that my heart was big enough to smoke with them all, but that tobacco made me sick, and therefore I never used it, but if they would permit me I would pass the pipes to Milor to smoke for me. All this met with approving grunts, and the ceremony terminated by the rest of the chiefs rising and coming to shake hands with me.

My reason for making the interpreter explain more

clearly what I had said was, that I had observed it was the invariable practice of white people who were unaccustomed to Indians, to go up to them, even if they were of the lowest class, and shake hands; and as it was evident that the effect of this running after the Indians indiscriminately had been to lower white men in their eyes, I thought it was best, seeing the insolent and overbearing carriage of these distant tribes, to give them a strong idea that I had an opinion I was able to protect myself. A white man who has no business to transact with them, and has not much to part with in the way of presents, acts imprudently if he shows a disposition to consider himself altogether dependent upon them. An Indian, though a savage, may be relied upon as having a tolerably just perception of what is due from one man to another; and nothing places a white man, who is amongst them, in a more dangerous situation, than sneaking and vacillating conduct on his part.

Renville now assigned me the magazine where he kept his merchandize as the place where my luggage was to be kept, and sent a cart and oxen down to the river to bring it up. The procession on our return was not as tumultuous as on the previous occasion. The agitation was over, I was an accepted guest, and the Indians contented themselves with looking at me and my dress. We had, however, a prodigious crowd around us when our men proceeded to unload the canoe; but, as we had nothing but trunks and bags of provisions, they were as much in the dark as ever as to the nature of the treasures they had once thought they were so near appropriating. As soon as the cargo was placed in the cart I had the canoe hoisted to the top of it, for I was determined to take care of our main chance if we returned the way we had come, and we then started for the fort; but such was the yelling and screaming of the young fellows, that the oxen took fright, ran off, and soon broke the pole of the vehicle. Fearing now that some confusion might arise out of this incident, I seized hold of the broken pole, and calling to the men to assist me, we began to drag it on; and Milor and a number of Indians going behind to push it, we at length reached the fort, and entering the stockade where the magazine was, we secured all our things, and put the canoe in a shed out of the sun.

Entertaining no longer any apprehensions of being plundered, I felt relieved from every care, and taking one of my own tins and towel and soap, I went to a small streamlet not far from the fort, and, having had a comfortable wash, I went to see Mr. or Dr. Williamson, who was here both in the capacity of missionary and apothecary, and found with him an out-and-out western Yankee of the name of Huggins, an odd, long-legged, sharp-faced, asparagus-looking animal, every portion of his body being as narrow as the head he bore at the top of it. This fellow being rather in the pious line, and professing to know something about farming, the missionary had brought him from Illinois to raise corn and vegetables, as well as to assist him in his other labours; but he was such an original, that the missionary himself stood no chance of being noticed where he was. I never saw a Yankee that so completely came up to those quaint, drawling, vulgar Jonathans, the idea of which is now so general. He always called the Indians "critturs," had got all their interjections and grunts, and used them instead of "Yes" and "No." He certainly knew more about the Indians than the missionary did, and was more constantly amongst them. Mr. Williamson was married, and had a motive for remaining at home, but Huggins, who was alone in the world, was in the habit of walking into the teebees without ceremony, and sitting down, would take his psalm-book and sing a few verses to the Indians, so that the women had got accustomed to him, and rather liked him. "Some folks is considerable curious," he once said to me, "to find out whar these ignorant critturs comed from. I am as sartin as death that they are the old Philistines of the Scriptures: they can't be the lost tribe of the Jews, bekase whar onder arth is their birds (beards) gone?" I asked him why he had not taken a young Indian girl to wife? "Stranger," said he, "I allow them har young painted Jizzabuls aint just up to missionarying."

Having got over the bustle of my arrival, Renville asked me to go to his house to take some refreshment. There I found his wife, an obliging Nahcotah woman, his son, a heavy-looking man, about twenty-six years old, two daughters not very prepossessing, and a young fair-haired maiden, about fifteen years old, the daughter of a white trader by an Indian woman. We all sat down to a table where we had something that was called tea, with maple sugar, some bear's meat, and other things I could not make out, with potatoes, which were excellent. I did some violence to my inclination in partaking of the other things, because I knew they were produced in honour of myself; but after making a meal of the potatoes, I made my retreat, and went to look at the plan of the village.

Gaining a mound on the upland prairie just above it, I had a charming view of Lac qui Parle and its whole neighbourhood. The valley, as usual about two miles wide, lay before me to the south. To the west was the lake, about eight miles long, all the lowlands adjacent to it being very well wooded, with the upland prairie in the distance. In front of the height where I stood was the alluvial land with the fort and the village, this last consisting of forty-eight Nacotah skin lodges, and twelve large bark-covered teebees, with Indians strolling about in every direction. Whilst I was sketching the scene, I observed several Indian women with bags on their heads and shoulders, appearing heavily laden, bent down, and not raising their faces from the path they were upon. I never saw individuals contend more with a load that almost mastered them than did some of these females. Following them a short distance to a place where they stopped, I found they were making a *cache* of the ripe maize of that season. A sort of cave had been hollowed out of the side of the hill, about eight feet in diameter at the bottom, and not more than two or three at the top. To this *cache* the women were bringing the corn a distance of about two miles, and some very young girls were in the cave stowing it away.*

These sacks of corn weighed about 80 lb., and some of the females whom I had observed staggering under them were young girls not more than sixteen years old. They seemed very much relieved when they had got rid of their loads, but were cheerful, and talked and laughed as if it was work they ought not to complain of. This sort of work, however, brings on premature old age; for an Indian woman of thirty years of age, who has been accus-

* This was the custom of the Indians in Massachussets when the whites first landed there, in 1620. The ears of maize are gathered and cured whilst the corn is in the milk, and the bags when filled with it are laid in the cave upon layers of dry grass, one layer above another. When the cave is full, straw is put in and covered over with dry earth. They cure the corn in the milk, because the blackbirds are numerous enough to devour it all if it were left to ripen in the field.

tomed to the severe labour which is imposed upon her, and who has borne children besides, becomes a perfect hag. Shrivelled, and disgustingly filthy, she is more like a fiend than one of the gentler sex, and receives neither sympathy nor assistance from the brawny fashionable bedaubed youths who are sunning themselves in the plain below, whilst these poor creatures are toiling.

From the upland I strolled down to the village, and found that I was free to go wherever I chose, my speech of the morning having removed all distrust. I therefore, following the example of the pious Huggins in part, entered the teebees of the chiefs, and lost no time in coming to a good understanding with the ladies, a piece of policy it is good to observe in all situations. To their wives I presented handsome new calico handkerchiefs, with the flags of all nations printed upon them. To the young girls I gave handsome necklaces of beads, and rings with sapphires, emeralds, diamonds, rubies, &c. of paste set in them, all manufactured for Indian commerce. I ventured also to sport some phrases which Milor had taught me to pronounce, and was not laughed at; indeed, the Indians never criticise or laugh at you, they are not civilized enough for that, but pay great attention to what you say, that they may understand what you mean. Having paid my respects in the most important quarters, I tried one or two of the skin lodges, but having only a few loose beads left to give to the children, I made no great progress here; indeed, I failed altogether in making myself understood, for the people of the lodges I had entered belonged to the Assiniboin country, and were only on a visit here.

On my return to Renville's, I partook of their evening meal, which was exactly like the first, and, as soon as it was over, I went to a scalp-dance to be celebrated in the village, some wild young fellows having come in with three scalps they had just taken from some Ojibways near Elk Lake. A circle was formed of twenty warriors painted and bedaubed in the usual manner, and thirty women and girls with their blankets on, a few of these last having the red beauty spot painted on their cheeks. In the centre of the ring three poles were held up, each with a hairy scalp depending from it, stretched out and gaily ornamented. The men who held the poles up were the Indians themselves who had taken the scalps. These had a song of self-glorification for themselves, the burden of which was, that "they were the bravest of all brave men." This song was varied twice, and the second time the first words were, "I have the proud Ojibway in my power, he cannot escape me."

But there were other songs in which all the circle bore a part; and more pleasing and animating Indian music I never heard. It was a loud strain of glorification, accompanied with a sort of drum or tambourine. The music rose and fell, and was loud and low, both sexes singing in the most exact concert. Sometimes the men, after a bold sustained strain, would let it die away; and as their voices began to sink, the drum beating louder was a signal to the women, who, taking the melody up with their soft and sweet voices, would continue it for awhile, when the men joining in with them once more, the women would give from time to time a curious cluck with their voices, producing a peculiar sort of harmony, when the whole would be suddenly concluded for two or three minutes by a war whoop and yells on the part of the men, and a general laugh. After resting a few minutes, they began again as fresh as ever.

PLEASING MANNER OF DANCING.

In dancing round the circle, the men, close together, advance in single file, treading gently with one foot after the other, and rather bending inwards; whilst the women advancing sidelong, and leaning against each other's shoulders, and still preserving an upright position, keep their small feet close together, and turning their toes in, glide over the ground without any violent motion of their feet, and scarce lifting them from the ground, the whole being done without any apparent personal effort. The measure of the dance was exceedingly well kept by all, the ring being almost in constant motion, whilst the scalp-takers were shaking their poles. It was a most exhilirating scene, even to me; indeed, I was so delighted with the music, that I remained with them until ten o'clock at night, in order to be able to note it down accurately. As to the Indians, they appeared to be full of enthusiasm during the dance; all ages engaged in it; and before I retired some of the mothers brought two or three dozen of young children, from four to ten years old, into the circle, all of whom joined in the dance most merrily.

Introduced into scenes of this kind at so early an age, and then trained up to the chase, it is not surprising that they should afterwards find such enjoyment in taking human life. With the pleasures of the scalp-dance impressed upon his memory, and habituated to the butchery of animals, the Indian youth takes up his tomahawk for the first time with about the same degree of feeling towards the individuals destined to be scalped, that an English boy entertains towards partridges when about to make his maiden effort in that line; and such is the intensity of the few pleasurable emotions which fall to the share of savage life, that, if we may judge from what we know of the ferocious indulgences they riot in when the excited warriors have an enemy in their power, they experience an unutterable delight in inflicting upon the conquered, torments the very recital of which fills us with horror.

Before going to my pallet I made another journey to the upland behind the fort, to see the prairies on fire. It is a spectacle one is never tired of looking at: half the horizon appeared like an advancing sea of fire, with dense clouds of smoke flying up towards the moon, which was then shining brightly. Here I remained enjoying this rare and glorious sight until a late hour, the distant yells and music of the Indians occasionally reaching my ears. At length, feeling fatigued with the exertions and spectacles of the day, I slowly descended the hill, and gaining the fort, went to the warehouse, and taking the key out of my pocket opened the door, succeeded in striking a light, unrolled my mattress, and crept under my buffalo robes to compose myself to sleep.

October 2.—I rose at 6 A. M., and not knowing where to get any water, put my brushes and towel in my pocket, and walked to the lake with the intention of making my *toilette* at the water-side; but the lake was low, the ground near it was swampy, and not being able to find clear water, I returned to the fort, and sent one of the Canadians to procure me some nice water from the brook above the village. With this I succeeded in making myself presentable, and went, according to invitation, to breakfast with Mr. and Mrs. Williamson. I found Mrs. W. an obliging, clever person, and made a comfortable breakfast with them. My friend Huggins, too, was of the party. As all three were enthusiastic religious Methodists, I soon found that it would not do to express any admiration of the Indian dancing and music of the preceding evening; the long prayer we had before breakfast was certainly not in harmony with the scenes I had witnessed, so I turned the conversation to missionary affairs, which I soon learnt made little or no progress. Mr. Huggins laid the whole blame upon Renville; " He hadn't it in him," he said; " he pretended to be a kind of Papist, but he had jist no more religion in him than there was in a pack of musk-rat skins." He added, that neither Renville nor any of his family had ever been at one of their prayer-meetings.

I could see at once that this was meant for me, who had omitted to go to their prayer-meeting the preceding evening. This was not altogether my fault; when they had asked me to breakfast, they had not asked me to assist at their evening prayer, taking it for granted I should be too happy to avail myself of the privilege. I was sorry for this incident, for they meant to treat me with great kindness, and I had inadvertently hurt their feelings. If they had mentioned it to me in season, I certainly should have joined them; but not having heard that they had a prayer-meeting, I was naturally glad of the opportunity of amusing myself with the Indians.

The missionary had to contend with great difficulties. Renville, in his youth, had been in a village where there was a French missionary, and amongst white men he called himself a Roman Catholic; but his religious feelings carried him no farther than to dislike every one who belonged to a different sect from himself; and not wanting the missionary to acquire any influence with the Indians, he probably did him as much harm with them as he could. On the other hand, I could easily see that the Methodists, whilst they professed to pity the Indians profoundly, did the "Papishes" the honour to hate them not a little. This was the situation of religious matters at Lac qui Parle, when my unexpected arrival was hailed by these good missionaries as a great stay and comfort to them. But I had disappointed them. I had been seen standing looking at and admiring the Indians for several hours; nay, some scandalous person had reported that I had joined in their music, and made an effort or two to keep up with them in their yells: of course, the Indians would conclude that I preferred their ceremonies to prayer-meetings. Nor was this all, for it appeared that when I did not make my appearance at the prayer-meeting, Huggins was despatched to find me, and invite me to join them, and that having traced me to the dance, he came up to me to deliver his errand, when, not suspecting the nature of it, and having a little touch of Indian enthusiasm about me at the moment, I unfortunately exclaimed, "Huggins, do you think you could manage to purchase those three scalps for me?" This did me up in the worthy Jonathan's good opinion completely, for he went back without mentioning the prayer-meeting, and no doubt reported me to be as considerable a reprobate as any of the Philis*tines*.

We had an explanation of this *mal entendu* afterwards, and I laid the blame upon him; assuring Mr. Williamson, that, if I had known of the prayer-meeting, I should have attended it, for although I was not a Methodist, I should always feel it my duty as a Christian traveller to confirm the Indians—as far as I could by my conduct—in an opinion of the great value and respectability of the religious character of such men as himself. The missionary was satisfied that I was sincere, and perhaps Huggins was equally so, for he was a very acute fellow; but he delighted in saying severe things, and when, at the close of this friendly explanation, I asked him if he thought it was not possible to gain over Renville and his family by kind and constant attention, he answered, "I calculate I'd jist as soon ondertake to convart all your canoe." Of course he included myself. Huggins persevered to the last in his intolerance; during the whole of my stay he repeatedly cast up to me my fancy for visiting the Indians and putting questions to them. "It beats all creation," he would say," to see you so a-haunting after sich *com*plete Phili*stines;* when you got the Doctor and me to talk to." But Mr. Williamson was more liberal, and admitted that it was natural I should avail myself of every moment to study what I had come so far to observe.

CHAPTER XXXII.

THE AUTHOR PERMITTED TO SEE THE BRAVES ATTIRE THEMSELVES FOR THE "DANCE OF THE BRAVES" IN HONOUR OF HIS ARRIVAL.—DANCE OF THE SQUAWS.—MATRIMONIAL NEGOTIATIONS.

On my return to Renville's, he informed me that the great dance of the braves was to be performed this morning in honour of my arrival, and that it would take place in the fort, in front of the warehouse where I slept. This was very intelligible; for I had seen a large mass of tobacco there, and had remembered my pledge when I saw it. I therefore went to an acquaintance I had made, who acted as a clerk to Renville, and kept his trading accounts, to concert with him what was to be done. This was a lively, mercurial little Canadian Frenchman, who had found his way into this part of the world by the way of Lake Winnipeg and Red River, and had got into the employment of Renville. How he attended to his own business I never learnt; but he had a singular talent for attending to everybody else's. "That er crittur," said Huggins, "is etarnally on the jump arter everybody's business but his own. If he lived in one of our large towns in the States, he'd ondertake to do everything for everybody, and keep school, and take in washing besides." But there was a circumstance in the domestic arrangements of this vivacious man of universal business, which almost threw Jonathan into a rage when he spoke of it. "The crittur," said he, "has actilly *jyned* with one of these female Jizzabels, and keeps her to hum as his wife; he won't let her do the least thing in the world; he's made her as fat as a ball of grease, and passes half the day sitting on the bed with her, painting her cheeks three times as big as a dollar, till she's as almighty a harlot as the Pope of Rome: and there she lies a-larfing and carrying on, and he won't let her get up, bekase he's afeard the paint'll come off." No doubt the little man was very uxorious; for when I asked him one day if he loved her very much, he answered, "Ah! Monsieur, elle est *terrible* bonne enfant."

From this person I learnt that Renville entertained a select company of stout Indians, to the number of forty, in a skin lodge behind his house of extraordinary, dimensions, whom he called his braves or soldiers. To these men he confided various trusts, and occasionally sent them to distant points to transact his business. No doubt he was a very intriguing person, and uncertain in his attachments. Those who knew him intimately, supposed him inclined to the British allegiance, although he professed great attachment to the American Government—a circumstance, however, which did not prevent his being under the surveillance of the American garrison at Fort Snelling. He was very obnoxious to the Ojibways, who slew his brother a short time ago; and being aware that he had many enemies, he had converted this band of braves into a sort of personal guard. These braves, it appeared, were now attiring themselves in the Great Skin Lodge for the dance; and, on my expressing to the little Frenchman a strong desire to witness their proceedings, he said they seldom permitted any male person to enter the lodge upon such occasions, and women never; but, as the dance was to be given in my honour, he thought they would not make any decided objections to my presence; so, taking him with me, I went to the attiring-room to see them dress.

Of all the methods that ever were devised of rigging out and bedevilling the human form divine, I should recommend what I saw here as the most extraordinary. Certainly it would make any set of theatricals, great or small, national or provincial, blush at the degenerate distance in which they stand from these savages in the art of decorating it. On reaching the lodge, my guide crept into it through a low door of skin at the bottom, and I followed him, without asking any person's leave, just as one drops in at a rehearsal. Having no definite idea of what I should see, my astonishment was great at finding the lodge almost full of stark-naked brawny savages, some with their backs towards me, others fronting me, and all of them so attentively engaged in what they were about, that our entrance hardly appeared to attract their attention. One fellow, who had got a regular suit of vermilion daubed upon him from head to foot, was streaking the faces and drawing rings round the eyes of others, with a whiteish bole or clay. Another, with half of his stalwart frame red, and the other half a clayey white, was giving the last touch to three stout youths, every one of them as black as the ace of clubs from the crown of their heads to their heels, every part of their bodies having been well rubbed in with powdered charcoal. The greater part of them were daubed with dull reddish clay, others whiteish and yellowish, but generally they were streaked, and lined, and spotted in a manner not to be explained. Some had black faces, with a white ring round each eye; in others there were black rings round a whitened face; and many had a line running from one eye to another across the nose, like a pair of spectacles. Exceedingly amused I was with one of the braves, who, having just had a fine suit of vermilion put on, turned his very fat and noble parts to me—not from irreverence, or for the purpose of attracting my admiration, but to give the opportunity to another artist, who was finishing in the white line, of signing him with the mark of good-fellowship, and who stepping forwards, with his open right hand wet with bear's-grease mixed up with white lead, gave the expectant protuberance such an effective spank, as not only to leave a clear impression of the hand and fingers, but to rouse perceptibly the nervous system of the individual who received it. This practical joke created a general laugh, in which the little Frenchman and myself heartily joined. This, when neatly done, is considered a handsome decoration.

Others were advanced so far in their *toilette* that they were arranging eagles' feathers and dirty ribbands in their hair. All were exceedingly busy, carrying on their occupations with great system, and constantly inspecting their own faces in the most minute manner, with a small looking-glass that each possessed. Those who had finished their *toilettes* seemed almost to feel as much complacent satisfaction as do the interesting and sentimental Narcissuses, who from behind the counters of Regent-street discuss the mysteries of dress with those fashionable ladies who pass so much of their time in conversing with the knights of the yard-wand.

Altogether it was a very unexpected treat, and I enjoyed it much, laughing immoderately, which seemed to give great satisfaction. Before I left the party, I desired the little Canadian to assure them of my unqualified admiration, and to state to them that I had never seen any of the warriors of my own country prepare themselves for a dance in any way to be compared with the one I had now witnessed, not even the royal guard of the King of England.

At the appointed time all the Indians of the village had assembled within the fort, painted and dressed more or less, myself and party standing with Renville upon a small platform, near the door of the warehouse. After waiting some time, the braves, all arrayed in their most captivating costumes, issued from their tent with two little boys, whom I had not seen before, painted and dressed as chiefs. It was a singular spectacle. They looked like fiends that had escaped from the infernal regions. Milor whispered to me that the three warriors in black were the braves who had scalped the three Ojibways, and thus I came to know that Renville was directly instrumental in keeping up the sanguinary feud with that nation. Each of these fellows bore one of the poles I had seen the preceding evening, with a scalp depending from it. Upon reflecting upon the part I was playing in this ceremony, I began to wish that I had given them the tobacco, and had excused myself from this great honour, for news flies very quick through the Indian country, and I might find it difficult upon a future occasion to justify myself with any living Ojibways I might fall in with.

Having formed a ring they began singing, but their music was very inferior to that of the night before, for want of the female voices, and their dancing was bad, consisting of the old step and the old antics, something resembling what we may suppose would become the fabulous drunken satyrs of old. To cut the performance short, therefore, I told Renville to throw them down about 12 lb. of tobacco, with some other things, and to state that it was a present of friendship to the braves. Near to us was standing a circle of elderly chiefs, not belonging to the braves, one of whom now jumped up, and addressed them and myself in a sort of song, in which many complimentary things were addressed to my generosity. To the braves he said, that, as I had come so far to see them, they must dance on like brave men, and show me that they were men to make a favourable report of. He sang, that when he was a young warrior he had taken scalps from the Ojibways, and for that reason he should like to smoke some of my tobacco. I therefore threw him down a roll, and told Renville to tell them that I was the friend of peace; that both they and the Ojibways were the children of Wakon, as well as myself, and that Wakon ordered us all to love one another. Another old chief now arose, and said that I had spoken the truth, and that for that reason he should like to smoke some of my tobacco. Having given to him, another and another arose to tell what feats they had performed; and one aged man became so excited with acting and reciting some daring act he had performed, that all, both old and young, full of enthusiasm, arose and began to dance together, just as old ladies sometimes do in a family party. They were fairly overpowered by their animal spirits, and conducted themselves as if they had been drinking. It seemed to me that even Milor and Renville were catching the inspiration; and as I had not much confidence in the scaffold we stood upon, I descended to the ground, and in the midst of the excitement made my retreat to the upland, to take a walk.

On my return I was called to another entertainment at Renville's, of bear's meat and potatoes; and maple sugar was placed upon the table. Having eaten as many potatoes as I had a fancy for, I tried one or two more with the maple sugar, by way of a dessert, without being at all sorry for it afterwards; and the fair-haired young girl being in the room, I asked some questions about her father, who, I learnt, was a Scotch trader, of the name of Jeffrey. He had died and was buried there, leaving four young children he had had by a Nahcotah woman, of which this girl was the eldest. The mother had brought them up in the Indian way, and, like Renville's children, they spoke no language but Nahcotah. Women of this class generally become the wives of white traders, or of half-breeds, there being perhaps some sympathy between them; and although they are sometimes abandoned, they certainly escape the fate of the hard-worked full-blood Indian woman. Whilst we were at this meal, the manager of the dance of the braves came in, dressed in an old British uniform coat; he was brother to Renville's wife, and Milor said he was considered to be a brave man, and was of great use to Renville. He was in high spirits, and evidently well satisfied with the performance of the morning.

The Indians, when left to their own humour, are laughing, jocular persons, fond of jokes and fun: but a traveller can only see them in their natural character when he is behind the scenes; in the presence of strangers they affect an indifferent, incurious character, which is the reason why they have often been represented as a grave, reserved people; but at such times they are actors.

Towards evening, the three heroes in charcoal came to the fort, and afterwards went round the village, to announce that a great dance was to be performed by the women, in honour of the day. I knew what this meant; but, as I had an unopened package of magnificent large printed handkerchiefs, of a very showy kind, which had not yet been seen, I felt confident that I should come off very well with the ladies. This dance differed from the other only in this, that the men first made a small circle round the scalp-poles, whilst the women formed a larger one outside, sidling around as they did before, with the men singing and beating the drums to them. The air which the women sang was pleasing, but the general effect was not equal to that of the preceding evening: the men first gave out the words, which formed a consummate glorification of themselves and their superlative bravery. In the scalp-dance, however, the day of my arrival, the men, after praising themselves, broke out into a most exaggerated eulogium of the unfortunate devils whose scalps were the subject of their triumph: they were the bravest men that ever lived; the prodigies of valour they were famed for were unutterable, and, of course, the heroes who could subdue these Hectors were equal to Achilles. In this particular case, however, Milor informed me that two of the scalps had belonged to a couple of Indians that had been shot from an ambush, and that the third had been taken from a woman who was with them, and whom they had tomahawked; so that poor savage nature, with all the virtues that some writers have imputed to it, makes but a sad figure in a fair estimate of human worth. From the experience I have had of the unwashed masses of mankind, I am inclined to think that real virtue is a very great stranger in all those strata of society, where that inestimable blessing, education, is wanting, and which is so essential to raise man above the condition of the Indian.

I soon became heartily tired of these dances. When the novelty of this monstrous sort of painting and dressing has passed away, the performance is as tedious as a bad ballet at a minor theatre. Nor are the Indians estimable in themselves; even these Nahcotahs —who are considered amongst the most decent of the nations—are idle, selfish, and insolent, and have boasted themselves into the belief that they are the superior beings they vaunt themselves to be. L'Amirant, who is a friend of the Ojibways, from having resided amongst them, says that he knows a dozen of that people that would lick all this village. It is probable that they are all alike, Ojibways and Nahcotahs; and that man, in his wild state, is a dirty, selfish, conceited animal. The women certainly are not as bad and disagreeable as the men; they are obliging, civil, and conversable. The very old ones, of whom I have already spoken, are anything but attractive: this is not the case with the young ones; they are often handsome, exceedingly well made, have fine full bosoms, and are quite lively and playful. Unfortunately, however, they are so frowsy, that they rarely, if ever, appeared to me desirable. Woman, if not brought up to cleanliness, is never what she ought to be; therefore, after all, "fix it how you will," as the Yankees say, it is mainly amongst the educated classes we are to look for examples proper to keep up the respectability of the human family.

During this afternoon a numerous band of Nahcotahs came in from *Minday Eatatenka*, or "Big Stone Lake," the women bending to the ground beneath their burdens, and the men strutting along with the most insolent air, and bearing nothing at all, except their guns, bow and arrows, &c. They had a great many indifferent-looking horses, with a panier on each side, the poles of their skin tents resting on the paniers, and trailing on the ground in parallel lines, united by cross pieces, extending beneath the tails of the horses. Upon these it is the practice to fasten the youngest children, with other articles belonging to their tents, as well as skins, if they possess any, for the purposes of trade. But the heaviest burdens are carried by the poor women. The moment they reached the village, the women went to work to set the lodges up; and if anything had been discovered to have been dropped on the road, the patient squaw was the person who had to go for it. In the meantime, the lordly brutes, for whose comfort these females were trudging, came one and all to the fort, each having a dirty blanket or buffalo skin, with the hair inside, on his back, the hair peeping out at the top, as if it were a tippet. At a distance, an Indian thus dressed looks well, for he carries his person erect, and keeps up various well-studied attitudes; but, on approaching him, the illusion is dispelled, for you behold nothing but an Indian with a dirty cow-skin next to his naked body, and that perhaps smeared over with mud.

As there was to be another scalp-dance at night, and as it was clear I was to be honoured in one way or another as long as I had anything to give away, I set about a negotiation for some horses to pursue the remainder of my journey, it being scarcely practicable to go any further with the canoe; and whilst Renville was engaged in this service for me, I called upon some of the principal ladies at their teebees, to make them parting presents. Soon after this the scalp-dance began again, and we had a perfect Bartholomew fair of it over again; nothing but dancing, singing, yelling, and beating of drums until near ten at night. Worn out with it, I left them at an early hour, intending to go to bed, but, on reaching the warehouse, I found Milor there waiting to speak to me.

It appeared that some of the squaws had taken into their heads that I was going to return to Lac qui Parle from the Côteau du Prairie, to stay all the winter; and they had come to the conclusion, that, if I wintered there, I *must* have a wife to take care of my tent, and be very agreeable. Milor had been consulted, and had promised one of the squaws to deliver a message on her part, which was, that if I would make her a present she would arrange that very important matter for me. I told Milor that really it was uncertain how the journey would end, but for the sake of amusement I wished he would desire her to point out to me which of the squaws she thought a suitable companion, and how much I should have to pay for her. In commencing a negotiation for marriage amongst the Indians, the custom is reversed from that which obtains in civilized society, and, instead of asking how much the lady will bring towards making the pot boil, you ask how much you are to give for her to boil your pot. Amongst these simple people the ladies have no fortune, "et les Messieurs font tous les frais de leur bonheur."

Milor came back in half an hour, and said there was the daughter of a chief called the *Prairie on Fire*, (it would have been an odd name for the daughter,) that was *washtay* ("good") in every sense of the word; that I probably remembered her, for I had given her a handkerchief, and when I spoke to her she had laughed. I told Milor I had given so many away, that I could not remember who had gotten them; upon which he asked me if I did not remember a young girl, with large vermilion spots on her cheeks, that sometimes walked with Renville's daughters. I now remembered her as one of the exclusives of the nation, a belle, in fact, of the first order, and a match only for a considerable personage. I became curious to know, therefore, upon what terms an alliance could be formed with the aristocratic daughter of the Prairie on Fire. Milor now said that the squaw had informed him that I should first* have to give her two pair of blankets as the negotiator; then three pair of the very best blankets to the young lady's mother; 15 lb. of tobacco to her brother; a rifle and a horse to her father; and that, as she was his daughter, it would be expected I should make him a present of six rat-traps besides.

This, I suppose, would be considered a fair settlement upon a young squaw of the first pretensions; but settlement it is not, in the proper sense of the word, for no part of it goes for the use of the girl herself. If she has any particular good qualities, every member of the family spunges out of the *futuro* as much as he can get; and, indeed, it is stipulated that all the children in the family are to have something or other; and all this without the slightest return, for when the purchase-money is paid, the mother of the bride takes her to the tent she is to inhabit, with nothing but a dirty blanket thrown over her shoulders, and turns her into it in the same state that the worms go to their mates.

* This provident disposition seems to be universal in the United States; for in all trials for small debts in the townships of the northern states, when the magistrate asks the jury, "Gentlemen, who do you find for?" the foreman answers, "We find *first* for ourselves!" which is sixpence for each of the jury at every trial.

Unfortunately for the further prosecution of this tender arrangement, it was unfeelingly nipped in the bud by the hard-hearted Renville, who, finding he could make a good job out of me by the hire of his horses, came to tell me that he had procured me a sufficient number, as well as a cart used in the fur trade, and that I could depart whenever I pleased. I, therefore, that there might be no misunderstanding with the illustrious family of the Prairie on Fire, sent Milor with a present to the old squaw, and a message, that, if I came to live there, I would employ her, and no one else, in my matrimonial arrangements, but that at present I was not going to pitch my tent anywhere. I further enjoined Milor to make her clearly understand that it was for the gratification of his own curiosity that he had asked her these questions, for I was not only desirous of not giving offence to the Indians, but to the missionary, who, if he had heard of the old squaw's benevolent intentions to me, and Milor's interviews with her, might have put a bad construction upon what was founded upon mere curiosity, which Huggins certainly would have done.

October 3.—Having determined to depart for Lake Travers this morning, I went to breakfast with the missionary and his family, who inhabited a part of Renville's building, that was, unhappily, too close to the large tent of the braves. During the praying and singing before breakfast, the Indians were drumming, screaming, and laughing in the tent in the most outrageous manner, an annoyance it was impossible to escape from, and which made Mr. Williamson exceedingly anxious to get into the log-house he was building, about a mile from the village. Huggins was in a very sad taking: besides his usefulness to the missionary as a farmer, it was his business to set the psalms when they were preparing to sing; and this morning, before he had got through the first line, the braves, hearing the drawling, broke out with their drums and yelling, and fairly overpowered us. I was sorry for this, as I perceived the Indians did it maliciously; but still I could scarce at times refrain from laughing, for, in proportion as Huggins screamed at the top of his voice, to make himself heard, the braves increased their yelling, so that truly it would have been better for us to have desisted, and have sat down quietly to breakfast. But Huggins was not of that opinion, and, as soon as he had got through the first verse, exclaimed, "Them ar critturs is as cont*rary* as the sarpints can be; but I guess we 'll try the next." And we did try it, with no better success; so the missionary closed our morning service with a short prayer, and we went to our repast. Mrs. Williamson said that when any of the Indians in the tent awoke in the night, they always began drumming; and, as Huggins said, "They han't no marcy upon nobody, and it ain't bearable no how." But the life of a missionary amongst such rude savages must always have a great deal that is painful in it; and in this particular case, judging from what I saw, there is little hope of converting this village, where Renville's braves have so decidedly the upper hand.

CHAPTER XXXIII.

LEAVE LAC QUI PARLE.—EXPOSED TO THE DANGER OF BEING FROZEN TO DEATH. — EXCELLENT CONDUCT OF MILOR.— REACH A FEW TREES, AND MAKE A FIRE.

At 8 a. m., preparations being made for my departure, I shook hands with these worthy people, who, I dare say, were not unhappy at my departure. My arrival had given a stimulus to the passion which Indians entertain for all sorts of dissonant noises; and if my going away procured them any cessation of the horrid disturbances that my coming had produced, they must have been delighted to get rid of me. Renville had procured me a *charette*, or cart, to carry the tent, baggage, and provisions: I was to ride an old grey mare, with a foal running alongside; one of the Canadians was to drive the *charette*, and Milor and the rest were to walk. The morning was exceedingly cold, and our road was along the prairie, parallel with the lake. All the country in every direction, having been burnt over, was perfectly black, and a disagreeable sooty odour filled the atmosphere. At the end of five hours of a very tedious march we reached a stream called *Wahbōptah*, which may be translated *Ground-nut* river, the savages being in the habit of digging up the *Psoralea esculenta*, a nutritive bulbous root which grows here. The stream was about thirty feet wide, and had some trees growing on its banks. Having built up a good fire, the men proceeded to cook their dinner, whilst I strolled up the stream and collected some very fine unios, although I found it bitterly cold wading in the shallow water to procure them.

Having fed our horses on the grass near the stream which had not been burnt over, we started again for *Les Grosses Isles*, which we were instructed were distant about seven leagues, at the foot of Big Stone Lake. During the first two leagues, the strong sooty smell of the country gave me a severe headache, and the weather became so cold that I was very uncomfortable: the fire, however, had not extended beyond this distance, for, in about an hour and a half from our departure, we came to the grass again, and I fortunately got rid of my headache. Our cavalry was exceedingly pleased by the change, the horses repeatedly winnowing to each other, as if to express their satisfaction. I here perceived a live gopher, or geomys, feebly running in the grass, and dismounting caught it. It apparently had strayed from its burrow, and had suffered from the weather. After examining it I let it go again, as it was impossible to take care of it, and I did not like to consign it to the men, as I knew they would kill and eat it, for they spared nothing.

As the evening advanced it became excessively cold, and a sharp wind, accompanied with frozen sleet, set in from the north-east: this soon became so thick, that I could scarcely look up, much more see anything in the direction in which I was proceeding. Securing my person and ears as well as I could with my blanket-coat, I left it to the mare — who Renville told me had been more than once to Lake Travers—to take her own course. At length the sleet became so dense, that I lost sight of everybody except the little foal, which generally lagging behind in the wake of its dam, occasionally trotted up to her when in her great anxiety she called for it. I never saw greater marks of maternal feeling in an animal than in this poor creature to her young one.

As we advanced, my situation became exceedingly painful: the frozen sleet came in streams upon my face and eyes when I looked up; my feet and hands were so cold, that I had scarcely any power over them; my whole exterior, as well as the head and neck of the mare, was covered with a glazing of ice; night was advancing, and we were without a guide, upon a dreary and shelterless moor of very great extent, and far beyond our present day's journey, with no prospect of an abatement of the storm. In the course of a somewhat adventurous life, I have occasionally had to meet with serious privations, and to look danger rather steadily in the face, but I had never been where there was so slight a chance of any favourable change. I had not even the comfort before me that every bleak moor in England offers under similar circumstances to the imagination,—some kind of shelter to receive us at last, if we were not overpowered by the inclemency of the weather. It became absolutely necessary to consider what it was best to do, if overtaken before dark by a deep snow. My first thought was, not to separate myself from my party, which I had not seen for some time, for they had the cart, and the tent, and the provisions; and if we failed in our attempt to reach the few trees that grew near Grosses Isles—the only chance we had of finding materials to make a fire—we could at any rate burn the *charette*, eat something, and cover ourselves as well as we could with the tent. This we inevitably should have to do if we missed the station we were aiming at, and of which there was imminent danger, as it was too thick for us to discern any trees at a distance. I therefore stopped the mare for a while, and turned our backs to the storm, which seemed to be a great relief to us both. I had not heard the voices of the men for some time, but I knew the cart was slowly following me, and I thought it best to wait awhile ere I advanced towards them, as it was quite possible that I might deviate from the direction they were advancing in, and separate myself from them altogether. In about a quarter of an hour the voices of the men answered to the shouts I had from time to time made, and soon after they joined me, all of them covered with ice and icicles. The men were afraid we had got into the wrong track, having passed one or two that forked different ways, and this would have been a most serious misfortune. Upon appealing to Milor, who was covered with ice, his answer was, "N'ayez pas peur, Monsieur; n'ayez pas peur." I was well aware that this opinion of a sagacious guide like himself, trained to all the difficulties and incidents of Indian life, was better than that of the others, and I had more confidence in his prudence and in his conduct than I had in them; but still I was not without fear that darkness would overtake us; and if it had been left to myself, should have been inclined to attempt to set up the tent whilst it was daylight.

But Milor kept walking on before the *charette*, acting up to his character of guide in the most thorough manner. I determined, therefore, to be governed altogether by him, and taking my place in the rear of the *charette*, thought, that, as I had now joined my party, I would alight, and endeavour, by running a little, to restore the circulation of my limbs; but my feet and hands were so benumbed, that I found it even difficult to dismount, or to stand when I reached the ground. As to the poor mare, she had icicles depending from her nose, six or eight inches long, which I broke off; and holding the bridle under my right arm, and averting my face a little from the storm, I tried to run and draw her into a gentle trot, but it was all in vain; she was too anxious about her foal, which was tired and becoming weak, and could scarce come up to her when she called to it. Full of anxiety as I was about myself, I could not but admire the solicitude of this good mother for her young, so earnestly does the voice of nature plead even with the inferior animals; that voice which God has planted in ourselves, no less for the safety of the species we are bound to protect, than to express the intensity of the love we bear to our offspring.

After trying in vain to get the mare out of her snail's pace without at all improving my own situation, I perceived that I must be making lee-way, for I had lost sight of the *charette*, so I determined to mount again and push her into a trot; we had got up a quasi-trot in the morning, and I hoped I might succeed in doing it again, but it took me a long time to do it. I was so benumbed that I could not regain my seat in the saddle until I had made several efforts, and then the adjusting my blanket-coat, and the covering my face to protect it from the cutting sleet, lost me so much time, that I was in a worse situation than ever,—separated from my party, night approaching, and somewhat apprehensive that in the grey light that was beginning to prevail I might wander from them, and be unable to rejoin them. Being already half frozen, and feeling rather faint at my stomach, it was clear to me that in that case I should certainly be frozen to death. Getting on as well as I could, and ruminating very unsatisfactorily upon these possible consequences, the storm began to abate, and the wind veered to the north-west: the mare knew this, and gave immediate signs of it by improving her pace. As we went on the weather began to clear up; and as I was straining my eyes to look for the *charette*, I heard the horse which drew it neigh several times; to this the mare immediately answered, and soon after came a cheer from the men. Milor was soon seen advancing to meet me, with the joyful intelligence that the trees at Grosses Isles were in sight. He said the horse in the *charette* was the first to see them, and to announce the discovery by neighing; so that, although horses have not yet reached the art, as some asses have done, of making long speeches, yet the epithet of dumb animals is not altogether appropriate to them.

All our anxieties were now at an end, and we soon terminated this distressing ride, and reached a spot near a marsh, where three or four trees were standing. Fortunately for us there was some dead wood on the ground, and some wild grass for the horses, which we immediately proceeded to tether and turn loose, that they might choose their own bite, for the night was too cold for them to stray far. Whilst the men were collecting wood, and pitching the tent, I endeavoured to produce a light; but my fingers were so benumbed, that after breaking several matches I gave up the attempt, and began to run backwards and forwards, and strike my hands together, to restore my natural warmth. The sickness at my stomach, from exposure and inanition, now increased upon me, and I felt persuaded that I should have perished if I had been obliged to lie out on the prairie without a fire. At length, the men having got a fire up, I gradually recovered from my indisposition, and having eaten part of a biscuit, felt much better. I was sorry, however, to receive bad accounts from the men about the water, which we so much wanted to make soup for themselves and for my tea. It appeared that the only water that was to be obtained was from a hole in the swamp, and that it was as black as ink. On inspecting it, it was so thick and disgusting, that I thought it impossible to use it; but remembering the saying of an old French fellow-traveller, "que tout est bon, quand il n'y a pas de choix," and knowing that nothing but a cup of tea would thoroughly revive me, and unwilling to send Milor a mile in the dark to Big Stone Lake to obtain clear water, I determined to make the best I could of it.

I had a large pot therefore filled, and boiled it, skimming it as the black scum came in immense quantities to the top; and having exhausted it of everything of that kind that it would yield, the very notable idea struck me to put a quantity of it into my kettle with some black tea, and boil it over again, which I did: and really, when I poured it out, it looked so like strong black tea, and was so good and refreshing, that I soon forgot everything about it, except that it had restored me to life and animation. How many dead newts, and other animals, that had perished in the desiccation of the swamp that had attended the late drought, went to form this tea-broth, would not be easily calculated; but I forgave them, and the sires that begot them.

Whilst we were at our meal, a half-perished Nahcotah Indian came to our fire, whom I saw at the dance of the braves the day before. I remembered him the moment he came up, from his having attracted my attention during the dance by firing his gun over the heads of the dancers, and then presenting it to one of the braves. Milor had informed me that it was not unusual upon such occasions for savages who look on to become so excited as to give everything away that they have. This was what this poor devil had done; he had parted with his gun and all his little property, and was now going a journey of six or eight days to the Shayanne river to kill buffalo, without any arms, and without anything to eat by the way. Some one had given him an old pistol, without a lock to it; and seating himself by the fire without saying a word, he after a while pulled it out, and asked Milor if I would repair it, and give him some powder and ball? I told Milor to inform him that people could not make locks for pistols when they were travelling on the prairie in such stormy weather; but that I would give him something to eat, and directed the men to give him some of the pork and biscuit out of their pot, which he seemed to enjoy very much.

Feeling once more comfortable after a hearty supper, I entered my tent, and remained there to a late hour bringing up my notes, which I had had few opportunities of doing at Lac qui Parle. Before I lay down, I could not help contrasting the cheerless prospect before me at sun-set, and the suffering I experienced, with the cheerful state of mind and body I had now returned to, and for which I trust I was most sincerely grateful to God, who had preserved me in continued health and safety. I felt completely wound up again, and ready to go on for any length of time, especially with the reasonable prospect of a good night's rest before me.

Such are the agreeable excitements attending this kind

of life, to those who can enter without prejudice into the spirit of it. Certainly whilst your progress is successful, it is delightful. You have plenty to eat, and you enjoy what you eat; you are amused and instructed: it is true it is often cold, but then it is not always so. You encamp when you please; you cut down as large a tree as you please, and you make as large a fire of it as you please, without fearing an action of trespass. You kill deer out of any park you are passing through, without being questioned; and you have the rare privilege of leaving your night's lodging without calling for the landlord's bill. All law and government proceed from yourself; and the great point upon which everything turns is the successful management of the party you are the head of. Prudence, consistency, firmness, and a little generosity now and then by way of condiment, will carry such a traveller through everything.

But there is a reverse to the picture. Days and nights exposed to cold soaking rains; want of food and water; unavoidable exaggeration of danger; painful solicitude for those dear to and absent from you, and most anxious moments when you occasionally feel that prudence is scarcely sufficient to ensure your safety. Even the intense and curious impatience to push on in the face of apparent danger, makes you at times feel a remorse on account of those whom you are leading into it. Such are the contrasts of feeling by which the wanderer in these distant regions, still unvisited by a ray of civilization, is frequently agitated.

October 4.—I arose refreshed by a long and sweet sleep; and now it became a question whether I should make myself cleaner or dirtier by washing in the swamp-water. I tried a little of it, however, and finding it without a bad smell, went on, and contrived to believe I had washed myself. It looked less inviting by daylight, but not knowing what sort of luck we might have further on, I boiled and skimmed a certain quantum, and filled two bottles with it, for it was by no means certain that I should meet with water where we should stop to breakfast. We started at 7 A. M., and having made about three leagues, passed some trees, intending to stop at a considerable grove we saw about a league off; but the track wheeling suddenly to the left, we rode on in the keen north-west wind, three leagues further, to a lake, that appeared in the distance like burnished silver. On reaching it, all of us very much fatigued, we found indeed that it was not a *mirage*, but, although a lake or pond in the wet season, was a large area covered entirely over with carbonate of lime, as white as chalk, and without a drop of water in it. This was a great disappointment to the men, and I gave Milor one of my bottles of black tea. A few willows were growing on the margin of the area, and we managed to get up a tolerable fire. What had added greatly to our belief that it was water which we saw as we were approaching it, was an immense number of white wild ducks with black-tipped wings, as well as wild geese, hovering over the place, themselves probably as much baffled as we were. The shore was covered with planorbis and lymnea of a large size, shewing how much the water when the pond is full must be impregnated with lime: indeed, from the circumstance of its being a granitic country, it is probable that a spring highly impregnated with calcareous matter may exist somewhere in the area, but I had no time to pursue any investigation of this kind.

CHAPTER XXXIV.

REACH THE SUMMIT LEVEL DIVIDING THE WATERS WHICH FLOW INTO THE GULF OF MEXICO FROM THOSE FLOWING INTO HUDSON'S BAY. — MIGRATION OF MUSK-RATS.—TWO BUFFALOES KILLED BY ONE DRAFT OF AN ARROW.—LEAVE LAKE TRAVERS.—BUFFALO SKELETONS.—REACH THE SOURCES OF THE MINNAY SOTOR ON THE COTEAU DU PRAIRIE.—MILOR ADVISES OUR RETURN.

Soon after leaving this place we saw the Côteau du Prairie for the first time on our left, looking very high. The name it bears is appropriate enough for its appearance, for, considering the prairies as an ocean of land, without any other horizon than that which appears at sea, an elevation like this *côteau*, which stretches up and down the country, stands in the relation of a *coast* to the universal low level.

The remaining part of our ride was bitterly cold, but a little after 2 p.m. I saw a few scattering trees, which Milor said were growing near Lake Travers; and before three o'clock we reached an edge of the prairie from whence I looked down upon the valley below, in which was Lake Travers, with real water in it, being the most southern source of the waters that flow into Hudson's Bay. The sources of the St. Peter's being close on our left, we were now on the summit of land that divides the waters flowing into the Gulf of Mexico from those flowing into Lake Winnipeg and Hudson's Bay. Near to the bank of the lake were some buildings called a fort, this being a trading post. I rode down the slope of the prairie to them, and there found Mr. Brown, (the identical Mr. Brown who is mentioned at page 253 as having abandoned his two wives,) the resident factor of the American Fur Company, who received me very cordially, and assigned me quarters in his house. As soon as I had got my luggage brought in and my *toilette* made, I walked down to the lake, and found its waters very dead and turbid. The drought had lowered its level to such a degree, that the channel by which it communicates with Red River, that flows into Lake Winnipeg, was dried up, and Lake Travers had consequently become stagnant. I found several species of anadonta and unio, some of the latter of the same species as those inhabiting the St. Peter's, which is accounted for by the circumstance of the south end of this lake being only divided from the north end of Big Stone Lake by a low isthmus, two miles broad, so that when the waters of Lake Travers are high, they flow into Big Stone Lake.

Lake Travers has received this name from the French from its lying *à travers*, or across the country, being at right angles with the course of the St. Peter's: it is about twenty miles long, and runs N. E. by N. by compass. It is probable the French have translated this name from some Indian term signifying the same thing, for Indian names are always significant of some natural circumstance, from the necessity of giving descriptive designations to localities. There were a few Indian lodges about this post, but not enough to make the place noisy. Being able now to converse a little with the natives, I visited some of the lodges, but, upon inquiry, found there was not a chief amongst them.

Whilst I was chatting with some of the women, a Canadian named François Frénier, who acted in the capacity of interpreter to Mr. Brown, came to me, and from him I acquired a good deal of geographical and other information about the country betwixt Lake Travers and the Missouri, as well as that further to the north. He informed me that the Côteau du Prairie was a beautiful upland country, containing an immense number of small lakes, some of which contained well-wooded islands, where the Indians in the season take great quantities of musk-rats. These animals, he assured me, sometimes migrate, and are often met at such times on the prairies in incredible numbers. I have very little doubt of the truth of his statement, for all the American animals, both large and small, possess—what is most probably an acquired intelligence—the sense of bettering their condition by emigrating from districts where their food is becoming scarce. I remember, when in the Indian country in Upper Canada in 1807, meeting with the most surprising quantities of fine glossy black-skinned squirrels, with singularly beautiful bushy tails: they had spread over an immense district of country, and were evidently advancing from Lake Huron to the south.

This man further informed me that three days' march upon the Côteau—which is only five leagues from Lake Travers—would bring me to the river *Chagndeskah,* or "White Wood," a tributary of the Missouri, which has been named by the French *Rivière Jacques;* and that four days further would bring me to the Missouri. Upon one of the day's march no water could be met with. The Shayanne river was only two days from Lake Travers; and *Pembināu,* or "Red River," where the British colony is, could be reached in ten days. All this was prairie country with occasional trees and small lakes. The information was very interesting, as none of us had any practical knowledge of the country; and after conversing a little more with him, I started with my hammer to look for rocks in place, and to consider with myself what it was best to do, in what direction to advance, or whether to advance or return, being somewhat disconcerted by the fact that all the upland water of the country was stagnant, and that probably in most instances we should find the lakes desiccated. It was a great object with me to advance to the Missouri; and so great was my anxiety, that I returned to my quarters earlier than I intended, to consult Milor.

October 5.—I rose early, after rather a hard lodging upon Mr. Brown's floor, and went out to look for some water. Fortunately there was a good spring near the fort, but it was too hard to wash with; so I went to the lake, where, although it was certainly not drinkable, yet I never met with such fine, slimy, viscous stuff as it was for my purpose, scarcely wanting any soap at all. On my return, Mr. Brown very kindly invited me to breakfast, and being rather tired of my black tea of the last day, I gladly assented. But I made a poor exchange of my own humble resources for his, which were of the coarsest kind, and as dirty as they were coarse: a few broken plates, placed on a filthy board, with what he called coffee, and maize bread to correspond. As I swallowed this disgusting food, I consoled myself by reflecting that it saved one repast out of my own stock. Upon inquiring of him who was his cook, he told me that she was a Nahcotah woman, the widow of that brother of Renville's whom the Chippeways had murdered, and that Renville had sent her here to live, and lament her widowhood. When she came into the room to remove the plates, I observed that she was tall and well made, with all the remains of a handsome woman. Like many others, she had been the favourite Indian wife of an American trader, and had had a daughter (by one Lockwood),—a pretty young girl, about fourteen, who afterwards came with some squaws to get handkerchiefs from me.

The moment I saw this woman, I perceived she had been accustomed to white people, and, upon subsequently inquiring her history of a squaw to whom one of the lodges belonged, I learnt that Renville had adopted her as one of his wives, and had sent her here to live in the cabin which he inhabited when he came to Lake Travers. As this, however, did not happen very often, Mr. Brown, who was distressed with a restless *penchant* for ladies, had done her the honour to remove her to his cabin, but this only *en attendant*, until he could persuade her daughter, the young beauty of fourteen, to live with him as his wife. He had made her various presents, but such was his notoriety for abandoning his ladies upon short notice, that she had hitherto resisted his cajolements. The girl was perfectly delighted when I presented her a handkerchief and some strings of beads; nor did I forget the mother, who took an early opportunity of asking Milor if I was going to stay all the winter; but whether she had an eye to herself, or to Prairie on Fire No. 2, I had no opportunity of ascertaining. Mr. Brown was evidently not very anxious that I should stay long with him; innocent as I was of offence, he saw that the women had commenced their intrigues, and was annoyed by it. As long as he had been the only person there, things went on quietly, and he could take his own time to carry out his plans of domestic happiness; but the arrival of my party had awakened amongst the women all their love for finery and intrigue, and it was evident that things would get into a mess of some kind or other if we staid. I determined, therefore, both for this reason and the more important one of losing no time, upon departing immediately.

After breakfast Mr. Brown shewed me some very rare furs he possessed, several very fine grizzly bear skins (*Ursus ferox*), one of which was a bright yellow, a rare variety. He had also an exceedingly large and rich otter skin, which, with many other things, I purchased of him. But my most valuable acquisition here was made from an Assiniboin chief, who came in about an hour before I departed. This was a fine bow, made of bone and wood, with a cord of very strong sinew. The chief had performed a feat with it for which Wānetáh, a Nahcotah chief, had been celebrated. He had killed two buffaloes that were galloping on a parallel with his own horse at one draft of his arrow, it having passed through the first, and inflicted a mortal wound upon the second. The chief was very unwilling to part with it: we tried him several times in vain; and at length I offered him five gold pieces, or twenty-five dollars. "Máhzázhee! Héeyah!" "Yellow iron! No!" he replied. At last Mr. Brown produced some brilliant scarlet cloth: the sight of it overcame his reluctance; it would make such beautiful leggings, and his squaws would be so delighted with it! So I gave him three yards of the cloth, and he delivered me the bow, a quiver of arrows, and a skin case, which contained it. Mr. Brown, of course, got his share of the amount, though he acted very fairly with me. Money is unknown to these savages, and they place no value upon it. He would not have taken twenty of these gold pieces for his bow, but thought he had made a good bargain with it for the cloth, although I have no doubt Mr. Brown would have sold it to any one for ten dollars. It was an affair of barter, where both parties were satisfied, which, under similar circumstances, is, perhaps, the best definition of value.

After acquiring as much information as I could at this trading post, I ordered the baggage and tent to be placed once more in the *charette*, and, remounting my mare, turned our faces to the Côteau du Prairie, shaping my course to the south end of Lake Travers, where there is a valley about one mile wide, down which its waters pass in the rainy season to Big Stone Lake. At this time the channel was dry, and, seeing a considerable Indian village about half way down it, I rode there, but its inhabitants were all out after buffalo, in the neighbourhood of the Shayanne. Seeing several mounds on the west side of Lake Travers, I proceeded in that direction, passing a great many stones that had been painted red by the Indians, as I afterwards understood, for their amusement. Having got upon the upland west of this valley, I followed the course of the north-west fork of the St. Peter's, on the brink of a deep ravine that it had worn, leaving the south-west fork to the left. We were now approaching the sources of the St. Peter's, where we could not have used our canoe, for the stream in the ravine in no place exceeded two yards in width, and in many places was almost dry. Having found a convenient place to cross the *charette*, I waited till the people came up, and, getting it down into the ravine with some difficulty, we contrived, by digging down the

IMPROVIDENCE OF THE INDIANS.

banks a little, and throwing bushes into the stream, to make it passable, and, having all crossed, proceeded towards the Côteau. Here we found the prairie completely black, having been thoroughly burnt over; and soon we came to where the ground was strewed over with countless bleached skeletons of buffaloes.

The poor improvident Indians, when they meet with powerful herds of these animals, and have a favourable opportunity of destroying them, kill as many as they can, frequently several hundreds in a day, and all for the sake of the skins, with which they liquidate their debts to the insatiate trader, leaving the carcases to rot on the ground and afford food to the prairie wolves. This had been the scene of one of these buffalo *battues*. At some future geological period, when another deposit is made on this part of the terrestrial surface, it may be that these remains may be discovered, and produce theories and conjectures as to the cause of the destruction that will greatly interest mankind, or whatever kind may then exist, until some Buckland *redivivus*, finding the barb of an arrow in the rib of one of them, will, with the same power of genius and fancy that once illuminated the obscurities of the Kirkdale Cave, people these prairies over again with butchering Indians and flying buffaloes. It was impossible to ride amongst these skeletons without thinking of the condition of the Indians, who are now paying for their folly in unprofitably destroying and frightening the buffaloes away, by having now to perform the most tedious journeys in the winter, to procure meat for the subsistence of their families.

Pleased at having one of the great objects of my journey—the Côteau du Prairie—so near to me, I rode on several miles in advance, on its east flank, and got insensibly entangled, towards evening, in a part of the country consisting of naked sand-hills, evidently thrown up by the wind. Hoping to find a grass prairie beyond them, I rode on in a N.N.W. course, until the whole country before me was nothing but sand, with here and there a leafless bush growing. Having alighted, and tied the mare to one of them, I got to the top of one of the loftiest sand-hills, to look for the *charette*. Nothing was to be seen but the Côteau and sand-hills; not choosing, therefore, to trust myself in the dark where there was neither wood nor water, nor anything to eat, I turned back and took a south-west course, in the hope of crossing the track of the *charette*, the general course of which I had agreed upon with Milor. At any rate the course I now took would bring me to the Côteau in a part where I had observed some trees growing, from which I had drawn the inference that water would be found there. Just as night was setting in, I came to a small ravine, where there were some bushes and dry wood, plenty of grass, and a little clear water trickling down, upon which I lost no time in alighting and tethering the mare, and made a fire, heaping sticks and grass upon it to make a large volume of smoke, for I was quite sure that Milor would keep a good look-out for me, and it was yet light enough for a column of smoke to be seen. Here I remained a couple of hours alone, changing my smoke to a bright fire, but being obliged to come to the conclusion that they had made their bivouac where they could not see my signals; and darkness having set in, I was reluctantly compelled to think I should see no more of my party that night. It being my own fault, I had nobody to blame but myself; so making up my mind to bear my privations as well as I could, and to pass the night where I was, I first took a hearty drink of water, then putting the saddle on the ground for a pillow, I arranged as well as I could a place to lie down upon, and muffling myself up in my blanket-coat, and placing my feet to the fire, I lay down and tried to sleep. But it was in vain. My mind was too busy. I had yet to determine whether to pursue my journey to the Mandans, or to turn back. This depended very much upon the men; they might not be willing to go, as many of them had families. I felt no inconvenience from having eaten nothing, an advantage I owed to a confirmed habit that has grown out of my manner of life: in fact, I never am hungry, or feel a desire to eat, until I have tasted the first mouthful, when I always eat anything that I like with great relish, but with moderation, and this only once during the day, after a slight breakfast. I had no concern on my mind about the *charette*, because I knew that in the morning one of the parties could not fail to see the other's smoke. Some of the stories I had heard of certain vagabond Indians frequenting the Côteau, who never failed to scalp those whom they could overpower, crossed my mind, and perhaps made me less desirous to fall asleep; but I had long ago made up my mind to do the best I could for myself upon every exigency, and, therefore, thinking that enough for the day was the evil thereof, I dismissed those thoughts, and turned to the more grateful occupation of carrying myself in imagination across the vast distance which separated me from my family. Whilst I was thus occupied, I was roused by a sudden yell, and starting to the ground I answered it with another, for I knew it was Milor, the very master who had taught me the yell with which I responded. He had been to various places where wood and water were to be found, to look for me; and having got upon the slope of the Côteau to give him the best chance of seeing my fire, he had at length discovered it. I was touched with the old man's fidelity, for he told me that his intention was to have passed the whole night looking for me, and I believed him. He said that the place the men had selected for their bivouac was not near so good as the one where he had found me, so I told him to return, and bring *toute la boutique* with him. In a little more than an hour they made their appearance with the *charette;* we got the tent pitched, a good fire built, and I was not at all sorry to see the frying-pan at work again. I made a most hearty meal, and soon went to sleep.

Some say that late dinners and suppers are unwholesome, which is very likely to be the case where these are luxurious meals; but when, at the close of a day's severe exercise, the traveller finds, that, after a simple and moderate repast, he can sleep soundly, and rise without being troubled with dreams, it may perhaps be taken as a proof that the practice is a salutary one, and consistent with natural suggestions, such as those which lead animals to eat their grass until they lie down for the night.

After a refreshing night's rest, I arose in excellent spirits: the morning was serene and beautiful; and striking our encampment, we got the *charette* in motion soon after 6 A. M., and began to ascend the Côteau by a very gentle slope. Having reached the crest of this upland, and seeing a fine bold eminence, distant about a mile and a half, I rode thither, and had a magnificent view of the country from the top. The Côteau du Prairie, called in the Nahcotah tongue *Chhra Tanka,* or the "Great

Hills," is, looking to the west, in everything like the other upland prairies, only a stage of elevation above them. Before we approached it, it had the appearance of a lofty range. Major Long's party, in 1823, who saw it at a distance of from thirty to forty miles, estimated it at 1000 feet high; but, as I have before observed, where there is nothing to compare an object with, it always appears of greater magnitude than it is. A knoll on the prairie, at the distance of two miles, will appear to have an elevation of 200 feet, and yet when you reach it, it is scarcely fifty feet above the general level. The ascent from the prairie below to the top of the Côteau was perhaps two miles and a half long, by a slope so gentle that in no place did it appear to exceed 250 feet to the mile, which would give 625 feet elevation for the summit of the Côteau, nor did I think it exceeded that height.

I found the surface of this upland very much broken up into knolls and inequalities; and in these depressions, small lakes or ponds, with a few trees growing near them, are found in great numbers. As I was riding along, I started a grey rabbit, with black-tipped ears and a white tail. I remarked, also, that there were no skeletons of buffaloes, as in the plain below; and, from the great deficiency of grass on the Côteau, I inferred that it would not be frequented by these animals. The surface was excessively rough and hummocky, so much so, that the men got the *charette* along with difficulty, the wheels constantly coming to the ground with a violent *sécousse*. One of these wooden wheels, ill adapted to such rough work, was already gaping and giving signs of weakness; and if the *charette* broke down, it was clear to the apprehension of every one, that the *butin*, consisting of the tent, a hamper, a trunk, two bags of provisions, one heavy bag of mineral specimens, a large package of curiosities, and the cooking utensils, would, save what we could get upon the horses, have to be carried upon the shoulders of the men. I heard nothing from the men but "Ce sacré Côteau va nous flamber au premier abord." Meantime we pursued our course, my mare floundering amongst the hummocks, Milor marching steadily on after me, and the men wondering where I was going, now that we had left all the trading posts behind, and *sacré*ing the Côteau and the day that they left their homes.

This was a state of things that could not last long, not longer than the *charette* at any rate, and therefore I consulted Milor. He said, if we were obliged to carry the *butin*, it would take us at least three weeks to reach the Mandans, and that there was one part of the route where we should be three or four days without water. That we might advance to the *Chagndeskah*, and scoop out a tree canoe, and descend in it to the Missouri; but what should we do with the *charette* and the horses? He said that the men were all desirous of returning to their families, as they never left them for the winter without an understanding to that effect, and making proper arrangements for them; they therefore considered me bound to take them back to their homes, the which if I did not do, he did not know what might happen. The snow, he said, would begin to fall in a week or ten days at farthest, and the men could not travel with the *butin* in the snow; indeed we might be caught in a deep snow, and find it difficult either to advance or retreat. And he finished by saying, "Monsieur, si cela lui plait soit, pourroit peutêtre retourner aux postes militaires avant le commencement de l'hiver ; qu'il avait beau temps pour cela. Mais si cela ne lui convenoit pas, il pourroit renvoyer les gens au Lac qui Parle ; qu'ils y trouveroient le canot pour retourner chez eux, et qu'il accompagneroit Monsieur où il voudroit. Que Monsieur n'avoit qu'à commander." Such was the prudence, good sense, and fidelity of this excellent man, that I had become attached to him, and was unwilling to desist from pursuing my journey to the Mandans whilst I could have the benefit of his judicious guidance ; but it was so late in the year, that, even if I had sent the men and *charette* back, and had undertaken to cross the country with him, we might have had to encounter very serious difficulties, carrying our own provisions, and liable to be surprised every day with a hostile change in the weather. I remembered the painful evening of the march from the Wahboptah to the Grosses Isles, and the practical conviction I received of its being possible to be frozen to death ; and believing it to be my duty to act with prudence, I told Milor that I was well satisfied with what he had said, and that he might direct the men to turn the *charette* round, for I should go to Big Stone Lake. This news was received with great joy.

CHAPTER XXXV.

REACH BIG STONE LAKE ON OUR RETURN.—SYMPTOMS OF WINTER.—IMMENSE MASSES OF GRANITE, FROM WHENCE THE LAKE TAKES ITS NAME.—PRAIRIES ON FIRE.—SUPPOSED ORIGIN OF THE WORD "MISSOURI."—REACH THE WAH-BOPTAH.—EGREGIOUS PRIDE OF THE MALE INDIANS.

WE now proceeded to the south along the crest of the Côteau, and from different points I had some exceedingly fine views of the country beneath me. Lake Travers was spread out in all its length; and to the south-east was another lake, called *Minday Wointzeah*, or "Rush Lake." Big Stone Lake was not visible, but, from particular indications, Milor knew exactly where it was; and we agreed to descend the Côteau, and try to make the lake in season to encamp there by daylight. We accordingly took leave of the Côteau and made for some trees at a distance, where we saw a smoke, thinking some Indians might be there. On reaching the place, we found that the smoke was occasioned by some embers of the prairie fire; and water being at hand we commenced preparations for breakfast; but the wind suddenly rising, the fire began to increase, and very soon such volumes of smoke came down upon us, that we were fairly driven off the ground just as everything was ready. As it was impossible to make our repast amidst a dense smoke, which began to extend upon a long line, we had only time to get the *charette* in motion, and snatching up the things, to make rather a confused retreat. My provision-basket was hastily rapacked and sent off; Milor bore off my boiling tea-kettle, and I followed him with the frying-pan, keeping it as well as I could in a horizontal position; — not from a particular *penchant* for taking a long walk with a hot frying-pan in my hand, but because I should have had some misgivings about its contents if such a fellow as L'Amirant had taken possession of it. After some time we gained a place where we were less annoyed, and getting through our repast not very comfortably, pursued our journey upon an E.S.E. course.

We had now to travel several hours over burnt ground, and my head-ache returned very painfully. At length, to the delight of my mare, I reached short sweet grass again, and dismounted to let her feed. Whilst I was waiting the arrival of the *charette* I was exceedingly amused with the movements of one of those antelopes which rove over these prairies. The graceful creature came bounding on in a singularly elastic manner towards the place where the mare was browsing, and where I was lying on the grass. Sometimes it reared itself up on its hind legs to get a good look at us, and then, if I lifted up my head, would wheel round and fly away with surprising speed; then again it would return and repeat its elegant motions.

These beautiful creatures often become the victims of their curiosity; for when the hunter conceals himself behind a knoll and waves a piece of cloth tied to a stick, so insatiable is their propensity, that they frequently approach too near for their own safety. This antelope, and some flocks of brown plover, were the only animals I saw during this ride. Having refreshed the mare, and seeing my party at a great distance coming slowly along, I mounted again, and with my sick head-ache went wearying along, making for some trees I had for a long time seen in the horizon. I think I never was more heartily tired with a ride than I was upon this occasion; it seemed as if there was no end to this interminable prairie. But the ride, like all other things, did come to an end; for about 5 P.M. I suddenly came to an abrupt and lofty bank, and looking down, beheld one of the most beautiful lakes I had ever seen in North America, describing for a great distance very graceful curves, with fine bluffs about 200 feet in height, and well-grown woods covering the slope beneath me down to the water's edge. I saw at once that this sheet of water was the remains of the river that once occupied the whole of this valley, just as Lake Pepin occupies the mean breadth of the Mississippi at the present day; the breadth of this lake, which is about two miles and a half, corresponding to the general breadth of the valley of the St. Peter's.

Having tethered my mare, and found an excellent situation for our bivouac somewhat down the bank, I lighted a fire and heaped some grass upon it as a signal to Milor. I now descended the slope to the bottom, with the intention of reaching the shore of the lake; but I found it impossible to get close to it, there being a great breadth of swamp betwixt the lake and the shore filled with canes eight feet high, so that it was impossible to see the state of the bottom, or to procure any unios. On my return to the camp I found a fine spring of cool and clear water; and the party having come up just about this time, I directed one of the men to it; and having pitched the tent and built up capital fires, we all made a very hearty and cheerful repast. A refreshing cup of tea cured my head-ache, so that I was able to devote a couple of hours to bring up my note-book before I lay down to rest.

October 7.—On rising at the dawn of day I found the spring water in my tent frozen across the pail, an unequivocal sign of what might be expected soon. At half-past six A. M. we were all again in motion, and gaining the upland, had a very beautiful ride along the west bank of this charming lake. Everywhere I found the soil of the richest quality; that on the adjacent prairie was generally black and fertile, so that this may become a delightful neighbourhood, if the country ever should be settled by people who know how to make a proper use of such advantages. I found the general direction of the lake to be north-west and south-east, being nearly at right angles with Lake Travers. Midway it bends east and by south.

In about a couple of hours' riding, I came upon an old *charette* track leading in the direction of an island in the lake, where there was an Indian village : it led across several deep gullies in the prairie, one of which formed an extensive cove of about 100 acres of land, reaching to the shore of the lake. The soil was exceedingly fertile, and the whole place was a perfect wilderness of trees and briars, with a fine stream of water running through it. I saw the remains of several lodges, but they did not appear to have been inhabited for a long time. On the south side of this curious cove, and near the top of the upland, I found some sepulchral mounds, one of them of a large size; and as it commanded a fine view of the lake and cove below, I made a sketch from hence.

At half-past nine A. M. we left the main prairie, and descended a convenient slope to the edge of the lake to breakfast. Here, on the beach, I found great quantities of unios and anadontas; and whilst I was engaged opening some of them, a beautiful large black marten came towards me, but ran off as soon as I stirred. On communicating this intelligence, the men left their avocations, and full of zeal and noise, set about his capture; but the fortunate animal had got into his hole and baffled them. We therefore left this place without the trophy, which even I was a little anxious to secure as a remembrance of the locality; and, pursuing our way, came at 1 P. M. opposite to some large islands, with teebees upon them, but we saw none of their inhabitants, who were probably at Lac qui Parle. We soon came to where the grass was very high; and as I was urging my mare through it, she almost placed her fore-foot upon a prairie wolf, who crouched and snapped his teeth, but sneaked off to his burrow as soon as he had recovered from his surprise. I could have shot him with a pocket-pistol if I had had one, for he was quite under my stirrup. In the course of the afternoon we descended again from the prairie, about a mile from the south end of the lake, where it was covered with tens of thousands of wild fowl, that made a noise like thunder when they rose. I never saw greater numbers together.

Big Stone Lake terminates in a plain flat marsh, and, by my computation, is about thirty-six miles long, and two miles broad. The northern part of its course is north and south, the central part east, and the southern part deflects to south by east. From the termination of the lake the valley continues with the same breadth to Lac qui Parle, but the channel which connects the two was, at the period of my visit, and owing to the drought, not even navigable for a canoe. From the point where we crossed it, Milor estimated the distance to Lac qui Parle to be fifteen leagues. We crossed over to the east side, about two miles from the termination of the lake, and soon after came upon a countless number of masses of granite in place, occupying an area of three or four

HOW TO PROCEED ON A BURNING PRAIRIE. 401

hundred acres of land. I got upon several of them that were at least twenty-five feet high. They were not boulders, though, viewed from a distance, they might, being isolated from each other, be taken for such. Many of them were separated from the rest fifteen to thirty yards; and what power could have removed the intervening portions, it would seem hopeless to conjecture at present. I certainly never saw a more curious spectacle, and perceived at once that the Indians had named the lake *Ea-tatenka*, or "Stones-big," from these masses. I afterwards saw similar masses in the valley for six or eight miles further down; and in one place I remarked that the valley betwixt the bluffs was about five miles broad. All this vale must have been at some period filled with water; indeed, I have no doubt that its whole line from the head of Lake Travers must have formed a mighty river.

As we proceeded we found the country on fire, and had to ride more than once through places where the grass was vigorously blazing. Upon these occasions, I remarked that the mare was very anxious about her young one; indeed, at one time the grass was so high, that the foal got a little singed. When the prairie is burning, and you are advancing to it, you can generally, by watching your opportunity, select a point to get through the line of fire to the burnt land on the other side of it, without injury. But where the grass on a dry rich fertile soil is as high as a man, it is very unsafe to attempt to meet the advancing conflagration; for a gust of wind will throw the fire in every direction, and perhaps cut off your retreat; and if you attempt to force your way through, the volume of smoke may be so powerful as to stifle both yourself and the animal you ride. Upon such occasions, the safest way is always to turn back until you get to short grass.

But, under any circumstances, nothing can be more disagreeable than passing from clean healthy grass through a line of fire to a dreary burnt plain, smelling strongly of soot, and without one verdant spot upon the dingy surface. As to myself, the odour of the smoke always produced immediate headache, and if obliged to endure it a long time, it increased until I was in great pain. I became quite of opinion upon this occasion, that, if Milor and myself had undertaken to go alone to the Mandans, and had had to encounter fire in the prairies, we could not have accomplished our intention.

About 5 P. M. we encamped on the left bank of the St. Peter's, on a clean grassy place, and found the stream not more than four inches deep, though I afterwards learnt that it was navigable for canoes betwixt the lakes when the water was high. We had passed in the course of the day the *Zoozoo Wâhpahdah*, or "Sandstone River," which comes into the St. Peter's on the right bank, and which in the wet season is a considerable stream coming down from the Côteau. Opposite our bivouac was another stream from the Côteau, called *Chhra Wakon*, or "Mount of the Great Spirit:" it takes its name from a lofty mound on its left bank up the country, which goes by that name, from a tradition of a miraculous nature respecting some Indian chief. The word *chhra* is pronounced rapidly, with a strong guttural burr, and signifies in the Nahcotah tongue any lofty hill.

While at Lake Travers I met with a rather intelligent Indian hunter, who was well acquainted with that part of the country; and inquiring about that portion of it which lies nearest to the Missouri, I asked him how the Nahcotahs called that river; when he answered *Minnay Shóshóh Chhráy*, which is literally "Water muddy Hill." I was puzzled at first, but when I came to understand his description of the country, I thought it not unlikely, that, as all the Indian names we are acquainted with are corruptions from the French, the word "Missouri" might have its origin in these three words. By itself it is not an Indian word, and therefore it is a fair inference that it is a corruption. This man said, that, in crossing the country to the *Chagndéskah,* you first came to *Chhray-tanka* ("Great Hill"), which is the general name for the Côteau du Prairie; that there was then a second *chhray* to cross: beyond that river was a third *chhray,* called *Minnay Shoshoh Chhray,* because you could see *Minnay Shoshoh,* or "Muddy River" (which is what is now called Missouri), from it. By abbreviating the first word, "Minnay," of its last four letters, and afterwards the others, according to the practice of the French, the word *Mi-sho-ray* is produced. It is far from being improbable that such is the origin of the word "Missouri," the river having perhaps received that name from those French adventurers who first traversed the country from Lake Travers to that fine stream.

The appearance of the line of fire on the prairie was very pleasing this night, and detained me a long time from my rest. In every direction the horizon presented brilliant spots, resembling the lamps in an illuminated garden, and would have made a curious and rare picture.

October 8. — We struck our camp about 6 A. M., and had a tedious ride over the dreary burnt prairie, having to cross an extensive morass into the bargain, from which we extricated the *charette* with difficulty. At the end of about five leagues we reached our old bivouac on the Wahboptah, where we found two Indians and their squaws, with a rather pretty girl of twelve years old. The poor creature was the daughter of a French trader called Martingère, and had been abandoned by her father. Soon after our arrival they took up their line of march for Lake Travers, the two females and the young girl almost bent to the ground with their heavy burdens, whilst the two males, totally regardless of the distress of the women, strutted on, with the air of princes, without any load whatever. So much for the unsophisticated and noble-minded savage, as some have been pleased to describe him. I gave the poor females some pork and biscuit, and desired Milor to tell them not to give their heroes the slightest portion of it. Whilst the men were breakfasting I went into the Wahboptah to get a few more unios; but the water was so cold that I was glad to get out of it again, and put on dry stockings by the fire.

CHAPTER XXXVI.

REACH LAC QUI PARLE.—AN INDIAN MARRIAGE.—DEPENDENCE OF THE INDIANS UPON THE TRADERS. — RE-EMBARK ON THE MINNAY SOTOR. — IMMENSE QUANTITIES OF WILD FOWL.—REACH MR. MOORE'S AND FIND PAH-KAHSKAH THERE.

HAVING made a hearty repast we proceeded with a bright cheerful sun. My mare now got into a capital humour: she knew she was near home, and with her foal went on in a quick ambling trot, as if purposely to show me what she could do when she chose. At 3 P. M. I reached Renville's fort again, and was glad to learn that the greater part of the noisy savages were gone upon various expeditions. Having refreshed myself with a complete change, I made all the arrangements for descending the St. Peter's the next day, having done which I went to Renville's in the evening, and made my last dirty meal there. Whilst we were at table I was surprised to hear some one groaning out some canticles to an air that was evidently meant for our national anthem of "God save the King," a tune which has been adopted at the old French missions. This proceeded from a sort of kitchen belonging to the house; but, as it is not etiquette to appear curious about the domestic manners of Indians when you are amongst them, I made no observation. After the meal, however, on going to the outside of the fort, I heard a most appalling and lamentable howling issuing from the woods on the border of the lake; and calling to

Milor, he informed me that the distressing sounds came from a squaw, whose daughter was going to be married, and that it was usual upon such occasions for the mother to express her sorrow for the loss of her child. I never heard a more woeful lamentation; it seemed to arise from the very inmost soul of the woman, and the effect was surprisingly increased by its proceeding from a wood in the darkness of the night. Ariosto could not have wished for a finer bass note to compose one of his vivid cantos upon.

Milor further informed me that the daughter thus lamented was at that moment in Renville's house, and that the happy bridegroom was Renville's stupid heavy son, who had bargained with the mother for her daughter to live with him as one of his wives. This egregious dolt of a fellow had already one wife, a good-looking young woman, who had brought him several children. To be sure a jumble of this kind could only be met with in such a state of society: a savage brought up by French missionaries singing canticles in the 96° of W. longitude, in North America, to the tune of "God save the King," as a religious preparation for a bigamy; and a mother, after screwing all she could get out of him for her daughter, going to the woods to scream in the dark as if her heart was broken. I remembered a tolerably good-looking Indian woman bringing in the potatoes to our evening meal, who appeared to think about nothing but her potatoes; but I now learnt that she was this man's first wife, and that she had already been to the teebee where the girl lived who was now to be married, to conduct her to her own husband, and that she had left her sitting in the kitchen listening to his frightful canticles. The consummation, it appeared, was not to take place until after a week's howling and singing, the first wife having the benefit of her husband's sweet society in the meantime. No wonder that Huggins called them Philis*tines*, and all sorts of hard names, for certainly nothing more egregiously absurd can be imagined.

The little Frenchman who acted as Renville's clerk came to see me when I went to my mattress at the warehouse, and I had some interesting conversation with him about the condition of the Indians. He confirmed the observations I had already made, that the Indians had entirely lost their ancient independent condition; that the race can no longer exist without blankets, guns, ammunition, and clothes for their wives, themselves, and their children; that upon all these things the traders put their own price, always increasing it when skins are plentiful, and seldom lowering it when the season is unproductive; that the Indians are always in debt to the traders, at least one year in advance—these last being obliged to advance them an outfit before they commence their hunting. Without this the Indian could not leave home on his now very distant expeditions, and consequently there would be no trade.

Sometimes the Indian dies in the trader's debt, and its amount is lost; the profits, therefore, must be in proportion to the risk which is run. No doubt the trader is vigilant, and takes care of his interests, but I certainly heard of no instance of the Indians being defrauded; perhaps it would be difficult to do this, although the Indians cannot write. The fact is, there is no money account betwixt them, it being kept in skins, and the Indian always remembers how many skins he owes to the trader, and that he must bring them to him the next year, or forfeit his credit. An Indian who breaks his engagement is never trusted again; and the understanding among the traders being general, an Indian cannot deceive one and then go to another. Some of them attempt to do this, and soon become vagabonds, especially if they can get rum or whiskey to drink; but the excellent regulations of the Government of the United States, in regard to the introduction of ardent spirits, seem to have entirely excluded them from this part of the country. At present the fur trade of the American Indians appears limited to musk-rat and buffalo skins: every year will diminish the supply of these last; so that, from the superior advantages which the Hudson's Bay Company enjoy, and their very liberal conduct to the Indians, it is probable they will soon engross all the fur trade of the north-west country.

The following account against one of the best hunters amongst the Nahcotahs is rather curious, and was extracted by me from the books of the American Fur Company at this place:—

Conte de *Táhtáywahkéeagn* ("*Le Vent de la Tonnerre*").

	Sinkcpáy ("Peau de Rats").			Sinkepáy ("Peau de Rats").
1 Blankette couvert de laine 3 points	70	7 Mésures poudre		70
1 Couvert drap	70	14 S. B. plomb		28
1 Broyois	20	2 B. Tavelle		8
1 Do. rouge	25	1 Darc		15
1 Capot	50	2 Couteau		8
1 Blankette 1 point	25	10 Pierres à fusil		11
1 Mitasse	30	2 Cassetêtes		30
1 Do.	20	10 Torquettes de tabac		10
1 Ceinture	6	1 Chemise		30
		1 Fusil		150
				676

To say nothing of other debts he might have, the *Wind of the Thunder*, to liquidate this account alone, was under the necessity of putting 676 musk-rats to their last squeak; and it is in this way that the white traders have converted these heroes of nature into a race of rat-catchers, amongst whom I understood Táhtáywáhkéeagn stood very high as a good and successful hunter, which I found was no small praise to a modern Indian, meaning, in fact, that he took care of his family and kept his word.

October 9.—We were up very early, and bustling to get off, and, being apprehensive that the river might be too low to get a heavy canoe down it, I sent the *charette*, with the heavy luggage, to Travers des Sioux by land, where the shallows terminated. Having taken a friendly leave of the missionary party, and recommended to Huggins to abate his dislike to the Philistines, who, I assured him, would never be converted by unkindness, I proceeded in fine spirits to the landing-place, and found my good old canoe afloat, with the men already in it. The population which remained at the place came *en masse* to see us depart, and amongst the rest was the new bride from Renville's, an exceedingly plain woman, with coarse, strong features and high cheek-bones. Before I stepped into the canoe, I distributed some handkerchiefs and beads amongst the youngest girls there, telling them they would live the longest to remember me, and, about 7 A. M., pushed off from the bank, delighted to find myself in the comfortable canoe again, where I could sit, and observe, and write, and read at my leisure.

Gliding with the current, and plying our paddles occasionally, we went quickly along, and had only made a very few miles when I observed the *Tetrao* in considerable quantities on the edge of the river's bank, for the country being burnt up for a great distance in the interior, they had come to the unburnt lowland close to the water, where there were seeds of various kinds. We killed a sufficient number of them from the canoe, and, on picking them up, found they were heavy birds, weighing about 2 lb. each. The men would willingly have waited until we had loaded the boat with them, but I told them that every half-hour we lost would bring us nearer to a snow storm; that I did not mean to eat those we had killed, but intended to carry them as a present to the commandant of Fort Snelling, and that, as they had plenty of pork to last them until they got back to their own country, the best way would be to eat it. Knowing that they had plenty to eat, they cheerfully assented to what I said; and we pursued our way amidst the most delightful weather, making, with the aid of the current, at the rate of from six to seven knots an hour, except when, tempted occasionally by the beautiful unios that were half buried in the clear sand, I stopped the canoe for a few minutes. It was a charming day's work, taking it altogether; and about half-past four P.M. we stopped for the night at a very comfortable place, where we set our regular establishment of frying-pans and kettles a-going, as in old times.

October 10.—I rose at peep of day after a comfortable night's rest, and had the canoe gummed, it having leaked in consequence of being dragged over some shallow places the day before. Again we found the moor-fowl ranged in rows along the banks of the river, and, as it was a very difficult thing to restrain the men, we stopped a short time to kill a few of them. The trees had now nearly lost their leaves, so that our tenure of the fine weather was at best precarious; and, remarking this to the men, they applied themselves vigorously to their paddles. We reached the first rapids before 9 A. M., down which we passed very pleasantly; the men shewing a great deal of skill, and accomplishing in ten minutes what it had taken them three hours to do when we ascended the river. We reached the *portage* about 9 A. M. Here I landed, and walked across in twenty-five minutes, pacing the distance, which I found to be 300 yards. The men were in such high spirits at the prospect of returning home, that, heavily laden as they were with the *butin*, they only took twenty minutes more than myself to cross it. The morning was sunny, and the heavy masses of lamellar granite, which, like those near Big Stone Lake, had the appearance of gigantic boulders, although they were merely outliers, looked very imposing on this treeless prairie.

The canoe having come round, and the party being united again, we were all very well disposed to breakfast, but we found it so inconveniently hot on the prairie, that we embarked and dropped down the river until we came to a shady place, where the grass was not burnt up. The whole of this part of the country had been fired, either through accident or design, since we ascended, an occurrence which Milor informed me was certain to take place annually. The Indians, some of whom are found wandering in every part of the country, often leave their fires, as likewise do the traders, to be blown about by the winds. In very dry seasons, a few sparks dropped from a tobacco-pipe are enough to set an extensive district in a blaze; but in most cases the natives fire the prairies to prevent the buffalo wandering too far from them,—a practice which answers their purpose for awhile, but, like everything that the untutored and improvident wild man does, is found very inconvenient in the end, for once on fire, the prairies are often burnt for greater distances than the Indian has calculated upon, and thus he loses sight of the buffalo for a long period of time. They hope that the fire will stop at such a river; but although that would generally be the case if the grass was uniformly low, yet now and then on the rich bottoms it is high and thick, and the conflagration rages to such an extent, that flakes of fire are sure to be blown across, and communicated to the other side. Had they but a little foresight, and would leave the grass unburnt, the buffalo would move from one part of the prairie to another, and return to that which they had first depastured. But his wants oblige him to procure skins, and the Indian goes the most ruinous way to work to supply the trader with them: the candle of his existence is in fact lighted at both ends, and must soon be burnt out.

At half-past three P. M. we came to the *Pahjeetah Zeezeehah*, twenty-five leagues from Lac qui Parle. The left bank of the river here was literally alive with *Tetrao* coming to feed and drink from the burnt prairie; they were so large and fat, that they looked like barn-door fowls. We stopped a short time to pick up a few of them; but having no means of roasting them, and being obliged to boil them, I found them so insipid that I cared no longer for them, except when fried with the ham, which I found the best way of preparing them. My rice was exhausted, which was a misfortune, the pillau being an excellent and convenient dish, as my men had already discovered, and had not scrupled to rob me of the rice I had laid in for my own use, to make pillaus for themselves with what L'Amirant called "les sacrés chats sauvages." About sun-set we came to a nice sweet clean place, and established our camp there.

October 11.—We left our encampment at *half-past*

five on a soft beautiful morning, and passed quickly down a great many of the rapids which had detained us on coming up, stopping to breakfast at 10 A. M. on a large flat granite rock. In an hour we were afloat again, and soon got into a clean grassy country, where the river was shallow. Finding the canoe grounded frequently, I put three of the men ashore to walk, enjoining them to keep up with us, and soon after looking back, I saw the vagabonds amusing themselves with setting fire to the prairie. I took them on board as quickly as I could, and bitterly reproached them with their misconduct, recalling to their recollection how much they had been annoyed by the burnt prairies near Big Stone Lake; but what I said made no impression upon them, men of their race and cast caring for nothing beyond present enjoyment. We stopped awhile near the Hahhahh to overhaul and repair the canoe, which leaked; and having cleared the cascade without difficulty, passed the Chagnshyapay before 4 P. M., and soon after reached the *cache* we had made on the 27th of September, which we found undisturbed: having transferred it to the canoe, we dropped down a little farther to a clean dry *batture*, or sand-bar, where we made our bivouac for the night.

October 12.—Nothing could be more beautiful than the succeeding morning; and pushing off at half-past five A. M., we soon came to a low sedgy part of the river, where there was a great deal of smoke, and an incredible quantity of wild ducks, many of them with exceedingly beautiful plumage. This was too much for my Frenchmen; the paddles instantly stopped, and all exclaimed, "Ah que *terrible* de canards." When our expedition first commenced, they were accustomed to express their admiration and surprise by those emphatic b——s and s——s they so much delight in; but, as I had positively objected to their being used when I was in the canoe, they had gradually taken to the word "terrible." Everything now was "terrible." Having supplied ourselves abundantly with the ducks, we hastened on, and in a short time became perfectly enveloped in a dense smoke that soon gave me a headache; even the men were exceedingly annoyed with it, for it got into their eyes and nostrils, and some of them withdrawing their paddles to wipe their eyes, exclaimed, "Ah, monsieur, que la fumée est terrible." "Yes," I replied, "et vous autres, vous êtes des imbeciles terrible; car c'est le même feu que vous avez allumé hier, et qui a gagné sur le pays dans la nuit." This was so evident to them all, that during the rest of the journey it was often a subject of bitter reproach from their companions to the three fellows who had committed the wanton act.

By hard paddling we at length got out of the smoke, and reached Mr. Moore's trading post an hour after sunset, where we encamped. He had got into his new dwelling, and we found him busily employed receiving parties of Indians who had returned from a distance, bringing packs of musk-rat skins. I observed several of them arrive heavily laden; throwing their packs down, they uttered a few words, and immediately lay down at full length on the floor. He told me that he never gave them anything to eat, lest, expecting anything, they should become idle and troublesome : by establishing this practice, he gets rid of them as soon as their business is transacted. Some of these poor creatures had walked seventy miles in the course of that day, and had still to search for the band they belonged to, before they could obtain anything to refresh themselves with. I learnt from one of them that this was a good rat season, but that sometimes they had very ill luck, for if the frosts set in before the small lakes and ponds were filled with the rains, they were often frozen to the bottom, when the rats perished in their houses, which occasioned a scarcity in the succeeding year.

Páhkahskáh, the half-breed white-haired girl, whom I saw on the 24th September, was here : she was on a dirty sort of bunk, laid upon some skins, with Mr. Moore's Indian children, but I at once recognised her by her hair. She was certainly a very pretty maiden, but, under an old filthy buffalo hide, did not look as sentimental and romantic as when I first saw her flaxen locks modestly hiding behind a tree. I gave her some biscuits, and asked her if she would like to go with me and live with the *Esontankahs* ("Long Knives"), where her father was ; and her answer was, that I had given her *coos coos* ("pork") as well as biscuits, when I saw her on coming up.

I perceived that Mr. Moore, who formerly resided several years at Lake Travers, knew the country well. He informed me that there were no banks at the head of Lake Travers, the country presenting a flat marsh, covered with tall aquatic grass, which continues some distance to *Otter-tail River*, a stream that flows out of *Otter-tail Lake* into *Red River* of *Lake Winnipeg*. He also stated that the Indians had cut the figure of a buffalo out of the sod there upon a large scale, which had occasioned the French *voyageurs* to name the locality "Le Lieu où ils font le Bœuf." This had produced an error in the maps of the country, a lake called Buffalo Lake being designated where the figure is cut. Mr. Moore further said that the Côteau du Prairie slopes down, and loses its elevation in the general prairie to the north in about lat. 46°, within a day's march of the head of the *Shayanne* and of the *Chagndeskah;* the sand-hills I fell in with abounding all along the east flank of the Côteau, with a prairie country extending as far as the *Assiniboin* river, destitute of trees, except where water is found.

October 12.—The wind had been very high in the night, and apprehensive of a change in the weather, I rose at the earliest peep of dawn, intending to start before any of Mr. Moore's party were stirring. Passing near his door, whilst the men were striking the tent, I observed through the window two Indians,—men at least thirty-five years old, and who had come in at a very late hour the preceding night,—already using their mirrors, and rubbing vermilion into their hair with great assiduity. They knew that a *Sontankah* was there, and intended no doubt to astonish him, for they consider a dirty head, well rubbed in with vermilion, quite irresistible; but their *toilette* was thrown away, for we were all in the canoe before half-past five A. M., and paddling stoutly along, for I observed the barometer sinking fast. Having breakfasted at one of our old bivouacs, we continued our course, every man plying his paddle with vigour, and at 3 P. M. passed the *Warhajoo*, or "Liards," where we found the country on fire on both sides. Stopping for a very short time at a clean place for the men to eat a morsel, we hastened on to a proper encampment, where we were glad to stop, having made by computation twenty-three leagues, each of us having laboured hard with the paddle all the day. The fire was raging on the other side of the river, within five hundred yards of us, and obliged us to keep an active look-out.

END OF THE FIRST VOLUME.

www.ingramcontent.com/pod-product-compliance
Lightning Source LLC
Chambersburg PA
CBHW031425160426
43195CB00010BB/611